Promoting the
Rule of Law Abroad

Democracy and Rule of Law Books from the Carnegie Endowment

Uncharted Journey: Democracy Promotion in the Middle East
Thomas Carothers and Marina Ottaway, editors

Critical Mission: Essays on Democracy Promotion
Thomas Carothers

Aiding Democracy Abroad: The Learning Curve
Thomas Carothers

Democracy Challenged: The Rise of Semi-Authoritarianism
Marina Ottaway

Open Networks, Closed Regimes: The Impact of the Internet on Authoritarian Rule
Shanthi Kalathil and Taylor C. Boas

Funding Virtue: Civil Society Aid and Democracy Promotion
Marina Ottaway and Thomas Carothers, Editors

The Third Force: The Rise of Transnational Civil Society
Ann M. Florini, Editor

Assessing Democracy Assistance: The Case of Romania
Thomas Carothers

To read excerpts and to find more information on these and other publications from the Carnegie Endowment, visit **www.CarnegieEndowment.org/pubs**.

Promoting the Rule of Law Abroad

In Search of Knowledge

Thomas Carothers

CARNEGIE ENDOWMENT FOR INTERNATIONAL PEACE
Washington, D.C.

Carnegie Endowment for International Peace
1779 Massachusetts Avenue, N.W., Washington, D.C. 20036
202-483-7600, Fax 202-483-1840
www.CarnegieEndowment.org

The Carnegie Endowment for International Peace normally does not take institutional positions on public policy issues; the views and recommendations presented in this publication do not necessarily represent the views of the Carnegie Endowment, its officers, staff, or trustees.

To order, contact:
Hopkins Fulfillment Service
P.O. Box 50370, Baltimore, MD 21211-4370
1-800-537-5487 or 1-410-516-6956
Fax 1-410-516-6998

Composition by Stephen McDougal
Printed by Edwards Brothers

Library of Congress Cataloging-in-Publication data

Promoting the rule of law abroad : in search of knowledge / Thomas Carothers, editor.
    p. cm.
Includes bibliographical references and index.
ISBN-13: 978-0-87003-219-6 (pbk.)
ISBN-10: 0-87003-219-4 (pbk.)
ISBN 13: 978-0-87003-220-2 (cloth)
ISBN-10: 0-87003-220-8 (cloth)
1. Rule of law. 2. Justice, Administration of. I. Carothers, Thomas, 1956– II. Title
K3171.P78 2006
340'.11—dc22   2005030472

---

11 10 09 08 07 06   1 2 3 4 5   1st Printing 2006

Contents

Part III. Regional Experiences

Part IV. Conclusions

Foreword

AS THOMAS CAROTHERS observes in the opening chapter of this book, the rule of law is often held out these days as the solution to almost every international policy problem, from consolidating shaky democratic transitions, establishing sustainable economic development, and stabilizing post-conflict societies, to fostering new global norms. A concept that one rarely heard much about in foreign policy circles during the Cold War is enjoying a heady run on the international policy stage.

With the rise of the ideal of the rule of law has come a mushrooming world of rule-of-law promotion. Almost every type of development organization, from the multilateral development banks and bilateral aid agencies to private foundations and international activist groups, has created programs to help revitalize laws and legal institutions throughout the developing world and the postcommunist countries. These programs often shine with promise, but profound questions exist about how much they really accomplish and whether this new rule-of-law community has rushed ahead with actions far in advance of any real understanding of the true nature of the problems to be solved.

In this book, Thomas Carothers, who has done so much in the past fifteen years to take the measure of democracy promotion, turns his sights on the burgeoning domain of rule-of-law assistance. In two magisterial opening essays he charts the rise of rule-of-law promotion then provocatively asks whether, despite all their activity and self-confidence, rule of law promoters really know what they are doing. There follows an absorbing series of commissioned essays by a group of unusually insightful rule-of-law practitioners and scholars who take up his challenge of searching for solid knowledge in this critical domain. The first set of essays presents penetrating critiques of different elements of what one author identifies as the "rule-of-law orthodoxy" prevailing in the international development community. The second set critically assesses the experience of rule-of-law promotion in different regions, ranging from the successful efforts by the United States to promote criminal procedure reform in Russia to the expanding world of programs to help China achieve the rule of law.

The result is a substantial step forward in the search for understanding of rule-of-law promotion. As with other books by Carothers and his colleagues in Carnegie's remarkably successful Democracy and Rule of Law Project, I have no doubt that this work will quickly be accepted as a standard reference in the field, one that establishes an incisive analytic framework for this new area of endeavor and establishes a foundation of knowledge that others will spend years building upon.

Jessica T. Mathews
President, Carnegie Endowment for International Peace

Preface

THOMAS CAROTHERS

THE FIRST TRIP I EVER TOOK for democracy promotion work was to Haiti in 1986 to assess that country's judicial system in the wake of the ouster from power of Jean-Claude Duvalier ("Baby Doc") several months before, and to come up with recommendations for a judicial assistance program. I was just out of law school and was serving on an assignment from the State Department's Legal Advisor's office in the newly established Office for Administration of Justice and Democratic Development in the Latin America bureau of the U.S. Agency for International Development (USAID). This was the first democracy promotion office in USAID since the end of the wave of political development programs of the 1960s and one of the starting points for what would soon become a large-scale expansion of U.S. democracy-related assistance.

As I interviewed judges, lawyers, ministry of justice officials, prosecutors, law professors, legal activists, and others in Haiti's justice sector, I was overwhelmed not just by the ruinous disorder and decay in the system but by the realization that the shortcomings of the system could not be reduced to a well-defined set of specific symptoms or factors, such as slow processing of cases, high levels of pretrial detention, inadequate judicial training, and so forth. Rather I saw that what was formally called a judicial system had only a nominal relationship to what I and my colleagues meant by the term. The system was an integral part of a predatory state that had long lived off the Haitian people for its own benefit, without any notion that a state might actually seek to serve the interests of its people. Although the devastating father–son Duvalier dictatorial reign was finally over, many parts of the Haitian state had survived the political transition intact. And thus, although one could talk about and work up plans for "judicial reform" and "judicial strengthening," trying to build the rule of law in Haiti, which was what our office at USAID believed it wanted to do, seemed to require something far deeper and more complex than the kinds of technocratic activities a judicial reform project was likely to entail.

When I returned to Washington and wrote up the report from my trip, I followed the conventional matrix our office had already developed in those early years of judicial assistance work, highlighting the many specific institutional challenges facing Haiti's justice sector and the array of training, material assistance, and other sorts of measures that might best meet those needs. However, when I handed the report to my boss, I told him that although I believed it was analytically coherent and factually accurate, at another level I felt it failed to convey a deeper and probably more important truth about what I had learned on my trip—that Haiti's justice system might be better thought of as an "injustice system" and that apparently uncontroversial concepts such as "reforming" or "strengthening" that system were completely inadequate descriptions of the task of promoting the rule of law in that profoundly troubled society. I also said that I did not know what assistance approach might be useful in a country that lacked even the basic conception of a state in the Western sense of the term.

My boss heard me out, having already developed an admirable patience with my tendency to question everything we did. After thinking over my comments for a few minutes, he answered with words to the effect that "you're saying that what we know how to do may not be that meaningful, but what would be meaningful we don't really know how to do." I agreed with that summary; he laughed wryly and thanked me for my report. Being in a bilateral aid agency with the usual imperatives to tackle the challenges at hand at high speed, we went ahead and oversaw the development and launch of a conventional judicial reform program in Haiti (one that ran into various problems, was relaunched and redeveloped several times over the next decade and a half, making progress in parts before ending up largely undermined by the broader, disastrous political problems in the country). I left the U.S. government not long afterwards, leaving behind the business of developing rule-of-law programs, but the dilemma that had surfaced at that time stayed in my thoughts.

I returned to rule-of-law work in the late 1990s as a researcher, as part of my broader efforts during that decade and since to analyze the world of Western efforts to promote democracy abroad. I carried out some research on what by then had grown into a large, active domain of rule-of-law assistance programs, carried out by myriad U.S., European, and multilateral organizations. I wrote up this research in two essays. The first, "The Rule of Law Revival," which appears as the first chapter in this book, attempted to take stock of the mushrooming world of rule-of-law aid, by highlighting the many different and often rather sweeping purposes that rule-of-law promotion was being asked to serve and by outlining the range of approaches that had come to make up the standard menu of such work. The article attracted a generally favorable reading in the community of rule-of-law promoters, who were happy to see their endeavors recognized as a field, one commanding increasing attention from the mainstream foreign policy community. As one U.S. lawyer working on rule-of-law projects in southeastern Europe said to me, "I sent your article to my parents so they can understand that I actually do something real for a living."

The second essay was another bird's-eye view of the field, but with a different focus. Entitled "Promoting the Rule of Law: The Problem of Knowledge" (chapter 2 in this volume), the essay rather bluntly argued that although promoting the rule of law has become a busy domain, full of activities and actors, it faces fundamental uncertainties that call into question whether it can be said to have yet coalesced into a coherent field. To start, it is not clear that the conception of the rule of law that aid providers tend to use is actually as well grounded or widely agreed upon as they seem to assume. One can ask for example whether the rule of law is best conceived of in terms of certain types or configurations of legal and political institutions, or whether it resides at a more basic level of sociopolitical relationships and norms, which may end up getting embodied in specific institutions. I also argued that rule-of-law promoters actually do not know very much about how and why the rule of law does or does not emerge in particular societies and what effects rule-of-law aid has beyond narrowly defined institutional outcomes. A persistent lack of basic research on rule-of-law assistance, I asserted, underlies the problem of knowledge and is stunting the development and consolidation of the domain.

This essay met a divided response from the rule-of-law aid community. Some aid practitioners, especially those in the larger aid institutions involved in rule-of-law programs, strongly disliked it. They felt that I failed to appreciate how much they and others had learned about this sort of work and that even if the learning was rarely written down, it did exist in practitioners' minds. Others, both some persons in aid organizations as well as some independent aid consultants and legal scholars familiar with this area, agreed with my thesis and in some cases felt I had not taken my critique far enough.

These diverse reactions prompted me to take this line of inquiry further. I commissioned several papers that went deeper into this question of the problem of knowledge, by authors in one of two categories— reflective practitioners of rule-of-law assistance or comparative legal scholars with a specific interest in rule-of-law promotion. The initial set of papers, which was also presented and discussed at a series of meetings of a practitioners' group on rule-of-law aid that I convened at the Carnegie Endowment, gained some attention in the rule-of-law practitioner world, in substantial part because almost no other such studies or writings were available. Over time, more papers started coming to me from other practitioners and scholars who felt they wanted to add their views to this debate. Eventually I realized I had a critical mass of writing on the subject and that it would make sense to put it together into a book, with my two initial essays as framing chapters.

I have grouped the contributions by other authors into two sets. The first set, chapters 3–7, are five essays that critically examine what one of the authors, Frank Upham, labels the rule-of-law orthodoxy, that is to say, the conventional approach to promoting the rule of law that the major aid organizations use. Rachel Kleinfeld starts off the section with an artful dissection of the vexing question of definition. She contrasts definitions of the rule of law that aid practitioners tend to use with those usually favored by scholars and philosophers and makes the case that practitioners are led astray by the types of definitions upon which they rely. Frank Upham draws on a searching analysis of the role of law in the economic development of both the United States and Japan to argue that the rule-of-law aid community is operating from a mythical imperative when it holds that a certain model of the rule of law is vital for a country to prosper. Stephen Golub mounts a broadside against the dominant top-down, institution-centric approach to rule-of-law promotion, arguing that it is unlikely to produce changes that will contribute to a better life for significant numbers of people in developing societies. Wade Channell presents an equally forceful critique of Western aid for law reform in postcommunist and developing countries. He examines why aid providers tend to violate well-known lessons about the pitfalls of exporting Western legal models and how they might do better. Golub then builds on his earlier chapter with a second one in which he proposes an alternative approach to aiding the rule of law, one that concentrates on legal empowerment of disadvantaged persons rather than the reform of state institutions.

The second set of essays, chapters 8–12, make up a regional tour of experiences with rule-of-law aid. Matthew Stephenson takes a look at the widening arena of U.S. efforts to promote the rule of law in China, focusing on the crucial question of whether attempts to support commercial law reform will likely have, as many aid providers hope, positive spillover benefits in advancing the rule of law in more political areas. Matthew Spence's chapter on rule-of-law reform in Russia highlights that outsiders (in this case the U.S. government) can play a valuable role in supporting positive changes but that the relationship between the external aid and the domestic gains is much more complex than usually anticipated on either side. David Mednicoff identifies important similarities and differences in Arab and American conceptions of the rule of law and proceeds from that analysis to explore the dilemmas that the United States faces in its newfound interest in trying to help strengthen the rule of law in the Middle East.

As Laure-Hélène Piron describes in her chapter, Africa has recently experienced a rapid increase in Western aid for justice sector reform. Although such aid is potentially valuable, she argues, donors are only just starting to grapple with a whole series of daunting challenges, including the extraordinary complexity of local legal systems, the formidable political obstacles to change, and the weakness of design and implementation of many aid programs.

Latin America has engaged in more sweeping criminal law reform efforts in the past two decades than any other region, with extensive donor support, making it a good candidate for assessing the long-term impact of such work. Lisa Bhansali and Christina Biebesheimer take up that challenge in their chapter, assessing the impact of criminal law reforms in Latin America through their effect on a set of quantifiable indicators of progress relating to due process and then assessing the broader significance of those changes.

Finally, in the concluding chapter, I extract some of the common themes and points of analysis from the different chapters and reflect on what they imply about the state of the field.

Given the importance and complexity of the task, the search for knowledge in promoting the rule of law abroad is certain to be long and difficult. Rule-of-law promoters are clearly gaining a greater appreciation of the disjunction between what is relatively easy to do and what is meaningful in advancing the rule of law in other societies. But they are also learning how hard it is to bridge that gap. This book is at most no more than a first step in addressing that challenge, but it may have value in framing the task and identifying some of the initial progress along the path.

Acknowledgments

I AM INDEBTED to several people at Carnegie for their help in getting this book ready for publication, including Patricia Mallan for her capable assistance with the manuscripts, Hania Kronfol for the thorough bibliography, Phyllis Jask for her highly skillful, diligent work on the whole production process, and Carrie Mullen for her knowledgeable help with the book production process overall. Jacqueline Edlund-Braun provided excellent copyediting. George Perkovich gave trenchant, helpful comments on several chapters in the draft stage. I am grateful to Richard Messick of the World Bank for useful advice at several key junctures. I also thank the William and Flora Hewlett Foundation for generous financial support at an early stage of this project.

PART I

Framing the Challenge

The Rule-of-Law Revival

THOMAS CAROTHERS

ONE CANNOT GET through a foreign policy debate these days without someone proposing the rule of law as a solution to the world's troubles. How can U.S. policy on China cut through the conundrum of balancing human rights against economic interests? Promoting the rule of law, some observers argue, advances both principles and profits. What will it take for Russia to move beyond Wild West capitalism to more orderly market economics? Developing the rule of law, many insist, is the key. How can Mexico negotiate its treacherous economic, political, and social transitions? Inside and outside Mexico, many answer: establish once and for all the rule of law. Indeed, whether it is Bosnia, Rwanda, Haiti, or elsewhere, the cure is the rule of law, of course.

The concept is suddenly everywhere—a venerable part of Western political philosophy enjoying a new run as a rising imperative of the era of globalization. Unquestionably, it is important to life in peaceful, free, and prosperous societies. Yet its sudden elevation as a panacea for the ills of countries in transition from dictatorships or statist economies should make both patients and prescribers wary. The rule-of-law promises to move countries past the first, relatively easy phase of political and economic liberalization to a deeper level of reform. But that promise is proving difficult to fulfill. A multitude of countries in Asia, the former Soviet Union, Eastern Europe, Latin America, sub-Saharan Africa, and the Middle East are engaged in a wide range of rule-of-law reform initiatives. Rewriting constitutions, laws, and regulations is the easy part. Far-reaching institutional reform, also necessary, is arduous and slow. Judges, lawyers, and bureaucrats must be retrained, and fixtures like court systems, police forces, and prisons must be restructured. Citizens must be brought into the process if conceptions of law and justice are to be truly transformed.

The primary obstacles to such reform are not technical or financial, but political and human. Rule-of-law reform will succeed only if it gets at the fundamental problem of leaders who refuse to be ruled by the law. Respect for the law will not easily take root in systems rife with corruption and cynicism, since entrenched elites cede their traditional impunity and vested interests only under great pressure. Even the new generation of politicians arising out of the political transitions of recent years are reluctant to support reforms that create competing centers of authority beyond their control.

Western nations and private donors have poured hundreds of millions of dollars into rule-of-law reform, but outside aid is no substitute for the will to reform, which must come from within. Countries in transition to democracy must first want to reform and must then be thorough and patient in their legal makeovers. Meanwhile, donors must learn to spend their reform dollars where they will do the most good—and expect few miracles and little leverage in return.

Legal Bedrock

The rule of law can be defined as a system in which the laws are public knowledge, are clear in meaning, and apply equally to everyone. They enshrine and uphold the political and civil liberties that have gained status as universal human rights over the last half-century. In particular, anyone accused of a crime has the right to a fair, prompt hearing and is presumed innocent until proved guilty. The central institutions of the legal system, including courts, prosecutors, and police, are reasonably fair, competent, and efficient. Judges are impartial and independent, not subject to political influence or manipulation. Perhaps most important, the government is embedded in a comprehensive legal framework, its officials accept that the law will be applied to their own conduct, and the government seeks to be law-abiding.

The relationship between the rule of law and liberal democracy is profound. The rule of law makes possible individual rights, which are at the core of democracy. A government's respect for the sovereign authority of the people and a constitution depends on its acceptance of law. Democracy includes institutions and processes that, although beyond the immediate domain of the legal system, are rooted in it. Basic elements of a modern market economy such as property rights and contracts are founded on the law and require competent third-party enforcement. Without the rule of law, major economic institutions such as corporations, banks, and labor unions would not function, and the government's many involvements in the economy—regulatory mechanisms, tax systems, customs structures, monetary policy, and the like—would be unfair, inefficient, and opaque.

The rule of law can be conceived broadly or narrowly. Some American jurists invest it with attributes specific to their own system, such as trial by jury, a constitution that is rarely amended, an expansive view of defendants' rights, and a sharp separation of powers. This alienates those from other societies who enjoy the rule of law but do not happen to follow the American approach in its many unusual particulars. Some Asian politicians focus on the regular, efficient application of law but do not stress the necessity of government subordination to it. In their view, the law exists not to limit the state but to serve its power. More accurately characterized as rule by law rather than rule of law, this narrow conception is built into what has become known as Asian-style democracy.

Transition Trauma

The rule of law is scarcely a new idea. It is receiving so much attention now because of its centrality to both democracy and the market economy in an era marked by a wave of transitions to both. Western observers say that enhancing the rule of law will allow states to move beyond the first stage of political and economic reform to consolidate both democracy and market economics.

Since the early 1980s dozens of countries in different regions have experienced political openings, held reasonably free and fair elections, and established the basic institutions of democracy. Some, however, particularly in Latin America and parts of the former Soviet Union, Eastern Europe, and Asia, are struggling with poorly performing institutions, citizens' low regard for governments, and the challenge of going beyond mere democratic processes to genuinely democratic values and practices. Other countries, in sub-Saharan Africa, Central Asia, and elsewhere, are not just stagnating but slipping backward as newly elected leaders fall into old authoritarian habits. For states grappling with democratic consolidation, fortifying usually weak rule of law appears to be a way of pushing patronage-ridden government institutions to better performance, reining in elected but still only haphazardly law-abiding politicians, and curbing the continued violation of human rights that has characterized many new democracies. For backsliding systems, strengthening the rule of law seems an appealing bulwark against creeping authoritarianism and the ever-present threat of a sabotage of constitutional order.

Many attempted economic transitions are at a similar dip in the road. Reform-oriented governments that have made it through the initial phase of economic liberalization and fiscal stabilization are now pausing before the second, deeper transitional phase, licking their political wounds and hoping for patience on the part of often unpersuaded citizens. As Moisés Naím has pointed out, the first phase of market reform turns on large-scale policy decisions by a small band of top officials. The second phase involves building institutions, such as tax agencies, customs services, and antitrust agencies, and the general amelioration of governance. Strengthening the rule of law is integral to this phase.

The challenges of the second phase are felt not only in Latin America and the former communist states, but also in Asian countries that have made considerable economic progress without the benefit of a strong rule of law. As Asia's recent financial woes highlight, if countries such as Indonesia, Thailand, and Malaysia are to move beyond their impressive first generation of economic progress, they will require better bank regulation and greater government accountability. More generally, economic globalization is feeding the rule-of-law imperative by putting pressure on governments to offer the stability, transparency, and accountability that international investors demand.

Shoring up the rule of law also helps temper two severe problems—corruption and crime—that are common to many transitional countries, embittering citizens and clouding reform efforts. Debate continues over whether corruption in government has actually increased in transitional societies or whether greater openness, especially in the media, has merely exposed what was already there. Skyrocketing street crime and civil violence are another unfortunate hallmark of many democratizing societies, from Russia to South Africa to Guatemala. Crime erodes public support for democracy and hurts the economy by scaring off foreign investors and interfering with the flow of ideas, goods, and people. Reform-oriented governments around the world are now adding crime and corruption reduction to their agenda for deepening reform. Rule-of-law development is an obvious place to begin.

For these reasons—political, economic, and social—Western policy makers and commentators have seized on the rule-of-law as an elixir for countries in transition. It promises to remove all the chief obstacles on the path to democracy and market economics. Its universal quality adds to its appeal. Despite the close ties of the rule of law to democracy and capitalism, it stands apart as a nonideological, even technical, solution. In many countries, people still argue over the appropriateness of various models of democracy or capitalism. But hardly anyone these days will admit to being against the idea of law.

The Reform Menu

Although its wonderworking abilities have been exaggerated, the desirability of the rule of law is clear. The question is where to start. The usual way of categorizing rule-of-law reforms is by subject matter—commercial law, criminal law, administrative law, and the like. An alternate method focuses on the depth of reform, with three basic categories. Type one reform concentrates on the laws themselves: revising laws or whole codes to weed out antiquated provisions. Often the economic domain is the focus, with the drafting or redrafting of laws on bankruptcy, corporate governance, taxation, intellectual property, and financial markets. Another focus is criminal law, including expanding the protection of basic rights in criminal procedure codes, modifying criminal statutes to cover new problems such as money laundering and electronic-transfer fraud, and revising the regulation of police.

Type two reform is the strengthening of law-related institutions, usually to make them more competent, efficient, and accountable. Training and salaries for judges and court staff are increased, and the dissemination of judicial decisions improved. Reform efforts target the police, prosecutors, public defenders, and prisons. Efforts to toughen ethics codes and professional standards for lawyers, revitalize legal education, broaden access to courts, and establish alternative dispute resolution mechanisms figure in many reform packages. Other common reforms include strengthening legislatures, tax administrations, and local governments.

Type three reforms aim at the deeper goal of increasing government's compliance with law. A key step is achieving genuine judicial independence. Some of the above measures foster this goal, especially better salaries and revised selection procedures for judges. But the most crucial changes lie elsewhere. Above all, government officials must refrain from interfering with judicial decision making and accept the judiciary as an independent authority. They must give up the habit of placing themselves above the law. Institutional reforms can help by clarifying regulations, making public service more of a meritocracy, and mandating transparency and other means of increasing accountability. The success of type three reform, however, depends less on technical or institutional measures than on enlightened leadership and sweeping changes in the values and attitudes of those in power. Although much of the impetus must come from the top, nonstate activities such as citizen-driven human rights and anticorruption campaigns can do much to help.

The Global Picture

Probably the most active region for rule-of-law reform has been Eastern Europe. Since 1989, most Eastern European societies have taken significant steps to de-Sovietize and broadly reform their legal systems. They have rewritten constitutions and laws and initiated key changes in their legal institutions. Many government officials have begun accepting the law's authority and respecting judicial independence. The Czech Republic, for example, has made major progress on judicial independence, and Hungary has recently launched a comprehensive judicial reform package. Thorough institutional reforms, however, are taking longer than many hoped, and some countries are falling short. The leaders of Croatia and Serbia continue to trample basic rights, and Slovak government institutions show contempt for the Constitutional Court's rulings. Nonetheless, the overall picture in the region has encouraging elements.

Latin America also presents a positive, if mixed, profile. Since the early 1980s constitutionally based, elected governments have been established almost everywhere in the region. Most Latin American governments have acknowledged the need for rule-of-law reform and are taking steps toward it, or at least proclaiming that they will. But judicial and police reform has run into walls of bureaucratic indifference and entrenched interests. A few countries, notably Chile and Costa Rica, have made progress, while others, such as El Salvador and Guatemala, may only now be getting serious about it. The will to reform has been lacking, however, in Argentina and Mexico, which have the necessary human and technical resources but whose political and economic development are being hampered by their weak rule of law.

Many Asian governments have begun to modify laws and legal institutions, primarily related to commercial affairs. This is the project of countries seeking to consolidate and advance economic progress, such as Malaysia, Taiwan, South Korea, and even China, as well as those hoping to get on the train, such as Vietnam. These reforms generally stop short of subordinating government's power to the law and are better understood as efforts to achieve rule by law than the rule of law. South Korea is almost alone in taking these efforts beyond the commercial domain and seriously attacking government impunity and corruption, as evidenced by the recent conviction of former South Korean Presidents Chun Doo-hwan and Roh Tae-woo on corruption charges. The Asian financial crisis highlighted the failure of the region's various rule-of-law reforms to bring transparency and accountability to the dealings of the ingrown circles of privileged bankers, businessmen, and politicians. Pressure for more reform, both from within Asia and from the international financial community, is growing.

The situation in the former Soviet Union is discouraging. Although the Baltic states have made major strides in depoliticizing and revitalizing their judicial systems, few other post-Soviet states have achieved much beyond limited reforms in narrow areas of commercial law. Their legal institutions have shed few of their Soviet habits and remain ineffective, politically subordinated, and corrupt. Russia's difficulties in achieving the rule of law are the weakest link in the postcommunist transformation of Russian society. The government has attempted a number of reform initiatives, including the drafting of new civil and criminal codes. These have been neutralized, however, by the ruling elite's tendency to act extralegally and by the new private sector's troubling lawlessness.

Although more than thirty sub-Saharan African countries have attempted political and economic transitions since 1990, rule-of-law reform is still scarce on the continent. The issue is coming to the fore in both those countries attempting to move halting transitions along and those hoping that "transitional justice" mechanisms such as truth commissions and war crimes tribunals can help overcome the bitter legacy of the past. By far the most positive case is South Africa, where a far-reaching program to transform the administration of justice is under way. In at least a few other countries, including Botswana, Tanzania, and Uganda, less dramatic but still important progress has been made toward the reform of laws and law-related institutions, including the modernization of some commercial laws and stronger support for the judiciary. But in many countries of the region, the legal systems remain captive of the powers that be.

The Middle East shows the least legal reform activity of any region. Some Arab countries, among them Jordan, Lebanon, and Kuwait, are at least attempting reform in the commercial domain, such as in the mechanisms necessary to establish stock markets or otherwise attract foreign investment. Institutional change is more sporadic, ranging from the surprisingly bold reform plans announced by the government of Oman to Egypt's judicial reforms, whose seriousness is still unclear.

Rule-of-law reform is at least a stated goal of many countries. Globally there has been a great deal of legal reform related to economic modernization and a moderate amount of law-related institutional reform, but little deep reform of the higher levels of government. Around the world, the movement toward rule of law is broad but shallow.

Legal Aid

Most governments attempting rule-of-law reform are not doing so on their own. Assistance in this field has mushroomed in recent years, becoming a major category of international aid. With a mix of altruism and self-interest, many Western countries have rushed to help governments in Eastern Europe and the former Soviet Union carry out legal and institutional reforms. Russia's legal and judicial reforms, for example, have been supported by a variety of U.S. assistance projects, extensive German aid, a $58 million World Bank loan, and numerous smaller World Bank and European Bank for Reconstruction and Development initiatives, as well as many efforts sponsored by Great Britain, the Netherlands, Denmark, and the European Union. Asia and Latin America are also major recipients of rule-of-law aid, with a focus on commercial law in Asia and on criminal and commercial law in Latin America. Africa and the Middle East have received less attention, reflecting the smaller degree of reform that countries there have undertaken.

A host of U.S. agencies underwrite such aid, including the U.S. Agency for International Development, the Justice and Commerce Departments, and the Securities and Exchange Commission. Coordination is poor and turf battles are common. The rapid expansion of U.S. rule-of-law aid exemplifies the only partially successful U.S. response to the challenges of the post–Cold War era. Many programs have sprung up to address these emerging issues, but officials have done far too little to ensure that they are well designed, consistent, and coherent.

Almost every major bilateral donor, a wide range of multilateral organizations—especially development banks—and countless foundations, universities, and human rights groups are getting into the act. In most countries, U.S. rule-of-law assistance is a small part of the aid pool, although Americans frequently assume it is of paramount importance. They mistakenly believe that rule-of-law promotion is their special province, although they are not alone in that. German and French jurists also tend to view their country as the keeper of the flame of civil code reform. British lawyers and judges point to the distinguished history of the British approach. Transitional countries are bombarded with fervent but contradictory advice on judicial and legal reform.

Donors sometimes determine rule-of-law reform priorities. Enormous amounts of aid are granted for writing or rewriting laws, especially commercial laws. Hordes of Western consultants descend on transitional societies with Western legal models in their briefcases. Judicial training courses run by Western groups have become a cottage industry, as have seminars on conflict resolution. Aid providers are expanding their rule-of-law efforts to reach parliaments, executive branch agencies, and local governments. Assistance also extends to civic groups that use law to advance particular interests and nongovernmental organizations that push for reform.

The Net Effect

The effects of this burgeoning rule-of-law aid are generally positive, though usually modest. After more than ten years and hundreds of millions of dollars in aid, many judicial systems in Latin America still function poorly. Russia is probably the single largest recipient of such aid, but is not even clearly moving in the right direction. The numerous rule-of-law programs carried out in Cambodia after the 1993 elections failed to create values or structures strong enough to prevent last year's coup. Aid providers have helped rewrite laws around the globe, but they have discovered that the mere enactment of laws accomplishes little without considerable investment in changing the conditions for implementation and enforcement. Many Western advisers involved in rule-of-law assistance are new to the foreign aid world and have not learned that aid must support domestically rooted processes of change, not attempt to artificially reproduce preselected results.

Efforts to strengthen basic legal institutions have proven slow and difficult. Training for judges, technical consultancies, and other transfers of expert knowledge make sense on paper but often have only minor impact. The desirability of embracing such values as efficiency, transparency, accountability, and honesty seems self-evident to Western aid providers, but for those targeted by training programs, such changes may signal the loss of perquisites and security. Major U.S. judicial reform efforts in Russia, El Salvador, Guatemala, and elsewhere have foundered on the assumption that external aid can substitute for the internal will to reform.

Rule-of-law aid has been concentrated on more easily attained type one and type two reforms. Thus it has affected the most important elements of the problem least. Helping transitional countries achieve type three reform that brings real change in government obedience to law is the hardest, slowest kind of assistance. It demands powerful tools that aid providers are only beginning to develop, especially activities that help bring pressure on the legal system from the citizenry and support whatever pockets of reform may exist within an otherwise self-interested ruling system. It requires a level of interventionism, political attention, and visibility that many donor governments and organizations cannot or do not wish to apply. Above all, it calls for patient, sustained attention, as breaking down entrenched political interests, transforming values, and generating enlightened, consistent leadership will take generations.

The experience to date with rule-of-law aid suggests that it is best to proceed with caution. The widespread embrace of the rule-of-law imperative is heartening, but it represents only the first step for most transitional countries on what will be a long and rocky road. Although the United States and other Western countries can and should foster the rule of law, even large amounts of aid will not bring rapid or decisive results. Thus, it is good that President Ernesto Zedillo of Mexico has made rule-of-law development one of the central goals of his presidency, but the pursuit of that goal is certain to be slow and difficult, as highlighted by the recent massacre in the south of the country. Judging from the experience of other Latin American countries, U.S. efforts to lighten Mexico's burden will at best be of secondary importance. Similarly, Wild West capitalism in Russia should not be thought of as a brief transitional phase. The deep shortcomings of the rule of law in Russia will take decades to fix. The Asian financial crisis has shown observers that without the rule of law the Asian miracle economies are unstable. Although that realization was abrupt, remedying the situation will be a long-term enterprise.

These lessons are of particular importance concerning China, where some U.S. policy makers and commentators have begun pinning hope on the idea that promoting the rule of law will allow the United States to support positive economic and political change without taking a confrontational approach on human rights issues. But China's own efforts to reform its law are almost twenty years old and have moved slowly, especially outside the economic domain. Statements by U.S. officials and increased flows of rule-of-law assistance are unlikely to speed up the process, judging from the rule-of-law programs that have been operating in China for years. Rule-of-law promotion should be part of U.S. policy toward China, but it will not increase U.S. influence over that country. Nor will it miraculously eliminate the hard choices between ideals and interests that have plagued America's foreign policy for more than two centuries.

Note

The Carnegie Endowment gratefully acknowledges the permission of the Council on Foreign Relations to reprint this article, which originally appeared in *Foreign Affairs* 77, no. 2 (March/April 1998).

CHAPTER TWO

The Problem of Knowledge

THOMAS CAROTHERS

WHEN RULE-OF-LAW aid practitioners gather among themselves to reflect on their work, they often express contradictory thoughts. On the one hand, they talk with enthusiasm and interest about what they do, believing that the field of rule-of-law assistance is extremely important. Many feel it is at the cutting edge of international efforts to promote both development and democracy abroad. On the other hand, when pressed, they admit that the base of knowledge from which they are operating is startlingly thin. As a colleague who has been closely involved in rule-of-law work in Latin America for many years said to me recently, "we know how to do a lot of things, but deep down we don't really know what we are doing." Although some practitioners harbor no doubts and promote the rule of law abroad with a great sense of confidence, most persons working in the field openly recognize and lament the fact that little really has been learned about rule-of-law assistance relative to the extensive amount of on-the-ground activity.

This fact raises an interesting puzzle. The current rule-of-law promotion field—which started in the mid-1980s in Latin America and now extends to many regions, including Eastern Europe, the former Soviet Union, Asia, and sub-Saharan Africa—is already older than its precursor was, the law and development movement of the 1960s and early 1970s, when that earlier movement ran out of steam and closed down. The law and development movement died out above all because of a too obvious gap between its ambitions and its achievements. Yet the current rule-of-law field—which has some important similarities to but also differences from the law and development movement—is still expanding as it approaches the end of its second decade, despite an apparent lack of knowledge at many levels of conception, operation, and evaluation.

The answer to the puzzle may lie not so much in differences between the substance of the two movements—though those differences are real—than in differing contexts. The law and development movement was launched in the optimistic days of the early 1960s, when hopes for democracy and development were high for the newly decolonized states of Africa and Asia, and for the developing world as a whole. Yet as the law and development movement unfolded, that broader context of optimism deteriorated quickly. Democratic experiments failed in many parts of the developing world in the 1960s and the broader hope for rapid developmental gains ran into contrary realities in many countries. By the end of that decade, the modernization paradigm on which U.S. foreign aid of the 1960s, including the law and development movement, had been based was already in serious doubt and a pessimistic assessment of foreign aid caused much retooling and retraction.

In contrast, the optimistic context of the crucial early years of the current rule-of-law aid movement—the heady period of the end of the Cold War—has held up somewhat longer. Although simplistic thinking about the ease and naturalness of the many dual transitions around the world to democracy and market economics has met with many disappointments, the international aid community has not (yet) experienced a major disillusionment with the underlying assumptions about aid for democracy and market economics from which the rule-of-law aid movement operates.

It may be then that a still-favorable, though increasingly shaky, context holds together the rule-of-law assistance movement. This should not prevent us, however, from pushing at this question about knowledge: What is the problem of knowledge that aid practitioners allude to in private? What is it that practitioners do not know that they feel they should know as they engage in rule-of-law promotion projects around the world? What about the many "lessons learned" that are dutifully reported in institutional documents? And to the extent there really is a problem of knowledge, what causes it and what might ameliorate it?

Self-Evident but Uncertain Rationales

The problem of knowledge in rule-of-law promotion can be considered as a series of deficits at various analytic levels, descending in generality.

To start, there is a surprising amount of uncertainty about the basic rationale for rule-of-law promotion. Aid agencies prescribe rule-of-law programs to cure a remarkably wide array of ailments in developing and postcommunist countries, from corruption and surging crime to lagging foreign investment and growth. At the core of this burgeoning belief in the value of rule-of-law work are two controlling axioms: The rule of law is necessary for economic development and necessary for democracy. When held up to a close light, however, neither of these propositions is as axiomatic as it may at first appear.

It has become a new credo in the development field that if developing and postcommunist countries wish to succeed economically they must develop the rule of law. One form of this economic rationale for rule-of-law work focuses on foreign investment: If a country does not have the rule of law, the argument goes, it will not be able to attract substantial amounts of foreign investment and therefore will not be able to finance development. Leaving aside the first question of whether foreign investment is really always a requirement for development (since it is not clear, for example, that the economic success of a number of the major Western economies, such as the American and Japanese economies, was based on substantial amounts of inward foreign investment), there is a notable lack of proof that a country must have a settled, well-functioning rule of law to attract investment. The argument has an undeniable common sense appeal—investors will want predictability, security, and the like. Yet the case of China flies squarely in the face of the argument—the largest recipient of foreign direct investment in the developing world happens to be a country notorious for its lack of Western-style rule of law. It is clear that what draws investors into China is the possibility of making money either in the near or long term. Weak rule of law is perhaps one negative factor they weigh in their decision of whether to invest, but it is by no means determinative. A recent study of the rule of law and foreign investment in postcommunist countries points to a similar conclusion. Weak rule of law is not a major factor in determining investment flows, and the more important causal relationship may be in the reverse direction: The presence of at least certain types of foreign investors may contribute to the development of the rule of law through their demands for legal reforms.[1]

A broader form of the argument about the relationship between the rule of law and economic development emphasizes an array of rule-of-law components—such as the need for legal predictability, the enforcement of contracts, and property rights—as necessary for the functioning of a modern market economy. Again the appeal of this argument is

obvious and probably contains elements of truth. But as Frank Upham
has argued in a study of the supposed relationship between an idealized apolitical, rule-based system of law and the economic development
of the United States and Japan, the relationship is by no means as clear-
cut as many might hope.[2] Similarly, a review by Rick Messick of studies
that attempt to find causal relationships between judicial reform and
development notes that "the relationship is probably better modeled as
a series of on-and-off connections, or of couplings and decouplings," in
other words the causal arrows go both directions and sometimes do not
appear at all.[3] It is not possible here to survey all the literature on what is
in fact an extremely complex, multifaceted question about the relationship of the rule of law and economic development. The central point is
that simplistic assertions such as have become common among aid agencies to the effect that the "rule of law" grosso modo is necessary for
development are at best badly oversimplified and probably misleading
in many ways. The case of China again points to some of the shortcomings of the assertion. Many countries being told that they must have
Western style rule of law before they can achieve significant economic
growth look with envy at China's sustained economic growth of the past
twenty years and wonder why the prescription did not apply there.

Things are similarly murky on the political side of the core rationale.
Unquestionably the rule of law is intimately connected with liberal democracy. A foundation of civil and political rights rooted in a functioning legal system is crucial to democracy. But again, the idea that specific
improvements in the rule of law are necessary to achieve democracy is
dangerously simplistic. Democracy often, in fact usually, co-exists with
substantial shortcomings in the rule of law. In quite a few countries that
are considered well-established Western democracies—and that hold
themselves out to developing and postcommunist countries as examples
of the sorts of political systems that those countries should emulate—
one finds various shortcomings: (1) court systems that are substantially
overrun with cases to the point where justice is delayed on a regular
basis; (2) substantial groups of people, usually minorities, are discrimi-
nated against and unable to find adequate remedies within the civil legal system; (3) the criminal law system chronically mistreats selected
groups of people, again, usually minorities; and (4) top politicians often
manage to abuse the law with impunity, and political corruption is common.

Of course one can interpret this to mean that because of the deficiencies in the rule of law these countries are imperfect democracies. This is

true enough, but the point is that they are widely accepted in the international community as established democracies. Yet their aid agencies are telling officials in the developing and postcommunist world that well-functioning rule of law is a kind of tripwire for democracy. It would be much more accurate to say that the rule of law and democracy are closely intertwined but that major shortcomings in the rule of law often exist within reasonably democratic political systems. Countries struggling to become democratic do not face a dramatic choice of "no rule of law, no democracy" but rather a series of smaller, more complicated choices about what elements of their legal systems they wish to try to improve with the expectation of achieving what political benefits.

In short, the axiomatic quality of the two core rationales of the current wave of rule-of-law assistance efforts—that the rule of law is necessary for economic development and democracy—is misleading when used as a mechanistic, causal imperative by the aid community. Rule-of-law aid practitioners can probably prescribe rule-of-law programs with a safe belief that these initiatives may well be helpful to both economic development and democratization, but they really do not know to what extent there are direct causal connections at work and whether similar resources directed elsewhere might produce greater effect on economic and political conditions.

The Elusive Essence

Rule-of-law aid providers seem confident that they know what the rule of law looks like in practice. Stated in shorthand form, they want to see law applied fairly, uniformly, and efficiently throughout the society in question, to both public officials as well as ordinary citizens, and to have law protect various rights that ensure the autonomy of the individual in the face of state power in both the political and economic spheres. Their outlook on the rule of law can certainly be criticized for its narrowness. They do not have much interest in non-Western forms of law, in traditional systems of justice, or, in the case of some American rule-of-law experts, even in civil law. But it is important to go beyond that fairly obvious weakness to a different aspect of the problem of knowledge: Rule-of-law aid practitioners know what the rule of law is supposed to look like in practice, but they are less certain what the essence of the rule of law is.

By their nature as practitioners intent on producing tangible, even measurable, changes in other societies, rule-of-law aid specialists need to concretize the appealing but inevitably somewhat diffuse concept of the rule of law. In the broader field of democracy assistance, the pattern has been for democracy promoters to translate the overarching idea of democracy into an institutional checklist or template that they can pursue through a series of specific aid intiatives.[4] Similarly, rule-of-law promoters tend to translate the rule of law into an institutional checklist, with primary emphasis on the judiciary.

The emphasis on judiciaries is widespread in the rule-of-law field, with the terms *judicial reform* and *rule-of-law reform* often used interchangeably. The emphasis derives from the fact that most rule-of-law promotion specialists are lawyers and when lawyers think about what seems to be the nerve center of the rule of law they think about the core institutions of law enforcement.

Yet it is by no means clear that courts are the essence of a rule-of-law system in a country. Only a small percentage of citizens in most Western rule-of-law systems ever have direct contact with courts. In a certain sense courts play a role late in the legal process—it might well be argued that the making of laws is the most generative part of a rule-of-law system. Yet rule-of-law programs have not much focused on legislatures or the role of executive branch agencies in law-making processes. The question of which institutions are most germane to the establishment of the rule of law in a country is actually quite complex and difficult. Yet for the last ten to fifteen years, rule-of-law programs have given dominant attention to judiciaries, without much examination of whether such a focus is really the right one.

The uncertainty goes beyond the question of "which institutions?" Indeed, doubt exists about whether it is useful to conceive of and attempt to act upon rule-of-law development in primarily institutional terms. Clearly law is not just the sum of courts, legislatures, police, prosecutors, and other formal institutions with some direct connection to law. Law is also a normative system that resides in the minds of the citizens of a society. As rule-of-law providers seek to affect the rule of law in a country, it is not clear if they should focus on institution building or instead try to intervene in ways that would affect how citizens understand, use, and value law. To take a simple example, many rule-of-law programs focus on improving a country's courts and police on the assumption that this is the most direct route to improve compliance with law in the country. Yet some research shows that compliance with law depends most heavily on the perceived fairness and legitimacy of the laws, characteristics that are not established primarily by the courts but by other means, such as the political process. An effort to improve compliance thus might more fruitfully take a completely different approach.

In sum, the question of where the essence of the rule of law actually resides and therefore what should be the focal point of efforts to improve the rule of law remains notably unsettled. Rule-of-law practitioners have been following an institutional approach, concentrating on judiciaries, more out of instinct than well-researched knowledge.

How Does Change Occur?

Even if we leave aside the problem of where the essence of the rule of law resides and accept the institutionalist approach that has become the norm, we see that rule-of-law aid providers face a problem of knowledge with regard to the very basic question of how change in systems actually occurs. Aid providers know what endpoint they would like to help countries achieve—the Western-style, rule-oriented systems they know from their own countries. Yet, they do not really know how countries that do not have such systems attain them. That is to say they do not know what the process of change consists of and how it might be brought about.

In launching and implementing the many rule-of-law programs of recent years, rule-of-law aid specialists have blurred this lack of knowledge by following what has been the approach to achieving change in the broader field of democracy assistance: attempting to reproduce institutional endpoints. This consists of diagnosing the shortcomings in selected institutions—that is, determining in what ways selected institutions do not resemble their counterparts in countries that donors believe embody successful rule of law—and then attempting to modify or reshape those institutions to fit the desired model. If a court lacks access to legal materials, then those legal materials should be provided. If case management in the courts is dysfunctional, it should be brought up to Western standards. If a criminal procedure law lacks adequate protections for detainees, it should be rewritten. The basic idea is that if the institutions can be changed to fit the models, the rule of law will emerge.

This breathtakingly mechanistic approach to rule-of-law development—a country achieves the rule of law by reshaping its key institutions to match those of countries that are considered to have the rule of law—quickly ran into deeply embedded resistance to change in many countries. The wave of judicial and police reform efforts in many Latin American countries sponsored by the United States in the second half of the 1980s, for example, initially bounced off institutions that had deep-seated reasons, whether good or bad, for being the way they were and little inclination to accept the reformist ideas brought from the outside.

The sobering experience with the early wave of efforts to promote institutional change produced two responses in the rule-of-law aid community. The first was a great deal of attention to what quickly came to be called "will to reform."[5] The new wisdom held that absent sufficient will to reform on the part of key host country officials, efforts to reform judiciaries, police, and other key institutions would be futile. It was up to rule-of-law aid providers to find and support "change agents" in the institutions, with the predominant assumption being that such agents would reside in the leadership of the institutions in question.

The sudden focus on will to reform was a way of restating the problem of how change occurs—aid providers should not presume change will naturally occur once institutions are introduced to the right way of doing things. Instead, change will occur when some of the key people inside the system want it to occur and those persons are given enabling assistance that allows them to carry out their will.

Though taken within the rule-of-law aid community as a crucial new in-sight, the focus on will to reform was a smaller step forward than it initially appeared. Major questions abound, still unanswered. For example, how does will to reform develop? Can it be generated and if so how? Should we assume that institutions change through gradualist reform processes willed by persons inside the system? Does public pressure play a major role? What about abrupt, drastic change provoked by persons outside the institutions who are dissatisfied with their function or who have their own goals about what institutions to have?

The other response to the initial wave of disappointments was the introduction within the rule-of-law aid community of the concepts of incentives and interests. After bouncing off a number of reform-resistant institutions, rule-of-law aid providers began saying that it was necessary to understand the underlying interests of institutional actors and to try to reshape the incentives to which these actors responded. This represented progress and allowed some analytic insights, which while rather basic were at least better than completely technocratic approaches. Aid providers began confronting the unpleasant fact, for example, that poorly performing judicial systems in many countries served the interests of powerful actors in various ways (for example, not serving as a means of justice for poor persons seeking to uphold land claims) and that the persons in those systems had no incentives to change their ways and had some significant incentives not to. But it was hard to go beyond new insights to new methods to produce change. Realizing that incentive structures are distorted is one thing; doing something about it is another. To some extent, casting the problem of change in terms of interests and incentives has ended up being more a restatement of lack of knowledge about how change occurs than an answer to it.

What Effects Will Change Have?

Although rule-of-law aid providers lack knowledge about what might produce broad-scale change in the role and function of law in a society that seems to lack the rule of law, they nevertheless do succeed in helping produce change in some specific areas. When they do, however, they often do not really know what effects those changes will have on the overall development of the rule of law in the country.

Consider several examples. A focus of many judicial reform programs has been to speed up the processing of cases by slow, inefficient courts. Such programs highlight administrative reforms, usually featuring the much-favored tool of case-tracking software. The aid providers' assumption is that efficient processing of cases is one small but vital element of the rule of law and improving that processing will improve the rule of law. Yet even in this well-defined, circumscribed area there is a surprising amount of uncertainty. For example, it is possible that if the processing of cases speeds up in a country where justice has long been quite poorly served, the number of cases filed with the courts might skyrocket, clogging the courts anew and effectively negating the reform achieved. Or, if the system has significant unfairness built into it, such as political bias or control, does increasing the speed of cases through the system actually represent a gain for the rule of law? This question arose vividly in Egypt in the second half of the 1990s where the United States devoted significant resources to helping the Egyptian judiciary improve its case management and speed up its processing of cases.

Another example concerns the spillover effects of improvement in one part of the system to other parts. A key belief animating some programs of commercial law reform in authoritarian or semiauthoritarian contexts is that if international aid efforts can help improve the quality of justice on commercial matters, this will augment justice in other domains and thus represent a kind of stealth method of promoting the rule of law in a broader political sense. The Western aid organizations supporting rule-of-law reforms in China and Vietnam regularly invoke this argument. It is of great appeal to donors who on the one hand seek to pave the way for business reforms that will facilitate commerce but on the other hand want to defend themselves against charges that they are assisting authoritarian regimes. Though attractive, the argument is not grounded in any systematic research and represents a typical example in the rule-of-law world of an appealing hypothesis that is repeated enough times until it takes on the quality of a received truth.

One more example concerns means of increasing judicial independence. Rule-of-law aid providers have given considerable attention to trying to find ways to increase judicial independence in Latin America and now are tackling the issue in other regions. Believing that one of the stumbling blocks is the hold on the process of judicial selection and promotion by politicized, corrupted ministries of justice, they have pushed for and supported efforts to establish semiautonomous judicial councils to take over these functions. The idea has common sense appeal, but despite an accumulating record of experience there has been little effort to date to examine in any systematic fashion whether the various new judicial councils have improved the situation. The first such study indicates that the results are not impressive.[6] Anecdotal evidence from Argentina and other countries suggests that as often happens with institutional solutions to deeper problems, the underlying maladies of the original institutions end up crossing over and infecting the new institutions.

These are just several of many possible examples that indicate that even when aid programs are able to facilitate fairly specific changes in relevant institutions, it is rarely clear what the longer-term effects of those changes are on the overall development of the rule of law in the country in question.

Limitations of Lessons Learned

In analyzing the levels and extent of the problem of knowledge in the field of rule-of-law assistance, I do not mean to imply that no learning is taking place. Aid practitioners, especially those who are close to the field efforts and have extensive experience in projects in at least several countries, often accumulate considerable knowledge about how to go about promoting the rule of law. Yet the knowledge tends to stay within the minds of individual practitioners and not get systematized or incorporated by the sponsoring institutions.

Aid institutions do seek to come up with "lessons learned" and to present them in official reports as evidence that they are taking seriously the need to reflect critically on their own work. Yet most of the lessons learned presented in such reports are not especially useful. Often they are too general or obvious, or both. Among the most common lessons learned, for example, are "programs must be shaped to fit the local environment" and "law reformers should not simply import laws from other countries." The fact that staggeringly obvious lessons of this type are put forward by institutions as lessons learned is an unfortunate commentary on the weakness of many of the aid efforts.

There is also the persistent problem of lessons learned not actually being learned. Experienced practitioners have consistently pointed, for example, to the fact that judicial training, while understandably appealing to aid agencies, is usually rife with shortcomings and rarely does much good.[7] Yet addicted to the relative ease of creating such programs and their common sense appeal, aid organizations persist in making judicial training one of the most common forms of rule-of-law assistance. Similarly, it has become painfully clear on countless occasions that trying to promote the rule of law by simply rewriting another country's laws on the basis of Western models achieves very little, given problems with laws not adapted to the local environment, the lack of capacity to implement or enforce the laws, and the lack of public understanding of them. Yet externally supported law reform efforts in many countries, especially those efforts relating to the commercial domain, often continue to be simplistic exercises of law copying. The problem of reforms being blocked by underlying interests and incentives turns out not only to apply to institutions in the aid-recipient countries but to the aid agencies themselves.

Obstacles to Knowledge

Confronted with the lack of systematic, well-grounded knowledge about how external aid can be used to promote the rule of law in other countries, aid officials have usually responded by arguing that the field is relatively young and still in the early stage of learning. As the years pass, however, this explanation is losing force. If one takes together the law and development movement and the current rule-of-law promotion field, over thirty years of activity are now under the bridge, surely enough time for real learning to take place. It is apparent therefore that some embedded obstacles to the accumulation of knowledge exist below the surface. At least five can be identified at a quick glance.

First, there is the unavoidable fact that the rule of law is an area of great conceptual and practical complexity. Understanding how law functions in a society, the roles it plays, and how it can change is extremely difficult, especially in societies that are not well understood by aid providers from many points of view. Foreign aid providers have found it hard enough to develop effective ways of analyzing and acting upon much more delimited challenges, such as increasing the supply of potable drinking water or vaccinations in poor societies. Grasping the problem of the shortcomings of law throughout the developing and postcommunist worlds is an enormous intellectual and practical challenge.

Related to this is a second problem—the tremendous particularity of the legal systems, or perhaps better stated, the functioning of law, in the countries of Latin America, Asia, Africa, Eastern Europe, and the former Soviet Union where rule-of-law promoters are at work. A rule-of-law aid provider traveling to Guyana, Yemen, Madagascar, or some other country to set up an assistance project is faced with the daunting challenge of understanding the realities of law in that particular society. He or she is unlikely to be able to draw much up-to-date, detailed, comprehensive, and insightful information about the problem because the availability of such knowledge tends to be highly sporadic. Even to the extent that some such information exists, drawing the connection between it and the question of "what to do?" is akin to stringing a very long, thin line between two distant points.

The third obstacle is that aid organizations have proven themselves to be ill-adept at the task of generating and accumulating the sort of knowledge that would help fill the gap. They profess great interest in lessons learned but tend not to devote many resources to serious reflection and research on their own efforts.[8] They are by nature forward-looking organizations, aimed at the next project or problem. Personnel tend to change positions regularly, undermining the building up of institutional knowledge. They are criticized by others if they are seen as devoting too much time to study and not enough to knowledge. And they work in a context of broader doubt about the value of aid, which has led to a tremendous set of conscious and unconscious defensive walls being built up around their activities, including rule-of-law work.

Fourth, if aid organizations are themselves not sponsoring the kind of applied policy research that would build knowledge in the rule-of-law promotion domain, neither are political science departments or law schools. This kind of research is eminently applied in nature and thus tends not to attract scholars, who have few professional incentives to tackle questions that arise from and relate to aid activities. Remarkably little writing has come out of the academy about the burgeoning field of rule-of-law promotion in the last twenty years. And only a small part of that existing literature is written by scholars who have had significant contact with actual aid programs.

A fifth obstacle is the fact that many lawyers—who tend to dominate the operational side of rule-of-law aid—are not oriented toward the empirical research necessary for organized knowledge accumulation. They often have relatively formalistic views of legal change and are slow to take up the developmental, process-oriented issues that have come to inform work in other areas of socioeconomic or sociopolitical change. Also, lawyers working on rule-of-law aid programs sometimes feel in tension with the aid organizations of which they are part. They are a minority legal subculture in organizations unfamiliar with and often not wholly comfortable with legal development work. This leads the rule-of-law aid practitioners to feel they lack the space necessary for searching studies of rule-of-law aid and to be wary of other development specialists attempting to raise hard questions about this work.

When Is a Field a Field?

The rapidly growing field of rule-of-law assistance is operating from a disturbingly thin base of knowledge at every level—with respect to the core rationale of the work, the question of where the essence of the rule of law actually resides in different societies, how change in the rule of law occurs, and what the real effects are of changes that are produced. The lessons learned to date have for the most part not been impressive and often do not actually seem to be learned. The obstacles to the accumulation of knowledge are serious and range from institutional shortcomings of the main aid actors to deeper intellectual challenges about how to fathom the complexity of law itself.

Thus far the field of rule-of-law assistance has expanded less because of the tangible successes of such work than because of the irresistible apparent connection of the rule of law with the underlying goals of

market economics and democracy that now constitute the dual foundation of contemporary international aid. With a recognizable set of activities that make up the rule-of-law assistance domain (primarily judicial
reform, criminal law reform, commercial law reform, legal education
work, and alternative dispute resolution), a growing body of professional
specialists, and a consistent place on the international aid agenda, rule-
of-law assistance has taken on the character of a coherent field of aid.
Yet it is not yet a field if one considers a requirement for such a designa-
tion to include a well-grounded rationale, a clear understanding of the
essential problem, a proven analytic method, and an understanding of
results achieved. Doubtless many types of work with law in developing
and postcommunist countries are valuable and should be part of the
international community's engagement with these countries. However,
whether rule-of-law promotion is in fact an established field of international aid or is even on the road to becoming one remains uncertain.

Notes

An earlier version of this chaapter was originally published as Carnegie Working Paper
no. 34 (January 2003).

1. See John Hewko, "Foreign Direct Investment: Does the Rule of Law Matter?" Carnegie
   Endowment Working Paper no. 26 (Washington, D.C.: Carnegie Endowment for International Peace, April 2002).
2. See Frank Upham, "Mythmaking in the Rule of Law Orthodoxy," Carnegie Endowment Working Paper no. 30 (Washington, D.C.: Carnegie Endowment for International Peace, September 2002).
3. Rick Messick, "Judicial Reform and Economic Development: A Survey of the Issues,"
   The World Bank Research Observer 14, no. 1 (February 1999): 117–36.
4. On the democracy template, see Thomas Carothers, *Aiding Democracy Abroad: The
   Learning Curve* (Washington, D.C.: Carnegie Endowment for International Peace, 1999),
   ch. 5.
5. The first major shift to a focus on will to reform came after a review in the early 1990s
   by the U.S. Agency for International Development (USAID) of its own rule-of-law
   programs. See Harry Blair and Gary Hansen, *Weighing in on the Scales of Justice: Strategic Approaches for Donor-Supported Rule of Law Programs*, USAID Program and Operations Assessment Report no. 7 (Washington, D.C.: USAID, 1994).
6. See Linn Hammergren, "Do Judicial Councils Further Judicial Reform? Lessons from
   Latin America," Carnegie Endowment Working Paper no. 28 (Washington, D.C.:
   Carnegie Endowment for International Peace, June 2002).
7. See, for example, the critical analysis of judicial training programs in Linn Hammergen,
   Judicial Training and Justice Reform (Washington, D.C.: USAID Center for Democracy
   and Governance, August 1998).
8. One noteworthy exception is the study of legal and judicial reform by Linn
   Hammergren, sponsored by USAID and released as four papers in 1998.

PART II

Questioning the Orthodoxy

CHAPTER THREE

Competing Definitions of the Rule of Law

RACHEL KLEINFELD

The rule of law bakes no bread, it is unable to distribute loaves or fishes (it has none), and it cannot protect itself against external assault, but it remains the most civilized and least burdensome conception of a state yet to be devised.

—Michael Oakeshott, 1983[1]

It would not be very difficult to show that the phrase "the Rule of Law" has become meaningless thanks to ideological abuse and general over-use. It may well have become just another one of those self-congratulatory rhetorical devices that grace the public utterances of Anglo-American politicians. No intellectual effort need therefore be wasted on this bit of ruling-class chatter.

—Judith Shklar, 1987[2]

DEVELOPED COUNTRIES and international organizations have spent more than a billion dollars over the last twenty years trying to build the rule of law in countries transitioning to democracy or attempting to escape underdevelopment.[3] Like a product sold on late-night television, the rule of law is touted as able to accomplish everything from improving human rights to enabling economic growth to helping to win the war on terror. The rule of law is deemed an essential component of democracy and free markets. The North Atlantic Treaty Organization (NATO) demands that all new members demonstrate their commitment to it, and the European Union (EU) requires its existence before a country can even begin negotiating for accession. Building the rule of law is a strategic objective of the U.S. Agency for International Development (USAID), a growth field for the World Bank, and a rhetorical trope for politicians worldwide.[4] So what is this magical elixir?

Read any set of articles discussing the rule of law, and the concept emerges looking like the proverbial blind man's elephant—a trunk to one person, a tail to another. In fact, the phrase is commonly used today to imply at least five separate meanings or end goals. One frequent usage implies a government that abides by standing laws and respects judicial rule—precisely what the International Bar Association found lacking when it chastised Zimbabwe for destroying the rule of law in that country.[5] By this same standard, neighboring South Africa is praised for its government's willingness to abide by the law. Yet USAID is sponsoring "rule-of-law" building activities there to counter high crime rates—under a definition of the rule of law that means "law and order."[6] An *Asia Times* writer uses the term to mean lack of equality before the law, stating, "If a case arises between two normal people, then the law is somewhat powerful. But if one person is a company official or from the government, then there is no power in the law."[7] The rule of law is also frequently used as a synonym for enforced human rights. Amnesty International, for example, is not alone in making statements such as, "The only way to make a break from the past, a time when human rights were routinely abused, is to establish the rule of law, with the protection of human rights at its center."[8] Meanwhile, under the aegis of rule-of-law building, the World Bank is providing computers to courts, printing laws, and establishing magistrates' schools to create its technocratic vision of the rule of law as efficient and predictable justice.[9]

Is the rule of law any of these bundles of goods, a set of goods lumped together, or a set of goods that must be related to one another in a particular way? Is it, in other words, a tail or a trunk, a bundle of elephant parts, or the whole elephant? Among those who define the rule of law by its ends—and thus argue about which ends deserve inclusion—this argument has raged since the ancient Greeks. The debate continues today, mainly among legal scholars.[10] Yet among others—particularly within the practitioner, political, and journalistic communities—the very question seems to have gone unnoticed. The five ends are jumbled together willy-nilly, any end may be implied when the phrase *rule of law* is invoked, and differences between ends are often ignored.

This conceptual confusion may have arisen because practitioners working to build the rule of law abroad have developed an entirely different way of looking at the concept, based not on end goals but on institutions to be reformed.[11] Few modern rule-of-law reform practitioners sat down and enjoyed a disquisition on classical rule-of-law conceptions before taking up their jobs; their efforts were developed in the heat of battle, as authoritarianism was pushed back, Communism fell, and countries had immediate needs for functioning economies, governments, and societies. In response to these unprecedented demands, aid agencies and their hastily employed lawyers tried to get a handle on the massive new undertaking by breaking the concept down into the concrete institutions that needed reforming. In Latin America, that meant a focus on "judicial reform," gradually expanding to law and then police reform. In Eastern Europe, legal change alone was thought sufficient in early years; when this approach failed to bear fruit, efforts expanded to reform other rule-of-law institutions. When the U.S. Government Accounting Office (GAO) was asked to evaluate U.S. rule-of-law assistance, for instance, they defined the scope of their work as many practitioners would:

> Throughout this report, we use the phrase "rule of law" to refer to U.S. assistance efforts to support legal, judicial, and law enforcement reform efforts undertaken by foreign governments. This term encompasses assistance to help reform legal systems (criminal, civil, administrative, and commercial laws and regulations) as well as judicial and law enforcement institutions (ministries of justice, courts, and police, including their organizations, procedures, and personnel).[12]

In other words, a parallel conversation has emerged in which the rule of law is defined not by the end purposes it is to serve in society but by what I will call its "institutional attributes." Creating the proper institutional attributes—the "necessary" laws, a "well-functioning" judiciary, and a "good" law enforcement apparatus—has become, for many practitioners, the goal of rule-of-law reform efforts.

Thus, there are two very different ways of defining the rule of law that are being discussed in parallel conversations.[13] The first style of definition enumerates the goods that the rule of law brings to society. A society with the rule of law is a society that instantiates these goods or ends, such as law and order, a government bound by the law, and human rights. The ends are the reason why we value the rule of law and are what most people mentally measure when determining the degree to which a country has the rule of law. Another type of definition describes the institutions a society must have to be considered to possess the rule of law. Such a society would have certain institutional attributes, such as an efficient and trained judiciary, a noncorrupt police force, and published, publicly known laws.

These two different ways of defining the concept are often conflated and confused. Current definitions of the rule of law used by organizations working to create it abroad tend toward ad hoc laundry lists of institutions to reform, mixed with high-flying rhetoric about the ends that the rule of law is expected to accomplish.[14] It is easy to accuse attempts at closer definition as pedantic, academic exercises. After all, even if current practitioners have not precisely defined their terms, they will know what they want when they see it.

If institutional reform led directly to improvements in rule-of-law ends, that would be true enough. Yet, because achieving such ends requires reform *across* institutions while institutional reforms are generally carried out *within* single institutions, institutional reform can be undertaken with no significant effect on rule-of-law ends. At the same time, definitions based on institutional attributes lead practitioners to measure the wrong things to determine success. Worse, poorly devised reforms of rule-of-law institutions can undermine rule-of-law ends. Therefore, the slant toward definitions that are based on institutional attributes or that amalgamate ends and institutions has serious repercussions for the success (or lack thereof) of rule-of-law building strategies. Improving our definitions is crucial to advancing our understanding of what it is we are trying to build and our ability to implement reforms. Before we can improve definitions, however, we must first consider each definition in turn.

Ends-Based Definitions

Already, in discussing the "ends" of the rule of law, I have gotten ahead of the general use of the phrase. In ringing policy pronouncements and membership criteria for exclusive "clubs" such as NATO and the EU, the rule of law itself is the desired end—singular. States can have more or less rule of law, and more is always better. Yet as the elephant metaphor indicates, by the time the field of rule-of-law building had gained steam, the concept was being used to imply at least five different goals:

making the state abide by law, ensuring equality before the law, supplying law and order, providing efficient and impartial justice, and upholding human rights.

Because these ends were never clarified or separated, practitioner organizations did not fully appreciate their distinctiveness. In their written definitions, practitioner organizations tend to mention some ends and forget others—often with little consistency in which they include and which they leave out from definition to definition. For instance, in the various USAID definitions cited in this paper, predictability appears in only one, while another leaves out law and order and touts a market-based economy as inherent to the concept.[15]

Clarity on the five end goals is important, however, because they are not the same: One cannot be reduced to another. On a theoretical level, some of these end goals have become generally accepted in Western legal and political philosophy over the last few thousand years. Others remain hotly disputed. Reining in the state by forcing it to govern through a known set of laws has been accepted as a goal of the rule of law since the ancient Greeks.[16] Meanwhile, whether human rights is an end of the rule of law—or whether the phrase merely implies technocratic procedures and institutions—has been contested from Aristotle to the present day. For modern practitioners, these disputes still affect the success of reforms but are often unrecognized: For instance, the kleptocrats in a transitioning country might happily accept limiting the power of a previously autocratic state (thereby enhancing their own economically based power), but they may balk at equality before the law.

In other words, clarity on the five ends we are now seeking from the pursuit of the rule of law is also important because each end goal touches on different cultural and political issues. Each is thus likely to meet different pockets of resistance from different portions of society in countries being reformed. Aid practitioners often talk about the importance of finding "political will" for rule-of-law reforms and overcoming resistance. Clarifying the actual ends being sought from various rule-of-law reforms highlights the fact that different elements of society are likely to have "will" for different sorts of reforms and that those resistant to one reform may be supportive of another.

Because rule-of-law ends are so contested and historically determined, they cannot simply be stated as given. They must be understood as varying greatly by context, culture, and era. Simply describing the ways in which the term is currently used lacks depth and provides no heft to argue against certain ways of using the term that are erroneous or unhelpful. Thinking about rule-of-law ends requires realizing that they are historically and culturally determined concepts. New ends can be discovered by reinterpretation or reemphasis of old ideas, but creating a new end is a lengthy and intellectually weighty proposition, not something that can simply be declared by practitioners.

I will therefore look at each of the current ends in turn, first describing their historical precedent and the societal goals they are expected to uphold. I will then consider which of the primary rule-of-law institutions (laws, courts, and law enforcement)—as well as which nonorganizational cultural and political structures—would need to be reformed to accomplish the end. Finally, for each goal I will discuss the power centers it affects, and the possible resistance for reform. By doing so, I hope to demonstrate why it is useful for practitioners to consider their reforms end by end, rather than institution by institution, so that they can accurately gauge the likelihood of their success.

Government Bound by Law

When the idea of the rule of law was first conceived, the original end was to make the state subordinate to law in order to prevent arbitrariness. Aristotle considered whether it was better for kings to rule with discretion or according to law, and determined that in a state governed by law "God and reason alone rule," whereas "passion perverts the minds of rulers, even if they are the best of men."[17] Solon provided Athens with laws so that they would have "the certainty of being governed legally in accordance with known rules."[18] The idea, naturally enough, fell out of favor during centuries of monarchical absolute rule, particularly in Europe. The Magna Carta introduced the concept in England, and the celebrated English Petition of Grievances of 1610 emphasized the basic notion of a government subordinate to law when it claimed that the most prized traditional right of English subjects was

> to be guided and governed by the certain rule of law, which giveth to the head and the members that which of right belongeth to them, and not be any uncertain and arbitrary form of government . . . [and that people should not be subject to any punishment] other than such as are ordained by the common laws of this land or the statutes made by their common consent in parliament.[19]

The idea that the monarch needed to act through parliament to suspend or create laws was enshrined in the English Bill of Rights of 1689.[20]

A government bound by law must act through pre-written laws in executing its decisions and change laws through established legislative means. Absolute governments, from Caligula to modern-day Myanmar, have taken the property of subjects without recompense, killed citizens at will, and destroyed economies on vanity projects and silly ideas. Governments bound by law must, at the very least, follow pre-written laws or pass general laws through separate legislative organs before undertaking such destructive activities. Under this end alone, however, governments would still be able to abrogate individual rights as long as they followed correct legal procedures: Upholding rights is a separate end and requires additional means to accomplish.[21]

Binding the government to rule *by* law is the sine qua non of the rule *of* law. Some would even argue that this end alone is enough to constitute the rule of law—although most scholars, lawyers, and rule-of-law practitioners hold a more expansive definition.[22] Regardless, this concept can hardly be described as technical; after all, restricting the powers of an otherwise absolute government is a highly political activity. In countries where the rule of law is being reformed, strong or absolute executives have usually held sway quite recently, either in communist or authoritarian systems. So real powers are being taken away from powerful individuals when judiciaries are strengthened and procedural laws that bind the executive are passed. Reformers would be naïve not to expect recalcitrance and evasion of reforms meant to achieve this end from those who stand to lose power. However, these reforms also strengthen other power centers—particularly the judiciary, which is often weak and subservient, commanding little respect under absolute regimes. For reforms that bind the government to rule by law, the judiciary is often a reform ally. Such a face-off does not necessarily make the judiciary more "reformist" than the government across the board; it simply means that on this dimension of the rule of law, the judiciary tends to benefit from supporting reform.

Often, binding a government to rule by law is treated as an issue of judicial independence and is therefore considered an issue of court reform. Obviously, as stated above, power plays a far greater role than mere court organization in limiting the government, although well-organized courts with self-confidence can play a strong role in curtailing government power. Laws must also codify the concept. Law enforcement is generally ignored in achieving this end, yet in any absolute government or captured state, one of the mainstays of extralegal power is having law enforcement bodies that answer to the government, not the people. In fact, the transfer of military and police allegiance from the regime to the citizens is often the first essential step in moving auto- cratic governments toward becoming governments bound by law.

Equality before the Law

Equality before the law also hearkens back to disputes among the Greeks. Plato insisted on a hierarchical society buttressed by an original myth, but Solon gave Athens, "equal laws for the noble and the base." Again, centuries of hierarchical monarchy halted further development of the concept, which revived during the Enlightenment and the French Revo- lution. When A.V. Dicey crafted his seminal modern definition of the rule of law, one of his three "kindred conceptions" was the idea that all people are equal before the law, and that all, particularly government officials and clergymen, must be tried under the same laws and in the same courts as ordinary men.[23]

Equality before the law ensures that all citizens—no matter how well- connected, rich, or powerful—are judged for their actions by the same laws, equally applied. Equality before the law is one of the core ways in which citizens can ensure that government officials, the rich, the power- ful, and the well-connected do not become a caste apart. It is also essen- tial for upholding the rights of marginalized groups, such as women and racial and religious minorities, who must also be treated as equal before the law. In transitional and developing countries, the lack of equal- ity before the law—the feeling that there are not "equal laws for the noble and the base"—is a prime complaint and is often believed so strongly that ordinary people do not even attempt to test the principle with a time-consuming and expensive court case.

As with reining in the government, creating equality before the law changes the balance of power in a society, giving far more power to ordinary people at the expense of the rich and powerful. It is therefore likely to meet with political resistance when it becomes successful enough to really threaten power holders. Nor is such resistance entirely self- serving: Those in politics are often most likely to be accused of misdeeds by political rivals; if equality before the law is not enforced by courts that are truly independent, politicians can face punishment for wrongs they may not have committed. Equality before the law can also meet cultural resistance. In many Islamic societies, giving women equality before the law is opposed by most interpretations of Sharia, the Islamic code. In other cases, equality before the law is de jure, but different justice prevails de facto. For example, even though India has formal equality before the law, caste concepts in villages remain strong; the idea that a low-caste person should be treated as the equal of a high-caste person is "unjust" in such contexts, as well as irreligious. The idea of equality would be seen as nearly inhuman in less individualistic societies. For example, the notion that a policeman should treat his mother caught in a crime as he would a stranger would be seen in the West as personally difficult but nonetheless a just ideal, whereas elsewhere it would be seen as manifestly unjust.[24]

Real equality before the law requires courts that are strong and independent enough to enforce it. It also depends particularly on a lack of corruption within the judiciary, because the rich can use bribes to escape equal justice. It is highly dependent on cultural factors that reinforce the notion and on a government strongly committed to upholding minority rights in this area. In other words, promoting equality before the law requires change across laws, courts, and even law enforcement, as well as alterations in the cultural and political fabric. Not only does it require a good system, but it also requires citizens who are willing to test the principle. Bringing a case to court is time consuming and expensive (just in opportunity costs alone); in many countries, the poor or marginalized will not risk bringing misdeeds of their "betters" before a court if they believe the courts will simply uphold the power structure of society. Thus, access to justice programs has proliferated as a means of helping to create de facto equality before the law.

Law and Order

Law and order did not form a major portion of the political thought of ancient Greek philosophers. Enlightenment thinkers, however, were influenced by the brutality of the English civil war and entranced by the idea of the newly explored "savage" America.[25] They began considering the origins of the state by contrasting it with the brutality of the state of nature. Hobbes stated that escaping the anarchy of a "nasty, brutish, and short" life subject to the crimes and whims of one's fellow human beings was the main reason people joined the state. In perhaps one of their few points of agreement, Locke assents: Why would people give up absolute liberty and be subject to a government? Because although they have the natural rights of freedom, property, and so on, "Enjoyment of it is very uncertain, and constantly exposed to the Invasion of others . . . the enjoyment of the property [they have] in this [state of nature] is very unsafe, very unsecure." People join society for the "mutual *Preservation* of their Lives, Liberties, and Estates, which I call by the general Name, *Property*."[26] Protection from one's fellow citizens—or law and order, as we would say today—thus became one of the ends that government was supposed to provide.[27] Law and order is central to the popular understanding of the rule of law. Most citizens within weak states see law and order as perhaps the main good of the rule of law. Law and order is essential to protecting the lives and property of citizens—in fact, it is a prime way of protecting the human rights of the poor and marginalized, who often face the greatest threat from a lack of security.[28] In this end goal, the rule of law is often contrasted with either anarchy or with a form of self-justice in which citizens do not trust in the state to punish wrongdoers and to right wrongs but instead take justice into their own hands and use violence to enforce the social order.

Law and order, however, came to the concept of the rule of law through the back door. As described above, it was never part of the philosophical basis of the rule of law but emerged from the way in which Enlightenment thinkers groped toward their political ideals. Although it pervades the common use of the term, it elided with the rule of law rather than finding a comfortable situation within Western jurisprudential definitions. Dicey, for example, left it out of his first modern attempt to pin down the meaning of the rule of law.

This "poor-cousin" historical status has had direct effects on the place of law and order in modern rule-of-law building efforts. Despite its importance to the popular conception of the rule of law, and its essential role in attracting foreign investment, ensuring the well-being of the poor, and promoting global security, law and order tends to be outside mainstream rule-of-law building projects. Ironically, although U.S. and EU rule-of-law assistance disproportionately flows to police reform and equipment (reflecting the fact that such aid serves donor countries' own security interests ranging from combating drug trafficking to countering terror), these programs tend to be separate from legal and judicial reform programs in the minds of scholars and practitioners; they are also administered by different agencies and farmed out to different contractors.[29] Police reform efforts are often oriented more toward border security or solving law-and-order problems that spill over and affect other states, such as smuggling and human trafficking, than they are geared toward promoting domestic law and order per se. Insofar as rule-of-law programs do consider the police, their focus tends to be human rights training, not law and order.

In the United States, part of the isolation of law and order from the mainstream rule-of-law building agenda can be attributed to U.S. law: Congress banned foreign development aid from being used for police training after U.S.-trained police in Latin America were found to be committing human rights abuses in the 1960s. Although the rules have been relaxed and many loopholes admitted, the stigma still remains. Professional balkanization likely plays a part as well: Lawyers, who make up the bulk of rule-of-law practitioners, tend to be different types of people and move in different circles from the security officials who focus on reforms more directly related to law and order.

As with the other ends discussed earlier, law and order requires more than institutional change; it also has political and cultural components and can meet resistance from any of these areas. States want the police strong enough to do their bidding and fend off threats to their power, but they do not want the police (who are often paramilitary in developing countries) to *become* threats to their power. Unless power backs a strong, professional police force, such a force is unlikely to emerge without a fight. Although law and order might appear to be a universal good, it also depends heavily on citizens' acceptance of laws and on the government's legitimacy to make laws that bind them.[30] Customs such as blood feud traditions can also undermine the imposition of a state-based law and order.

The split between law and order and other rule-of-law ends is pernicious for two reasons. First, because this end conflates easily with an institution, law and order is often viewed solely as police reform efforts. But as with the other ends, improving law and order requires cooperation across all rule-of-law institutions. Police reform alone can do nothing to quell crime if police capture criminals and then corrupt judges release them, if prisons allow prisoners to enlarge their criminal empires while behind bars, or if laws do not exist to keep criminals in jail for significant periods of time.[31]

Second, high degrees of crime tend to undermine other rule-of-law reforms. Crime is often better remunerated than magistracy in many developing countries, and criminals try to bribe judges to evade imprisonment. In many countries with law-and-order problems, judges are afraid to dispense equal justice to members of the military, organized criminals, or gangs for fear of reprisal or that they will not survive the sentencing.[32] At its worst, criminals buy politicians to gain security for their enterprises or buy political seats to gain immunity to distort the system. Moreover, organized criminals and drug gangs can abuse human rights on just as wide a scale as any government. Thus, high crime rates not only harm law and order but can also corrupt or overwhelm all rule-of-law institutions and undermine all other rule-of-law ends. By treating law and order as an institutional reform of the police and leaving it to the police and security reformers, those working on other rule-of-law goals practically ensure that they will not achieve their own ends.[33]

Predictable, Efficient Justice

The idea of efficiency had been implicit since the Magna Carta, which first hinted that justice would neither be denied nor delayed.[34] In 1693, William Penn wrote, "Our law says well, 'To delay justice, is injustice.'"[35] By the time the famous aphorism "justice delayed is justice denied" was (mis)attributed to Gladstone and the first legal case cited it as precedent, the idea that the rule of law required some form of efficiency in decision making was fairly settled.[36] In part, efficient justice was seen as a way to uphold other rule-of-law ends, such as discouraging the tried-and-tested method of delaying cases to extort bribes from those who most wanted a decision. Delay could also be used to subvert justice, such as when delays intrinsically favored one party and therefore acted as a penalty to the other party before a judgment was even announced.[37]

Hayek, meanwhile, did the most to revive the notion of predictability, hinted at by the earliest Greek thinkers, as a stand-alone element of the rule of law. Although Hayek's writings stress that the rule of law is about binding the government to rule through legislated laws, his underlying interest is in how the rule of law buttresses the market economy. One of the primary by-products of the rule of law, in Hayek's mind, is that it provides predictability—it allows one to "plan one's individual affairs."[38] But Hayek's antipathy to judicial discretion meant that predictability gained a prominent place in his argument.[39] Hayek's followers cemented the idea. What had been part of the outcome of the rule of law, in Hayek's definition, had become an element of the rule of law by the time Ronald Cass defined the concept in 2001 as: (1) fidelity to rules, (2) *of principled predictability*, (3) embodied in valid authority, (4) that is external to government decision makers (emphasis added).[40]

A predictable, efficient legal system allows businesses to plan, enables law-abiding citizens and businesses to stay on the correct side of the law, and provides some level of deterrence against criminal acts. It enables a free market by providing for efficient adjudication of contract disputes. Efficiency is relative and differs widely in countries that see themselves as having the rule of law. What is important in both cases is that the majority of people see the judicial system as a viable means for solving disputes so that they are not forced to use extrajudicial means—ranging from only doing business with trusted family members to hiring contract killers—to attain the same ends. Predictability and efficiency are thus closely linked with law and order and with equality before the law. A lack of either law and order or equality can harm predictability and efficiency, while a lack of predictability and efficiency can undermine law and order by forcing citizens to bypass courts and take justice into their own hands.

Predictability and efficiency are typically seen by practitioners as attributes of the judiciary alone. However, laws and law enforcement are also needed to support the end goal. If laws are not relatively known and settled, it is difficult for courts to rule with predictability. Overzealous legal reform, such as occurred in Romanian commercial laws, can wreak havoc on predictable decisions—not only because the laws are changing, but because it is difficult for overtaxed and understaffed judges to keep up to date on these legal changes. Moreover, judges are not the only possible source of legal delay; clerks can "lose" files, and law enforcement agencies can delay investigations in return for bribes just as easily. In Moscow during the roaring 1990s, for example, the going rate for stalling a criminal investigation was claimed to be $50,000.[41]

Current rule-of-law building organizations such as the World Bank, with a vested interest in making the concept as technocratic and apolitical as possible, have further elevated the ideas of predictability and efficiency as central pillars of the rule of law.[42] When the World Bank pushes the rule of law for development, for instance, they couch their thinking in Hayek and label their internal think-tank Legal Institutions for the Market Economy. Many of their legal development specialists fail to consider whether, for instance, rampant law-and-order problems might be dampening foreign investment in Africa or Russia more than a weak system of commercial law.[43] Development technocrats push for predictability and efficiency as their primary—and often only—rule-of-law goal, hoping that the more political issues such as limiting government or the more cultural issues such as human rights will come in on the same tide. Yet these are separate ends, and although there are relationships among them, as discussed above, there is no reason to assume that pushing one will help all of the others.

In fact, predictability and efficiency are often used by local power brokers as code words to achieve their own goals, which can undermine other rule-of-law ends. Ministries of justice can advance predictability, for instance, by holding anticorruption drives that let them purge courts of independent judges, or they can promote efficiency by delivering computers to those justices who promise them allegiance. Although real reform would reduce the executive's control over the judiciary, a reform that only half accomplishes its goals will often increase executive control—hence the support many ministries of justice give to these programs and the waffling that can occur later. Judiciaries tend to balk at these reforms because, when successful, they reduce chances for corruption, patronage, and the less pernicious but often equally Byzantine immemorial customs that judiciaries the world over uphold. Determining exactly who is balking at what reform can be difficult in such circumstances. For example, a Romanian minister of justice who appeared to this author and to many Romanian liberals as genuinely committed to helping the judiciary reduce its case backlog, improve its skills, become less corrupt, and promote younger, more honest and liberal judges, used means that were nearly the same as those used by his successor—an ex-Communist who was, by all accounts except her own, attempting to regain executive control over the judiciary and reduce its independence.[44] Predictability and efficiency are important and accepted rule-of-law ends. But they, in particular, show the hazard of not recognizing the tension between ends, and their irreducibility.

Lack of State Violation of Human Rights

The Enlightenment revival of the rule of law expanded the idea of individual rights nascent in the previously cited English Petition of Grievances. Locke asked the question: Why should rulers not have absolute power over their subjects—why should rulers not be arbitrary? Because all humans have natural rights that proceeded his rule, he answered. People join the state voluntarily to protect those rights, and thus it makes no sense for the state to be able to abrogate them. Making a ruler bow to law thus became intertwined with the end goal of individual rights, including the right to preserve "lives, liberties, and estates."[45] By positing natural rights, Enlightenment thinkers added substantive content to the procedural ideals of the rule of law. The importance of individual rights was upheld in Dicey's first modern conception of the term, which lauds the common law as a way of ensuring that individual rights are not only established but also enforced.[46] Because the modern rule-of-law building field grew in large part out of a desire to improve human rights in

Latin America in the 1980s and to create liberal democracy in Eastern Europe in the 1990s, getting states to recognize and not violate human rights was from the beginning a core reason for undertaking rule-of-law reforms.[47]

Yet human rights are the most contested end of the rule of law. A debate has raged for centuries between substantivists, who believe the rule of law must contain some content and some limits on what the government can *ever* legally do, and formalists, who claim that the rule of law is simply about procedure, not content. Formalists such as U.S. Supreme Court Justice Antonin Scalia have argued that there "are times when even a bad rule is better than no rule at all."[48] Experience in countries where the government is above the law, where anarchy has taken hold, or where laws change so frequently that businesses cannot plan and individuals cannot even know what justice would be gives this view weight. For formalists, the rule of law is useful because it provides the four goods mentioned above. Insofar as it provides justice, it does so procedurally, through efficiency and equality before the law. The rule of law cannot be expected to provide just outcomes such as human rights. Human rights may be a laudable goal, but they are seen as separate from the rule of law.[49]

Substantivists believe the formalist definition amounts to rule *by* law, which strengthens the government, not a rule of law meant to bind it to certain acceptable ways of treating citizens.[50] Aristotle was the first substantivist, stating that his *Politics* showed nothing more than that "laws, *when good*, should be supreme" (emphasis added), raising the question of what a "good" law entailed.[51] Locke's definition of rule-of-law institutions quoted above concludes with the statement, "all this is to be directed to no other *end* but the *Peace, Safety*, and publick good of the People."[52] This definition suggested that the rule of law was intended to have content that would protect the citizens of a state; therefore, states such as Nazi Germany or apartheid South Africa (which were run by law but used that law as an instrument to deprive some citizens of peace and safety) were not governed by the rule of law at all.

Those rule-of-law practitioners who include human rights in their goals are thus taking a side in this debate—they are not promoting a technocratic ideal, but a cultural idea with substantive, values-driven content. The problem with human rights as an end, of course, is that different cultures—and different countries, even within the developed world—differ on what they see as human rights. Even when general concepts can be universalizable, particulars, such as the death penalty,

social and economic rights, or even the practice of female genital mutilation, are disputed. Some in the United States see a Scandinavian-style
system of social and economic rights as undermining property rights
through excessive taxation. Europeans see the U.S. death penalty as a
human rights violation. In Romania, the EU pushed very hard for the
legislature to repeal laws criminalizing homosexuality—a human rights
issue essential to the rule of law to the European Commission, but a
moral issue that had nothing to do with the rule of law to the indignant
Romanians.

As with all the other ends, human rights require reforming many rule-
of-law institutions, as well as establishing new cultural norms. Laws can
and must be established to promote these rights, but laws are among the
weakest instruments for protecting human rights. It was precisely because laws alone are such poor defenders of human rights, particularly
when they get ahead of social and government intuition, that Dicey championed the common law—which by definition enforced rights at the time
they are proclaimed. Police must be trained to uphold human rights and
watched to ensure that they do so. Unfortunately, they are often among
the worst abusers of human rights. The judiciary has traditionally been
a bastion for the protection of individual liberties and minority rights
against encroachment from the government and the uncaring majority,
but in developing countries, the judiciary can only serve this function to
the extent that its members uphold liberalism over traditional or
majoritarian values.[53] Culture generally matters a great deal in proclaiming and promoting human rights. Governments can get ahead of their
citizenry, as occurred in the American south with *Brown v. Board of Education*, but they rarely go too far outside culturally set boundaries, and
when they do, these rights tend to be de jure alone.

A Note on Ends-Based Definitions

As shown above, defining the rule of law based on the ends it is intended to achieve within a society provides more clarity and focuses
practitioners more on their end goals than defining it by institutional
attributes, which are just means to these ends. Moreover, achieving any
end requires reform across multiple rule-of-law institutions. Reforming
a single institution or even reforming laws and courts but not law enforcement will rarely be able to further rule-of-law ends.

Considering rule of law by its ends also illuminates one of the major
difficulties with rule-of-law reform: All good things do not go together.

These ends are not part of a unified concept that emerged whole; rather they grew piecemeal in response to different historical needs over a period of millennia. They represent distinct societal goals, and work toward one goal will not necessarily lead to success in the others. Moreover, these ends are often in tension: Improving one can often make success in another more difficult—a point to which I will return when discussing implications.

Institutional Approach

Although most legal scholars define the rule of law by its ends, most programs to build the rule of law implicitly define the rule of law by its institutional attributes. Although they cite the rule of law as their ultimate goal, practitioners almost immediately turn to institutions not as means, but as intermediate or measurable ends. Internally, most practitioner organizations rarely use the words *rule-of-law reform* and instead discuss legal reform, judicial reform, and police (or law enforcement) reform.

Institutional definitions of the rule of law are not new. Their heritage stretches back to ancient Greek discussions of the need for standing laws, impartial courts, and enforcement mechanisms (although the latter were often religious, political, or cultural strictures, not modern law-enforcement bodies). The three primary institutions that modern-day rule-of-law programs focus on were first enumerated by John Locke, who stated that legitimate governments were:

> bound to govern by establish'd *standing Laws*, promulgated and known to the People, and not by Extemporary Decrees, by *indifferent* and upright *Judges*, who are to decide Controversies by those Laws; and to imploy the force of the community at home only in the execution of such Laws.[54]

Modern rule-of-law practitioners still define the rule of law as a state that contains these three primary institutions:

- **Laws** themselves, which are publicly known and relatively settled;
- A **judiciary** schooled in legal reasoning, knowledgeable about the law, reasonably efficient, and independent of political manipulation and corruption; and
- A **force able to enforce laws**, execute judgments, and maintain public peace and safety: usually police, bailiffs, and other law enforcement bodies.

As practitioners have tried to reform these primary institutions, however, they have found that they rely on the proper functioning of a large and ever-growing array of essential supporting institutions. Laws are supported by institutions ranging from legislatures to land cadastres and notary publics. The judiciary is reliant on magistrates' schools, law schools, bar associations, clerks and administrative workers, and other supporting groups. Police require prisons, intelligence services, bail systems, and cooperative agreements with border guards and other law enforcement bodies, among other institutions. As new supporting institutions are discovered and deemed to be essential, they are added to the list of areas in need of reform.

From Institutions as Means to Institutions as Ends-in-Themselves

When ancient Greek or Enlightenment philosophers discussed the rule of law, these material rule-of-law institutions were considered means to overarching societal ends, such as order, rights, and justice. Aristotle, for instance, discussed various forms of political arrangements, as well as the institutions of the magistrates and juries, and cultural and personal values, as enforcement mechanisms—all of which were judged on how they would affect the end goals that the rule of law was supposed to accomplish.[55]

Similarly, when the rule of law first came into the development field through the work of Douglass North and his fellow new institutional economists, they meant to underline the importance of both means and ends. The new institutionalists used the term institution in a broad and new way to mean "the humanly devised constraints that shape human interaction."[56] Recognizing the importance of institutions so construed was not meant to imply that aid workers focus on the *material* organization of such legal institutions, such as laws and judiciaries, but that they recognize the importance of political, social, and cultural structures—such as a set of social patterns and interactions that serve to limit the acceptable areas of government control.

Yet when practitioners turned these ideas into practice, they inevitably had to simplify such nuanced theoretical concepts. Because programs to build the rule of law are most easily oriented around reforming concrete problems within material things such as laws or organizations, it was all too easy for means to become conflated with ends and eventually made into ends in themselves. Rather than considering from scratch, each time one enters a new country, how organizations, cultural interactions, and government agencies can be made to function in a system that supports human rights, for example, it is simply easier to write human rights laws, train police in human rights norms, and establish legal clinics that enable the poor to enforce their rights. Such a move is an inevitable part of rule-of-law reform.

This move would not be problematic if it were true that when organizations are made to function properly, or laws are better written, the means become the end. But, in fact, it is the ends to which they will be put that determines what it means for these institutions (as the word is commonly used) to function well. Even an impartial, efficient judiciary, for instance, is not of value in and of itself; if a society never had a dispute to solve, such a judiciary would simply be a ceremonial cost. It is of value because we believe that such a judiciary will enable disputes to be resolved efficiently and without recourse to violence, will create predictability, and will provide like judgments for like cases.[57] It is these ends, among others, that compose the intrinsic goods that the rule of law brings. Moreover, as shown above, even if reformers can make a single institution function well, they will not necessarily achieve any rule-of-law ends because each requires reform across *multiple* institutions.

The problem, therefore, is seeing the creation of such laws, training programs, and clinics as ends in themselves. Yet that step is an easy one to take. In many states, the problems with these institutional attributes are broad and deep. After the fall of the communist regime in Albania, for instance, laws were not published or distributed. Judges without high school degrees had been appointed from the hometown clan of the prime minister; their inability to reason through judicial precedent, their lack of knowledge of the laws, and their frequent corruption rendered fair justice impossible. Moreover, the sudden downfall of the government had been followed by widespread looting, and government arms caches had thus been redistributed to most men in the country. Poorly equipped bailiffs and police were scared to enter heavily armed villages, making the enforcement of civil claims or criminal justice nearly impossible. In rural areas, old forms of tribal justice—made more brutal and arbitrary from their reintroduction by drug and human traffickers with goals other than the rule of law in mind—had taken over in the face of government inability to enforce the laws. Similar problems are repeated in countries worldwide.

The solution, to any well-meaning and time-pressed reformer, seems obvious. Laws should be published and disseminated, judges should be trained, police should be armed and citizens disarmed, court procedures should be made efficient and corruption reduced—the list may be enormous, but it is, at least, self-evident. Improving flawed primary and secondary institutions appears to be a fairly straightforward process of skill building and technical reform.[58] The question then becomes one of sequencing: Where does one start?

The tendency to move directly into institutional reform, without considering the overarching end goals of such reforms, is exacerbated by the practical problems of expertise. Breaking down the rule of law by the institutions that must be improved in order to build it makes practical sense, given how expertise is allocated. Consultants on police reform tend to be retired police officers, police commissioners, and scholars of criminology. Lawyers alone have the expertise for legal reform, and judges, magistrates, and lawyers tend to be involved in most judicial reform projects. Meanwhile, a person who can advise on police reform will probably have little to say about the judiciary and vice versa. Other than political theorists and legal scholars, few presume to be expert in the rule of law, and their ability to transform this theoretical knowledge into pragmatic procedures for addressing the practicalities of institutional reform in developing countries is limited, to say the least. For such mundane reasons, the rule-of-law field tends to be subdivided into different areas of expertise, and bringing these fields together to consider how they can work toward joint ends based on a unified definition and understanding of overarching goals is difficult.[59] It is easy to take the next step and simply focus on making each field function "properly" as an end in itself.

It is quite understandable why practitioners have made this simple move in their need to accomplish a particular goal. Most have ended up betwixt and between: Their formal definitions mix ends and institutions, the distinction is never clarified, and in practice, they tend to focus on institutions as ends in themselves. The reasons are understandable, but explanation is not exculpation. Organizations working to build the rule of law abroad could insist that institutional reform always occurs under a distinct and clear understanding of the end it is intended to serve. Reformers could measure ends, rather than institutional reforms, in judging their success. They rarely do. Instead, reform of institutional attributes is treated as the end goal of rule-of-law reform—a definition that has real, negative impact on the success of rule-of-law reform efforts.

Problems with Institution-Based Definitions

When the rule of law is implicitly defined by its institutions, rather than its ends, the latter tend to be assumed. Rather than considering the desired goals we are trying to achieve through the rule of law, and then determining what institutional, political, and cultural changes best achieve these ends, practitioners are tempted to move directly toward building institutions that look like those reformers know. Practitioners engaged in such institution modeling tend to compare institutions in the country that need to be reformed with their counterparts in developed countries and then provide the resources, skills, and professional socialization to help each local institution approach Western models.[60] However, judiciaries can be impartial, trained, efficient, and able to dispense honest justice whether they are working within an Anglo-Saxon adversarial system, a Continental prosecutorial system, or even are constituted as a group of tribal elders working with known customary law within a *panchayat* (village council) in India. A government can be reined in by a constitution, but sometimes, as Montesquieu made clear, custom or a type of "English constitution" works just as well, if not better, than paper laws that are not obeyed. Not only are innumerable institutions to be reformed not necessarily essential to rule-of-law reform, but they can even impede it, by insisting on a model that is either unnecessary or unsuited to the political and cultural landscape.

Defining the rule of law by its institutions also slants practitioners toward overly technocratic models of reform. As discussed in the section on ends, the rule of law is as much a cultural and political model as a technocratic or even legal institution. The Greeks recognized that the rule of law rested on more than correctly constituted legal institutions, and their enforcement ideas tended to emerge out of religious strictures far more than human institutions.[61] For this reason, Aristotle claimed that "customary laws have more weight . . . than written laws."[62] And, as Isaiah Berlin observed, "What makes [Great Britain] comparatively free, therefore, is the fact that this theoretically omnipotent entity is restrained by custom and opinion from acting as such. It is clear that what matters is not the form of these restraining powers—whether they are legal, or moral, or constitutional—but their effectiveness."[63] Even the *Economist*, in a recent article on crime in Argentina, discusses the need not only for improved institutions but also for cultural change among the citizenry to curb crime and corruption.[64] Many modern practitioners recognize the cultural dimensions of the rule of law in theory, but their definition of the concept and means of attacking it impede this realization from seriously impacting reform efforts.

An institutional attributes type of definition also fails to ask why institutions are so bad—and whose interests are served through weak rule-of-law institutions. Often, there are quite rational political reasons for appointing ill-trained judges who, as a result, lack independence or for keeping police underequipped with arbitrary career paths so that they are not tempted or able to form a power center separate from their government benefactors. Practitioners are often following an idealized blueprint of their home system that ignores its own difficulties and flaws, such as the intense political involvement in the picking of the U.S. judiciary or the corruption residing in some European judiciaries. Therefore, many reformers ignore the issues of power and politics inherent in all developed rule-of-law systems. The very question "how should this institution be reformed?" ignores larger political changes that may be far more important than institutional tweaking in achieving rule-of-law ends. As in the establishment of the court in the *Eumenides* or the historical case of the Magna Carta, politics and power matter a great deal in establishing the rule of law.[65] Michael Oakeshott correctly noted that the rule of law cannot protect itself against external assault. It must have powerful defenders or interests who gain from supporting it. Reform programs that focus on providing computers to improve court efficiency in the midst of a political autocracy, for example, seem rather like treating heartburn in a patient suffering from cancer.

Another problem that arises from such institutional modeling is that reformers tend to waste time and scarce legal resources within developing countries in efforts to make laws and institutions look like those in their own system. Delegates from the EU speak constantly of bringing the legal systems of Balkan countries "up to European standards" and suggest that they adopt the entirety of European law, regardless of their ability to enforce it, as a first step. Lawyers from the United States hold mock trials to teach adversarial litigation techniques to law students in countries with prosecutorial legal systems. There is a theoretical basis to some of these efforts: The Balkans may eventually need European law, and the adversarial, oral litigation system, for instance, is argued to be more transparent and less confusing, particularly for illiterates, than prosecutorial, written procedures. Even so, fights often break out between reformers from different nations who argue over whether to use German bankruptcy laws or American, or whether the constitution should uphold case law versus code law, when in reality either would be sufficient for achieving the ends that these reforms are supposed to serve. Reform can then become a process of substituting one workable law with another, perhaps slightly "better," that emanates from a different legal system.

Part of the reason for such arguments is that many supposed rule-of-law reforms stretch the concept to encompass not only the minimal ends of the rule of law but also values and institutions that are cutting-edge or not even agreed upon within countries with a developed rule of law. The poor, for instance, did not get free legal counsel in criminal cases before the 1960s in America, but such counsel is considered essential to declare that a developing country has the rule of law. Human rights laws that far exceed those of Singapore, or even of the United States, are considered essential for legal reform in Europe. These reforms may well be very good things, but they are not necessarily essential for the rule of law, and by stretching the point they can cast doubt on the more core attributes of the concept.

In fact, by claiming that institutional reform is an attempt to bring institutions in line with those in developed countries, reformers open themselves to charges of hypocrisy. Judicial and criminal legal reform in Russia is engaged in overturning a system that is *de rigueur* in Japan, which has a 99 percent conviction rate and allows citizens to be held without reason for 23 days.[66] The highly political process of judicial choice in the United States would never be permitted by reformers elsewhere. Neither would an institutional arrangement such as that in Great Britain that leaves the police answering to three different masters, none of them the public. In fact, since Hayek, there has even been an active debate about whether the United States and Great Britain, by allowing too much administrative discretion or by using the law to advance social goals, are moving away from the impartial rule of law.[67] Many legal professionals in the developing world know that the rule of law is a goal toward which even Western institutions are still evolving. Using Western systems rather than universally accepted ends as models leaves the reforms themselves open to question when flaws in the "model countries"—corruption, the death penalty, prison abuse—come to light.[68]

Most pernicious, depending on how they are implemented, institutional reforms carried out under the banner of rule-of-law reform can actually undermine rule-of-law ends. For instance, in Romania, businessmen have pleaded for an end to legal reform: They can live with bad laws, but the constant "improvement" of key property laws by various bilateral and multilateral aid agencies creates an unpredictable legal environment. An end good of the rule of law—a stable, predictable legal system—has been undermined by the so-called reform process. If legal reforms are forced on other countries through conditionality, as they often are, executives may be forced to pass laws by decree rather than through the legislative process.[69] In many Latin American and Eastern European countries, for instance, strong World Bank and International Monetary Fund conditionality for various commercial legal reforms forced the growing use of executive ordinance in the face of a recalcitrant parliament. The growing habit of the executive to bypass parliament and rule through decree was noted with alarm in the EU progress reports on Romania's rule of law.[70] These apparent reforms threatened the very idea of a government bound to pass laws through a standing legal process, a particularly worrisome occurrence in a new democracy emerging from overly strong executive rule.

These criticisms of an institutional attributes style of definition may appear strong on paper, but in the field, it is easy to shrug off these thoughts as pedantic. When institutions are extremely flawed, fixing some of the problems seems like a move in the right direction, regardless of whether rule-of-law ends have been thought out. Yet the effects of such breezy thinking should be seriously considered. Real, negative outcomes, such as pushing institutional reforms in ways that actually undermine rule-of-law ends, demonstrate the serious repercussions of too-easy thinking.

Implications of Competing Definitions

This chapter has sought to make two core points: first, that the rule of law is more usefully defined for the international development community by its ends, not by its institutional attributes; and second, that these ends are manifold, separable, often in tension, and affect different segments of the society to be reformed. Taking these two conceptual steps has many repercussions for the rule-of-law reform community, including the following:

1. For any rule-of-law end, all institutions must be reformed.

Fulfilling any rule-of-law end requires work across the three primary rule-of-law institutions. Even the most frequently undertaken reform, achieving predictable and efficient justice, which may appear to involve judicial reform alone, in fact necessitates legal reform to ban activities such as judicial corruption, bribery, and threatening public officials, as well as police reform to ensure that appropriate evidence is collected for use in cases, to avoid investigation delays, and to protect judges from threats that could affect their decisions.

Not only does each of the major rule-of-law ends require reform of and coordination among laws, the judiciary, and the police, it also requires reforms across the spectrum of supporting institutions for all three, such as prison reform (to keep prisoners in jail and prevent them from perpetrating crimes from inside), notary public reform (to reduce corruption and forgery of legal documents used in court), and law school reform (to ensure that lawyers are a professional class trained to argue cases based on law, rather than "fixers" who win by connections and bribes).

On the ground, coordination between some types of legal reform and judicial reform occurs regularly, but coordination between these two reforms and police reform almost never takes place. Moreover, coordination of any of these three areas with the reform of supporting institutions is ad hoc, at best. When reform of any one institution gets too far ahead of the other, achieving rule-of-law ends becomes less likely, because of the interdependence among rule-of-law institutions. For instance, in Panama, a decade-long reform effort moved the police from being one of the least trusted and most corrupt institutions in the country, to being among the most highly regarded. Police reform in Panama was successful, and now people turn to the police for help. However, law and order there has barely improved; the corrupt judiciary tends to release prisoners, particularly drug traffickers and organized criminals. And although the state may abuse the human rights of the citizenry somewhat less (never a huge problem before), individual criminals now do so more.

Obviously, country-specific empirical research is necessary to address the practical implications of this point, such as which areas should be prioritized, or where scarce resources should be allocated. The overarching point, however, should be heeded: Organizations such as USAID that are leaning ever further toward sector-specific reform, where one contractor focuses solely on the judiciary and another on the police, should reconsider their model.

2. Achieving rule-of-law ends requires political and cultural, not only institutional, change.

Reform must occur across all primary institutions to achieve any rule-of-law end, but even such widespread institutional reform will rarely be enough to ensure real change. As alluded to throughout this chapter, many rule-of-law ends are upheld even when institutional arrangements are far from supportive, if countries have social and political cultures that place a premium on the rule of law. The converse is also true: Recalcitrant cultures or balking politicians can undermine even well-organized rule-of-law institutions. Institutional reform can be a lever of change that pushes culture and politics in the right direction, but this outcome is neither assured nor particularly likely to occur unless reformers have their eye on using institutions to leverage wider change in this way.

Alexis de Tocqueville probably saw this issue most clearly. Visiting England just after a trip to Switzerland and following his famous travels in America, he wrote:

> Whoever travels in the United States is involuntarily and instinctively so impressed with the fact that the spirit of liberty and the taste for it have pervaded all the habits of the American people. But if violence were to destroy the Republican institutions in most Swiss Cantons, it would be by no means certain that after a rather short state of transition the people would not grow accustomed to the loss of liberty. In the United States and in England there seems to be more liberty in the customs than in the laws of the people. In Switzerland there seems to be more liberty in the laws than in the customs of the country.[71]

In other words, while customs without material institutions can manage to uphold some rule-of-law ends (here described as the "spirit of liberty"), institutions without customs are weak and easily circumvented by raw power.

Well-planned institutional reforms can certainly affect political culture and change societal expectations. And most practitioners realize the importance of culture, power, and politics. But the institutional attributes style of defining the rule of law minimizes the importance of these levers of change and obstructs clear thinking about how to address them.

As already discussed, looking at distinct ends one by one illuminates the political and cultural cleavages that will affect reform success. By adopting this nuanced view of rule-of-law ends as distinct goals, reformers could better anticipate obstruction and could begin to take power and politics into account on the practical, planning level. Moreover, a clear consideration of ends would remove the ability of some practitioners to deny the fact that their work is inherently about changing the cultural and political values of other countries. The self-deception endemic in the field regarding this issue raised obstacles in project after project.[72]

3. Not all work to reform legal institutions is rule-of-law reform.

Rule-of-law reformers believe, by definition, that they are trying to create the rule of law. Yet the field of rule-of-law reform grew not out of a desire to create the rule of law abroad but out of a need to find solutions to myriad international needs and problems. The United States and Europe hit on the rule of law as one solution to many needs: creating liberal democracies in Latin America and Eastern Europe, providing global security against drug cartels and organized criminals, and helping poor countries develop. Piecing together preexisting programs and creating new ones, the field of rule-of-law reform was born. Yet the field of rule-of-law reform did not replace these primary policy motives—it was a means to these larger ends. When strict rule-of-law procedures would impede the passage of laws or the construction of agencies desired for development, security, and so on, they tended to be ignored. Thus, these public policy goals that motivated the creation of the field sometimes also motivate action outside of it—as is shown by the acceptance of using executive decrees to achieve supposed rule-of-law goals.

One of the key problems with defining the rule of law by institutional reform rather than end goals is that it makes such conceptual conflation easier. Any work to reform laws, any change to police policy, is considered rule-of-law reform. This is not true. For instance, goals such as improving global security through police reform and antiterrorist laws are accomplished by reforming rule-of-law institutions—but they are targeted not at improving the rule of law *within* a particular state, but at achieving security for *other* states. When the EU pushes acceding countries to adopt the entire legal *acquis communitaire*, it is not building the rule of law through all these legal changes; it is simply helping them create a legal system that can mesh with its own, which is often tilted in ways that benefit current members. In the past, such activity was known as "gunboat diplomacy." Simply because it is now undertaken by aid agencies and lawyers instead of generals does not elevate it to a dimension of the rule of law.

Conflating all institutional reform with rule-of-law reform leads to two problems. First, the rule of law winds up being defined so broadly that it takes in all sorts of reforms pursued for other reasons, including the self-interest of the aiding state. Second, reformers can believe that they are working toward the rule of law, when in fact their goals require reforms that are other than, and at times opposed to, the rule of law.

A common example of the first mistake is conflating the desire to build the rule of law to enable a market economy—which is certainly helped by forwarding these five rule-of-law ends—with building a particular type of laissez faire economy, a separate goal from building the rule of law. Law reforms to enable large-scale privatization activity, reduce business regulations, float prices on basic goods, and create certain types of bankruptcy and credit procedures are encouraged, often in the name of legal reform for the rule of law.[73] Because this work is done by those agencies engaged in other rule-of-law reform projects, and because they are using the instruments of rule-of-law reform to press their case, practitioners frequently confuse "building the rule of law" with enacting a particular vision of economic life.[74] These reforms may all be economically useful, but even Hayek (under whose name such reforms are frequently conflated with the rule of law) distinguished between reforms that improved economic efficiency, and the far narrower range of economic activities that the state had to be restricted from to maintain the rule of law. Germany and the United States, for instance, are both viewed as rule-of-law societies, despite the fact that bankruptcy is a more difficult procedure in the former than the latter. Scandinavia can be more socialist, and France can favor greater agricultural tariffs, without either having less rule of law than more open, laissez faire economies.[75] Misdefining the rule of law in this way breeds cynicism and resistance in states to be reformed. Politicians in states that are being reformed can end up believing, rightly or wrongly, that rule-of-law reform is used as a guise for developed countries to tie the developing state more closely to their own legal and economic system.[76]

Equally important, rule-of-law reformers may not actually want the rule of law, a point obscured by institutionally based definitions that count all reform of rule-of-law institutions as rule-of-law reform. Reformers engaged in the rule-of-law field primarily to improve global security may support some rule-of-law ends but be less excited about others, such as human rights or due process that would bind the executive to act through law. Other reformers may want some of the ends some of the time but not all of the time. Frank Upham describes an early case in the United States in which judges use some tricky legal footwork to abrogate one individual's property rights to allow for large-scale development that would create growth and jobs for many more.[77] The case could easily mirror the development desires that the World Bank, USAID, or EU holds for many countries today. These development goals lead these organizations, which theoretically favor rule-of-law ends such as binding the executive, to push executives to use unlawful decrees to pass desired reform legislation, rather than upholding rule-of-law procedures as their primary end.

In other words, the rule of law is often desired by rule-of-law reformers not as an end in itself but as a means to other ends. In such cases, the rule of law, the means they are using to try to achieve their other goals, is under some definitions in opposition to them and certainly likely to slow them down. In fact, it is arguable that reformers often do not want the rule of law at all—or at least not the technocratic, proceduralist version they proclaim.[78] The lack of hard evidence that the rule of law, in and of itself, procedures and all, actually does bring improved economic growth in the long run or better international security contributes to the ambivalence over actual end goals within the rule-of-law building field.[79]

4. *Rule-of-law ends are in tension—particularly in poor societies or societies with a weak rule of law. Improvements in one end goal can decrease success in others.*

If we are going to pursue an ends-based definition, we must acknowledge that it is not easy. A key point that must first be understood is that all good things do not go together: Rule-of-law ends are in tension, particularly in the development stages.

The rule of law is about both limiting the power of the state and empowering it to protect the rights of the citizens against lawbreakers and rebels. Fostering the judicial independence required to bind the government can work against rooting out corruption within the judiciary. A country with scrupulous human rights norms may have difficulty maintaining law and order in the face of a heavily armed citizenry and organized gangs without similar scruples. Conversely, citizens wanting social order may demand the weakening of regulations protecting civil and political rights. In working rule-of-law systems, the five elements of the rule of law support one another. In nascent or poorly functioning systems, the five elements can and do undermine one another. While the ends of rule of law are not opposed in theory, in practice, they often come into conflict.

Poverty is one exacerbating factor. Countries are better able to enforce law and order while respecting human rights if the police are well paid, well trained, and properly equipped, and prisons are well built and undercrowded. When judges are underpaid and underrespected, corruption can take hold, forcing difficult choices between increasing judicial independence and achieving predictable, equitable justice. Poor countries are more at risk for civil wars and rebel movements and therefore are more likely to need to invoke overwhelming executive powers and martial law to create law and order.[80]

In fact, in countries where the rule of law is not well developed, vicious cycles can emerge where the lack of one good leads to the lack of another: Human rights abuse, for instance, breeds a rebel movement that causes the government to attempt to reassert public order by acting further outside the law and further harming human rights. In countries where multiple elements of the rule of law are lacking or out of sync, rebuilding them often requires choices between valuable goods. For example, forcing the government to abide by law may allow the rebel movement to get out of hand, which itself creates law-and-order problems—and can lead those victimized to take the law into their own hands.

Sequencing of reforms is yet another difficulty. Attempts to reform aspects of the rule of law that focus on one end can be undermined by reform efforts concerned with another. For instance, efforts to increase predictability and efficiency in the judiciary through anticorruption drives, skills testing, and other measures can be used by local ministries of justice to increase the grip of the executive over the judiciary. Precisely this fight played out in Albanian reform efforts. Reformers from the World Bank, working with the Ministry of Justice, wished to institute a skills test for judges to weed out those who had been appointed with no training. They were opposed by reformers from the Council of Europe, who believed that a skills test instituted by the Ministry of Justice set a bad precedent for executive interference in the judiciary. In Albania, a smart solution was found: The test was held but was closely monitored by international reformers, watered down considerably, and few judges were expelled. This outcome both reduced the precedent of executive interference and ended up improving judicial skill levels to some extent, because international reformers spent the weeks before the test providing judges with copies of the laws and helping them study.[81]

Most of the time, states and international organizations working to build the rule of law avoid the implications of this tension, instead taking the approach that "all good things go together" and that a little bit more rule of law is better than none at all.[82] Yet because these goods are often interrelated in tension, progress on one front without progress on the others will lead not to partial progress (all other goods being held equal while one improves) but to an entirely different animal (where the improvement in one good pushes some of the others up and others down).

Far from the current belief among aid practitioners that some reform is better than none, reform may occasionally create worse, less liberal outcomes.[83] For example, improved human rights laws and norms in a society suffering from law-and-order problems can erode cultural support for human rights, if they are seen as getting in the way of the rights of "ordinary" citizens to live free from crime.[84] Greater efficiency without improved laws can lead not to a liberal rule of law but to an autocratic rule *through* law that is not founded on liberal norms, as exemplified by regimes such as the Third Reich. The U.S. Institute of Peace report on the rule of law in Afghanistan, in discussing the lopsided work in law enforcement versus human rights and judicial reform, notes,

> at best, such a [law enforcement] force will be able to provide some public order; at worst, the international community will have enhanced the ability of power-holders to control and abuse the population without creating mechanisms to protect the rights of Afghans. A substantial investment in one area of rule of law will not have a meaningful pay-off in terms of real democratic governance and stability unless other pieces of the puzzle are put in place as well.[85]

One reform effort can also undermine another. For instance, a subsector of many rule-of-law reform programs is making justice more accessible. Those working for predictable, efficient justice tend to see this end largely in terms of making justice more accessible so that the market economy might function more efficiently.[86] They therefore tend to create small claims courts, which both serve the ends of making justice more affordable and efficient for those with small stakes to settle and move those cases that would have been brought out of the regular courts. Yet other accessibility reforms can undermine this end. Accessibility programs championed to help the poor ensure their human rights or gain real equality before the law often use the regular court system, and if the programs are successful, they can overwhelm courts at all levels with suits that would not have been brought previously, reducing court efficiency.

5. We should measure the ends of the rule of law, not the institutions. Given the tension between goods, we will gain clarity if instead of measuring the rule of law, we measure achievement in each end of the rule of law.

As discussed above, end goals of the rule of law can be achieved even when institutions vary widely. Moreover, whether institutions are properly aligned or not cannot be measured by considering the state of the institution itself; the measurement only makes sense against the end the institution is intended to serve. Any anxious tourist to an exotic locale knows that if one is worried about law and order, it is more telling to measure crime statistics, not to count how many police have graduated from the academy. An investor does not read the constitution of an emerging market economy but asks other businesspeople whether contracts are enforced fairly and predictably. Having the aforementioned institutional

Figure 3.1. Rule of Law Measurement

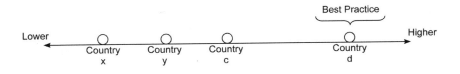

attributes may be necessary to these outcomes, but they are not the way in which we determine whether the rule of law is present.

When the United States, the EU, or the World Bank tries to measure success in building the rule of law, or the Millennium Challenge Account attempts to measure a country's "rule of law" as one of its criteria for aid, it tends to be one of a number of goods they are measuring. They generally divide the dimensions of the manifold goods they are looking at along different lines, where the rule of law is a unified good, and is placed under the umbrella of "governance," which includes other measures such as regulatory quality and control of corruption.[87] Their rule-of-law measurement thus looks unitary, as in figure 3.1.

Yet the fact that the rule of law has five distinct ends means that it is not a unitary whole, but a set of five distinct goods that can advance at different rates. If we agree that the five ends described above should be the measurement of rule-of-law achievement, we must then determine how to weigh them against one another. Does improving one end create more rule of law? Or must all five be advanced together, or be related in a particular way? Many U.S. and EU interventions to build the rule of law do not work at pushing all five ends but are geared toward improving some institutional attribute aimed primarily at one of these ends, though often affecting a few of them simultaneously. This interdependence, along with the fact that the five ends are complementary but often in tension, means that progress in one area alone rarely occurs with all other goods being held constant. If one goes up, the others may rise with it, but they may also fall as a result.

For instance, Russia under Putin has had more predictable and efficient justice than it did under Yeltsin (see figures 3.2 and 3.3). The reduction in corruption has helped to ensure that the central government can rule, regular businesses can operate, and local government officials do not have impunity before the law. However, Putin accomplished this feat by amassing more power at the central level, reestablishing executive control over the Duma and much of the judiciary, and reinstating

Figure 3.2. Rule of Law in Russia under Yeltsin

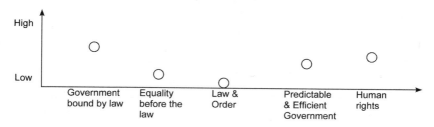

elements of state power such as the reformed KGB.[88] Is this more rule of law, or less? The question, actually, is incoherent, because the rule of law is not a unified good. Instead, it makes more sense to see these five aspects of the rule of law as independent elements—like five dimmer switches that control different lights.

Under Putin, law and order has improved, as has the predictability and stability of legal institutions (figure 3.3). Yet the executive is less bound to law. Meanwhile, human rights are now more threatened by the state, but less by anarchy, leaving that measure fairly steady.

These five goods can be added together, of course, to get a single rule-of-law "score" for a country; a higher score would mean a greater level of rule of law, but the additive number would be fairly meaningless. If one country has serious law-and-order difficulties and another has an authoritarian government, but their final scores even out, do they have the same rule of law? The answer is not worth giving: They have different types of rule of law, and different societies have different levels of tolerance for different rule-of-law problems.[89]

Finding the proxies to measure these end goals is a huge undertaking and outside the scope of this chapter. Here, it is enough to suggest that we need to be looking for proxies to measure the right things: The ends—not the institutions or an amalgamation of the two—are the proper goals to measure. The actual measurement proxies within efforts such as the World Bank Governance Indicators are a good first step, but by amalgamating ends and institutions and by making the rule of law unitary, these indicators hardly serve any clarifying purpose.

Conclusion

When Dicey described the rule of law a hundred years ago, he wrote that "whenever we talk of Englishmen as loving the government of law,

Figure 3.3. Rule of Law in Russia under Putin

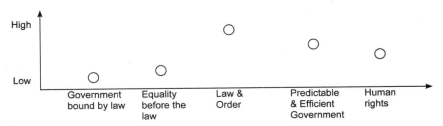

or of the supremacy of law as being a characteristic of the English constitution, [we] are using words which, though they possess a real significance, are nevertheless to most persons who employ them full of vagueness and ambiguity."[90] This pleasant fog had not improved significantly
at the time that the field of rule-of-law reform was born.

The new field of rule-of-law reform did not emerge slowly after years
of academic discourse. It grew from action—action needed right away—
as states tried to keep regions from falling into poverty and anarchy,
organizations jockeyed with one another for primacy in a new and growing field, reformers tried to create new polities out of crumbling states,
and the United States and Europe fought for influence over the newly
unallied states of Eastern Europe through legal systems, as well as
through NATO and the EU. Few, except perhaps practitioners on the
ground, noticed that they were working for different goals under the
rubric of rule-of-law reform—and that they were too busy acting to comment.

After twenty years of such fevered activity toward ambiguous ends,
however, it is time to take a step back and reflect.[91] Rule-of-law reformers have been working to improve an ever-growing number of rule-of-
law institutions. But the ends these institutions are intended to serve in
society have become obscured. Rule-of-law reformers are trying to build
a system that is better seen not as a set of institutions but as a set of
distinct but interrelated end goals. When the system is properly balanced,
these ends are mutually supportive. But when the system is in its in-
fancy or when these goods are improperly aligned, they can undermine
one another.

By treating the rule of law as a set of institutions, reformers handicap
themselves in bringing about the end goals of the rule of law—all of
which require reform across institutions, as well as cultural and political
changes that lie outside the concrete institutional realm. By treating the

rule of law as a single good rather than as a system of goods in tension, reformers can inadvertently work to bring about a malformed rule of law, such as one in which laws that overly empower the executive are applied and enforced more efficiently.[92]

The difficulties of turning a definition of the rule of law based on ends into a practical method of tackling rule-of-law reforms are real. Acknowledging the need to do so and developing a measurement system that orients reformers toward this realization are first steps.

Notes

An earlier version of this chapter was originally published as Carnegie Paper no. 55 (January 2005).

1. Michael Oakeshott, "The Rule of Law," in *What Is History? and Other Essays* (New York: Barnes and Noble, 1983), 119 at 164.
2. Judith N. Shklar, "Political Theory and the Rule of Law," in *The Rule of Law: Ideal or Ideology?* ed. Allan C. Hutchinson and Patrick Monahan (Toronto: Carswell Legal Publications, 1987), 1.
3. See Thomas Carothers' chapter 1 in this volume.
4. USAID defines a strategic objective as "the most ambitious result that a U.S. Agency for International Development operating unit, such as a country mission, can materially affect, and for which it is willing to be held accountable." See U.S. Government Accounting Office, "Former Soviet Union: U.S. Rule of Law Assistance Has Had Limited Impact and Sustainability," GAO-01-740T (Washington, D.C.: GAO, May 2001), 3. For examples of rhetoric, see Brian Z. Tamanaha, "The Rule of Law for Everyone?" St. John's Legal Studies Research Paper (Jamaica, NY: St. John's University School of Law, n.d.), available as Social Science Research Network Working Paper at http://ssrn.com/abstract=312622.
5. International Bar Association, "Report on Zimbabwe" (London: International Bar Association, 2001), available at www.ibanet.org/misc/zimbabwe_report.asp.
6. Remarks by Jeffrey N. Bakken, "Remarks at the Judicial Symposium Banquet" (Washington, D.C.: USAID, 2003), available at www.sn.apc.org/usaidsa/speech54.html.
7. Ram Gorni, "China: Rule of Law, Sometimes," *Asia Times Online*, July 3, 2003, available at www.atimes.com/atimes/China/EG 03Ad03.html. In addition to citing inequality before the law, the article describes all five senses of the rule of law in turn.
8. Amnesty International, "Afghanistan: Police Reconstruction Essential for Human Rights" (New York: Amnesty International, March 2003), 1, available at http://web.amnesty.org/library/index/engasa110032003.
9. In a single extended article, the *Economist* manages to use the rule of law to demonstrate each of these meanings. It begins by stating that in Argentina, "the rule of law has been repeatedly trumped by executive power." It then repeats the need for the rule of law in its claim that "Argentines are demanding something new from their government: law and order." The article goes on to quote the deputy foreign minister, who says, "Argentine society is convinced that the impunity of the army's crimes facilitated corruption and lack of respect for the rule of law," referring both to the lack of equality under the law and the army's impunity for human rights abuses. Then the article quotes Roberto Sava of the Association for Civil Rights as saying, "a politician who wants public support has to adhere to an agenda of the rule of law,

fighting corruption, and promoting open government and human rights." *Economist,* "Becoming a Serious Country" and "Crimes Past, Crimes Present," June 5–11, 2004.

10. For a survey of how the term has been used in Germany, France, the United Kingdom, and the United States, see Rainer Grote, "Rule of Law, Rechtstaat and Etat de Droit," in *Constitutionalism, Universalism, and Democracy—A Comparative Analysis,* ed. Christian Starck (Baden-Baden: Nomos Verlagsgesellschaft, 1999), 271. Friedrich Hayek traces the history of the phrase in his book *The Constitution of Liberty* (Chicago: University of Chicago Press, 1978). A. V. Dicey attempts the first modern definition in his book *Introduction to the Study of the Law of the Constitution* (Indianapolis, IN: Liberty Fund, 1982). Also see Matthew Stephenson, "The Rule of Law as a Goal of Development Policy" (Washington, D.C.: World Bank, n.d.), available at www1.worldbank.org/publicsector/legal/ruleoflaw2.htm. Grote concludes that the idea "belongs to the category of open-ended concepts which are subject to permanent debate."

11. *Institution* is a term packed with meaning for international relations scholars and those familiar with the new institutional economics, from whence much rule-of-law building activity sprang. Because this chapter is dealing with precisely the misuse of the term by rule-of-law practitioners, I use the terms *institutions* and *institutional attributes* to refer to concrete, material organizations and sets of concretized interactions, such as laws. I will discuss the new institutional economics and its intended use of this terminology, which refers more generally to customs and patterns of interaction, in the section on definitions based on institutional attributes.

12. GAO, "Rule of Law Funding Worldwide for Fiscal Years 1993–1998," GAO/NSIAD-99-158 (Washington, D.C.: GAO, June 1999).

13. There are, of course, dozens of ways to classify definitions of the rule of law, depending on the purpose the definition is meant to serve, or what divisions it is intended to clarify. Brian Tamanaha divides the concept between preliberal and liberal ends (see Tamanaha, "Rule of Law for Everyone?"). Others divide it between formalist and substantivist definitions, or proceduralist and substantivist modes. I have chosen the following means of definition because it best illuminates the dilemmas faced by the rule-of-law building project.

14. The World Bank's Comprehensive Development Framework states, for example, that

> Without the protection of human and property rights, and a comprehensive framework of laws, no equitable development is possible. A government must ensure that it has an effective system of property, contract, labor, bankruptcy, commercial codes, personal rights laws and other elements of a comprehensive legal system that is effectively, impartially and cleanly administered by a well-functioning, impartial and honest judicial and legal system. [See James Wolfensohn, *Proposal for a Comprehensive Development Framework: A Discussion Draft for the Board, Management, and Staff of the World Bank Group* (Washington, D.C.: World Bank, January 1999).]

USAID, when asked by the GAO for a definition of the rule of law, responded that

> The rule of law embodies the basic principles of equal treatment of all people before the law, fairness, and both constitutional and actual guarantees of basic human rights; it is founded on a predictable, transparent legal system with fair and effective judicial institutions to protect citizens against the arbitrary use of state authority and lawless acts of both organizations and individuals. (GAO, "Rule of Law Funding Worldwide," 13.)

The European Union, in its 1998 Commission Communications to the Council and the European Parliament, makes the greatest attempt to delineate between ends and institutions but suggests that the latter are implied by the former—a misunderstanding that I will discuss later. They declare that

> The primacy of law is a fundamental principle of any democratic system seeking to foster and promote rights, whether civil and political, or economic, social, and cultural. This entails means of recourse enabling individuals to defend their rights . . . The principle of placing limitations on the power of the State is best served by a representative government drawing its authority from the sovereignty of the people. The principle must shape the structure of the State and the prerogatives of the various powers. It implies, for example:
>
> - a legislature respecting and giving full effect to human rights and fundamental freedoms;
> - an independent judiciary;
> - effective and accessible means of legal recourse;
> - a legal system guaranteeing equality before the law;
> - a prison system respecting the human person;
> - a police force at the service of the law;
> - an effective executive enforcing the law and capable of establishing the social and economic conditions necessary for life in society.

[See European Initiative for Democracy and Human Rights, "1998 Commission Communications to the Council and the European Parliament: Presentation on the Rule of Law" (Brussels: European Union), available at http://europa.eu.int/comm/europeaid/projects/eidhr/pdf/presentation_rule_of_law.pdf.]

15. Compare the USAID definition in note 14 above to the definition used in its *Handbook of Democracy and Government Program Indicators:*

> The Rule of Law ensures that individuals are subject to, and treated equally according to the law, and that no one is subject to arbitrary treatment by the state. A rule of law that contributes to the building of sustainable democracy is one that protects basic human rights . . . It is one in which market based economic activity is enabled, and freely operates. It is one in which the processes and institutions of justice are available to all individuals . . . A democratic Rule of Law is also one in which the processes and institutions of justice work efficiently and effectively to establish justice and resolve disputes. [See USAID, *Handbook of Democracy and Government Program Indicators*, Technical Publications Series no. PN-ACC-390 (Washington, D.C.: USAID, August 1998), available at www.usaid.gov/our_work/democracy_and_governance/publications/pdfs/pnacc390.pdf.]

16. Tamanaha, "Rule of Law for Everyone?" 11.
17. Aristotle, *Politics*, III, 15, 1286a-16, 1287a, in *The Complete Works of Aristotle*, ed. J. Barnes (Princeton, NJ: Princeton University Press, 1995).
18. Quoted in Hayek, *Constitution of Liberty*, 164–5.
19. Quoted in Hayek, *Constitution of Liberty*, 168.
20. See the English Bill of Rights, 1689.
21. Brian Tamanaha separates these senses and suggests (1) that a government bound by law must follow the law or change it, and, more robustly, (2) that there are certain actions that even the government cannot make "legal." I separate these concepts into the end of human rights and the end of a government limited by law, in order to draw the distinction, discussed later, between those who advocate for the "formal" rule of law in which rights are not included, and those who take a substantivist position in which both procedure and content matter. This debate is discussed later in the section on human rights.

22. Some strict formalists and certain strands of Rechtstaat theory would posit rule by law as the rule of law—although this substance-less definition is rebutted by substantivists and often by the underlying assumptions of formalists themselves. More on this debate is found when the end goal of human rights is discussed later.

23. Dicey, *Introduction to the Study of Law*.

24. Cultural values, in other words, permeate most of the ends we desire out of the rule of law—and not just human rights issues. Montesquieu discusses this idea in depth and saw little hope for success in legislating what were properly cultural and social matters. This realization is important to understanding why legal reform, as pursued under the institutional attributes definition discussed later, has failed to live up to its promise. See Montesquieu, *Spirit of the Laws*, ed. Anne Cohler, Basia Miller, and Harold Stone (Cambridge: Cambridge University Press, 1994).

25. See, for example, Thomas Hobbes, *Leviathan* (New York: Hackett, 1994), ch. XIII; and John Locke, *Two Treatises of Government* (Treatise II), ed. Peter Laslett, Raymond Geuss, and Quentin Skinner (Cambridge, UK: Cambridge University Press, 1988), 46–9, for references to the United States, and commentaries for the effects of the English civil war on Hobbes' thinking, in particular.

26. Locke, Treatise II, 123.

27. Ibid., 131, 353.

28. See Deepa Narayan, with Raj Patel, Kai Schafft, Anne Rademacher, and Sarah Koch-Schulte, *Voices of the Poor* (New York: Oxford University Press, 2000), 183–7, available at www.worldbank.org/poverty/voices/ reports.htm, which features thousands of interviews with poor individuals in developing countries; see particularly the case study on the police.

29. For U.S. figures, see GAO, "Rule of Law Funding Worldwide," 8, 11. Although numbers are for Latin America alone, the author's research into other areas and into EU funding demonstrates similar funding levels. See also GAO, "Foreign Aid: Police Training and Assistance," GAO-NSIAD/92-118 (Washington, D.C.: GAO, March 1992).

30. Most laws are followed not out of fear of force but out of general acceptance. Where large law-and-order problems prevail, either a society has reached a tipping point where social strictures no longer serve this self-policing function, or large portions of the citizenry do not accept the government's legitimacy in governing them. The former frequently occurs in impoverished areas; the latter in separatist or tribal regions with a strong sense of customary law.

31. In Panama, for instance, a decade-long effort at police reform has been quite successful in creating a trained, respected corps of police officers, but lagging judicial reform means that criminals simply bribe judges and evade imprisonment.

32. In Russia, judges were regularly bribed, and at least one judge was beaten, see Bernard Black, Reinier Kraakman, and Anna Tarassova, "Russian Privatization and Corporate Governance: What Went Wrong?" *Stanford Law Review* 52 (2000): 1755–6. Even in Italy, the famous "clean hands" judges who tried to go after the mafia and connected politicians found their ranks decimated by murders that went unsolved.

33. Black, Kraakman, and Tarassova, "Russian Privatization," 1757.

34. Magna Carta, 1215, c1. 40. "To no one will We sell, to no one will We deny or delay, right or justice."

35. William Penn, *Some Fruits of Solitude* (1693), ed. Eric K. Taylor (Scottsdale, PA: Herald Press, 2003).

36. *Bartlett's Familiar Quotations* attributes the quote to Gladstone, but it does not seem to be found in his writings. The first case to cite the idea is *Gohman v. City of St. Bernard*, 111 Ohio St. 726, 737 (1924).

37. Obviously, civil settlements that are delayed earn the winner less money, given inflation and the opportunity cost of investment. A better example might be the recent

contestation of a local election in the Philippines where the court eventually overturned the results and gave the seat to the plaintiff—on the last day of his term. See *Economist*, "Democracy as Showbiz," July 1, 2004.

38. F. A. Hayek, *The Road to Serfdom* (Chicago: University of Chicago Press, 1994), 80.

39. Hayek is participating in a fight between proceduralists and substantivists that is described later in note 78.

40. Ronald Cass, *The Rule of Law in America* (Baltimore, MD: Johns Hopkins University Press, 2001).

41. Lee S. Wolosky, "Putin's Plutocrat Problem," *Foreign Affairs* (March/April 2000): 27.

42. The World Bank has a vested interest in making the rule of law appear technocratic because the organization is caught in a quandary. Their research arm shows that the rule of law and other highly political issues they now term *governance* are crucial to successful development, but their mission precludes them from taking a stand on political systems. Thus, they are trying to approach these sticky governance issues as technocratic problems so that they can address them without overstepping their legal bounds.

43. Even though the World Bank has a new and cutting-edge program to consider the problems of insecurity on development, the Legal Department that advises on most rule-of-law reforms is not connected to this line of thinking within the Bank. For the problems that law and order, not efficiency and predictability, have on foreign investment, see Black, Kraakman, and Tarassova, "Russian Privatization," 1758–60.

44. The story, based on field research and interviews, is contained in the author's unpublished master's thesis, Rachel Kleinfeld, *Diplomacy and Development: The European Union's Efforts to Build the Rule of Law in South Eastern Europe, 1997-2001*, Master's thesis, University of Oxford, Oxford, UK, 2002. Parts can also be gleaned from successive European Commission, *Progress Reports on Romania, 1999–2002*: "Regular Reports on Romania for 2000, 2001, and 2002," available at http://europa.eu.int/comm/enlargement/romania/index.htm; and "Progress Reports on Romania, 1999–2002," available at http://europa.eu.int/comm/enlargement/romania/index.htm

45. Locke, Treatise II, 131.

46. Dicey, *Introduction to the Study of the Law*, 107–22. Dicey upholds human rights by stressing that the common law is the preeminent means of creating the rule of law, because rights are less easily abrogated when they emerge through precedent, and because rights proclamation comes simultaneously with a means to enforce them. Many commentators confuse this third of his "kindred conceptions," believing that it is about the necessity of the common law, and miss the focus on individual rights. Yet Dicey specifically cites the United States as having the rule of law, despite proclaiming rights constitutionally and in the Bill of Rights rather than solely having them evolve from precedent, because the American system had numerous methods to ensure that rights were realized and enforced. Dicey's point in stressing the common law is that he believes the rule of law requires individual rights to be enforced, not simply proclaimed. He fears that when rights are declared by constitution rather than emerging from precedent, it is more likely that they will become empty statements rather than enforced liberties.

47. Not any human rights reform would necessarily count as a rule-of-law issue. The idea is not simply the growth of human rights, but the notion that the state should be reined in by the law and that law should have content to it—that is, the state cannot violate intrinsic human rights of individuals. Thus, the rule of law is historically about negative rights, not positive rights or so-called economic and social rights. There is also a strong connotation of physical or property violence to human rights as a rule-of-law issue. A state violates the rule of law when it abducts and

extrajudicially executes citizens or appropriates citizens' property; it is not as intuitive that a state violates the rule of law when it places curbs on free speech.

48. Antonin Scalia, "The Rule of Law as a Law of Rules," *University of Chicago Law Review* 56 (1989): 1179.

49. Joseph Raz, "The Rule of Law and Its Virtue," *Law Quarterly Review* 93 (1977): 195. This chapter will later argue that even the apparently value-neutral institutional attributes actually carry a liberal Western value set, but this is not generally recognized by the field and not part of the debate between formalists and substantivists.

50. Empirical work on growing authoritarian tendencies in Russia shows the danger to rule-of-law reformers of not using a substantivist definition of the term that includes a full range of human rights. See Jeffrey Sachs and Katharina Pistor, *Rule of Law and Economic Reform in Russia* (Boulder, CO: Westview Press, 1997).

51. Aristotle, *Politics*, III, 11, 1282b-III, 12, 1283a and IV, 8, 1294a.

52. Locke, Treatise II, 131, 353.

53. A recent news account, for instance, describes how marriage-through-kidnap-and-rape, a traditional practice in Ethiopia, was banned by law but was not enforced because most people were unwilling to protest through the courts, and judges did not believe in the right enough to uphold it. See Emily Wax, "Ethiopian Rape Victim Pits Law Against Culture," *Washington Post*, June 7, 2004.

54. Locke, Treatise II, 131.

55. *Aristotle, Nicomachean Ethics* V. 6, 1134a-b; see also Aristotle, *Politics*, III, 11, 1282b.

56. Douglass North, Structure and Change in Economic History (New York: W. W. Norton, 1981), 344.

57. USAID and the EU both imply the distinction in their definitions. USAID declares that the rule of law "embodies" some things and "is founded on" others, whereas the EU notes that the rule of law is "a fundamental principle" and then describes institutions that it "implies." Amnesty International actually captures the distinction best, stating in its report on Afghanistan that, "the institutions essential to implement the rule of law and to protect human rights are weak. The reconstruction of a professional police force, as an important enforcement mechanism for the rule of law across the country, needs urgent attention."

58. See chapter 1 in this volume.

59. A similar problem can be seen in economic development, a field in which identifying the connections among education, infrastructure, governance, environmental health, and economic policy, to name just a few, has been notoriously difficult.

60. Thomas Carothers coined the term institutional modeling to describe this process; see Thomas Carothers, "Democracy Assistance: The Question of Strategy," *Democratization* 4, no. 3 (Autumn 1997): 116.

61. Aristotle, *Nicomachean Ethics* V. 6, 1134a-b; see also Aristotle, *Politics,* III, 11, 1282b. Of course, Plato's entire idea of enforcement of social hierarchy through the noble lie (in which a society's rulers tell the people that the social hierarchy reflects God's intervention) is such an example. Brian Tamanaha describes numerous cultural and social strictures that upheld parts of the rule of law during the medieval era, even when rule-of-law institutions did not exist; see Tamanaha, "Rule of Law for Everyone?" 15.

62. Aristotle, *Politics*, III, 16 1287b.

63. Isaiah Berlin, *Four Essays on Liberty* (Oxford: Oxford University Press, 1969), 166.

64. *Economist*, "Crimes Past."

65. In The Eumenides, the third play in Aeschylus' *Oresteia*, Athena creates a court to rule on the case of patricide, taking the right of such decisions away from the ancient Furies, who she then placates in a most political way with a host of other nonlegal powers. The Magna Carta was famously forced on the English King by the growing

power of the aristocratic landowners. See Aeschylus, *The Oresteia*, ed. David Grene and Richmond Lattimore, trans. Richmond Lattimore (Chicago: University of Chicago Press, 1983); and Fredrich Pollock and Fredric William Maitland, *The History of English Law before the Time of Edward I (1898)* (Union, NJ: Lawbook Exchange, 1996).

66. *Economist*, "The People Come to Court," March 4, 2004, available at www.economist.com/world/asia/displayStory.cfm?story_id=2479774.

67. Hayek, *Constitution of Liberty*, 172; this problem was also mentioned by Dicey.

68. Frequent references to the U.S. Supreme Court's "independence" after their intervention in the Bush v. Gore electoral battle, comments on the highly political judge-picking strategies in the United States, evidence of police use of torture in New York, and notorious corruption cases in Italy, France, and the United States are often mentioned as asides by legal professionals in developing countries, as if to say, with a wink and a nod, that we all know no state can really practice the rule of law. We would have more credibility if we acknowledged that all of our systems are evolving attempts toward ideals.

69. All governments now use executive decrees to some extent, and they are quite common in the United States. At issue is the use of executive decrees to evade the parliamentary legislative process for laws that would be unlikely to pass otherwise, or the use of such decrees to unlawfully amass extra powers to the executive.

70. See European Commission, "Regular Reports on Romania for 2000, 2001, and 2002." The overuse of executive decrees to meet conditionality has been recognized by many observers of other countries as well. See Poonam Gupta, Rachel Kleinfeld, and Gonzalo Salinas, "Legal and Judicial Reform in Europe and Central Asia" (Washington, D.C.: World Bank, Operations Evaluations Department, 2002).

71. Alexis de Tocqueville, Complete Works, viii, 455–7, quoted in Dicey, *Introduction to the Study of Law*, 109.

72. Admittedly, much of this self-deception is forced on practitioners by the obvious political difficulty of admitting that they are meddling with the politics and cultures of other countries (for bilateral aid agencies) or by a mission that proscribes such work (for multilateral groups). Nevertheless, it impedes clear thinking.

73. Sometimes, regulations are reduced in an effort to reduce corruption; where there are no rules, there are no rule-breakers, and every regulation is an opportunity for corruption. What I am criticizing is not such reasoned efforts, but the ideology that sometimes leads to blind activity without reasoned thought to guide it—an ideology criticized by Joseph Stiglitz in *Globalization and Its Discontents* (New York: W. W. Norton, 2003).

74. The World Bank is particularly guilty of ascribing to this fallacy. Its Comprehensive Development Framework, for instance, states that "Without the protection of human and property rights, and a comprehensive framework of laws, no equitable development is possible." Fair enough, so far. It then states, "A government must ensure that it has an effective system of property, contract, labor, bankruptcy, commercial codes, personal rights laws and other elements of a comprehensive legal system that is effectively, impartially and cleanly administered by a well-functioning, impartial and honest judicial and legal system." In practice, this rarely means simply that a country must have rules of the game for commercial life and property, as well as the institutional attributes already agreed upon; instead, it means that a country must have the particular rules preferred by the World Bank and International Monetary Fund.

75. In part, the confusion between the rule of law and a particular system of law has arisen, particularly in the United States, because Americans misread Dicey, fail to read Hayek, and thus view the rule of law as a particularly Anglo-Saxon concept.

76. It may be easy to dismiss these beliefs as conspiracy theory—but they affect our success in convincing local elites to support reform. Moreover, they are not wholly off

the mark. Many rule-of-law programs are sold on a domestic political level through claims that improving the rule of law abroad will lead to greater market opportunities for the country ponying up money for the reform.

77. See Upham's prologue for a case study involving a Mrs. Sanderson in Frank Upham, "Mythmaking in the Rule-of-Law Orthodoxy," Carnegie Working Paper no. 30 (Washington, D.C.: Carnegie Endowment for International Peace, 2002).

78. In fact, by actually preferring various public policy outcomes over rule-of-law procedures, rule-of-law reformers may unwittingly be stepping into the center of one of the bitterest debates over the rule of law. A current argument is raging over how much discretion judges have to decide cases on public policy grounds. Substantivists such as Dworkin and Tremblay see a large role for judicial discretion: When laws are not "good," the spirit of justice, they argue, not the written word, should be supreme. Proceduralists, such as Hayek and even Aristotle (see his *Rhetoric* 1354ab), believe that such judicial discretion overturns the rule of law by allowing judges to make, as well as decide upon, law. They believe this situation undermines both equality before the law (because such decisions would require the state to determine how particular individuals should be situated) and the notion that the state must be reined in by law. In their rhetoric, rule-of-law practitioners echo the beliefs of proceduralists, who believe that to uphold the rule of law, the elected legislature must make the rules, and the judges must decide upon them narrowly. If the outcome of a case appears "unjust," it is a sign for the legislature to rewrite the laws in a general, impartial way, and the judge is not allowed to amend judgment on public policy grounds that would make laws specific to individual circumstances. In practice, however, rule-of-law practitioners are generally happy with having the executive bypass the legislature or judges overstep the limits of the laws, if these abrogations of the rule of law help them achieve their public policy desires.

79. Although numerous economists have tried to demonstrate these correlations, the facts are still unclear. See Thomas Carothers, chapter 2 in this volume.

80. Paul Collier and Anke Hoeffler, "Greed and Grievance in Civil War," World Bank Working Paper no. 2355 (Washington, D.C.: World Bank, May 2000), available at http://econ.worldbank.org/docs/1109.pdf. Their findings on the links between poverty and rebellion are upheld by many scholars in this burgeoning field.

81. Kleinfeld, *Diplomacy and Development*.

82. Thomas Carothers cites the "all good things go together" mentality in his book, *Aiding Democracy Abroad: The Learning Curve* (Washington, D.C.: Carnegie Endowment for International Peace, 1999), 56.

83. Pilar Domingo, "Judicial Independence and Judicial Reform in Latin America," in *The Self-Restraining State: Power and Accountability in New Democracies*, ed. A. Schedler, L. Diamond, and M. F. Plattner (Boulder, CO: Lynne Rienner, 1999), 164; David M. Trubek and Marc Galanter, "Scholars in Self-Estrangement: Some Reflections on the Crisis in Law and Development" *Wisconsin Law Review* 4 (1974): 1075–6; and Elliot M. Burg, "Law and Development: A Review of the Literature and a Critique of 'Scholars in Self Estrangement,'" *American Journal of Comparative Law* 25 (1977): 518.

84. Some of the backlash against human rights norms in Eastern Europe and the former Soviet Union can be attributed to this problem of pacing: Cultural norms widely accepted before they were implemented have fallen into disfavor as international groups preach human rights and ordinary people feel preyed upon by increased criminality.

85. Laurel Miller and Robert Perito, "Establishing the Rule of Law in Afghanistan," Special Report no. 117 (Washington, D.C.: U.S. Institute of Peace, March 2004).

86. Their line of thinking is generally inspired by Hernando de Soto, whose groundbreaking book, *The Other Path*, demonstrated how a lack of legal title, overregulation,

and inaccessible justice kept small businesses from growing and the poor from gaining credit. See Hernando de Soto, *The Other Path: The Invisible Revolution in the Third World* (New York: Harper Collins, 1989).

87. See the indicators used for the Millennium Challenge Account, or those now advanced by the World Bank in Daniel Kaufman, Aart Kraay, and Massimo Mastruzzi, *Governance Matters III: Governance Indicators for 1996–2002* (Washington, D.C.: World Bank, June 2003). The World Bank indicators actually do measure a number of the dimensions of the rule of law that I am talking about, but they obscure the fact by placing them under different subheadings of governance, all of which are made to sound technocratic. Human rights indicators slip in under political stability and voice and accountability. The predictability of law is sandwiched into regulatory quality. Law and order is placed under the rule-of-law criteria but also emerges under political stability and lack of violence. Thus, the requisite points are measured, but not as elements of the rule of law, in such a way that obscures all of the gains to be made from recognizing the different types of desired ends and the tensions between them.

88. For an appraisal of Russia's standing on a variety of rule-of-law measures and appraisals of judicial corruption, see Katharina Pistor, Martin Raiser, and Stanislaw Gelfer, "Law and Finance in Transition Economies," European Bank for Reconstruction and Development Working Paper no. 48 (London: European Bank for Reconstruction and Development, 2000), 6–7, available at http://papers.ssrn.com/paper.taf? abstract_id=214648; and Jeffrey M. Hertzfeld, "Russian Corporate Governance: The Foreign Direct Investor's Perspective," in Conference Proceedings of Corporate Governance in Russia (Paris: Organization for Economic Cooperation and Development, 1999).

89. For more on how liberal societies hold opposing or equally valued goods in tension, see Berlin, *Four Essays on Liberty.*

90. Dicey, *Introduction to the Study of Law,* 110.

91. There is no easy start date for rule-of-law reform activities. Developed countries have affected reforms of weaker states since the era of Rome, or even ancient Greece. The law and development movement of the 1960s heralded some of the first modern efforts at rule-of-law reform in countries that were not colonized or occupied. Rule-of-law reform started incrementally in Latin America with various legal reform programs in the 1980s and then grew rapidly with the end of the Soviet Union and the need to move states from communism to market-oriented democracies in the 1990s.

92. Jeffrey Sachs and Katharina Pistor make the important distinction between the rule of law and rule *through* law, in which law functions as an administrative device, not as a set of rules binding on state officials. The rule through law can entrench autocracy in law. See Sachs and Pistor, *Rule of Law and Economic Reform,* 24. Because reformers tend to favor technocratic reforms that improve efficiency and judicial functioning, this is precisely the problem many "successful" reforms risk. See Domingo, "Judicial Independence," 164.

CHAPTER FOUR

Mythmaking in the Rule-of-Law Orthodoxy

FRANK UPHAM

THE MANIFOLD EFFORTS by Western development institutions to encourage and sometimes compel developing countries to create the rule of law often rest on a very formalist conception of the goal—that is, regimes defined by strict adherence to established legal rules and freedom from the corrupting influences of politics. Rule-of-law promoters contend that such reforms are essential to establishing stability and norms that encourage investment and sustainable economic growth in the developing world. In evaluating this new rule-of-law orthodoxy that has emerged in the development business in the past decade and a half, I question some of its underlying assumptions, including this idea that economic development requires formalistic rule of law and the notion that the rule of law is actually apolitical in economically developed democracies like the United States.

The foundation of my argument is that law is deeply contextual and that it cannot be detached from its social and political environment. This is just as true in developed countries as in developing countries, but this truth is absent from the new rule-of-law orthodoxy. Two important consequences follow from this failure to acknowledge the political nature of law, particularly of U.S. law. First, it leads to an underestimation of the difficulty and complexity of legal development.[1] If law can be seen as a set of neutral rules, or at most institutions, different national legal systems can be formally compared and modeled, and successful models can be transplanted into countries with failed systems, much as businesses adopt "best practices" in manufacturing processes, inventory management, and so on. Law, in other words, is seen as technology when it should be seen as sociology or politics. Second, the denial of the universally political nature of law has led aid providers to act as though law is good and politics is bad. Besides the irony of a movement that advocates democracy while denigrating politics, the result is the quixotic quest for an impossible ideal where impoverished developing countries are expected to strive for a pristine rule of law that their developed counterparts have not achieved. More important, the distaste for politics has led legal reformers to avoid it and to try to build legal systems outside of and in opposition to it, where property and contract rights are seamlessly enforced without reference to their political and social consequences. Not only will such an enterprise inevitably fail, but also it would often be undesirable even from the largely economic perspective of the institutions that dominate the law and development movement.

The Rule-of-Law Model

Given the substantial attention and money that development organizations now direct to rule-of-law assistance, one would assume that there is a carefully elaborated model of law and development based on empirical evidence from the developmental periods of Western economies, what has worked and not worked in the developing world over the last fifty years, and the experience of the previous period of law and development in the 1960s. If such a model exists, however, I have not found it.[2] Instead, one finds a series of assumed legal systems that seems to have emerged fully formed from the pages of a high school text on U.S. democracy, and not a very sophisticated text at that. Advocates of rule of law extrapolate from Weberian sociology and the imagined experiences of Western capitalism to the rest of the world. Universal theories of the interdependence of legal form and economic activity lurk behind the rhetoric of the rule of law without a great deal of intellectual agonizing over exactly what this form of law entails, how it relates to economic activity, or how it fits in different political, social, and institutional contexts. The result is a formalist model of law detached from the social and political interconnections that form actual legal systems everywhere.

This view of law rests on two assumptions about law and society. The first is that the description of law as a system of rules can be a reliable guide to understanding legal systems. The second assumption has two parts: one, that law's primary role in society is dispute resolution; and two, that society depends on formal legal adjudication for stable and predictable dispute resolution. I examine each of these assumptions in turn, not in the abstract but by drawing on the writings of two prominent advocates for legal reform in the developing world: Ibrahim Shihata, former general counsel of the World Bank, and Hernando de Soto, Peruvian author of *The Other Path*.

The World Bank Model

At the end of the 1980s, in an effort to increase the effectiveness of the World Bank's development loans, its legal staff began to address what it calls "governance" issues in borrowing countries. Concerned that the way power is exercised in developing countries may contribute to the inefficient use of World Bank funds, yet constrained by its Articles of Agreement from considering political criteria in its lending, the general counsel of the World Bank in those years, Ibrahim Shihata, drafted a memorandum that distinguished governance from politics and identified the former as a legitimate consideration in the awarding of bank loans.

In general terms, Shihata equated governance with "good order"; in more specific terms, he called it the rule of law, which he defined at one point as a "system based on abstract *rules* which are actually applied and on functioning *institutions* which ensure the appropriate application of such rules" (emphasis in original). Such a system, Shihata claimed, provides a legal foundation for social stability and economic growth and is a prerequisite for the effective use of World Bank assistance:

> Reforms cannot be effective in the absence of a system, which translates them into workable rules and makes sure they are complied with. Such a system assumes that: a) there is a set of rules which are known in advance, b) such rules are actually in force, c) mechanisms exist to ensure the proper application of the rules and to allow for departure from them as needed according to established procedures, d) conflicts in the application of the rules can be resolved through binding decisions of an independent judicial or arbitral body, and e) there are known procedures for amending the rules when they no longer serve their purpose.[3]

Shihata went on to state that, in the absence of such a system, the fates of both individuals and enterprises will be left "to the whims of the ruling individual or clique" and that only such a system can provide the "general social discipline" that makes economic reform possible.

Shihata's views are echoed throughout subsequent World Bank literature. A few excerpts from the Bank's website are illustrative:

> Legal and Judicial systems that work effectively, efficiently, and fairly are the backbone of national economic and social development. National and international investors need to know that the rules they operate under will be expeditiously and fairly enforced. Ordinary citizens need to know that they, too, have the surety and protection that only a competent judicial system can offer.[4]

> Without the protection of human and property rights, and a comprehensive framework of laws, no equitable development is possible. A government must ensure that it has an effective system of property, contracts, labor, bankruptcy, commercial codes, personal rights law and other elements of a comprehensive legal system that are effectively, impartially, and cleanly administered by a well-functioning, impartial and honest judicial and legal system.[5]

> A competitive business and corporate sector is built on the foundation of strong property rights, ease of company formation, corporate governance, the availability of flexible collateral mechanisms to support the availability of credit, and reliable insolvency systems to minimize lender risk and encourage the rehabilitation of viable firms in financial difficulty. Laws and legal institutions also underpin fund raising and securities trading through well-regulated securities markets.[6]

It is hard to argue that an effective, efficient, and fair judicial system is not a good thing or that a country will be better off without "an effective system of property, contracts, labor, bankruptcy, commercial codes, personal rights law and other elements of a comprehensive legal system that are effectively, impartially, and cleanly administered by a well-functioning, impartial and honest judicial and legal system," and I will not attempt to do so. Later in this chapter, however, I will elaborate on my objections to the type of rhetoric exemplified by the above quotes, but at this point, three observations will suffice:

- These statements are platitudes, with no more precise meaning than "a well-educated citizenry is the first guardian of democracy" or "ask not what your country can do for you, but what you can do for your country."

- They present an exclusive path to development, using phrases like "a government *must* ensure" and "investors *need* to know" and statements that legal systems "are *the* backbone of national economic and social development" without which "no equitable development is possible." They leave no sense that there may be other paths to development other than through an effective, efficient, and fair legal system, and they imply that nothing can happen until these institutions are perfected. There is no acknowledgment of the variety of types of development or the possibility of different sequences within the development process.
- These statements are evangelical. They advocate a course of action based on faith in social perfection, in this instance, a perfect legal system, which in turn produces a transparent and equitable order. There is no room for ideological compromise, no hint that building such a system might be difficult and costly, or that other necessities of development might have to be sacrificed to build it.[7]

The World Bank is by no means alone in this embrace of the new rule-of-law orthodoxy. "The rule of law, not men" is a standard maxim of U.S. politics. Politicians of every stripe repeat it as a mantra, perhaps sincerely, while running on platforms that explicitly promise a political makeover of the current judiciary. Law professors urge the protection of the fragile institution of the rule of law in the face of centuries of political manipulation of the U.S. judiciary. "Rule of men" has the connotation of arbitrariness, corruption, and instability; "rule of law" promises procedural fairness, honesty, and consistency. Justice Antonin Scalia has also weighed in favor of a rule of law that is a "law of rules," as opposed to a more sloppy law that allows "men" to influence outcomes.[8] There is also a general agreement that markets and rule of law go hand in hand. Without the slightest textual basis in the U.S. Constitution, the U.S. Supreme Court has declared that special efforts should be made to preserve economic rights because markets require stability.[9] For other types of rights, stability is apparently less important. Returning to the law and development context, the U.S. Congress has most recently put these sentiments in statutory form in the African Growth and Opportunities Act.[10] In other words, the World Bank and other international development institutions are not plowing new ground; they are simply attempting to put into action some of the central platitudes of U.S. legal and political ideology.

De Soto and the Evils of Informalism

The rhetoric of the rule of law does not emerge solely from Washington sources. It has eloquent advocates elsewhere, the most powerful of whom is Hernando de Soto.[11] De Soto has provided an empirical basis for the assumptions of the World Bank model of the rule of law, but he has done so in a deeply paradoxical way—not by describing the failure of development without law but by describing its triumphs. As such, de Soto provides an extremely revealing example of how the imagined world of the rule of law blinds us to the reality of economy and society and makes it impossible to imagine alternative sources for the stability and fairness that all the participants in this debate desire.

In *The Other Path*, de Soto describes the success of informal elements in Peru's economy in achieving economic growth and social mobility, despite the lack of formal legal protections. He convincingly claims that Peru's official economy had become so encrusted with legal and regulatory formalities that virtually all economic growth within the official sector had ceased. He describes the success of informal actors, usually poor immigrants to Lima from rural areas, in establishing stable systems of production and exchange without rules to define entitlements or formal institutions to settle disputes. Although de Soto sees informality as ultimately limiting growth, he contrasts the vitality of the informal sector with the stagnation of Peru's formal economy.

The phenomena that de Soto describes provide powerful evidence of the possibility of sustained and complex economic activity, at least on an individually small scale, without structure or protection provided by a formal legal system. The lesson more commonly drawn from de Soto's work, however, is that the isolation of poor Peruvians from law has seriously limited their economic opportunities and, in turn, the general economic growth of Peru. Instead of weakening their faith in the need for formal law, de Soto and those influenced by him call for the official recognition of the informal economy and its inclusion within a dramatically restructured formal legal system. They argue that legalization of the rights of those in the informal sector under this new regime would give them greater access to credit and legal protection for large-scale investment.

De Soto envisions a legal system that would operate within a deregulated economy stripped of virtually all of the government intrusion that has stifled the Peruvian economy and outside of which the informal economy flourished. It would be an economy much like that envisioned by Shihata. The market would allocate resources efficiently through the operation of Adam Smith's invisible hand. Individuals and corporations would have clear property and contract rights that would be more or less seamlessly interpreted and enforced by the courts. Government's role would be limited to responding to instances of market failure.

So far, so good. It would be hard to dispute that vigorous entrepreneurs who have thrived under a thoroughly corrupt regime without any legal rights whatsoever would not do even better under an honest pro-market regime. I may argue that de Soto and his followers are naïve in dreaming the same dreams as Shihata or the U.S. Congress, but that is not what is most perplexing about this school of thought. What is most perplexing is that they have amassed rich empirical data about economic and social success in the real world of corruption and government incompetence and yet appear totally uninterested in the lessons that these data may hold for developing countries. More specifically, they seem uninterested in the possibility that a formal legal system of the type they advocate could stifle growth or that courts would face the apparent conflict between the application of rules and economic growth. Nor do they consider the possibility that the formal legal system they envision could not exist within the context of real-world politics. They seem to assume that those whose interests would suffer from the mechanical operation of the market and the rule of law either would not have legitimate avenues to oppose its operation or would choose not to do so out of an appreciation of the greater good. Also left out of the calculus is any cost-benefit analysis. Even if one assumes that a formal legal system of this type is possible and that it contributes to economic growth, it remains an open question whether it is worth the cost, including of course, the opportunity cost of the financial and human resources necessary to establish and maintain such a system.

However, the apparent disinterest in investigating the practices that have provided social stability and investment security and fostered growth in the informal sector in Peru is the most surprising omission of de Soto and his followers. In seeming defiance of their own evidence, they leave untouched the assumption that productive capitalism cannot develop without formal adjudication, scrupulously enforced contracts, and inviolable property rights. They are not interested in whether the informal practices that supported growth in Lima could be replicated elsewhere or whether they might be superior, at least in a cost-benefit sense, to a formal legal system. De Soto never considers, for example, whether it might be more cost effective to introduce some of the successful informal mechanisms into the stultified formal sector, instead of formalizing the informal sector.

Equally striking is the failure, not only of de Soto but also more puzzling of Shihata and the World Bank, to investigate examples of informal economic growth in other parts of the world. There is a substantial literature on the possibility of social order and economic growth in the absence of formal law in the United States (and in Japan, which I discuss in the next section), but it is worth noting here the experience of the People's Republic of China (PRC) and the Chinese diaspora.[12] It is difficult to imagine a developing country of any size that has outperformed the PRC economically or socially over the last two decades. China's economy grew on average 9.7 percent from the beginning economic reforms in 1978 to the late 1990s.[13] Nor has China had any difficulty attracting foreign capital, with more than $53 billion in foreign direct investment in 2003 alone. Furthermore, although China is suffering from growing social dislocation, disparities of wealth, and official corruption, its record in these areas is better than that of most developing countries. Most important for our purposes, the PRC has achieved this growth without a legal system worthy of the name. No one would claim that China has had the legal institutions envisioned by the World Bank during most of this period, and yet, except for a series of conferences by the Asian Development Bank, there has been little interest in finding out how this has been done or whether it can be replicated elsewhere.[14]

Nor has the rule-of-law movement paid much attention to the economic success of ethnic minorities. Although this general topic is too extensive to deal with here, the experience of the Chinese in Southeast Asia presents an example of "lawless" growth that is even more striking than China's recent successes. In China, at least the economic growth was legal in the sense of taking place with the approval of the regime; for the overseas Chinese, economic success has frequently taken place in defiance or circumvention of formal legal norms, so much so that one commentator has referred to the Chinese in Malaysia as "guerilla capitalists."[15] Some observers of overseas Chinese capitalism share de Soto's concern that doubtful legal status limits growth and technological innovation, but it is unclear whether these problems arise from legal informality or the constant political uncertainty and racial hostility that the Chinese have faced in most of Southeast Asia. It is clear, however, that the overseas Chinese within these societies have had economic success despite legal uncertainty and that their success has often, if not universally, outpaced that of the ethnic majorities, who have enjoyed full legal protection.[16]

It is possible, of course, that overseas Chinese and the PRC might have enjoyed even greater economic success had they had the advantage of a fully functioning legal system of the World Bank type.[17] Indeed, it may be impossible to argue in the abstract with the desirability of the characteristics and results that Shihata and de Soto ascribe to the rule of law: that contracting parties should be required to perform the substance of their promises or pay compensation, that business people should be able to predict the requirements of licensing procedures and to receive the license when they are able to meet those requirements, or that investors should not be surprised by rule changes that deprive them of a return on their investment or, worse, the value of the investment itself. But even if we assume that these are theoretically attractive attributes, before we conclude that the rule of law should become an immediate goal for developing societies, we must be convinced that it is a possible goal and the benefits of achieving it will be greater than the cost. Rule-of-law building is not worth spending money on unless the imperfect institutions created by such expenditures will have beneficial effects that outweigh their costs and any harm they create. To investigate the possibilities, costs, and varieties of the rule of law, in the next two sections I examine two highly successful economies of the twentieth century—those of the United States and Japan. Through an examination of their legal systems and their relationship to the rule-of-law ideal, we can get a more sophisticated sense of what the role of law is, what it entails, and what alternatives may exist. I start with the United States, the most vigorous advocate and practitioner of the rule-of-law development model.

Myths and Realities of Law and Practice in Developed Countries (I): The United States

The rule-of-law ideal might be summarized as universal rules uniformly applied. It requires a hierarchy of courts staffed by a cadre of professionally trained personnel who are insulated from political or other nonlegal influences. The decision-making process must be rational and predictable by persons trained in law; all legally relevant interests must be acknowledged and adequately represented; the entire system must be funded well enough to attract and retain talented people; and the political branches must respect law's autonomy. To casual observers, the epitome of the rule of law is the United States, and the United States is a leading exponent of the new rule-of-law orthodoxy. When we look closely at the U.S. legal system, however, we find few of these characteristics.

Rule by Politicized Judges, Not Law

The judiciary is a good place to begin. The U.S. judiciary is permeated by politics, especially when compared with the judiciary in legal systems influenced by the civilian tradition of continental Europe. Most state judges are elected and serve for a term of years. They belong to political parties and are chosen for their allegiance to partisan platforms. If they are not constantly aware of the effect of their important rulings on the electorate and their party's leaders, they will not be reelected, and they will cease to be judges.

The case of Rose Bird, the Chief Justice of the California Supreme Court who was removed from office by California voters for her stubborn opposition to the death penalty, is one of the best-known instances of judges being punished for fidelity to their vision of the law, but more typical is the recent transformation of the Texas judiciary at the hands of competing commercial interests.[18] In the early 1980s, wealthy trial lawyers succeeded in transforming the historically pro-business Texas Supreme Court into an "all-Democratic, lawsuit-friendly court that began upholding enormous jury verdicts against corporate and medical defendants." In response, corporations and doctors struck back and reversed the court's politics, again through partisan elections, so that by the mid-1990s, the winning record of defendants before the court had risen from 40 to 83 percent. By 2000, with a governor running for president as a "compassionate conservative" using his interim appointment powers to portray a picture of moderation, the pendulum had swung back once again toward the center.

All parties to such controversies claim that their position is faithful to the correct interpretation of the law and that their opponents' positions are politically motivated distortions of the law. What is striking about these arguments and vital to understanding the psychological hold of the rule-of-law orthodoxy is that many, if not most, of the participants on both sides sincerely believe that their side alone is being faithful to the letter of the law and that the other side, most charitably put, is mistaken. The sincere belief in these claims and their effectiveness as political tactics does not, however, make them true.

If we move from the state to the federal judiciary, the picture is more complicated but fundamentally similar. Federal judges are appointed, not elected. They serve for life, subject only to impeachment for egregious misbehavior, and the story of the politically conservative judge becoming a liberal on the bench (or the reverse) is rare. The inspiring stories of life tenure giving judges the security to grow in their jobs or to adhere to principle should not blind us to the reality of the appointment process, however. It is overwhelmingly political, and, the occasional Earl Warren or Hugo Black notwithstanding, federal judges rarely experience substantial conversions. It would be difficult to imagine it otherwise, because they are usually appointed when they are in their fifties, after decades of professional and political activity. Of course the ultimate proof of the infrequency of judicial bench conversions is the role of judicial appointments in federal politics, both during presidential elections and in the relationship between the president, who nominates federal judges, and the Senate, which must confirm them. If judges often acted inconsistently with their prior political views, judicial appointments would not loom so large in political campaigns.

More striking, if less obvious and well known, than the open political behavior of those appointing judges is the political engagement of sitting U.S. judges. Judge Richard Posner of the Court of Appeals for the Seventh Circuit, for example, published a book in 2000 arguing for the prosecution of President Clinton for perjury in the Monica Lewinsky affair while the Office of Independent Counsel was considering that very issue. Although controversial, this action was not generally criticized as crossing the bounds of judicial propriety. Indeed, after the remarkable case of *Bush v. Gore* that decided the 2000 presidential election, several Supreme Court justices took to the road to discuss the decision.

Despite unending proclamations of fidelity to precedent, political neutrality, judicial restraint, and other legal virtues, U.S. judges overwhelmingly follow their political preferences when the opportunity presents itself. As mentioned above, the most powerful evidence of this fact is the amount of attention given to judicial appointments in presidential campaigns and Senate confirmation hearings, but more direct examination of judicial behavior bears out this common-sense observation. A 1993 study by social scientists Jeffrey Segal and Harold Spaeth on the implementation of judicial restraint by Supreme Court justices between 1953 and 1989 serves as an example.[19] The authors studied the voting patterns of justices on the Warren, Burger, and Rehnquist courts in cases involving labor rights, civil liberties, federalism, and economic regulation and compared them with the justices' professed fidelity to judicial restraint. The result was that justices, whether liberal or conservative, were only restrained when it suited their preexisting political preferences. Otherwise, they found some reason to overcome their devotion to restraint. In a testament to the power of the myth of the apolitical, formalist rule of law, one of the worst "offenders" was Justice Felix Frankfurter, an icon of judicial restraint in the eyes of generations of law professors and students.[20]

Structured Irrationality

It is not just the politicization of the judiciary that contradicts the formalist model. Four fundamental aspects of the structure of the U.S. legal system make the World Bank version of the rule of law literally impossible. First, federalism guarantees, indeed celebrates, national inconsistencies in legal rules and results. Each state enjoys its own legislative and judicial sovereignty, limited only by the supremacy clause of the federal Constitution. As a result, most laws governing commercial or financial activity are state laws and vary throughout the fifty-one jurisdictions. Model codes such as the Uniform Commercial Code substantially reduce the disparities in many areas but do not eliminate them. Nor do they touch the procedural and institutional differences that make "forum shopping" an integral part of much commercial and products liability litigation.

It is not, for example, coincidence that the vast majority of large American corporations are incorporated under the laws of Delaware. Nor is it because most major corporations are headquartered in Delaware. Delaware has triumphed in the interstate competition to attract corporate registration fees and related business because it created a legal regime that most corporations have found more attractive than those found in their states of origin. Far from being condemned by legal scholars or politicians, this type of interstate legislative competition is valued as creating a series of laboratories of legislation on the one hand and preventing states from stifling economic activity by creating legal regimes less favorable to corporations on the other.

The second structural aspect of the U.S. legal system that deviates substantially from the rule-of-law orthodoxy is the jury system. As with federalism, there are myriad reasons why one might want a jury system, particularly in criminal trials, but fidelity to the rule of law is not one of them. Whether one defines the rule of law as the rational application of rules to facts or more abstractly as the rule of law, not men, juries simply do not fit. Juries are in theory limited to deciding questions of fact and are generally prohibited from relying on their own interpretation of legal rules. Even if the distinction between law and fact were clear—and dozens of scholarly careers have been made disputing that point—it is quite likely that many juries do not even understand the law that they are to apply.

This lack of understanding has nothing to do with intelligence or good will. It is structural and, at least in that sense, intentional. Lawyers spend three postgraduate years learning the techniques necessary to analyzing, interpreting, and applying legal rules in a professionally acceptable manner. Judges usually have decades of practice honing these skills. To expect a jury to understand legal rules in the same way and depth just because a judge patiently explains them borders on the fantastic. A jury may well have a good, common-sense understanding of the judge's instructions, and hence a good, common-sense understanding of the legal rules, but it is imperative to note that a common-sense understanding of the law is most definitely not what is required by the rule of law. Common sense varies from person to person and context to context; it is not a sound basis for the rule of law, however defined. Indeed, the supposedly "common-sense" decision making of the anthropological stalwart village elder or neighborhood boss is precisely the image against which the rule of law is most frequently contrasted. If one argues for a common-sense application of the law, one is arguing against the rule of law.

The third structural aspect of the U.S. legal system that leads to deviations from the rule-of-law orthodoxy is its system of civil procedure, specifically the adversary system. Here there are two aspects that deviate from fidelity to rules: the lawyers' obligations to their clients and the passive role of judges. Ethical rules require lawyers to represent their clients zealously, to keep virtually all information received from clients confidential, including information of illegal acts, to work to discredit the opposing party's evidence regardless of its truth, and, perhaps summing up the result of all the other duties, to give their primary loyalty to their client, not to truth or law.

As with federalism and juries, there are powerful arguments for requiring attorneys to give their primary loyalty to their clients. Many of these, however, relate to political theory, rather than the rule of law as defined as an accurate mechanism for the uniform application of rules to facts. It is true that many attorneys and law professors defend adversarial procedures by arguing that zealous advocacy by two equally talented partisans is the best path to truth. Even if one accepts this position in theory, the social reality is that opposing sides are rarely represented by equally talented lawyers with equal resources. All too often one side has vastly more talent and money than the other, so much so that the weaker party is not likely even to bring the matter to litigation, much less win if it did.

One might expect in instances in which one party has markedly greater resources or a clearly more effective attorney that the judge would have an obligation to step in to correct the imbalance. Such is not the case in common law legal systems, in which the judge plays a role more akin to a referee than to a seeker or guarantor of justice or fidelity to rules. The judge is not ethically required to redress inequalities of resources, talent, or dedication that threaten to lead to inaccuracy or injustice. Nor is he or she to structure the trial so that truth will emerge or prevent an advocate from misleading the jury with a deceptive cross examination that remains within the bounds of legitimate zealousness. The judge's role is to create a space where the opposing lawyers can compete, within the rules to be sure, but with their primary obligations to their clients, not to the law. Then, at the end of the competition between frequently mismatched lawyers, the judge turns the result over to a group of citizens whose legal education is usually limited to television shows.[21]

A final anomaly of the U.S. legal system as an exemplar of the new rule-of-law orthodoxy is the extreme reluctance on the part of federal or state governments to make the law available to people with little or no means.[22] Perhaps the most fundamental norm of the rule-of-law ideal is the uniform application of the law, without which the universality of norms, their rationality, indeed their substantive content, mean nothing. Society will not reflect the benefits of the rule of law if the rules are not enforced evenhandedly or if one side to a dispute does not have the resources to bring the matter to the attention of the law. Despite the simplicity of this concept, the U.S. government has never devoted even a fraction of the resources necessary to ensure that the poor have access to the courts. In recent decades, the United States, for example, spent approximately one-ninth as much per capita on civil legal services for lower-income persons as England.[23] The implication is that the uniform application of law is not important enough to spend significant resources on, which is a policy judgment that seems unlikely if Americans were as convinced as Shihata and de Soto that the rule of law is indispensable to economic growth or stability.

Legitimately Politicized Institution

The above discussion is intended to convince the reader that the U.S. legal system is a thoroughly and intentionally politicized institution. It is emphatically not intended to portray the legal system as in any way illegitimate, ineffective, or undeserving of political or intellectual support. It is important in this context to remember several aspects about politics. Politicization is not equivalent to corruption. Also, politics is the lifeblood of all regimes, especially democratic ones. Unfortunately, the rule-of-law orthodoxy equates politics with corruption. Law and judging are supposedly clean, procedurally transparent, and stable; politics is dirty, procedurally opaque, and chaotic. Consequently, the sins of corrupt judges in developing countries and elsewhere are conceived of as the result of political interference, and an "independent judiciary" is defined as one free of any political influence, without any consideration of whether such a judiciary is even possible or advisable. Instead of this focus on the depoliticization of the judiciary, international financial institutions and other international purveyors of the new rule-of-law orthodoxy should be concerned with the judiciary's legitimacy and effectiveness, not its political purity.

The question then becomes not whether courts play a political role but how that role is structured and managed. In the United States, it appears to be handled very well. Politics in the U.S. judiciary has not led to the "telephone justice" of Russia, where the judges sometimes change their minds at the order of a politician, or the "local protectionism" of China, where the courts favor local enterprises because local governments control their budgets. U.S. justice is a deeply institutionalized form of politics that operates over relatively long time spans—either the terms of elected state judges or the political cycles of presidentially appointed federal ones. More fundamentally, it operates within a very narrow political spectrum. The difference between Democrats and Republicans is tiny compared with the differences among political interests in many other countries, and judges, whether elected at the state level or appointed at the federal, are likely to be moderates within their parties. In most U.S. jurisdictions, it is also true that parties rotate in power, so that the judiciary is not totally dominated by one party or one political view.

Important consequences flow from political stability. Because judges' political preferences are concentrated at the middle of the political spectrum, their socialization to their roles as judges, although superficial compared with civil law countries such as Japan, is more successful in overcoming personal preferences than it would be if political differences among them or within society were more dramatic. Equally important, most cases will not pose issues that appear political to most judges. As opposed to persons at more extreme ends of the political spectrum, they accept the legitimacy of both positions in the vast majority of cases brought before them. The result is a stability of doctrine that appears like "the rule of law" but owes more to the political stability of the United States than to the political independence of the U.S. judiciary.

The difference between U.S. judges on the one hand and Russian or Chinese judges on the other, therefore, is more complicated than might first appear. If the "telephone justice" of Russia is motivated by a financial interest in one of the litigants' success, the issue is one of corruption and is distinct from questions of the neutrality of the judiciary, politics, or the rule of law. For example, corrupt Russian judges who affirm the decision of a corrupt bureaucrat are more like that bureaucrat than they are like an honest judge. If, however, judges decide for one litigant over the other because they are convinced that that decision is better for society and will strengthen their political allies, then the comparison with U.S. judges becomes more a matter of degree and institutional style than one of principle. Similarly, if Chinese judges decide for a local litigant because otherwise their budget will be reduced or they will not be able to get desirable housing, this is corruption, and it is the equivalent of a bureaucrat denying a license because the licensee would compete with local industry. If, however, the conference of judges within the particular court discusses the case and decides that one result is more consistent with the guidelines set out by the National People's Congress as interpreted by the Chinese Communist Party, then we again have an institution that is comparable to U.S. courts and particularly to appellate courts, where negotiated, collegial decisions are the norm and where political preferences are arguably even clearer than at the trial level.

This discussion may seem both shocking and wildly implausible. How could the Russian or Chinese judiciaries be compared to the American? I agree that the U.S. legal system is incomparably better, but the reason is not that the U.S. judiciary is independent of politics and the Chinese and Russians are enmeshed in it. It is that the Chinese and Russian judges are much more likely to be corrupt, to be part of corrupt institutions, and to be so poorly paid and educated that resisting corruption simply does not make practical sense. Although this distinction may make little difference if you are a politically naïve and unconnected litigant—as most foreign enterprises or financial institutions are likely to be—it makes a great deal of difference if one is prescribing a formula for China or Russia to use in building an effective judiciary.

Myths and Realities of Law and Practice in Developed Countries (II): Japan

One would think that postwar Japan would be an obvious model for the rule-of-law movement. Japan was the first non-Western economy to develop, it did so relatively quickly, and it did so under a democratic regime. To my knowledge, however, legal reformers seldom consult the Japanese experience. A possible reason is lack of knowledge about Japan, but rule-of-law advocates are not generally known for letting a lack of local knowledge stop them from advising on appropriate strategies. A more likely explanation is the institutional structure of the movement, particularly its fragmentation into national factions. A U.S. aid organization is not likely to approve a contract for the dissemination of the Japanese model. Perhaps most important, however, is the general sense, often encouraged by the Japanese themselves, that Japan is culturally unique and that whatever happens there is of little practical use to others. Closely related is the argument that consulting Japan's legal experience would be worthless because Japanese life is hardly affected by law, that law is irrelevant to most Japanese and disfavored as a means of dispute resolution, and that the Japanese economy is ruled by powerful bureaucrats unhindered by legal restrictions.

I agree that law has played a less visible role in Japan than in the United States but not for the cultural reasons assumed. Much of this conventional wisdom is either exaggerated or simplistic, and I will try briefly to correct some of these misunderstandings in the next section.[24] My purpose here, however, is not to argue that Japan should be a model for legal development, although I see no reason why Japan should be less relevant than the United States. My primary point here is that the Japanese experience stands, as does the American, in sharp contrast to the assumptions of the rule-of-law development discourse.

Inadequacy of a Cultural Explanation

In the Middle Ages, when the English were still throwing litigants into rivers to see if they would float, Japan had developed a legal system to adjudicate competing land claims that valued procedural regularity, the right to confront hostile witnesses, and objective third-party adjudication based on evidence instead of magic or divine ritual.[25] Even during the Tokugawa period (1600 to 1867), seen largely as the heyday of neo-Confucian authoritarianism and the flat prohibition of the legal profession, formal legal institutions were overloaded with lawsuits, legal advice was a significant industry, and legal justice was not impossible for even the most downtrodden. By number of cases, commercial matters and debt collection cases dominated, but the courts were used for disputes concerning property rights and personal status as well.

Law continued to play a significant role in the eighty years of Imperial Japan, and not solely as a superficial ornament borrowed from the West. Legal rules and litigation to enforce them became an important tool in defending privilege and challenging it.[26] Landlords exploited their rights under the civil code, demanding rent legally, although perhaps not morally, due, and tenants sued landlords for overreaching. Husbands exercised their rights to quick and simple divorce, and wives countered with suits for damages suffered because of their husbands' adultery. Contracting parties sued each other for default, and neighbors sued each other for irritating and harassing land use practices. Lawyers were numerous, litigation was common, and the results were not always to the liking of the political elite. The one exception was litigation against the government, especially any direct challenge to the legality of government action. There the courts were more circumspect. Some courts provided relief in the nature of torts, but success against the government in administrative cases was rare.

The leading politicians within the Imperial Diet reacted to this blossoming of legal activity with horror. By the 1920s, they were passing progressively harsher statutes to restrict litigation and protect the "beautiful customs" of Japan's imaginary past from the corrupting influences of law, individualism, and modernity, but to little avail. Eventually the onset of militarism brought litigation rates, and not incidentally the number of lawyers, down drastically, but it was not until the advent of postwar democracy that the government's efforts bore fruit in a more conventional sense. The number of lawyers relative to population or gross national product plummeted through the simple device of a legal limitation on their number. For most of the second half of the twentieth century, the government simply set the maximum annual production of legal professionals, including judges and procurators, at five hundred. The result was dramatic but entirely predictable. The number of lawyers in the country actually shrank from the 1930s to the 1960s despite significant population growth in those years.[27] The number of attorneys rose slowly but steadily thereafter and by 1995 had more than doubled in absolute numbers, although the increase in per capita terms was significantly less. Litigation rates are harder to characterize, but by one count they dropped by 75 percent between 1883 and 1990.[28] The absolute number of cases, as opposed to per capita rates, varied during that period, ebbing and flowing in rough but clear positive correlation with economic recessions. The number of judges and procurators remained virtually constant from the immediate postwar period through the 1990s.

What is remarkable about this shrinking of the legal sector is that it occurred at a time of rapid economic expansion and demographic dislocation. That is well illustrated by the share of the national budget spent on the court system, which went from an already low 0.91 percent in 1955 to an infinitesimally small 0.36 percent in 1999.[29] Also striking is the fact that from 1950 to 1970, the percentage of Japanese living in cities practically doubled, presumably increasing the need for the social ordering of formal law.[30] Put simply but accurately, during the very same period that the economy boomed and society underwent substantial changes, the number of legal professionals per capita declined, the litigation rate fell, and the size of the formal legal system relative to the economy shrank substantially. It is difficult to exaggerate the importance of the juxtaposition of these phenomena to the topic of this chapter. If formal legal institutions were necessary for either social order or economic growth or even just weakly associated with it, one would expect the de-emphasis of formal law to have hindered growth. Instead, in Japan a shrinkage of legal institutions is positively correlated with growth, although no causal connection—that the lack of attention to formal legal institutions created growth—can be proved.

Regulatory Environment

How could the Japanese economy have flourished in the face of a set of formal legal institutions that were steadily shrinking in relationship to the level of economic activity, social change, and population? Although rule-of-law advocates would not argue that economic policy should be governed by courts and policy decisions made through litigation, an important tenet of the rule-of-law orthodoxy is that there should be a clear separation between private and public in the economy. In Japan, however, a legally established and maintained system of private incentives is not the dominant explanation for the rapid economic growth over the last fifty years.

Although there are forceful exceptions, the conventional explanation is that the Japanese economy developed under the strong guidance of a dedicated and talented cadre of powerful central governmental bureaucrats that created what has become known as the developmental state.[31] In this world, the bureaucrats of the Ministry of International Trade and Industry (MITI) and the Ministry of Finance (MOF) decided where Japan's resources should be invested. In the argot of industrial policy, they picked winners and then did their best to make sure their choices were correct. The market played a crucial but passive role; it was there to ratify MITI's choices and to reward the winners, but it did not allocate investment resources as assumed by economists. On the contrary, according to this view, the market had to be bypassed and distorted both to provide emerging sectors the necessary resources and to provide a soft landing for the losers. For the proponents of the developmental state model of Japan, the law played virtually no role.

The accuracy of this characterization of the Japanese state and economy is strongly debated, with a major focus being the role of the bureaucrats and whether they deserve credit for Japan's success or whether they acted at the behest and under the control of Japanese politicians. Although potentially crucial for a general model of development and the question of the relative roles of democracy and expertise, this issue is not central to our immediate purposes. In fact, I would argue that these two viewpoints underestimate the role of private third parties in the formation and implementation of economic policy.[32] Whether Japanese bureaucrats acted on their own, as agents of elected politicians, or in cooperation with the private sector, the crucial point is that they largely acted outside of the formal legal system and were unaffected by it. Again, it is important to note that I do not mean that they deprived individuals or corporations of property or profits, although this did happen on occasion.[33] My point is that economic policy was discussed, formed, and implemented largely through informal mechanisms that were consciously shielded from the interference of the formal legal system.

The administrative actors in this process were MITI and the MOF, for industrial and financial policy, respectively, and whatever other ministries were involved in a particular question. The private actors were the trade associations of the involved industry or some similar ad hoc group, in some cases bridging two or more affected industries or sectors. The implementing agents were most frequently cartels, facilitated by MITI but directly enforced by the trade associations. These cartels were sometimes legal, formally approved by MITI or the Fair Trade Commission (FTC). At other times, the cartels were legally informal, created through consultation between the industry and MITI, sometimes with the understanding of the FTC, sometimes without. On rare occasions, the FTC would object to a cartel's formation or attack an existing one.

What was almost completely missing during the entire postwar period through the 1980s was intervention by the courts in the implementation of economic policy on behalf of private parties. Individual banks undoubtedly chafed under some of the restrictions of the MOF, and industrial firms certainly disagreed with the cartel allocations of MITI and trade associations and with the need for cartels in general. Disagreements led to fierce and bitter battles among the players in a given industrial field, but they rarely took their grievances public and even less frequently to the courts. In fact, those few times when firms went public, much less litigated, became legends known by nicknames like "the Naphtha War," the "Lions Oil Incident," and the "Sumitomo Metals Incident" and are recounted in the popular media in the breathless terms usually reserved for sports or soap operas.

In short, it is hard to argue that the regulation of the Japanese economy for the first three to four decades of the postwar period had many of the institutional characteristics called for by the rule-of-law orthodoxy. Yet it would be equally difficult to argue that the Japanese system was not successful, not only in achieving economic growth but also in preserving civil order and a high degree of social justice. Although this chapter is not the place to discuss in depth the factors that made this possible, a few are worth mentioning. First, the actors involved in economic policy formation and implementation were stable institutions staffed by dedicated and competent private and public bureaucrats. Whether it was the corporations themselves, the trade associations that represented them, or the ministries that had responsibility for their regulation, their staffs were well educated and trained and usually stayed at or close to the institution for their entire career. Second, there were pervasive and institutionalized means of communication between the public and private institutions. The most famous is the *amakudari* (descent from heaven) system—the process through which top ministry bureaucrats received senior management positions in the private sector upon retirement from public service. There was also informal interaction on an almost daily basis between regulated and regulator. Third, there was little direct corruption in the public sector. *Amakudari* might be interpreted as a form of corruption, but its effect was indirect and in any case far from the massive and explicit corruption of many public bureaucracies. Fourth, the politicians and the voters behind them always had a veto power if policy failed disastrously or important interests were ignored.[34] Fifth, in some big disputes between economic powerholders and victims of their predatory practices, the courts intervened at crucial times and provided an outside limit to the flexibility and arrogance of the insiders. Finally, as we see in the next section, these regulatory institutions existed within a society where most conflict was handled by informal mechanisms consciously created to channel it away from the courts and other public institutions that might bring it into the public sphere.

Dispute Resolution

Japan has managed conflict that fell outside of the regulatory context described above through myriad informal mechanisms generally lumped under the rubric of alternative dispute resolution. Japan is rightfully renowned for such devices, but it will suffice here to look briefly at two instances: one in the politically charged area of environmental disputes and the other in the routine area of automobile accidents. They will give us some sense of the way that Japan has dealt with the inevitable social dislocation of economic growth without a legal system that fits the rule-of-law development model.

Prior to the current decade-long recession, perhaps the greatest social crisis faced by Japan in the postwar period was the environmental degradation of the 1950s and 1960s. The Japanese government was unable to respond decisively to pollution, despite clear evidence that unrestrained industrialization was destroying Japan's social fabric. The postwar pro-development consensus made protest unpopular, and pollution victims had few allies in the Diet or the powerful ministries. Opposition parties were able to control many local governments but unable to take effective action.

In the end, it was a litigation campaign that broke the political logjam and forced the central government to respond. The result was effective and comprehensive regulation of industrial pollution that was stricter than that of the U.S. and most of Europe, including schemes for the compensation of pollution victims that for a time were considered models for the rest of the developed world. What interests us here, however, is the mode that Japan chose to deal with environmental disputes subsequent to that era. Despite the demonstrated success of tort litigation in exposing and redressing pollution, the Japanese government explicitly rejected using the legal system for future conflict. Instead it established bureaucratically managed compensation and mediation schemes to channel disputes out of the courts.

The environmental dispute system was a direct response to a political crisis, but it is representative of similar informal systems that cover virtually every field of social interaction conceivable in a modern polity. From divorce or adoption to human rights or employment, there is a government-created conflict resolution scheme ready for potential litigants. They range from conciliation attached to family courts to local human rights committees under local government supervision. Many casual observers of Japan attribute these devices to a cultural preference among the Japanese for harmony and consensus over the divisiveness of litigation. Others see a political conspiracy to use references to culture and tradition to keep political issues out of the courts, where they may escape elite control. Undoubtedly both views have some currency: There are historical antecedents for mediation in the Tokugawa period, and the political advantage of bureaucratically administered mediation is clear. What is of interest to us, however, is the success of these devices in managing social conflict without direct resort to the formal legal system.

Traffic accidents provide an excellent example of how this has been achieved in Japan. As Tanase Takao, a leading Japanese sociologist of law, put it:

> [W]hile in the United States, except in minor injuries, people routinely bring their claims to lawyers, in Japan nearly all the injured parties handle compensation disputes themselves without the aid of lawyers. Only when they encounter extraordinary difficulty and feel that, as a very last resort, they will have to use the court, do the Japanese ask the help of lawyers.[35]

In his account, less than one percent of total accidents end up in court and no more than two percent involve private attorneys at any stage. For those who believe that harmonious dispute resolution is the natural result of Japanese culture, it is striking that such was not always the case. Litigation was common in the 1960s and peaked in 1971. Thereafter, the government, the police, insurance companies, bar associations, and the courts took measures that reduced the number of absolute cases by two-thirds in a decade. It is not necessary to go into the details of how this was accomplished, but it is important to note that there was nothing spontaneous or uniquely Japanese about the process. On the contrary, it was carefully structured to provide adequate compensation to accident victims without the expense of the formal legal process. Nor was it developed without attention to legal rules. A key aspect of the process is the provision of free legal consultation by police, insurance companies, and even bar associations, but the emphasis in these consultations is on the ability of the parties to handle the vast majority of accident claims without litigation or professional involvement. The judiciary played a role by carefully and consistently simplifying liability rules and compensation formulas, a task well suited to the Japanese judiciary because it more closely resembles a tightly controlled and regimented bureaucracy than does its U.S. counterpart.

As is implied by the involvement of the bar and the judiciary in the automobile accident scheme, legal institutions can play important supporting and enabling roles in Japan's informal dispute resolution mechanisms. Family court conciliation is another such example, although in this instance the goal has often been the processing of complaints rather than even rough fidelity to legal rights. In other areas, especially those under the jurisdiction or policy sphere of particular ministries, processes are conducted with considerably less involvement of legal rules, institutions, or personnel. The common denominator for all dispute procedures, however, is a concerted and largely successful effort to avoid the cost and formality of litigation; and, to this extent, informal mechanisms such as these and similar ones in every developed country may be a more attractive route for developing countries to pursue than relying on the creation of a full-blown "rule-of-law" legal system. Again, it is necessary to stress that these systems have not arisen spontaneously from the depths of Japanese culture but were specifically designed by the government to discourage parties from litigation. They are not, in other words, uniquely Japanese; nor do they depend on a culturally submissive population ready to compromise its interests in the name of harmony. They may depend, however, on a degree of internal social cohesion that many developing countries do not currently have. Even more important, they clearly require an effective bureaucracy, another state institution that is in short supply in much of the world. Even so, informality may still be preferable to the formality of a rule-of-law judiciary, which is at least equally dependent on social conditions and vastly more expensive.

Implications for Developing Countries

Both the formal legal mechanisms of the United States and the largely informal mechanisms of Japan have served these two societies well in the period under review, despite deviating from what the new rule-of-law orthodoxy would assume is necessary for economic growth.[36] What lessons do these two examples have for contemporary developing countries?

The first and most important lesson may be that neither the Japanese nor the U.S. legal system is likely to provide a useful model for other societies. The U.S. legal system deviates substantially from the rule-of-law ideal; it is massively expensive in terms of human capital, as well as in purely financial terms; and its primary features are at least as attributable to political goals, ideals, and compromises as they are to efforts to promote economic growth. The Japanese system was certainly created with economic growth in mind and has operated with that goal foremost, but the institutional requirements of the Japanese system seem almost as historically dependent as the American. The relatively balanced interaction of political, governmental, and private institutions, each component of which was characterized by competence and stability, seems more suitable as a goal of development efforts than the means.

Furthermore, each system has substantial flaws. The details of the U.S. legal system are as likely to be cited as a politically created impediment to economic efficiency than as a foundation for it. Indeed, the Japanese government has repeatedly claimed that the U.S. legal system is so ineffective and unfair that it constitutes a nontariff trade barrier. The Japanese system is also currently under siege, blamed for contributing to the decade-long recession that has tarnished the country's economic "miracle." Indeed, it could be argued that the very institutions that served Japan so well while it was a fast-growing economy are no longer suitable now that it is a mature one.

A second lesson is that the creation of a formal rule-of-law system of the type advocated by adherents of the new rule-of-law orthodoxy may well not be worth the cost. As I have argued, even the United States, the country most insistent on the virtues of the rule of law for developing countries, has chosen to depart from the model in fundamental ways, and Japan was able to grow economically with a relatively shrinking legal sector. If these societies grew without a formalist rule of law, why should a developing country consider it a necessity? Of course, this does not mean that the protection of basic rights is not necessary. Nor does it mean that an effective formal legal system may not be politically desirable or that political stability may not be a prerequisite to growth, but it does not appear that the formalist rule of law has been a major immediate factor in economic growth in these two countries. In fact, if one had to choose, it would be the informal systems of Japan that would seem most useful to developing countries. One would urge caution, therefore, before recommending that a developing country divert significant resources from more directly productive activities or, more important, attempt to replace effective and inexpensive means of social order with any formalist rule of law.

The last point—that legal transplants may displace indigenous institutions—deserves elaboration. The cost of importing a formalist legal system is not solely the expense of courthouses and legal education or the diversion of human talent into the legal profession. A more important cost is the risk to existing informal means of social order, without which no legal system can succeed. Although it is highly unlikely that the transplanted system will operate as it did in its country of origin or as intended by the borrowing country, it does not follow that it will have no social effect.[37] A legal system provides a powerful set of resources, and those who see themselves as benefited will use such resources to their own advantage. That is, of course, precisely what the creators of a legal system wish for. But if the social context of a legal system is not able to support the individual exercise of rights or if the incentives governing the use of the resources are not finely calibrated, the results can be far from those intended. In other words, unless the creators of the legal system get it exactly right, unexpected consequences will occur. In a mature system, established institutions can deal with negative consequences. However, in countries with new legal systems, especially ones imposed or imported from abroad, preexisting institutions often lack the experience, expertise, and, most seriously, political legitimacy necessary to deal with unforeseen consequences of reform. Legal anarchy can result in a society that has a new, formal legal system but lacks the social capital, institutions, and discipline to make use of it.

The reason that advocates of the new rule-of-law orthodoxy are willing to take this risk, in my opinion, is that they view the rule of law as an indicator of social development.[38] Such advocates hold a relatively unvarying vision of the end product of legal reform efforts, without requisite attention to the social, cultural, economic, and political contexts within which such efforts take place. Legal systems are so complex and so intertwined with these contexts that the chances of large-scale legal transplantation performing in the way intended, especially right off the bat, are slim. Because the reformers are focusing on the expected result—the formalist rule of law—rather than the new institutions' interaction with the social context, it is difficult for them to perceive problems and react effectively to the inevitable surprises, which are certain to arise, particularly if contextual factors are ignored.

I do not intend to discourage legal reform or the borrowing of legal rules or institutions from other countries. Indeed, some have argued that legal transplants are the main source of legal change, not only in the developing world, but everywhere. It would be foolish and futile to argue against it, and it would mean arguing against transnational legal learning. My point is a much more limited one and one that seems self-evident to most students of the actual role of law in society. A legal system is too complicated to be planned from the top down. Any group of competent legal scholars with the necessary audacity could devise a formal legal system that would work well on paper, making the various assumptions about human behavior, institutional capacity, and incentive structures necessary to implement their worldview.

Unfortunately this exercise is akin to what the planners of the former Soviet Union did with their economy. I doubt that we can expect any greater success from the proponents of the new rule-of-law orthodoxy. The problem with centralized economic planning, after all, was not that the planners were stupid, ignorant, or corrupt; it was that an economy is too complicated to be effectively directed over the long term by a central authority. The design of a legal system faces the same issues. Even if the assumptions about human behavior are correct, the knowledge of social context is insufficient to calibrate perfect rules, and the legal institutions are too weak to implement them on their own. As Robert Putnam has eloquently demonstrated about Italy, legal rules do not operate in a social vacuum. Identical rules can exist in dramatically divergent societies.[39] The secret to legal borrowing and to legal reform in general, therefore, is not merely attention to the foreign model or the institutional goal; it must include close attention to, genuine respect for, and detailed knowledge of the conditions of the receiving society and its preexisting mechanisms of social order.

Notes

An earlier version of this chapter was originally published as Carnegie Working Paper no. 30 (September 2002).

1. The record of externally imposed law reform is dismal. For recent commentary on Russian failures, see Merritt B. Fox and Michael Heller, "Corporate Governance Lessons from Russian Enterprise Fiascoes," *New York University Law Review* 75, no. 6 (December 2000): 1720–80. For more comprehensive accounts, see Thomas Carothers, *Aiding Democracy Abroad: The Learning Curve* (Washington, D.C.: Carnegie Endowment for International Peace, 1999); and Yves Dezalay and Bryant Garth, *The*

Internationalization of Palace Wars: Lawyers, Economists, and the International Reconstruction of National States (Chicago: Chicago University Press, 2002). For a human rights perspective, see Lawyers Committee for Human Rights, *Building on Quicksand: The Collapse of the World Bank's Judicial Reform Project in Peru* (New York: Lawyers Committee for Human Rights, 2000).

2. There are excellent studies of past experience, such as Kevin Davis and Michael Trebilcock, "What Role Do Legal Institutions Play in Development?" draft prepared for the IMF Conference on Second Generation Reforms, Washington, D.C., November 8–9, 1999, but they do not yet rise to the level of accepted guides for lending institutions.

3. Ibrahim F. I. Shihata, "The World Bank and 'Governance' Issues in Its Borrowing Members," in *The World Bank in a Changing World* 1, ed. Franziska Tschofen and Antonio R. Parra (Boston: Martinus Nijhoff, 1991), 85. For similar ideas, see Edgardo Boeninger, "Governance and Development: Issues and Constraints"; Pierre Landell-Mills and Ismaïl Serageldin, "Governance and the External Factor"; and Denis-Constant Martin, "The Cultural Dimensions of Governance," in *Proceedings of the World Bank Annual Conference on Development* (Washington, D.C.: World Bank, 1991), 267; and Clive S. Gray, "Reform of the Legal, Regulatory, and Judicial Environment: What Importance for Development Strategy?" Development Discussion Paper no. 403 (Cambridge, MA: Harvard Institute for International Development, September 1991).

4. Available at www1.worldbank.org/legal/legop_judicial.html.

5. James D. Wolfensohn, then president of the World Bank, quoted from the World Bank's Comprehensive Development Framework, available at www.worldbank.org/legal/ljrconference.html.

6. Available at www4.worldbank.org/legal/legps.html.

7. For a description of this urge for order across subject matters and ages, see James C. Scott, *Seeing Like a State: How Certain Themes to Improve the Human Condition Have Failed* (New Haven, CT: Yale University Press, 1998).

8. Antonin Scalia, "The Rule of Law as a Law of Rules," *University of Chicago Law Review* 56 (Fall 1989): 11754–88.

9. Six justices—Rehnquist, Kennedy, O'Connor, Scalia, Souter, and White—agreed that "Considerations in favor of *stare decisis* are at their acme in cases involving property and contract rights, where reliance interests are involved . . ." *Lawyer's Edition* (2nd) 115 (1996): 737.

10. Available at the African Growth and Opportunities Act web site: www.agoa.gov/About_AGOA/agoatext.pdf.

11. Hernando de Soto, *The Other Path: The Invisible Revolution in the Third World*, trans. June Abbott (New York: Harper & Row, 1989). De Soto has since written a sequel, *The Mystery of Capital: Why Capitalism Triumphs in the West and Fails Everywhere Else* (New York: Basic Books, 2000). Although significantly more sophisticated in its description of the nature and role of property rights in the informal economy, his emphasis on the importance of formal legal institutions remains fundamentally unchanged.

12. For literature on the United States, see Robert C. Ellickson, *Order without Law: How Neighbors Settle Disputes* (Cambridge, MA: Harvard University Press, 1991).

13. Official Chinese government date, reported by the World Bank, *World Development Report* (New York: Oxford University Press, various years).

14. The failure to investigate has not been total. See Katharina Pistor and Philip Wellons, *Role of Law and Legal Institutions in Asian Economic Development, 1960–1995* (Manila: Asian Development Bank, 1998).

15. K. S. Jomo, "A Specific Idiom of Chinese Capitalism in Southeast Asia: Sino-Malaysian Capital Accumulation in the Face of State Hostility," in *Essential Outsiders: Chinese and Jews in the Modern Transformation of Southeast Asia and Central Europe,*

ed. Daniel Chirot and Anthony Reed (Seattle: University of Washington Press, 1997), 237–57.

16. Gary G. Hamilton and Tony Waters, "Ethnicity and Capitalist Development: The Changing Role of Chinese in Thailand," in Chirot and Reed, *Essential Outsiders*, 258–84.

17. It is also possible that minority status, if not illegality, was instrumental in the success of overseas Chinese. For several reasons why minorities may be culturally and structurally advantaged in economic activities, see Hamilton and Waters, "Ethnicity and Capitalist Development."

18. Jim Yardley, "Bush's Choices for Court Seen as Moderates," *New York Times*, July 9, 2000, A1. Also representative are William Glaberson, "Fierce Campaigns Signal a New Era for State Courts," *New York Times*, June 5, 2000, A1; and Kevin Sack, "Judge Trades on Renown in Race," *New York Times*, June 5, 2000, A22.

19. Jeffrey A. Segal and Harold J. Spaeth, *The Supreme Court and the Attitudinal Model* (New York: Cambridge University Press, 1993). See also Jonathan D. Casper, "The Supreme Court and National Policy Making," *American Political Science Review* 70, no. 1 (March 1976): 50–63; and Robert Dahl, "Decision-Making in a Democracy: The Supreme Court as National Policy-Maker," *Journal of Public Law* 6 (1958): 279–95.

20. Segal and Spaeth, *Supreme Court*, 316–9. Segal and Spaeth discovered a number of other interesting surprises. For example, despite the rhetoric of state sovereignty and federalism, justices were less deferential to state government decisions than to those of the federal government, p. 311.

21. The reader should not take from this comment any bias against television dramas. As indicated in the text, the television version of law may have a great deal more to do with common concepts of the rule of law than does the professional version.

22. I am referring here to civil cases only. Legal representation is provided to criminal defendants, although with varying degrees of success. Civil cases are of more direct interest to the present topic, because civil law largely shapes the economy and provides the framework that economic actors rely on for their activities. For a comparison of U.S. provision of civil legal services with those of European countries, see the symposium issue of the *Maryland Journal of Contemporary Legal Issues* 5, no. 2 (1994). Statistics in this chapter are drawn from Earl Johnson Jr., "Toward Equal Justice: Where the United States Stands Two Decades Later," *Maryland Journal of Contemporary Legal Issues* 5, no. 2 (1994): 199.

23. The comparisons with some of the other North Atlantic societies were better, but the United States was still outspent by a factor of 2.5:1 by France and Germany, the next lowest two countries on the list of per capita expense. Johnson, "Toward Equal Justice," 212. Japan, however, through the 1990s spent even less than the United States.

24. It is also outdated and more representative of the first three decades of the postwar period than of the last two, but because we are concerned primarily with Japan's period of high growth, the outdated nature of these assertions is largely irrelevant to us.

25. The reference is to the *shiki* system of land rights adjudication developed during the Kamakura period. See Jeffrey Mass, *The Development of Kamakura Rule, 1180–1250* (Stanford, CA: Stanford University Press, 1979). For discussions of the role of law and legal institutions in later periods of Japanese history, see, for example, Frank K. Upham, "Weak Legal Consciousness as Invented Tradition," in *Mirror of Modernity: Invented Traditions of Modern Japan*, ed. Stephen Vlastos (Berkeley: University of California Press, 1998), 48–64; and Herman Ooms, *Tokugawa Village Practice: Class, Status, Power, Law* (Berkeley: University of California Press, 1996).

26. Sources include J. Mark Ramseyer, *Odd Markets in Japanese History: Law and Economic Growth* (New York: Cambridge University Press, 1996); and John O. Haley, "The Politics of Informal Justice: The Japanese Experience, 1922-1942," in *The Politics of Informal Justice* 2, ed. Richard Abel (New York: Academic Press, 1982), 125–47.

27. The precise figure was 7,136. Dan Fenno Henderson, "The Role of Lawyers in Japan," in *Japan: Economic Success and Legal System*, ed. Harald Baum (Berlin: Walter de Gruyter, 1997), 40.

28. I cite these statistics for dramatic purposes only. Comparing lawsuits is as good an illustration of the adage, "lies, damn lies, and statistics," that I know, especially when the comparison crosses eras or jurisdictional borders. The most recent attempt to evaluate Japanese litigiousness that I know of is Christian Wollschläger, "Historical Trends of Civil Litigation in Japan, Arizona, Sweden, and Germany: Japanese Legal Culture in the Light of Judicial Statistics," in Baum, *Japan*, 89–142. The figures for the 75 percent drop come from Wollschläger, figure 1, p. 94. The specific figures are virtually meaningless, but they express both the direction and degree of litigation rates.

29. Curtis Milhaupt and Mark West, "Law's Dominion and the Market for Legal Elites in Japan," unpublished paper.

30. Japan Access, "The High Growth Era," Mainichi Interactive, available at www.jinjapan.org/access/economy/grow.html.

31. Chalmers Johnson, *MITI and the Japanese Miracle* (Stanford, CA: Stanford University Press, 1982) is the classic. Ironically, Johnson and his followers are known as revisionists, but within Japanese studies, both of the academic and popular varieties, it is those who argue that economic orthodoxy works as well with Japan as with anywhere else that are the outsiders. A prominent example of this heterodoxy is J. Mark Ramseyer and Frances McCall Rosenbluth, *Japan's Political Marketplace* (Cambridge, MA: Harvard University Press, 1993).

32. Frank K. Upham, "Privatized Regulation: Japanese Regulatory Style in Comparative and International Perspective," *Fordham International Law Journal* 20, no. 2 (December 1997): 396–511.

33. Frank K. Upham, "The Man Who Would Import: A Cautionary Tale about Bucking the System in Japan," *Journal of Japanese Studies* 17, no. 2 (Summer 1991): 323–43.

34. The seemingly total failure of financial policy throughout the 1990s and the political turmoil that followed may be illustrative of this democratic oversight, although the changes in electoral rules may be more directly responsible.

35. The system for automobile accidents is beautifully described by Japanese legal sociologist Tanase Takao in "The Management of Disputes: Automobile Accident Compensation in Japan," *Law & Society Review* 24, no. 3 (1990): 662. His article puts the automobile accident scheme in the context of general conflict control and is an excellent source for understanding the Japanese approach to litigation and social conflict.

36. Of course, it is theoretically possible that both societies developed despite their respective modes of economic ordering and that legal systems more closely resembling the rule of law would have resulted in even more impressive performance. Because this possibility is purely hypothetical and speculative, I do not address it here. It is also possible that the respective legal systems played a minor role in economic growth.

37. The experience of Japan's Civil Code of 1889 is illustrative. The Meiji leaders may well have intended their new legal system primarily as a demonstration to foreign powers of their modernity, but the code was taken seriously by the Japanese people. They used its provisions in the courts to pursue their own interests in ways that political leaders of Japan had not anticipated and did not welcome. The result was a flurry of legislation in the 1920s to "correct" the excessive individualism of the Japanese by limiting the peoples' rights under the code and requiring prospective plaintiffs to use "traditional" means of dispute resolution in place of litigation.

38. I have borrowed this idea from Michael Dowdle, "Rule of Law and Civil Society: Implications of a Pragmatic Development," unpublished paper.

39. Robert D. Putnam, Robert Leonardi, and Raffaella Y. Nanetti, *Making Democracy Work: Civic Traditions in Modern Italy* (Princeton, NJ: Princeton University Press, 1993).

CHAPTER FIVE

A House without
a Foundation

STEPHEN GOLUB

THE RULE-OF-LAW ORTHODOXY, the dominant paradigm followed by development organizations seeking to promote the rule of law in developing countries, is a flawed and incomplete approach.[1] As principally practiced by multilateral development banks, which are major sources of rule-of-law aid, it concentrates on the reform of laws and legal institutions, particularly judiciaries.[2] It is state-centered and "top-down" in nature, focusing funds on government institutions and usually working through their top officials to design and implement projects. It conversely minimizes support for civil society or building the legal capacity of the poor. To the extent it does touch on such issues, it does so as adjuncts to state-centered activities. The World Bank and to some extent the other multilateral development banks apply the orthodoxy to build more business-friendly and investment-friendly legal systems that presumably help spur economic growth and reduce poverty. Other development organizations, such as the United States Agency for International Development (USAID) and other bilateral aid agencies, sometimes use the rule-of-law orthodoxy to promote such additional goals as good governance and public safety, whether as ends in themselves or as steps toward reducing poverty. The problems with the orthodoxy are not these economic and political goals, per se, but its questionable assumptions, unproven impact, and insufficient attention to the legal needs of the disadvantaged.[3]

The substantial resources that development organizations have poured into the dominant paradigm, to the relative exclusion of alternatives, represent a great gamble—or, as McAuslan puts it, "an act of faith."[4] Today's heavy emphasis on judges, lawyers, and courts is analogous to what the public health field would look like if it mainly focused on urban hospitals and the doctors staffing them, and largely ignored nurses, other health workers, maternal and public education, other preventive approaches, rural and community health issues, building community capacities, and nonmedical strategies (such as improving sanitation and water supply).

In fact, donors' faith in the rule-of-law orthodoxy reflects a "build it and they will come" mentality that flows from a series of flawed assumptions. If judges and police receive training, they supposedly will do their jobs better—despite powerful pressures and incentives to the contrary. If laws are reformed, they presumably will be used and not abused—although such reforms often mean nothing to disadvantaged populations lacking the knowledge, organization, and power to obtain justice. If development agencies pour funds into state justice institutions, those institutions will serve the disadvantaged—despite civil society's superior track record in improving access to justice. Many aid practitioners are not blind to these problems, but a diversity of influences keeps them from grappling with them.

Furthermore, such assumptions overlook a fundamental fact: The central challenge for making the law a positive reality for the poor is not achieving formalistic institutional or legal reforms but spurring the actual implementation of existing laws in a pro-poor manner. In many developing countries, laws benefiting the poor exist on paper but not in practice unless the poor or their allies push for the laws' enforcement. And to the extent that other laws are enforced, it is to the detriment of the disadvantaged. In failing to fortify the capacities and power of the poor, the orthodoxy emphasizes formal structures and ignores underlying realities. It is a house without a foundation.

Despite its critical stance, this chapter does not assert that the dominant paradigm is worthless or counterproductive. Enhanced laws, courts, business climates, and investment definitely are important for a host of reasons. I certainly do not claim that the rule-of-law orthodoxy is the wrong path to take under all circumstances. Those of us concerned with law and development do not know enough to be so absolutist about these matters.

But we do know enough to raise questions—and that is precisely the point: The orthodoxy's many problematic features make its dominant position in the field a remarkable state of affairs. In numerous countries, law-oriented development aid goes mainly to a narrow range of state institutions, whereas the legal priorities of the poor often lie elsewhere. The issue, then, is one of emphasis and resources. The rule-of-law orthodoxy devotes too much attention to building formal structures and state institutions, and too little to civil society and direct impact on the poor.

Key Features of Rule-of-Law Orthodoxy

The programs and goals that donors pursue in the rule-of-law orthodoxy are not confined to the economic sphere, although that is often the main focus of the multilateral financial institutions that are among the largest sources of assistance funds for rule-of-law work. This central stream of the rule-of-law orthodoxy considers the rule of law essential for long-term development because it provides security for foreign and domestic investment, property and contract rights, international trade, and other vehicles for advancing economic growth. Martinez accordingly asserts that "the liberalization of market economies . . . requires a legal order that is fair, efficient, easily accessible, and predictable."[5] This line of thought further holds that properly functioning courts and other legal institutions nurture a favorable business climate by protecting investments and by enforcing contracts and property rights. Foreign and domestic enterprises are more likely to establish and expand operations that manufacture goods and provide services under such circumstances, the reasoning goes. Among other benefits, this in turn provides jobs, increases the output of goods and services, yields a ripple effect of additional business for and employment by local enterprises that serve expanding domestic and foreign firms, brings about technology and skills transfer, and increases foreign exchange reserves.

The rule-of-law orthodoxy has an even wider reach, however, in that it is applied by some donors in pursuit of a diversity of goals beyond building better business environments. It infuses many law programs supported by USAID, for example, which seeks to advance the rule of law as part of its support for democracy and good governance.[6] Much of the law-oriented work of the United Kingdom's Department for International Development (DFID) emphasizes state institutions as vehicles for promoting the poor's personal safety, security of property, and access to justice (SSAJ).[7]

USAID and DFID do not pursue orthodox approaches exclusively or everywhere (nor do other aid agencies that focus on state legal institutions). In a number of countries, both of these donors fund legal services for the disadvantaged. Furthermore, DFID's SSAJ program explicitly aims to address the poor's urgent legal needs. In prioritizing personal safety, for instance, the program certainly responds to many disadvantaged populations' vulnerability to criminal violence, but it mainly works through the state in doing so. This is despite the fact that informed, organized citizens may be as essential as training or pay raises to deterring police misconduct or encouraging police professionalism. Rural residents whom law enforcement personnel extort rather than serve when they seek their help are in a far better bargaining position if they belong to a well-connected, well-informed farmers' association. More generally, the point is that law projects undertaken under the rubrics of democracy and governance, SSAJ, and other rationales nevertheless manifest the rule-of-law orthodoxy where they exhibit its top-down, state-centered emphases, even though the underlying justifications differ from those of the multilateral banks.

To be fair, international aid agencies increasingly consult with the disadvantaged and civil society in setting priorities, and a few are broadening their perspectives on legal systems. DFID's policy papers, for example, emphasize how crucial it is to ascertain the legal needs of the poor and the multifaceted ways in which dysfunctional legal systems perpetuate their poverty.[8] But civil society consultation is far different than supporting civil society to serve the disadvantaged and build their legal capacities. DFID, USAID, and a limited number of other organizations also have expanded their characterizations of the justice sector to embrace traditional dispute resolution mechanisms. However, they still tend to exclude administrative agency and local government decisions that boil down to matters of law and that the poor often consider crucial matters of justice.[9]

In short, key features of the orthodoxy include:

- A focus on state institutions, particularly judiciaries.
- This institutional focus is largely determined by the legal profession, as represented by a nation's jurists, top legal officials, and attorneys, and by foreign consultants and donor personnel.
- As a result, a tendency to define the legal system's problems and cures narrowly, in terms of courts, prosecutors, contracts, law reform, and other institutions and processes in which lawyers play central roles.

- Where civil society engagement occurs, it usually is as a means toward the end of state institutional development: consulting nongovernmental organizations (NGOs) on how to reform the (narrowly defined) legal system, and funding them as vehicles for advocating reform.
- A reliance on foreign expertise, initiative, and models, particularly those originating in industrialized societies.

These features translate into funding a distinct array of activities, including:

- constructing and repairing courthouses;
- purchasing furniture, computers, and other equipment and materials;
- drafting new laws and regulations;
- training judges, lawyers, and other legal personnel;
- establishing management and administration systems for judiciaries;
- supporting judicial and other training/management institutes;
- building up bar associations; and
- conducting international exchanges for judges, court administrators, and lawyers.

Questionable Assumptions

The rule-of-law orthodoxy is built on a whole series of questionable assumptions. Not all are necessarily invalid in all contexts, but they are all problematic in some substantial ways and merit careful, critical scrutiny.

Assumed Impact on Poverty Alleviation

The bottom line for assessing the dominant approach to promoting the rule of law must be its impact on the poor. Poverty alleviation is the main goal of many development organizations. The desire to reduce poverty is the greatest reason why donor governments and international institutions contribute substantial funds for development aid generally and rule-of-law work as a subfield of that greater endeavor. But so far, at least, there is a paucity of proof to support the assumption that strengthening the rule of law necessarily reduces poverty. There is evidence that the rule of law goes hand in hand with favorable development indicators, such as lowered infant mortality and higher incomes and literacy.[10] What such evidence does *not* demonstrate is cause and effect: whether strengthened rule of law brings about poverty alleviation, or vice versa.

There is some historical evidence and analysis arguing for a causal connection between the establishment of the rule of law and overall socioeconomic development, not least Weber's linking of law and legal systems to the growth of capitalism in Europe. But why assume that what (presumably) transpired in Europe several centuries ago applies to Asia or Africa or Latin America today? As North points out, "Economic (and political) models are specific to particular constellations of institutional constraints that vary radically both through time and cross sectionally in different economies."[11] A fundamental tenet of development principles and practice is that the elements of success in one society do not necessarily translate into success elsewhere—particularly where the gap between the two comprises several centuries, thousands of miles, and vastly different political, economic, and cultural contexts.

Thus, as Perry argues in summarizing literature challenging the notion that developing countries must adopt Western laws and legal institutions, "Law reform projects seem to be based on the unspoken Weberian assumption that because a particular legal system is found in countries which are developed, that legal system will help countries to be developed. There is no proof of this."[12] She also notes that those projects "ignore evidence [such as businesses' informal commerce-facilitating and development-promoting practices] which demonstrates, as a matter of fact, that there are limits to the importance of law in economic transactions."[13]

In a separate summary of relevant research, Messick similarly finds that "the question of the direction of causality" has not been settled by cross-country regression analysis.[14] Reviewing what we do *not* know about law and development, Carothers, in chapter 1 of this volume, sees "a surprising amount of uncertainty [about whether] . . . promoting the rule of law will contribute to economic development and democratization . . . [and] about how the rule of law develops in societies and how such development can be stimulated." Other sources agree that we lack evidence to know whether legal reform and legal systems improvement spur development,[15] or suggest that such legal change may be an effect of development rather than a cause of it.[16]

Actual experience in today's developing and transitional societies also undercuts the Weberian model. Several nations that have achieved significant economic growth and attendant poverty alleviation in recent decades have done so in the absence of Western-style rule of law. China is a leading example.[17] Indonesia, Thailand, and South Korea also thrived for years—and were hailed as success stories by international institutions—before the 1997–1998 Asian economic crisis (which was brought on by factors other than the flawed legal systems of these countries).[18]

Indeed, the success of the East Asian model was rooted in good policy decisions and other factors, not the rule of law. And even as recently as a decade ago, some observers argued that authoritarian governments, regimes often quite abusive of the rule of law, are inherently better than democracies at implementing successful economic policies. Haggard laudably challenges that conclusion, but it is noteworthy that the rule of law does not figure in his analysis.[19] In a study for the Asian Development Bank, Pistor and Wellons suggest that law (both on the books and in actual practice) is more a dependent than causal variable, asserting that it is "embedded in culture" and that "to be effective law has to be embedded in the overall economic policy framework."[20] Frank Upham points out in chapter 4 in this volume that neither the United States nor Japan, two of the most successful economies of the twentieth century, embody what he calls "formalist rule of law—that is, regimes defined by their absolute adherence to established legal rules and completely free of the corrupting influences of politics." Perry's case study of foreign enterprises in Sri Lanka, which includes a survey of those enterprises, disputes an important element of the "rule of law alleviates poverty" argument: the assumption that the rule of law is a crucial factor affecting foreign direct investment (FDI). She concludes that "the role of legal systems as a determinant of FDI is neither straightforward, nor proven, nor uniform."[21] Drawing in part on his work as a practicing lawyer in Eastern Europe, Hewko agrees. He asserts that "the existence of real business opportunities and the overall visceral perception . . . of a host country" are much more important to many foreign investors than extensive rule-of-law reforms.[22] Hewko argues, in fact, that once such investors set up operations on the ground they can identify specific FDI-facilitating changes better than can foreign aid institutions and their consultants.[23] At the very least, it would seem that the supposed link between the rule of law and investment has not been demonstrated.

Rule-of-Law Aid Often Makes a Difference

Even if assuming that strengthening the rule of law helps reduce poverty sometimes holds true, it would not verify a second problematic assumption: the belief that external aid for rule-of-law promotion actually alleviates poverty or otherwise makes a difference. Rather it seems likely that the rule of law and its attendant benefits flow primarily from a society's internal changes rather than external inputs such as foreign aid.

What is the impact of rule-of-law assistance? There is no evidence of poverty alleviation and little evidence of other substantial positive results relating to other development goals. External reviews of rule-of-law aid efforts have been highly critical. The U.S. General Accounting Office found serious flaws in USAID's largely state-oriented rule-of-law work in parts of Latin America.[24] In a book on various Latin American countries' progress in (often donor-supported) judicial reform, Prillaman offers a bleak assessment of all except Chile, which he views as having a mixed record.[25] Summing up the track record of U.S. government work with judiciaries across the globe, Carothers asserts that "what stands out about U.S. rule-of-law assistance since the mid-1980s is how difficult and often disappointing such work is."[26]

As critical as Prillaman and Carothers are, there are respects in which they may be too charitable in their assessments. Prillaman sees Chile as a partial, favorable exception to the rule of collapsing reform efforts. Yet Chile and other partial success stories, such as Costa Rica, may be exceptional not because of donor efforts, but rather because of underlying, enduring legal cultures that transcend reform strategies or even regimes. For his part, Carothers concludes that "some learning is occurring, particularly among aid officials and consultants working in Latin America, the region in which the United States has labored most intensively on rule-of-law aid."[27] Whether that learning is translating into actual impact on Latin Americans' lives is a matter he does not substantially address. In addition, it is worthwhile to ask whether the foreign "aid officials and consultants," rather than domestic actors, do most of the learning under orthodox rule-of-law programs (I return to this issue of intellectual ownership below).

Blair and Hansen's USAID-commissioned study of rule-of-law assistance in six Latin American and Asian countries advises against a "legal system strengthening/institution building strategy"—and implicitly, against the rule-of-law orthodoxy, which resembles that strategy—unless a number of elements already are in place in a country.[28] The most fundamental of these elements are the absence of rampant corruption in its justice system and the absence of major human rights violations in the society. Where such abuses are prevalent, they argue against any rule-of-law assistance.

Blair and Hansen more specifically advise against the top-down, institution-oriented strategy where a country's political leadership lacks the will to pursue reforms. They further find that this crucial political will is missing in most situations. They reluctantly maintain that in many countries "constituencies and coalitions may be so fragmented and fractious, and the political environment may be so inimical to judicial reform (perhaps even to the notion of [the rule of law]), as to eliminate any effective program activity."[29] These conclusions—that rule-of-law assistance will prove unproductive under many circumstances and (implicitly) that the rule-of-law orthodoxy is inappropriate in even more situations—both weigh against the dominant paradigm.

Despite this bleak assessment, there may be respects in which Blair and Hansen, like Prillaman and Carothers, may be too optimistic about the prospects for rule-of-law programs producing large-scale change. Even the greatest amount of political will is sometimes insufficient to implement lasting legal system reforms in the face of recalcitrant bureaucracies and improper but powerful external influences.

Hammergren's subsequent 1998 USAID review in effect seeks to rebut elements of the Blair/Hansen study but essentially is much more a thoughtful "how to pursue reform" document rather than a documentation of impact.[30] She asserts that by addressing more technical and politically manageable issues, practitioners of rule-of-law assistance can establish progress, credibility, and insights that help them tackle more fundamental obstacles to reform.[31] In effect, they can build political will even where it is missing. This is a credible argument, but whether it will prove true in practice in many places, particularly to help alleviate poverty, is questionable. It optimistically implies that foreign reformers will outlast and outsmart domestic opponents in a process that can take many years or will cultivate domestic allies who can sustain change in challenging contexts. It also represents a programmatic gamble on the ability of reformers to cultivate local political will.

The consulting firm Management Systems International (MSI) recently undertook for USAID an explicitly achievement-oriented assessment of USAID's rule-of-law programs.[32] In addition to describing some support in some countries for civil society and legal services for the poor, the study reports apparent progress with state institutions—the kind of results Hammergren refers to as "system changes (such as shifts from written to oral testimony in court cases) or first level behaviors (number of bankruptcies filed and settled following the passage of a new law, reduction in time to judgment, etc.)."[33] Other changes are more a matter of outputs than outcomes—cross-border cooperation and training involving the U.S. and Mexican judiciaries, for example.[34]

Although the assessment represents a thorough effort to tackle a daunting task, various sources' analyses cast doubt on whether many of the beneficial changes it detects are truly significant or lasting. Prillaman sees a downward spiral in Latin American judicial reform, MSI's favorable findings about USAID's work in that region notwithstanding. Bohmer implicitly differs with MSI's conclusions concerning Argentina, criticizing the "many top-down approaches to legal reform" in that country's history, "which focus entirely on government institutions" but which have largely ignored the country's legal culture and the anti-reform incentives in those very institutions and the legal community.[35] And as described below, Blackton's perspective on the Egyptian judiciary and the impact of his work on a USAID-supported project in that country is much more critical than that of the MSI assessment. Finally, as Carothers suggests in generally commenting on USAID's rule-of-law efforts, beneficial changes may pale in comparison with enduring realities: limited access to justice, vested interests devoted to the status quo, corruption, clientelistic appointments, and so on.[36]

Carothers is not alone in this critique. Other observers imply or assert that the kind of impact that programs based on the rule-of-law orthodoxy achieve may not address the fundamental problems plaguing many countries' legal systems. In one of the most in-depth scholarly studies of a given judiciary's operations—a scrutiny of the civil courts in the Indian state of Uttar Pradesh—Moog concludes that the "conventional explanations for the functioning of the district-level courts [too few jurists, insufficient funding, inadequate rules of court, overly complex legislation, excessive litigiousness] are largely unsatisfactory."[37] He points instead to a host of external and internal forces that constrain the courts' performance.

Kauffman similarly

> challenge[s] the prominence given to the traditional 'long list' of obstacles to proper rule of law/judiciary performance in the literature and in practitioners' writings—such as the conventional focus on budgetary resource constraints, cumbersome procedures, process delays, caseload management, traditional training approaches, study tours, and the like.[38]

He asserts that "there are forms of corruption (such as state capture) which rather than being a *symptom* of more fundamental weakness, can in themselves be the *cause* of a dysfunctional judiciary" (emphasis in original).[39] The upshot of these analyses is that the rule-of-law orthodoxy's impact might reflect winning some battles but losing the war—or even perhaps fighting the wrong battles.

Thus, what is seen as progress in terms of the rule-of-law orthodoxy does not automatically translate into more general advances for development. For instance, USAID boasts of its role in helping to increase judicial budgets in parts of Latin America. Yet an application of the analyses of Moog and Kauffman suggests that in at least some settings this is an inappropriate focus. The funds might be better devoted to other needs outside the legal field (such as education or health), within it (legal services for the poor), or issues that straddle legal and other fields (such as targeting the widespread problem of violence against women). The more general point is that working with the courts is not necessarily the most effective, efficient, or viable method of addressing the legal needs of the disadvantaged in ways that alleviate poverty or serve other development goals.

In addition, with the exception of support to legal aid and related services for the disadvantaged, the MSI-documented impact on the actual lives of the poor ranges from scattered to indiscernible. To be fair, as Hammergren correctly points out, "the impact [of law projects] on economic variables, whether of the growth or poverty type, is really hard to trace . . . We are not even terribly clear about how improvements in court performance will affect the poor or any other economic group."[40] And as the World Bank's Legal Vice Presidency notes,

> the [law and justice] sector poses certain special problems for measurement, not the least of which are the lack of any consensus on what a well-functioning system looks like, uncertainties as to the extent of its impact on extra-sectoral goals, and the fact that a large part of its success ultimately comes down to what it deters (conflict, illegal behavior), not what it does.[41]

These are valid points. But if "lack of consensus" on the nature of a well-functioning justice system and uncertainty of "its impact on extra-sectoral goals" (such as poverty alleviation) are the case, they are problems not just for measuring impact but for undertaking the rule-of-law orthodoxy at all. The presence of so much uncertainty weighs in favor of diversifying the international community's approaches to integrating law and development.

State Institutions Are Key

The rationale for the rule-of-law orthodoxy also has intellectual roots in a general emphasis on the roles of institutions in development. In the last two decades the idea has taken hold in the development literature that well-functioning institutions are fundamental for development.[42]

But there is a difference between how the concept of institutions is considered in development literature and how it is applied in development practice, at least in the legal field. North defines institutions as "the rules of the game in a society, or . . . the humanly devised constraints that shape human interaction . . . both formal constraints—such as rules that human beings devise—and informal constraints—such as conventions and codes of behavior."[43] He further distinguishes between *institutions* as "the underlying rules of the game" and *organizations* (legislatures, regulatory bodies, firms, universities, unions, and so on) that both influence and are influenced by institutions.[44] In rule-of-law programs, however, the emphasis on institutions typically reflects how the term is commonly used—including how I use it here: institutions *as* organizations, with a particular focus on state institutions/organizations such as judiciaries.

This is not to suggest that a divergence between development theory and practice is at play in the rule-of-law orthodoxy, hinging on a semantic distinction. But the way in which this matter plays out in the legal sphere merits attention. The programmatic focus of the dominant paradigm is on the judiciary and other state organizations, as well as laws as institutions. The result is that the paradigm places great faith in a narrow view of the legal field: worshipping at the altar of institutionalization, as it were.

In contrast, a full-fledged scrutiny of how a society's "rules of the game" affect the poor would consider the historical, cultural, social, and political factors that shape both the formal and informal manifestations of how the poor interact with the law and would take both formal and informal types of law into account. That analysis might in turn learn from and apply strategies that enable the poor to affect the rules of the game. Formal laws and state organizations of course would play important parts in this analysis. But the view of how they operate—and whether and how they can be reformed—would only be part of the picture. Underlying factors that shape their operations and alternative strategies that do not wholly or mainly rely on state organizations would be taken into account.

An additional difficulty with the focus on state institutions is that it ignores the institutional flaws in the very international development agencies that maintain this focus. As a USAID colleague remarked to me several years ago, "Given the way this institution works, I can't believe we're in the business of institutional development." Critics of the World Bank, some with experience working there, offer comments such as "there's a big disconnect between World Bank operations and World Bank research," and "you get the sense that the left hand doesn't know what the right hand is doing at the World Bank."[45]

Of course, such problems are not confined to the development community: One can find insiders making analogous comments about the U.S. Congress, the Pentagon, many corporations, and a host of other entities. Furthermore, personnel at USAID, the World Bank, and other aid organizations can justifiably boast of organizational strengths and successes, despite institutional flaws. But it is ironic and perhaps a bit self-deluding to aim for sweeping reforms in developing countries' legal institutions when many funding agencies are themselves so resistant to change.

A final problem with the focus on state institutions is that it ignores the opportunity costs of pursuing alternative strategies, such as focusing directly on the poor as a means of improving justice delivery (with related impact on poverty alleviation and other goals). Where donors provide support, civil society can and does play a central role in such strategies. Under the rule-of-law orthodoxy, however, civil society is at most an adjunct to state-oriented institutionalization: useful for building up constituencies for reform so that the "real work" of changing legal institutions can take place. That NGOs, community-based organizations (CBOs), informal institutions, and religious institutions can facilitate the delivery of justice is minimized. Similarly, the actual and potential roles of media and elements of the private sector are relegated to supplementing state-centered initiatives.

The Judiciary Is Central to Rule-of-Law Development

A key assumption of the orthodoxy is that the judiciary is central to serving society's legal needs: Unless we fix the courts, the thinking goes, many other legal reforms will fail. As the World Bank's Legal Vice Presidency puts it, "The rule of law is built on the cornerstone of an efficient and effective judicial system."[46] Applying similar reasoning that many development organizations use, the Asian Development Bank asserts that "although a daunting task, Cambodia has no alternative other than to overhaul the current judicial system if it is to lay a strong foundation for the nation's future development."[47] These claims tie in with related assumptions that neither alternative roads to justice nor dysfunctional judiciaries are usable. This package of assumptions, however, is fatally flawed.

Even within the realm of formal legal systems, and assuming the (unclear) causal link between the rule of law and development, there are many nonjudicial institutions and processes that affect economic progress. These include administrative law, national and local governments' legislation and legal decisions, and the many arrangements through which international trade and investment disputes are handled by forums outside developing countries.

Moreover, as a review for the Danish International Development Agency (Danida) of its judicial and related aid concludes, support for the formal legal system "does have important limitations and trade-offs: the majority of the population is often not in a position to access the formal legal system for various cultural, linguistic, financial or logistical reasons . . . Their access to justice largely depends on the functioning of informal systems, which have been neglected in terms of external support."[48] Although the report stops short of challenging Danida's attention to the formal system, it nevertheless finds "little connection between the justice, constitution and legislation assistance and the overriding poverty orientation of Danish assistance."[49]

DFID concurs with the Danida evaluation's assertion about the limits of the formal system, estimating that "in many developing countries, traditional or customary legal systems account for 80% of total cases."[50] This clearly is not a precise calculation. But taken together with the many disputes and other legal matters handled by formal but nonjudicial forums, one can reasonably conclude that perhaps 90 percent or more of the law-oriented problems involving the poor are handled outside the courts in much of the developing world. One could argue that judiciaries are nevertheless more important than these alternatives—an assertion that, to make a very long debate short, might be true in some respects and false in others. The point simply is to put the courts in perspective, particularly the perspective of the poor.

Interest in informal systems is slowly growing. DFID recently completed a multicountry study of the subject. There is a stirring of interest in the matter within the World Bank. Some donors are supporting NGO efforts to use and reform these mechanisms.[51] But although informal systems are the main avenues through which the poor access justice (or injustice), such systems remain programmatic stepchildren to the judiciary and other official institutions.

Judicial Reform Is a Valuable End in Itself

Proponents of the orthodoxy may argue that although a well-functioning judiciary may not be a direct path to poverty reduction, it is still a worthwhile development priority in and of itself.[52]

This argument, however, bumps up against the need to set priorities. It would be one thing to pursue judicial reform in a world of unlimited resources. It is quite another matter to invest so heavily in the courts when there are many other legal options for serving the poor, particularly in view of the opportunity costs of excluding those options out of preference for judiciaries. The opportunity cost problem becomes all the more acute in view of the questionable track record of judicial assistance programs.

Moreover, the notion of judicial reform as a developmental end in itself conflicts with the explicit goal of many development institutions: poverty alleviation. Entering the World Bank lobby, one sees large, stirring words about the Bank's vision for a world free of poverty, not a world free of judicial delay.

Societywide Impact Is Possible

The faith in state institutions partly stems from donors' assumption that they can bring about societywide impact despite the huge obstacles they face and the relatively limited resources they possess. In certain contexts the international community may be up to this challenge. But those situations are exceptions to the rule.

It may be possible, for example, for a sizeable, armed UN force to stabilize Kosovo and train a new local police force, given that the United Nations was able to start with a clean slate (in the sense that it did not need to work with a preexisting police institution and leadership) and administrative control over a population of less than two million—though the ultimate effectiveness of that effort remains to be seen. The typical development or transitional context, however, involves far larger polities, no administrative control by international agencies (although such control would not guarantee wise or successful programs by any means), and deeply ingrained forces dictating the operations of judiciaries, police, and other justice institutions. As Anderson notes, "Constitution-alism and the rule of law depend upon sustained political support."[53] Such support is lacking in many societies, not least among those persons responsible for upholding the rule of law.

A summary of the Egyptian judiciary's entrenched tendencies toward patronage and clientalism offered by former USAID official John Blackton conveys a picture of a self-serving institutional culture in the develop-ing country that receives the largest amount of U.S. aid, including sub-stantial rule-of-law assistance:

> One area in which the [Supreme Judicial] Council is very active is in protecting the "family guilds" within the Egyptian judiciary . . .
>
> The council is cautious in approving disciplinary actions against the "sons of counselors" and sympathetic to requests for multi-year leaves of absence and overseas secondments for these favored members of the judicial family . . .
>
> Family influence and gratuities are significant elements in the assignment process, first at the Ministry where assignment lists are prepared and later amongst members of the Supreme Judicial Council where the log-rolling is intense and the final lists are ap-proved . . .
>
> The Ministry of Justice and the Judges Clubs are institutional mechanisms for accessing scarce government resources—apart-ments in Cairo, villas on the Mediterranean and the Red Sea, sub-sidized automobile loans, free medical care in Europe or America for a judge or a judge's family member.[54]

Half a world away, in the Philippines, Soliman similarly portrays an institutional culture whose undue influences similarly transcend wide-spread corruption:

> A chief obstacle to judicial independence is the pervasive culture of personalism, and the repetitive cycle of debt-of-gratitude (*utang na loob*) that besets public service. Personalism refers to decision-making based on personal, kinship, familial or other ties (coming from the same province, ethnolinguistic group, sorority, fraternity or social club), rather than on the merits of the case, the evidence presented and the impersonal application of the law on the facts. Personalism is aggravated by perceived debts-of-gratitude, ex-tended to persons who have helped the judge along his profes-sional career . . . Personalism is further reinforced by feelings of

guilt, shame or embarrassment (*hiya*) when the judge does not render a decision in favor of the person to whom he owes the debt-of-gratitude. Filipino social norms dictate that the proper behavior is to return the favor (*pagbigyan*) to persons to whom we owe such "debts."[55]

Where problems run so deep, even well-conceived reforms may themselves prove problematic. A UN Development Program (UNDP) paper finds reported corruption in the Indonesian court system "so pervasive that proposals have been put forward recently to dismiss the entire judiciary," with other justice sector institutions similarly infected.[56] Recent reform efforts have perpetuated or exacerbated the problem. Rather than improving its performance, a judicial independence law instead served to insulate the institution from accountability. And "the new commercial courts, which were intended to serve as a model in which cases are handled competently, expeditiously, transparently and with integrity are developing a reputation for delivering similar standards of justice as those elsewhere in the court system."[57]

Some donor personnel and agencies simply overlook such problems by viewing legal systems development as a purely technical, rather than political, task. They undertake superficial international exchanges, such as high-profile conferences of supreme court justices, whirlwind tours for top officials, and consultancies that involve boilerplate transfer of laws from industrialized societies to developing ones. Even when limited technical approaches are pursued under the rationale that judiciaries must walk before they can run, it is doubtful that these efforts can make a dent in the endemic corruption, bias, and other deep deficiencies plaguing these systems. And there are also the opportunity costs of such a course and the question of the doubtful sustainability of technical improvements once foreign aid ends.

Other rule-of-law orthodoxy proponents recognize the tremendous forces at play and correctly portray them in political and not just legal or technical terms. Yet they may still underestimate the power of those problems, ignore how they shape their organizational and individual partners, and overestimate their own capacities to analyze and overcome the obstacles. Proceeding with the best intentions, they nevertheless may skate along the surface of how a foreign society operates.

Soliman highlights this issue in pointing out that "the sources of judicial interference [in the Philippines] . . . may not be openly opposing the reform measures (in fact, nobody in his right mind would dare oppose these measures). It is just that these measures will be disregarded or slowly be implemented, to the point that it becomes meaningless."[58]

Many development practitioners can tell tales of misplaced faith in local partners who paid lip service to reform. My own experience includes work by my (then) office with Filipino judicial reformers subsequently identified with criminal conduct—in one case a supreme court justice who was forced to resign and in another a trial judge who was involved with covering up violent assaults by a relative (the son, in fact, of a former chief justice). In evaluating work with the Cambodian judiciary, I was told by a U.S.-based NGO of its great progress with courts in a particular province, only to have independent Western and Cambodian sources volunteer (without prompting) that those courts were particularly corrupt. Although technical progress can take place even in the face of undue influences, where such influences are widespread they tend to trump the value of the technical change.

Perhaps the most illuminating illustration of this point, however, comes from a different end of the rule-of-law field: drug control. For a good part of the late 1980s and early 1990s, the U.S. government's efforts to staunch the flow of illegal drugs from Mexico relied considerably on Mexico's top officials. That confidence culminated in U.S. drug policy chief Barry McCaffrey praising Mexico's top anti-drug enforcement officer as "an honest man and a no-nonsense field commander."[59] The commander was arrested eight days later and subsequently charged with having protected a top drug lord. In such a high priority arena and with all of its intelligence resources at its disposal, the U.S. Drug Enforcement Agency could not detect the true nature of its hero. Operating with much less information and funding, what are the prospects for practitioners of the rule-of-law orthodoxy to know the real intents of the government officials who are their local partners? This is particularly challenging when the real issue is not whether such officials are corrupt—in many or most instances they are not—but whether they really are dedicated to reform. Although the same can be said of NGO personnel, it is often easier to observe their direct work with the disadvantaged than it is to assess high officials' dedication to reforms that constitute only a part of their jobs.

There are certainly numerous honest, sincere chief justices, attorneys general, and other justice sector officials across the globe. But in working with them, even those donors who acknowledge the shortcomings of an institution-centered approach still tend to underestimate the problem: The challenge is not just the institutional culture itself, but also the societal milieu from which the institution springs. Egyptian and Filipino judges frequently favor their relatives and others with special connections because that is what one does to be a good family or community member in Egypt and the Philippines. Personal probity or even sincere dedication on the part of a high official may not be sufficient to outlast or outwit influences that are societal, rather than organizational, in nature. Thus, strengthening the Indonesian judiciary's independence and organizing a new commercial court there do not reform that judiciary's injustices out of existence.

The tendency to underestimate the obstacles to institutional reform is mirrored by an inclination to overestimate the potential impact. The dominant paradigm promises the realization of the rule of law. Yet it is unclear how the multilateral development banks' business-promoting version of the paradigm can even theoretically bring about the equal treatment, dignity, and access that the rule-of-law orthodoxy promises. Furthermore, even proponents of the orthodoxy grant that this is inevitably a slow, problem-plagued process.

Of perhaps even greater importance, there is often less than meets the eye in the nominal successes along the way. The adoption of a new law or new rules of court may be hailed as a great step forward, but the reality in many developing and transitional societies is that laws and rules are only rarely enforced. Training of judges might seem an important endeavor, unless of course most judges make little use of their new knowledge. Simply working with a national institution such as the judiciary can become confused with bringing about national changes in its operations or can trigger changes that do not necessarily benefit the poor. Thus, reforming a law or ostensibly revamping a judiciary offers the allure of national impact but in reality may affect few judges, cases, or citizens.

Institutional Reform Is Sustainable, Civil Society Strengthening Is Not

An important argument for investing in state legal institutions is that only such a course can offer sustainable development. The assumption is that, once reformed, the institutions will deliver improved services without continued donor input. The converse assumptions are that NGOs and other civil society groups do not merit ongoing development support because they are inherently unsustainable organizations or that they must generate funding themselves after a few years of donor financing.

The DFID Bangladesh (DFIDB) office accordingly illuminates a tension and assumption that many development agencies struggle with in many countries:

A striking conclusion is that there are few DFIDB projects with government that are making a higher-level impact for poor people . . . Thus, DFIDB faces a dilemma; it can achieve a more direct impact on poor people in the short term (possibly up to 2015) by working outside government, but for the long term only sustained improvement in delivery of public services will reach the majority of the population. A balance needs to be struck between the short and long-term goals.[60]

At least as applied to the legal field, three development myths account for this understandable but questionable assumption about the nature of sustainable change. The first is that support for state legal institutions will yield self-sustaining reforms and enduring improvements in services. As already suggested, however, the undertow of societal forces may undo promising changes: If legal systems' operations are in fact more the effect than the cause of social conditions, many systems that experience temporary improvements may revert to form. In addition, the chief justices, ministers of justice, and other officials who lead or agree to reforms often come and go rather rapidly—ironically, more rapidly than the leaders of supposedly unsustainable NGOs. The dedication to reform sometimes resides in those officials, not their institutions.

Often, however, even that personal dedication is not present. Commenting on a USAID project's short-term cuts in delay in pilot courts in Egypt, John Blackton asks:

Will that hold up when we leave? Will our changes move from our court clusters to the nation as a whole? Have we brought about a genuine change in judicial culture—one in which reducing case delay is valued? I fear that the answer will, three years after we are gone, be "no" to most if not all of my questions. The expat and Egyptian professionals organized within the construct of "the project" are the ersatz substitute for political will and a new judicial culture. We [the project team] are in fact, variables in the experiment. Our presence strongly impacts the results. Donors don't like to admit how much this is true, but in justice projects in settings like Egypt, I believe it is significantly so.[61]

This problem often manifests itself from the very outset of projects, with donor organizations and personnel, rather than those of recipient countries, initiating and driving rule-of-law programming. It is not as though chief justices, ministers of justice, and their staffs typically analyze their legal systems' problems on their own and present resulting proposals to funding agencies. More frequently, the agencies initiate the dialogue, commission the consultants, and design the projects. Of course, donors often have access to the intellectual capital that can undertake these tasks. And recipient institutions' personnel certainly are consulted and in some cases become very engaged in the planning and implementation of projects. But to return to Blackton's point, the funding agencies often supply "the ersatz substitute for political will and a new judicial culture." The result is a lack of intellectual ownership among recipients.

Proponents of the rule-of-law orthodoxy sometimes acknowledge that short-term reforms may hinge on persons rather than institutions and that intellectual ownership is an issue, but they legitimately argue that legal systems development must be seen as a long-term process. It accordingly will take many years or even decades before it becomes clear whether and to what extent sustained impact transpires. Fair enough, but this argument exposes a second sustainability myth: the notion that government initiatives should always be seen as potentially sustainable and that civil society efforts should not. If state institutions merit such ongoing support, especially with highly uncertain outcomes, then why exclude civil society from the long-term mix?

In reality, legal services NGOs and other civil society groups can outlast the appointments of the personnel heading and staffing many government agencies and acquire a greater knowledge of their fields. Over the course of many years, such NGOs often develop track records that enable them to obtain funding from a range of donors. It is even conceivable that long-term societal changes could generate in-country resources for them in some countries, whether from their governments or private sources. With support from the Ford Foundation and other sources, over the past several years the Asia Foundation has pursued an initiative to encourage the growth of indigenous philanthropy in many Asian nations.

The third sustainability myth is that, such philanthropy-promoting efforts aside, legal services and related NGOs in many developing nations must have the potential to become wholly self-supporting if medium-term outside support is to be justified. In fact, NGOs engaged in challenging the status quo may always depend on foreign sources for funding in many parts of the developing world, just as equivalent groups depend on foundations and other outside sources in many far more affluent societies. It is questionable whether developing country NGOs should even seek government or private money in many contexts, in view of the strings and uncertainty that could come attached.

This does not mean that a given funder should automatically commit itself to many years of support to a given NGO. But it should be open to the possibility of such ongoing assistance if the recipient shows sufficient promise and impact. It *does* mean that donors and other development agencies should move beyond repeatedly uttering the "NGOs must make themselves sustainable" mantra and take more responsibility for assisting worthwhile partner organizations to move toward sustainability. This can include providing support that expands the fundraising and financial management capacities of civil society groups, as well as connecting such groups with industrialized society donors that otherwise would be logistically unable to support overseas development.[62] Yet another mechanism is self-sustaining endowments. Organizations such as the Ford Foundation, USAID, and most recently the ADB have established such funds for selected high-impact organizations and important fields in certain countries.[63] The endowment approach merits further, broader consideration as a mechanism for ensuring ongoing funding of civil society efforts in the legal field.

We also need to rethink what we mean by sustainability. Rather than *organizational sustainability*, which biases funding toward often ineffective state institutions, a key consideration should be *sustainability of impact*. If a given legal services NGO serves enough people, or builds enough capacities for the poor to effectively assert their own rights, or affects enough laws—such impact is sufficient to justify past and future donor investment. It would be unfortunate for such an organization to cease operating down the line, but its existence would still be validated by the poverty it has helped alleviate and the justice it has helped secure. This patient approach has implicitly guided some of the better donor support for NGO legal services and has enabled recipient NGOs to build expertise and experience that translate into impact over time.

Additional Factors Behind the Orthodoxy

Given the problematic nature of its underlying assumptions, it is important to ask why the rule-of-law orthodoxy has taken hold so strongly. Some reasons lie in the assumptions themselves, of course. Many individuals and organizations operating in this field manifest a sincere dedication to the paradigm because they believe in many or most of its premises. But it would be misleading to attribute the orthodoxy's predominance to these intellectual viewpoints alone. Other factors are at work.

Rule of Lawyers

One reason that so much Western rule-of-law aid focuses on judiciaries and other formal legal institutions (for example, ministries of justice, prosecutorial services, police) is that the main actors involved in designing and carrying out the aid are lawyers and judges. Unlike the development professionals who dominate many other areas of development aid, many Western rule-of-law aid practitioners have little or no prior experience in developing and transitional societies before they enter the aid domain. They naturally see the problems and prospects for legal systems development in terms of their experience in their own countries, experience that typically features the courts and other forums through which they work with legal colleagues. The single greatest category of funding, then, focuses on assistance for judiciaries.

The upshot for the field is the "rule of lawyers." It carries with it the powerful tendency to minimize, usually not intentionally, the many other factors and actors that affect legal systems development and that can be brought to bear to improve it. Attorneys and judges are not blind to such considerations, but their perspectives and experience undercut giving nonlawyers and nonlegal tools the full weight they deserve.

The rule of lawyers also overlooks the ways in which attorneys are sometimes part of the problem rather than part of the solution. Bar associations in some societies are self-serving guilds that effectively limit access to justice, or that work against social and economic equity. These associations may vocally advocate political freedoms and judicial independence but be much less sensitive to the needs and priorities of the poor, particularly where those priorities challenge the interests of prosperous clients or the attorneys themselves.

Of course, all persons who get involved in development work tend to view the world through the lens of prior experience and professional orientation, so lawyers and judges are by no means unique in this regard. The impact, nevertheless, is that the rule-of-law orthodoxy is guided by a perspective that is either blind to the many influences and possibilities that lie beyond a narrow institutional perspective, or that can see such factors only dimly. Ironically but not coincidentally, some of the best people involved with funding agencies' law-oriented programs are nonlawyers. The Ford Foundation, for example, has employed a number of such individuals as program officers engaged in its human rights and social justice work.

This is not to dismiss the roles of lawyers and judges, of course. They are crucial for an array of purposes pertaining to the poor, not least as part of legal empowerment mechanisms that I discuss in a subsequent chapter of this book (chapter 7). They serve a vast array of other societal purposes. But the development community does, after all, prioritize poverty-alleviation, pro-poor programs, and community-driven and rights-based development to various degrees. This is not reflected in the kind of work that the lawyers who dominate rule-of-law aid tend to emphasize.

Bureaucratic Inertia

Another influential factor fueling the rule-of-law orthodoxy is bureaucratic inertia. As with most institutions in most fields, initial programs, personnel, and perspectives can lead to similar subsequent initiatives, regardless of whether they are appropriate to new contexts (or were appropriate in the first place). As U.S. rule-of-law aid first got under way in Latin America in the 1980s, the dominant organization behind this work at the time, USAID, followed a strongly top-down, state-centric approach. As USAID expanded its rule-of-law work to other regions in the 1990s, this initial orientation tended to reproduce itself around the world. And other development organizations joining the field in those years were influenced by USAID's example as well.

Institutional inertia may also play a role in many organizations on which USAID has no influence. In many cases, other funding agencies commissioned lawyers and judges to offer advice and design programs as the agencies initially explored work in this field. The legacy of their initial rule of lawyers, then, was to set in place programs and personnel that continue to shape priorities and perspectives.

Improper Incentives

Although many development practitioners trying to support institutional reforms talk in terms of "getting the incentives right" in developing country governments and systems, an irony of the orthodoxy is that it is substantially a product of improper incentives in funding institutions. In

some cases, career rewards are more closely linked to initiating programs—which is primarily done through making loans in the case of the
multilateral banks—than whether the programs eventually benefit the
poor.

A related improper incentive, perhaps particularly at the banks, is
that the dominant paradigm can easily consume large amounts of money
and that this is considered a good thing. Some funding agencies present
their personnel with de facto "use it or lose it" requirements. That is, a
given field office's or division's future resources hinge partly on whether
it spends all of what it has been allocated during the fiscal year. Many
activities supported by the rule-of-law orthodoxy—constructing courthouses, buying computers, training judges, retaining consultants, and
the like—can be funded in ways guaranteed to exhaust annual allocations. This creates an additional incentive to pursue this approach.

Political pressure also drives rule-of-law programming. Particularly
in the wake of wars or sudden transitions away from dictatorship, there
are demands from high officials in donor governments to help new leaders turn around their nations' ineffective legal institutions. Those officials may evince little patience for sound programs that take proper account of constraints and opportunities. This typically translates into a
"don't just stand there, do something" perspective, even in situations
where, realistically, the obstacles for actual systemic reform are still considerable.

Structural Biases

Various structural biases built into aid organizations also push rule-of-
law assistance toward the dominant orthodoxy. Due to explicit mandates and governing structures, some organizations view national governments, rather than the poor, as their partners. It is no coincidence,
then, that some of the more effective multilateral agencies, such as the
UN High Commissioner for Refugees and the UN Children's Fund
(UNICEF), focus on serving particular populations, rather than governments.

The multilateral development banks labor under an additional, obvious structural burden: Recipient governments naturally require control
over how their loans are spent. Most governments are much more prone
to use these resources for state projects and personnel, rather than having them diverted to potentially troublesome civil society groups. In
addition, policy parameters dictate that development banks sometimes

can more easily fund capital projects or offer lower rates on loans for such projects.

In reality, the situation of the banks is a bit less rigid than their loan-making nature implies. They have increasing access to grant funds, largely from bilateral donors, that can complement loans in a flexible manner. They also have some leeway in negotiating loans with recipient governments, not least because of many loans' heavily discounted nature and repayment terms. Whether they are prepared to use the grant funds and leeway to move beyond the rule-of-law orthodoxy is another matter.

Another structural bias stems from constraints on taking a political approach to development work. The World Bank's mandate is economic development, not political development. The other multilateral banks (with the partial exception of the Inter-American Development Bank) are similarly oriented. In reality, as the staffs of these institutions acknowledge, their work is politically charged in countless ways. And over the past decade the World Bank and, to varying degrees, the other multilateral banks have begun to grapple explicitly with politically sensitive issues such as corruption and human rights that were previously taboo. But the economic focus nevertheless acts as a brake on confronting some of the most pervasive problems that usually impede the rule of law in developing countries.

Yet another structural shortcoming is the project approach, the way many development agencies plan how to spend their funds. Tremendous amounts of time and resources go into designing projects, often leaving too little flexibility to respond to new developments or to learn and apply lessons as the projects unfold. This is an issue that reaches far beyond the legal field, but it strongly resonates in this field. Once a project has started, it is very difficult to back away from work with chief justices or government ministers even if they fail to demonstrate the desired political will. Barring extreme circumstances, the funding organization is "locked in," both politically and financially.

A related bias stems from what might be called "the view from the hotel window." Particularly during project development, when the very nature of the project is decided, many agencies rely on visiting consultants rather than in-country staff. This can lead to a superficial analysis of what ails a legal system and what legal issues confront the disadvantaged. To put the point mildly, a society seen from a hotel is far different from one experienced every day.

As a consultant myself, I may be in the position of the person living in a glass house (or hotel) throwing stones at its windows. But the visiting consultant bias is exacerbated when taken together with the other influences that steer rule-of-law work toward a state-centered approach. Because the rule-of-law orthodoxy is geared toward working with state institutions, the visitors' meetings with NGOs and representatives of disadvantaged populations (to the degree that such meetings take place at all) focus on how to fund those state institutions, rather than whether to do so and what alternative initiatives might be possible. The typical judicial administration consultant, for example, does not go tromping through the boondocks to learn how the poor perceive the judiciary, what their lives are like, what legal problems they face, or how they handle those problems.

A fundamental structural barrier involves the sectoral walls that divide much development work. Even though development issues often transcend sectors such as irrigation, natural resources management, urban housing, education, and the like, there is relatively little cross-fertilization of ideas, not to mention integration of approaches between rule-of-law work on the one hand and other areas of development aid on the other. Again, this is not unique to the legal field but severely constrains integration of law and development.

Lack of Applied Research

In many organizations that support law-oriented work, there often is a reluctance to support research that will scrutinize whether and how such work is doing any good or that will otherwise inform its efforts.[64] It is ironic, in fact, that some organizations that fund extensive research on legal systems or human rights conduct virtually none on the impact of their own law-oriented programs. It can be far more rewarding for a program officer or aid official to report anecdotal progress to the higher levels of an institutional hierarchy than it is to undertake the kinds of in-depth quantitative and qualitative inquiries that might contribute to learning and impact, but that also might yield negative results. This is not confined to the rule-of-law orthodoxy, but it is most striking in view of the resources it consumes.

In fairness, as discussed above, constructing studies that would probe the successes, failures, and lessons of rule-of-law initiatives is no easy task. And as the aforementioned divisions within the World Bank demonstrate, there is no guarantee that applied research will actually inform programs. Nevertheless, until such research is valued as contributing to progress even if it reveals problems, law-oriented work will lag behind other development fields in terms of both sophistication and impact.

Implications for Rule-of-Law Aid

Despite this chapter's critical tone toward the rule-of-law orthodoxy, it does not aim to dismiss all assistance to state legal institutions. The objective, instead, is to press for a more skeptical stance toward and a better balance in rule-of-law aid. The best intentions of some donor and government officials notwithstanding, state institutions often are burdened by counterproductive incentives and constraints that outweigh or outlast efforts to ameliorate them. These include entrenched bureaucratic structures, inefficient use of resources, corruption, patronage, gender bias, general aversion to change, and other factors that work against, rather than for, the disadvantaged. Many aid organizations' law programs either do not address the legal priorities of the poor or do so ineffectively because of excessive reliance on state institutions and top-down approaches. Although precise calculations are beyond this analysis, some international agencies could be spending as much as 90 percent of rule-of-law funds on activities that address only 10 percent of disadvantaged populations' greatest legal problems.

In view of the dominant paradigm's problematic assumptions and track record, it is best to raise the bar in deciding where and to what degree to work with state legal institutions. The political will for reform should be strong, not simply acquiescent. We should be modest about our expectations for generating and sustaining that political will where it is lacking. Even under the limited circumstances where long-term cultivation and support of local reformers in state institutions makes sense, this also weighs in favor of long-term funding of civil society forces that act on their own justice agendas, hold those state institutions accountable, and help them do their jobs better.

Notes

This chapter was adapted from Stephen Golub's *Beyond Rule of Law Orthodoxy: The Legal Empowerment Alternative,* Carnegie Paper no. 41 (October 2003).

1. The term *rule-of-law orthodoxy* was coined by Frank Upham in *Mythmaking in the Rule-of-Law Orthodoxy,* chapter 4 in this volume. Upham characterizes rule-of-law orthodoxy as contending "that sustainable growth is impossible without the existence of the rule of law: a set of uniformly enforced, established legal regimes that clearly lay out the rules of the game." I expand the definition so that it includes not just this underlying rationale, but the set of rule-of-law programs and activities geared toward achieving sustainable growth and other goals. In this chapter, then, rule-of-law orthodoxy is the same as the dominant paradigm for integrating law and development, and not just the intellectual basis for the paradigm.

2. In ascribing certain orientations to the multilateral development banks and other aid institutions, I of course am generalizing about organizations that have different units proceeding in different ways, some in more creative and less orthodox manners than others.

3. I use the term *disadvantaged populations* in the legal empowerment definition because it could be considered a broader class of persons than the poor. The concept includes the poor, but also those who face discrimination or abuse as a result of their gender, race, ethnicity, or other personal attributes. Still, as discussed in this chapter, the consensus characterization of poverty has broadened to include lack of opportunity and power, so that it comes closer to the notion of disadvantaged persons. To avoid further splitting of definitional hairs, however, I use the terms *poor* and *disadvantaged* interchangeably.

4. Patrick McAuslan, "Law, Governance and the Development of the Market: Practical Problems and Possible Solutions," in *Good Government and the Law: Legal and Institutional Reform in Developing Countries*, ed. Julio Faundez (London: Macmillan, 1997), 25–45, at 30–1.

5. Nestor Humberto Martinez, "Rule of Law and Economic Efficiency," in *Justice Delayed: Judicial Reform in Latin America*, ed. Edmundo Jarquin and Fernando Carrillo (Washington, D.C.: Inter-American Development Bank, 1998), 3.

6. See www.usaid.gov/democracy/index.html. Democracy and governance programs' link to the rule of law is reflected in the fact that the name of the USAID unit that originally promoted the rule of law in the 1980s was the Office of Administration of Justice and Democratic Development. However, although USAID's democracy and governance goals are not inherently business-oriented, one assumption is that good governance creates the proper environment for business to flourish.

7. See, for example, UK Department for International Development (DFID), *DFID Policy Statement on Safety, Security and Accessible Justice* (London: DFID, 2003).

8. See, for example, DFID, *Justice and Poverty Reduction* (London: DFID, 2000).

9. For a thoughtful but nevertheless narrow list of the main components of the justice sector, see DFID, *Safety, Security and Accessible Justice: Putting Policy into Practice* (London: DFID, July 2002), 12.

10. See, for example, Daniel Kauffman, *Misrule of Law: Does the Evidence Challenge Conventions in Judiciary and Legal Reforms?* Draft for discussion, July 2001, available at www.worldbank.org/wbi/governance/pdf/misruleoflaw.pdf.

11. Douglass C. North, *Institutions, Institutional Change and Economic Performance* (Cambridge: Cambridge University Press, 1990), 110.

12. Amanda Perry, "International Economic Organizations and the Modern Law and Development Movement," in *Making Development Work: Legislative Reform for Institutional Transformation and Good Governance*, ed. A. Seidman, R. B. Seidman, and T. Walde (New York: Kluwer Law International, 1999), 19–32, at 28.

13. Perry, "International Economic Organizations," 26.

14. Richard E. Messick, "Judicial Reform and Economic Development: A Survey of the Issues," *World Bank Research Observer* 14, no. 1 (February 1999): 117–36, at 122.

15. See, for example, McAuslan, "Law, Governance," 30–1.

16. See, for example, Richard Posner, "Creating a Legal Framework for Economic Development," *World Bank Research Observer* 13 (Washington, D.C.: World Bank, 1998).

17. China is not an unalloyed example of success, however, in that growing prosperity for hundreds of millions of citizens is partly offset by economic insecurity and even deprivation stemming from loss of jobs and the removal of the "iron rice bowl." The positive and negative developments are products of the shift from socialism to capitalism, however, rather than any efforts to institute the rule of law.

18. For an analysis that places responsibility for the crisis mainly on U.S. government and International Monetary Fund decisions rather than East Asian nations' laws and institutions, see Joseph E. Stiglitz, *Globalization and Its Discontents* (New York: W.W. Norton, 2002), ch. 4, 89–132. Stiglitz, recipient of the 2001 Nobel Prize for Economic Science, was World Bank chief economist during the crisis.

19. Stephen Haggard, *Pathways from the Periphery: The Politics of Growth in the Newly Industrialized Countries* (Ithaca, NY: Cornell University Press, 1990).

20. Katarina Pistor and Philip A. Wellons, *The Role of Law and Legal Institutions in Asian Economic Development: 1960–1995* (New York: Oxford University Press, 1999), 19.

21. Amanda Perry, "An Ideal Legal System for Attracting Foreign Direct Investment? Some Theory and Reality," *American University International Law Review* 15, no. 6 (2000): 1627–57.

22. John Hewko, *Foreign Direct Investment, Does the Rule of Law Matter?* Carnegie Working Paper no. 26 (Washington, D.C.: Carnegie Endowment for International Peace, April 2002), 4.

23. Hewko, *Foreign Direct Investment*, 5.

24. U.S. General Accounting Office (GAO), *Foreign Assistance: Promoting Judicial Reform to Strengthen Democracies*, GAO/NSAID-93-140 (Washington, D.C.: GAO, 1993).

25. William C. Prillaman, *The Judiciary and Democratic Decay in Latin America: Declining Confidence in the Rule of Law* (Westport, CT: Praeger, 2000).

26. Thomas Carothers, *Aiding Democracy Abroad: The Learning Curve* (Washington, D.C.: Carnegie Endowment for International Peace, 1999), 170.

27. Carothers, *Aiding Democracy Abroad*, 176.

28. Harry Blair and Gary Hansen, *Weighing In on the Scales of Justice: Strategic Approaches for Donor-Supported Rule of Law Programs*, USAID Development Program Operations and Assessment Report no. 7 (Washington, D.C.: USAID Center for Development Information and Evaluation, February 1994).

29. Blair and Hansen, *Weighing In*, 51.

30. Linn Hammergren, *Rule of Law: Approaches to Justice Reform and What We Have Learned: A Summary of Four Papers*, USAID Center for Democracy and Governance (Washington, D.C.: USAID, April 1998). Another thoughtful report in this vein is Madeleine Crohn and William E. David, eds., *Lessons Learned: Proceedings of the Second Judicial Reform Roundtable*, Williamsburg, Virginia, May 19–22, 1996 (Washington, D.C.: National Center for State Courts, USAID, and Inter-American Development Bank, November 1996).

31. Hammergren, *Rule of Law*.

32. USAID, *Achievements in Building and Maintaining the Rule of Law*, Occasional Paper Series, Office of Democracy and Governance (Washington, D.C.: USAID, November 2002).

33. Linn Hammergren, e-mail correspondence with author, December 16, 2002.

34. USAID, *Achievements in Building*, 79.

35. Martin Bohmer, "Access to Justice and Judicial Reform in Argentina," in *Fifth Annual Colloquium on Clinical Legal Education* (Warsaw: Columbia University Budapest Law Center/Public Interest Law Initiative, Open Society Institute, and Fundacja Uniwersyteckich Poradni Prawnych, 2002), 32. In fairness, the MSI report briefly notes apparently modest USAID support for civil society in Argentina (p. 35), though this seems limited to civic education and public information about judicial performance.

36. Carothers, *Aiding Democracy Abroad*, 170.

37. Robert S. Moog, *Whose Interests Are Supreme? Organizational Politics in the Civil Courts in India* (Ann Arbor, MI: Association of Asian Studies, 1997), 63.

38. Kauffman, *Misrule of Law*, 2.

39. Ibid.

40. Hammergren, e-mail correspondence.
41. World Bank Legal Vice Presidency, *Legal and Judicial Reform: Observations, Experiences, and Approach of the Legal Vice Presidency* (Washington, D.C.: World Bank, 2002), 65.
42. Although there is some movement by DFID and other donors toward a sectorwide approach in the legal field, this promising development often translates into a focus on specific state institutions.
43. North, *Institutions, Institutional Change*, 3–4.
44. Ibid., 5.
45. Former World Bank official William Easterly and Scott Pegg, respectively, in Daphne Eviatar, "Striking It Poor: Oil as a Curse," *New York Times*, June 7, 2003.
46. World Bank Legal Vice Presidency, *Legal and Judicial Reform*, 5.
47. Asian Development Bank (ADB), *Cambodia: Enhancing Governance for Sustainable Development* (Manila: ADB, October 2000).
48. Danish Ministry of Foreign Affairs and Danida, *Evaluation: Danish Support to Promotion of Human Rights and Democratisation, Volume 2: Justice, Constitution and Legislation* (Copenhagen: Evaluation Secretariat, Ministry of Foreign Affairs, 2000), vi.
49. Danish Ministry of Foreign Affairs and Danida, *Evaluation*.
50. DFID, *Safety, Security and Accessible Justice*, 58.
51. See, for example, Stephen Golub, "From the Village to the University: Legal Activism in Bangladesh," in *Many Roads to Justice: The Law-Related Work of Ford Foundation Grantees Around the World*, eds. Mary McClymont and Stephen Golub (New York: Ford Foundation, 2000), 127–58.
52. The aforementioned Danida evaluation, for example, more generally asserts that "a well-functioning, formal legal system is a pre-requisite for establishing a 'modern' society." Danish Ministry of Foreign Affairs and Danida, *Evaluation*, vi.
53. Michael R. Anderson, *Access to Justice and Legal Process: Making Legal Institutions Responsive to Poor People in LDCs*, IDS Working Paper no. 178 (Brighton, U.K.: Institute of Development Studies, February 2003), 12, box 4.1.
54. John Blackton, "Egypt Country Report," 6–8, unpublished background paper prepared in 2000 for USAID and International Foundation for Election Systems (IFES), *Guidance for Promoting Judicial Independence and Impartiality*, revised ed. (Washington, D.C.: USAID Office of Democracy and Governance, January 2002).
55. Hector Soliman, "Philippines Country Report," 3, unpublished background paper prepared for USAID and IFES, *Guidance for Promoting Judicial Independence*.
56. UNDP, *The Status of Governance in Indonesia: A Baseline Assessment*, draft report produced on behalf of the Partnership of Governance Reform in Indonesia, October 2000, 11.
57. UNDP, *Status of Governance in Indonesia*, 12.
58. Soliman, "Philippines Country Report," 5.
59. Tim Golden, "Mexico and Drugs: Was U.S. Napping?" *New York Times*, July 11, 1997, at A1, A11.
60. DFID Bangladesh (DFIDB), *Country Strategy Review: 1998–2002 Bangladesh* (Dhaka: DFIDB, August 2002), 22.
61. John Blackton, written interview with author, May 8, 2001.
62. Save the Children, CARE, and other development and relief groups are well known for their efforts in this regard, but in recent years other organizations, such as the Asia Foundation, have taken on such facilitating functions.
63. In connection with an approximately $330 million loan to Pakistan, the Asian Development Bank is establishing a $24 million endowment for an Access to Justice Department Fund. Although two-thirds of the annual interest income will go to conventional judicial development activities, from 15 to 20 percent will be spent on legal

empowerment (sub-)fund (largely for legal services and public awareness activities). Smaller sub-funds will support legal and judicial research and legal education innovations. See ADB, *Report and Recommendation of the President to the Board of Directors on Proposed Loans and Technical Assistance Grant*, RRP: PAK 32023 (Manila: ADB, November 2001), 60–64.

64. One partial exception to this rule can be found within the World Bank's Poverty Reduction and Economic Management Network (PREM), which actively facilitates and disseminates very useful research on legal systems development experience (as well as many other topics).

CHAPTER SIX

Lessons Not Learned about Legal Reform

WADE CHANNELL

THE FALL OF THE BERLIN WALL in 1989 and the subsequent breakup of the Soviet Union presented an unparalleled opportunity for fundamental political and economic change in more than two dozen countries. As postcommunist countries sought to attain the economic development of their Western neighbors, it became clear that the existing framework of laws and institutions would not support the desired growth. Reformers and development experts soon identified a panoply of gaps and shortcomings in financial resources, human resources, and organizational capacity, all of which appeared ripe for outside assistance.

North American and Western European governments responded rapidly to the fall of communism by creating a variety of financial and technical assistance programs for both Central and Eastern Europe and the former Soviet Union. Working through international financial institutions such as the World Bank and bilateral donor agencies such as the United States Agency for International Development (USAID) and Germany's Gesellschaft für Technische Zusammenarbeit (GTZ), among others, they have sought to ensure successful transitions to free-market economies and democratic government. A priority area for donor efforts has been the establishment of the rule of law, which donors commonly define as accountable, transparent government that equitably enforces laws and regulations through an independent judiciary to create a "level playing field" for economic actors.

Promoting the reform of commercial law has been a major focus within the broader rule-of-law aid endeavor. Early in the postcommunist period, it was obvious that commercial laws needed to be rewritten, replaced, or reformed to unleash market forces for growth and development. Consequently, donors provided numerous experts to help countries identify, adapt, and transplant best practices from a number of successful models. These experts have drafted countless laws and trained thousands of people in legal institutions in the recipient countries.

The results have varied widely. In some countries, little actual change has taken place other than the passage of new legislation. Even in the more successful transition countries, many of the new commercial laws now on the books are not effectively or consistently implemented, despite additional assistance to support and reform implementing institutions. In some cases, application of well-crafted laws has been hijacked by vested interests to attain advantages through market manipulation. Countless stakeholders have summarized the problem simply: "The new laws are fine; they're just not enforced."

Those who work in the legal reform business generally expected greater impact from this investment in new laws. Analysts, drafters, and project implementers often assumed that market forces would propel a greater level of implementation once the right laws were in place. Instead, a number of common problems repeatedly appear as counterparts in beneficiary countries have moved from legislation to implementation.

These problems have been independently identified by numerous legal reform professionals. They can be summarized as follows:

- *Lack of ownership:* Laws are often translated or adopted wholesale from another system as "hasty transplants," without the necessary careful, patient adaptation to the local legal and commercial culture and without substantial involvement by the stakeholders most directly affected, including the private sector and nongovernmental organizations (NGOs), not simply government counterparts.
- *Insufficient resources:* Law reform projects are too short term and too lightly funded to create the needed mechanisms and processes that would permit sufficient absorption through broad-based discussion and sustained participation in the process of reform.
- *Excessive segmentation:* Overly narrow diagnoses and responses to legal shortcomings produce projects that ignore systemic problems and fail to add up to an integrated, effective whole.

These are not revolutionary insights. Similar critiques were made of the law and development movement of the 1960s and 1970s. World Bank rule-of-law specialist Richard Messick has found a wealth of analysis documenting these same shortcomings twenty years ago.[1] Earlier critics were concerned with overemphasis on top-down, state-centered approaches, use of "transplanted" laws, and reliance on the adoption of laws to drive change in the culture and habits of the local marketplace.

In many if not most cases, the lessons of the law and development movement have simply not been learned by practitioners in the new rule-of-law reform enterprise of the last two decades. Clearly, this is not due to a lack of existing research and writing on the earlier efforts or to a lack of awareness of the issues: Messick describes a number of debates in the early to mid-1990s on whether the new movement was likely to repeat the mistakes of the earlier one. It has.

If the current generation of rule-of-law aid specialists is aware of the problems and had access to a wealth of materials on these problems, why did they not learn from the earlier mistakes? I believe that the failure to learn has two root causes: first, rule-of-law aid practitioners tend to hold some core mistaken assumptions about the role of law, government, and culture in the development process; and second, the incentive structures within the legal reform industry do not encourage learning. Before turning to those root causes let me consider first in more detail the three basic problems cited above.

Core Problems

The three core problems of legal reform assistance—ownership, resources, and segmentation—are interrelated. Inadequate resources, for example, contribute to the difficulty of nurturing ownership. Nevertheless, each core problem merits separate elaboration.

Lack of Ownership: Whose Reforms Are They, Anyway?

The "hasty transplant syndrome" is a critical problem in legal reform assistance. It involves using foreign laws as a model for a new country, without sufficient translation and adaptation of the laws into the local legal culture. In some egregious cases, reformers simply translate a law from one language to another, change references to the country through search-and-replace commands, and then have the law passed by a compliant local legislature. The result is generally an ill-fitting law that does not "take" in its new environment as evidenced by inadequate implementation.

The syndrome is often, rightly, seen as a flaw caused by foreign drafters who naïvely bring their own laws or their last drafting project and reformulate them for the new location. But this same approach is also sometimes reproduced by local drafters. In Croatia, for example, several respected drafters have translated German laws and submitted them successfully for passage based on the premise that Croatia shares the same legal tradition as Germany. Unfortunately, the transplants have been beset by problems, in part because German and Croatian legal systems and traditions have taken significant detours from their common sources over the past seventy years. The common root, modified by a multitude of different influences, does not produce the same fruit in different locations.

The crux of the problem is not the origin of the law per se. Indeed, German company law may be the best model for Croatia to use. Rather it lies in the pursuit of law reform processes that generally do not permit users to participate in adapting the draft—whatever its origin—to local conditions. Donor-sponsored legislative reform projects frequently use what could be called a star chamber system in which a small working group of experts quietly drafts new legislation chosen in part by outside donors, which is then rapidly adopted by the legislature with little meaningful public comment. Lack of local input, not transplantation, is the problem. The process does not permit sufficient understanding of local needs for effective drafting to address those needs. Insufficient understanding is compounded by unnecessary speed in getting laws adopted without public input or public education. And those excluded from the process have a tendency to resist changes imposed without their knowledge or informed consent.

An additional challenge is the problematic, externally driven reform agenda. Many of the new laws are hastily produced because of donor pressures to pass laws or donor-sponsored assistance that make a new law possible. As a result, policy makers are not using a reasoned, cost-benefit, socioeconomic analysis of where the reform priorities lie but are instead responding to external needs and pressures. Reformers in several countries have reported that they have *never* seen an economic benefit analysis to support legal reforms.

One of the most striking examples of the ownership problem can be found in Albania. Albania ended almost fifty years of intense isolation to reenter the community of nations in late 1980s and early 1990s.

Developed countries quickly provided assistance for Albania's transition, in part through extensive legal reforms. Albanian lawyers today often speak proudly of the new system, noting, however, that the new laws are European, not Albanian, and that they are not actually being applied. This is an extreme case of hasty transplantation on a massive scale.

A more specific example of externally driven reform priorities can be clearly seen in reform of Albania's bankruptcy laws. Albania first adopted a market-oriented bankruptcy law in 1994, which combined elements of German and U.S. statutes and principles. The law was inspired in great part by conditionalities for loans and assistance from the international financial community, not by internal need. Recently a new project was undertaken to replace this law with a purportedly better one as part of a new set of loan conditionalities, not because the commercial sector wanted the change. There is a theoretical need for a proper law.[2] Albania, however, still does not have much practical use for such a law: Bankruptcy is the unwanted handmaiden of commercial debt, and Albania still has no significant level of commercial lending. When 60 percent of Albania's gross domestic product (GDP) was lost in the mid-1990s after the collapse of a national Ponzi scheme, only one bankruptcy case was ever brought because the massive national losses resulted in very little commercial default. Even so, Albania has dutifully acquiesced to replacement of one unused law with an arguably unneeded second law to satisfy donor priorities.

It is hard to imagine any rule-of-law aid specialist pursuing law reform in his or her own country in this fashion. If I assembled half a dozen recognized European or U.S. specialists to redraft the U.S. Code of Judicial Ethics and then tried to get it passed by the U.S. Congress with little or no input on the proposed draft from congressional committees, the judiciary, the bar, business interests, law schools, or other stakeholders, I would be looking for a new career rather quickly. Based on many current practices, however, that career could easily be found abroad "helping" transition countries with the same process.

Insufficient Resources: Never Enough Time or Money

It is a common complaint within the rule-of-law aid community that the time and money afforded to the process of reform are insufficient. Most donor-sponsored law reform projects run from two to five years, but it is also common to see tightly focused task orders of only one to two years. Some projects start with specific objectives, for example, reform of the company law. Others allow the implementer to determine need by working with local counterparts to identify priority laws and then reform them. The project will commonly require establishing a professional working group, drafting the law, getting the draft approved by the legislature, and providing some form of education to the legal community about the new law. These steps make sense, but they are not normally sufficient to produce any meaningful change, other than the passage of a new law, which may or may not be meaningful.

The resources problem also has a financial side. It is much cheaper to fund a few expatriate experts with a small local staff to draft a law than to fund a wide-ranging program of public education, institutional reform, and association building, which form the foundation for implementation.

By comparison with the most generous law reform project timeline (five years), legislative changes in the United States often require anywhere from two to seven years to move from submission of a well-written draft to passage of legislation. Preparation of a draft can easily take a year, and this after a year or more of policy debate. Although all of these processes can move more quickly, it is noteworthy that the United States, with a well-developed drafting and reform system, will often take five to ten years from inception to law.[3] In postcommunist and developing countries, where there is little or no history of deliberate policy development, public discussion, or legislative debate (in other words, democratic lawmaking processes), legal reform is expected to move much faster. And unfortunately it can.

Nondemocratic lawmaking can move more quickly than democratic lawmaking because it is not hampered by the need for cost-benefit studies of different approaches to law. Nor does it involve serious policy debate, which, once settled, must be translated into legal drafts. It usually skips public review and debate of drafts by interested stakeholders—as well as searching discussion and analysis by the legislators charged with voting the law into existence. It simply needs a strong "champion," a few efficient drafters, and a compliant legislature. For many in the industry, this is the expected, if not preferred, model. One project officer in the Balkans reportedly complained that the implementers of a legal reform project "have been working for six months and haven't passed a single law." In some projects, laws are passed in less than six months.

So what is the problem? If laws can be passed that quickly, why not just do it? The apparent efficiency of command-style, authoritarian lawmaking breaks down at the implementation level. There is wide agreement that many of these "efficient" laws that have been recently adopted in postcommunist countries are not implemented sufficiently, if at all, in a reasonable time frame. Some can sit on the books for five to ten years with little actual enactment in practice.

Excessive Segmentation: Losing Focus through Hyperfocus

Segmentation is a useful tool for analysis: Divide a system into its component parts to identify gaps and problems and then work on the weak components. Applied to aid programs, this approach permits well-focused interventions, which can be very effective in a narrow sense. But it can also produce hyperfocused approaches that ignore systemic problems and fail to add up to an integrated, effective whole.

Judicial reform provides a good example of the problem of segmentation. The transition away from communism opened up the possibility of fundamental judicial reform throughout Central and Eastern Europe and the former Soviet Union. In the field of commercial law, poorly functioning, politicized courts can create serious problems for economic development by hampering business through delays and unpredictable outcomes. Consequently, numerous aid projects have been established to address weaknesses in decision making and court administration.

These programs are clearly needed. Poor court management can be addressed in a number of ways, and substantial progress can be made through adoption of new technologies in combination with modern management techniques. Judges can be educated to understand the commercial concepts now before them, so that they can make better decisions.

Though necessary, court reform and judicial education are not at all sufficient. In fact, the Achilles' heel of the system is not in the courtroom but in the enforcement division. Where court reform programs have been effective, they have resulted in faster, better, more predictable decisions that *still cannot be enforced*. In Bosnia today, for example, enforcement of a final judgment can take several years. Aid providers have helped to redraft enforcement laws, civil procedures, and court processes over the past five years, but until very recently, no one had ever spoken to enforcement officers regarding much simpler, practical problems that keep them from completing their work. The net result in Bosnia as elsewhere is no real improvement—aid providers have narrowed the ambit of reform too much and missed crucial segments. Today, enforcement issues

are being addressed, but five to ten years after initial court modernization programs began. Logically, it would make sense to work on enforcement first or even simultaneously. Instead, rule-of-law aid providers segmented the analysis, prioritized external needs, and missed the
opportunities that could have been available through a systemic approach.[4]

Another problem arises through hyperfocus on seemingly distinct
areas of law that are, in fact, deeply intertwined with related laws. For
example, bankruptcy is frequently treated as a stand-alone discipline
despite its strong interdependence on other disciplines. Early bankruptcy
reforms in Russia failed to recognize overlapping reform needs in the
company law and thus ignored crucial fiduciary duty and corporate
governance issues. As a result, directors of recently privatized enterprises were at times able to loot the company, transferring corporate
assets to themselves directly or through shell companies, and then hiding behind an unpierceable corporate veil to maintain their gains while
shareholders and creditors lost heavily. Elsewhere, bankruptcy programs
have sometimes focused on the bankruptcy law by itself, without attention to separate laws on secured transactions, the code of civil procedure, execution and enforcement laws, and other fundamental segments
of the overall system. Recently, specialized work on Bosnia's lease law
undermined secured transaction priorities in the bankruptcy regime
because of a piecemeal approach to reform.

Problem of Learning (I): Mistaken Assumptions

One major reason that the rule-of-law aid community fails to learn from
the lessons of the past and of the problematic recent experience in
postcommunist countries (and elsewhere) is that aid practitioners hold
a set of mistaken assumptions about the importance of laws, the role of
government, the impact of culture, and the level of existing knowledge
about rule-of-law change.

Mistaken Assumption 1: New Laws Are the Answer

Underlying the core problems with many legal reform programs of the
past two decades is the mistaken assumption that new laws in and of
themselves are the solution. Laws, however, have no intrinsic value. They
are nothing more than tools—only one of many types of tools—used for
the design and implementation of socioeconomic policy. A society that

wishes to improve its economic performance will inevitably use these tools, along with other policy tools, to improve the commercial climate. Having the right laws is not the same thing as having an attractive investment environment, especially if the process of policy making is not functioning effectively. One Eurasian business executive recently told me that he could personally get the laws passed that he wanted but so could his competitors. Having the "right" laws for the moment was not enough to increase his investments.

When aid providers assume that new laws are the essence of the solution, they improperly limit the scope of their assistance. Effective policy making—which results in lawmaking—is normally based on some form of social discourse between the government and numerous interest groups, which leads to selection of appropriate tools to accomplish the agreed changes. Implementation then flows from the agreement between the government and the governed. Simply reforming the tools, absent underlying policy dialogues and processes, is insufficient.

Much of the legal reform work attempted in postcommunist societies arises from an understandable but insufficient analysis of the role of law in economic development. Comparing the world's developed economies makes clear that they share common legal frameworks, including similar approaches to bankruptcy, company law, capital markets, real property, pledges of movable property, competition, and a host of other laws. Those concerned with rule-of-law reform have been able to assemble best practices and devise model laws based on these commonalities, all of which are useful references in the reform process.

Up to this point, the analysis is essentially sound. The breakdown occurs in moving from what is to what should be. The rule-of-law aid community seems to have assumed that if they simply help countries adopt the laws that have been proven to support economic development, such development would follow. Unfortunately, passage of legislation is not the same thing as implementation of policy. In some sense, this approach could be compared to a hypothetical orchard development program, in which analysts recognize that healthy orchards all have a certain quality of apples. The analysts then fly in apples, tie them to the local trees, and momentarily assume success because the result looks like an orchard.

In legal reform projects, passage of new laws is a "deliverable"—a measure of the success of the project—rather than a way of describing a policy outcome that is needed but not yet functioning. Projects are graded on their ability to get laws passed. Aid projects are built on the assumption that new laws will be implemented after they have been passed, with some unspecified mechanism, perhaps public education or continuing legal education (CLE) courses, providing the necessary basis for implementation. But implementation is a function of consensus on the ends and means of the law. When law reform projects fail to forge consensus, they mistakenly rely on enforcement to bring the recalcitrant into line.

Passing a law is only one step, and not necessarily the largest or most important one, in creating and implementing *policy*. If rule-of-law law aid practitioners see themselves as engaged in a policy development and implementation process—which includes research, debate, negotiation, public education, outreach, institutional capacity building in parliament, development of skills in translating policy into legislative drafts, revision of drafts based on local political compromises, and a host of other steps—then the role of laws falls back into its proper place and allows them to build projects more likely to bring the results they have inaccurately assumed that laws alone would achieve.

Mistaken Assumption 2: Governments Are the Key to Achieving Legal Reform

The need for government involvement in legal reform programs is undebatable; the extent and nature of that involvement are not. Rule-of-law aid practitioners have assumed too great a role for governments in the law reform process—underemphasizing the role of the private sector and civil society—and have assumed too quickly that postcommunist governments are ready to oversee well-conceived legal reform projects. Although many postcommunist governments have made important strides in creating formal democratic institutions, too few have developed adequate mechanisms of political transparency and accountability. As a result, the input, feedback, and accountability that often characterize lawmaking processes in Western democracies are feeble or nonexistent in the postcommunist legal reform environment. One Macedonian practitioner characterized a common sentiment for her country, noting that many Macedonians see the state as "someone else's government." After 400 years under Ottoman rule and 50 years under Tito, a culture has developed for defending oneself against government, not engaging with it.

Mistaken Assumption 3: Cultural Issues Are Peripheral to Legal Reform

Rule-of-law aid specialists often assume that cultural issues are of peripheral importance to their work. Consequently, they lack a vital analytical component when they seek to understand why new laws are not implemented. Sometimes the resistance to implementation and acceptance comes from cultural predispositions, not some technical failure of implementing and supporting institutions.

Examples of the adverse effects of certain cultural factors can be seen in a number of judicial reform projects. Throughout the Balkans, court procedures are delayed excessively through well-developed tactics of lawyers. Failures to appear, to produce evidence, or to meet deadlines generally result in a grant of extensions without sanctions. As a result, even simple cases can be tied up for years in court. Judicial reform projects rightfully focus on improving case and court management but do not necessarily work from a cultural understanding of those delays.

This culture of delay within the courts of some transition or developing countries arose, to some extent, during a period in which judges and attorneys for private sector litigants attempted to mitigate authoritarian rule by hobbling the state's ability to prosecute claims through the courts. Judges and lawyers won respect by protecting individuals, not by efficiently enforcing unpopular policies. This protective approach also appears in "debtor-friendly" practices that inhibit enforcement by larger concerns (banks) against less powerful, unfortunate figures (debtors). A local drafter in the Balkans has noted that certain provisions of a recently enacted enforcement law were designed to prevent rather than enforce repossession of land and personal property.

This problem is highlighted in Bulgarian literature. In the 1950s, Bulgarian author Elin Pelin published the short story titled *Andreshko,* in which the principal character became a hero through resisting enforcement. The protagonist, Andreshko, is a poor farmer who picks up a traveler while driving his horse cart back to the village. As they converse, Andreshko discovers that the traveler is an enforcement judge who is going to Andreshko's village to seize the assets of a neighbor in satisfaction of a tax lien. Torn between his legal duties and his loyalty to a friend, Andreshko decides for the friend. He pretends to take a short cut but instead drives the cart into a swamp until it is mired. He then unharnesses the horse and rides home alone, abandoning the enforcement judge. This story has been taught to schoolchildren for over forty years. Today, Andreshko is the patron saint of resistance to enforcement, the heroic defender against attachment. Overcoming his legacy will not be met simply through better written laws.

The implications of such cultural barriers are significant. Some can be addressed through public education. For example, Bulgarian legal reformers would do well to distinguish Andreshko's resistance to tax liens from liens based on a debtor's nonpayment, showing that a lack of enforcement reduces credit availability and economic growth. Likewise, overcoming court delays must include reorientation of practitioners to the economic benefits of speed, especially in suits between private parties and against the state.

Cultural considerations can also shape the way in which reforms are presented and developed. Croatia is well known among implementers for its pride in Croatian solutions. Officials and others involved in the reform process regularly announce that no foreign input into laws or policies is needed, stating, in essence, that Croatia is intellectually self-sufficient. Assistance, therefore, must be carefully provided so that it is seen as coming from local resources. When a foreign expert insists on public credit for an idea, Croatians listen, publicly reject the assistance, then wait a few years until the foreigner leaves before they use the information.

By neglecting serious study of cultural barriers and differing values, rule-of-law aid practitioners often find themselves at cross purposes with those they are attempting to help. The emphasis on improving enforcement mechanisms for laws—including greater utilization of police and other enforcement agents—without building consensus for the changes to be enforced ignores the fundamental fact that many of these countries have finally thrown off a strong state after years of oppressive enforcement. There is widespread, unspoken, internalized resistance to empowering the state. It should not be surprising when efforts to restore dismantled structures are not immediately welcomed.

*Mistaken Assumption 4: The Processes of Legal Changes
Are Well Understood*

Rule-of-law aid providers often act as though they have a scientific basis for their work. They believe that a bankruptcy regime will help accelerate reallocation of productive assets in support of privatization programs, or that each country needs its own stock exchange for capital markets to develop. Millions of dollars have been spent on the basis of both beliefs, but is there any evidence to justify this? In my experience (equally unscientific), privatization cases overwhelm the courts because of their political implications, and new stock exchanges do not produce a return on investment sufficient to justify the expenditures. As Thomas Carothers has argued convincingly in chapter 2, the legal reform industry does not yet have a solid, scientific basis for the various approaches and ideologies used in attempting to bring postcommunist and developing countries into the world of democratic, market-oriented systems.

Without better analysis, current knowledge will remain insufficient to inform changes or judge success. But even when rule-of-law reformers begin to establish a better knowledge base, there will be a second danger. Practitioners tend to misconceive the nature of their endeavors, believing that they are applying scientific knowledge instead of testing hypotheses. The fact is that those in the rule-of-law aid community are experimenters in a new discipline. They may understand what an average legal framework looks like in an advanced economy, but they are still trying to understand how those advanced economies came into being. They simply do not know whether lessons and laws can be successfully transplanted or whether there are negative side effects from their approaches.

Learning is hampered when practitioners take as proven something that is hypothetical. Such presuppositions retard and misdirect analysis. If one can honestly approach projects as experiments based on reasonable hypotheses, then one can more accurately determine whether the hypotheses are correct. Experiments do not fail; they provide information on whether a hypothesis fails under given circumstances. Perhaps this problem, as much as any other, has contributed to repetition of the mistakes of the law and development movement. Specialists in the rule of law simply did not recognize the experimental nature of their work and thus have failed to look for the wealth of existing information on earlier failed hypotheses.

Problem of Learning (II): Lack of Effective Incentives

The persistent lack of learning within the world of commercial law reform projects and other rule-of-law assistance is not merely due to stubbornly held mistaken assumptions on the part of practitioners. Another major factor is a lack of proper incentives in the aid community for learning. Generally speaking, rewards are available for those who know, but not necessarily for those who learn. Project design and selection processes reward repetition, not innovation. Attempts to change this process have failed because they do not take into account that the contractor side of the aid industry is also hampered by a counterproductive incentive structure. When lessons are actually learned, they are not shared, because the incentives only encourage production and storage of knowledge, not publication.

Incentive Problem 1: Incentives for Knowing, But Not for Learning

The legal reform industry regularly recruits and attracts experts and specialists with ten to twenty years of professional experience in both developing and transition countries. This is appropriate. These experts are then expected to report for duty with a full understanding of what needs to be done under their terms of reference and begin doing it. This is inappropriate.

Each new assignment should require extensive preparation for the new conditions, cultural variations, and demands on the otherwise qualified specialists who will implement the project. Most will learn on the job, correcting mistakes as they go, but very few will be paid for learning as part of their job. Many mistakes could be avoided through preparation, especially structured preparation, but very little preparation is contractually permissible.

In ten years of recruiting and fielding consultants, especially for short-term work, I have generally had to fight for permission to provide those consultants with more than two days of preparation time, even when my team has assembled hundreds of pages of reports, studies, and documents for them to use in their work. In many projects, expatriate consultants can be paid only for time spent in the field, not for work done elsewhere, including the work of preparation. It is not surprising then that many of these consultants show up insufficiently prepared for the specific setting, though well versed in their subject matter specialty. As a result, much learning is done through mistakes that could have been avoided through preparation based on the wealth of published knowledge.

This problem is partly financial and partly semantic. Obviously, it costs more to pay people to engage in structured learning. In an award system based on competitive pricing, it is unlikely that many implementers will reduce their opportunity to win contracts by elevating the price to cover the cost of ongoing training for their project personnel. Contractors who keep their prices down by bidding experts with no assumed need for more learning will always have a competitive advantage in the bidding process.

The definition of expertise, then, becomes a key consideration. In many venues, an "expert" is expected to know all that should reasonably be known about a given subject. To admit that something is not known is to admit weakness. Although such caricature seems laughable, it is often the norm. Those funding the experts expect certain results without further investment in learning. Many experts are loath to admit that they do not know something about their area of expertise because it could affect a decision to hire them again, especially when they are billing maximum rates. Experts who freely admit that they need to do further study are rare, even though anyone asked to work in a new context is likely to need additional study. Perhaps it is time to reconsider what is expected from experts.

In the broader market for legal services, there are a number of incentives that motivate lawyers to participate in ongoing education and learning, which could be expected to promote continuing education with legal reform experts. First, competition makes it necessary for lawyers to stay abreast of developments lest their clients leave them for better service providers. Second, law schools update their teaching and curricula on a constant basis for similar reasons, so that baseline knowledge continues to advance. Third, there is a continuing legal education industry that meets the demand for new courses and new information, fueled in part by mandatory ongoing education requirements. None of these incentives is in place for legal reformers.

Education and training in legal reform have not, to my knowledge, been institutionalized. Although some donors or contractors offer occasional in-house seminars for their employees, and some law schools examine the impact of law in developing or transition countries, I know of no structured program for legal reformers nor of any consistently available system of continuing education in this field. Market analysis suggests that there is no such program because there is insufficient demand, and such demand is depressed because the marginal return on investment in such education is insufficient. Legal reform practitioners do learn, but they learn individually and have few if any avenues for passing that knowledge on to others. Although they write papers and reports on lessons learned, very few people read them. The information produced is passive, awaiting discovery. There is no significant system of structured learning in which such information is actively analyzed, critiqued, and presented to those whose task is to apply the lessons.

Incentive Problem 2: High Incentives for Repetition,
Low Incentives for Innovation

Within the legal reform industry, most projects are awarded through a competitive procurement system in which various service providers offer technical and cost proposals in hopes of winning work. (On occasion, donors will issue a sole source award, but this practice is quite limited and is generally reserved for less expensive projects.) Such competition helps to keep the service providers sharp. One might expect this competition to inspire creative, innovative offerings that challenge and advance industry knowledge as lessons learned from past projects are incorporated into bids for new projects. Unfortunately, this is frequently not the case.

Competition is desirable, but it is also expensive. Individual firms and consortia will often spend 5 to 10 percent of the value of a contract on their proposal effort. For larger projects, such as USAID's multimillion-dollar indefinite quantity contracts, the cost of submitting a proposal can easily run from $50,000 to $100,000. As a result, the bidders seek to keep their risks low to improve their chances of success.

The higher the cost of a proposal, the greater the strategic effort to reduce risk. This often includes careful analysis of those who have written the request for proposals or who are likely to grade the proposals, in addition to very close analysis of the tender documents. Why the emphasis on those behind the request? Successful bidders understand that those who wrote the request have biases and preferences, and that they are seeking "correct" answers that meet their expectations.

It is an open secret among contractors that a proposal should not challenge or contradict any significant assumptions incorporated into the request for proposal or espoused by those likely to be involved in awarding the contract. Instead, the recipe for success is to slavishly give back what is asked for in order to win the bid, then negotiate a different approach at the contracting stage, or simply implement based on the contractor's approach, not on the award. "Win it now and fix it later" best expresses the strategic approach of contractors.

At one level, this makes complete sense. If a buyer wishes to purchase a product through competitive bidding, then an intelligent seller will offer exactly what is being asked. If the seller truly believes that the requested product will not achieve the ends sought, it would seem appropriate to discuss the assumptions with the buyer. Indeed, donors (buyers) often expect to see innovation and new approaches in the bidding process. However, if the rest of the competitors are expected to regurgitate the underlying assumptions, then such innovation will increase risk for any competitor breaking ranks by challenging assumptions.

In other words, the bidding process does not encourage any serious discussion of lessons learned, especially from mistakes of the past. (Indeed, to admit mistakes is to suggest that the contractor should not have been paid for the past contract and is not qualified for the next.) Bidding success is based on regurgitation and repetition—a reasonable attempt to match offer with expectations, not to encourage new thought.

There is one exception, however. Often, contractors will share insights gained from prior implementation as they pursue new contracts. Contractors will highlight these best practices or lessons learned in the proposal to set them apart from their competitors. Evaluators may then have several approaches to consider, which, if shared broadly, could enrich the overall pool of knowledge. Unfortunately, however, these innovations are not shared, because proposals are proprietary and confidential. The award takes the form of a contract to implement the statement of work in the request for proposals, which does not lead to publication of the winner's approach. Such innovations are treated as trade secrets.

Incentives for innovation would be better placed outside the bidding process. This, however, has its own difficulties. Several senior USAID project developers have tried seeking input from the consulting industry. Partly in response to the criticisms raised above and partly in an admirable quest for better input and design, they have circulated drafts for comment before issuing a final request for proposals. The results have been disappointing.

The consulting industry is unlikely to invest much time in commenting on a draft for two important reasons. First, analysis and comment cost money. Those assigned to the task must be pulled off other billable work or off analysis of actual (not draft) requests for proposals and preparation of bids. The cost will not necessarily be recovered when the draft becomes final, because the draft may never become final and the comments may not be accepted or incorporated. Although it is reasonable to expect development professionals to provide input to improve the system, it is unreasonable to expect them to do so in this way. Financial incentives are needed to cover financial losses.

A second constraint on input is that many contractors feel that any lessons they have learned can be used to give them a competitive advantage once the proposal is issued. It is therefore self-defeating to improve the overall proposal process if it reduces their competitive edge. Legal reform is a business. Although it is heavily populated by dedicated individuals who would like to see all reforms done more effectively, these individuals need jobs, and withholding valuable information until the bidding stage is perceived as one means of increasing the likelihood of continued employment.

Incentive Problem 3: High Incentives for Guarding Information

Theoretically, each new legal reform endeavor deepens the overall body of knowledge about such work. In reality, a number of people do learn something, probably even something useful, but the lessons are unlikely to be shared widely. Most donors and projects have information management or sharing directives, and these often result in the creation or enlargement of report libraries but seldom in any significant increase in knowledge among implementers.

The value of a library is not just in the quantity of volumes it stores but also in the quality of those volumes and the number of people who use them. The legal reform industry has produced thousands of reports and other materials, many of them stored in donor libraries, which are increasingly accessible on the Internet. Virtually every topic of law has been assessed, analyzed, and opined upon, but very few ever read this material. Why not?

As already noted, few practitioners have the time to research and analyze existing literature because they are paid to know and not to learn. For those who have the time, or who are paid to study, much of the available literature is not worth the effort, and many of the better documents are unavailable. Both quality and availability are influenced by incentives.

Reports are written primarily by people who are paid by those who receive the reports. The writer's job is to provide information in such a way as to meet the client's expectations. One of those expectations is implementation success that will justify ongoing or new funding. If a report points out that some aspect of a project is not successful, this may affect the flow of funding. Thus, there are very few reports detailing mistakes or failures. Where they exist, implementers know how to describe them as successes.

It would seem that the project managers of the funding organization could overcome this self-serving trend, but that too is difficult. A manager's job is to make sure that implementers stay on course, avoid mistakes, and use funds well. If that has not happened, then managers may be subject to career setbacks. Their bosses could also provide safeguards against self-serving assessments, but they too must answer to someone higher with similar expectations. In short, there is an unintended but natural "conspiracy" all along the funding chain to characterize weakness as strength and failure as success to avoid sanctions perceived as inherent in telling the truth. As long as mistakes are considered sins, almost no one is going to admit them. Hiding mistakes, rather than learning from them, is the norm.

Lessons from mistakes often may not be documented, but many other lessons are. Donor shelves are replete with excellent analyses and insightful assessments that could be useful to others pursuing the same reform goals. But very few of these documents journey from the shelves—whether physical or electronic—to a wider audience, for several reasons.

Some of the best analyses are withheld by the donors due to political sensibilities. Critical assessments that include open, honest assessments of counterparts (including government, private sector, donor, and other counterparts) are withheld or sanitized to avoid controversy. For World Bank projects, this is particularly problematic, as almost all useful analysis is deemed to belong to the government of the country being analyzed and often unavailable to the broader legal reform community. Information flow is thus cut off at the outset.

Reports prepared by contractors are a somewhat different matter. In the USAID context, all contractor work product belongs to the public, unless withheld by USAID. It is difficult to believe this, however, when trying to obtain copies from competitors. Contractors frequently treat work-for-hire under USAID projects as privileged information to be withheld from competitors, even if not being used for competition. As noted previously, such information is believed to give a competitive edge for winning additional work, and there is no perceived upside to sharing it openly if it may lower the chances of winning. Most contracts require all technical reports to be filed directly with USAID, but that does not make the information any easier to find or retrieve. Guarding information is still seen as a useful and necessary competitive strategy.

Information can be shared in numerous ways, not only through reports. One popular approach among donors and some government counterparts is to organize structured collaboration between various implementers. This often takes the form of "donor coordination meetings" among multiple donors or similar events among multiple implementers of one donor. But the more official these meetings are, the less information is exchanged. Once again, the incentives are going in the wrong direction.

Donors and their implementers compete with each other. Although they readily espouse common goals, they just as readily work at odds. Formal meetings breed formal presentations, in which each presenter puts the best face forward to impress their superiors, counterparts, and other participants. They do not admit difficulties or shortcomings in these settings, fearing the consequences of showing weakness. These consequences can be economic (contractors regularly lobby to get donors to reassign resources to them from someone else's struggling project) or simply embarrassment among peers. If the emperor has no clothes, it is pretty certain that no one will point this out during a collaboration meeting.

Despite these constraints, collaboration does occur—among friends. In my experience, the best information exchange happens among implementers, counterparts, and consultants who get to know one another informally. The relationship provides a context of trust in which individuals can openly explore their assumptions, difficulties, and challenges without concern for negative career impact. It is hard to institutionalize such trust, but considering how to encourage relationship building should be part of project design.

Incentive Problem 4: Disconnection between Performance and Awards

In a normal market for services, demand precedes and defines supply, with suppliers rewarded based on their ability to satisfy the needs of the buyers. This feedback loop allows for correction and learning as buyers communicate satisfaction and dissatisfaction to the suppliers. Legal reform is not a normal market, however, because supply and demand are not sufficiently connected.

The problems arise at various levels. First, the market is not sufficiently based on demand but is driven by suppliers of legal reform assistance. Donor nations compete to provide assistance based on their own need to influence the beneficiary for any number of reasons: altruism in improving socioeconomic conditions, self-interest in improving markets, or foreign policy concerns of rewarding collaboration. In the end, recipient countries are not generally shopping for services in a competitive market but are being offered free or subsidized assistance on a take-it-or-leave-it basis. As one Macedonian colleague put it, "How can we possibly say 'no' to a donor?"

Second, the beneficiaries are often insufficiently or incorrectly identified, so that suppliers are not necessarily getting feedback from the right parties. Legal reform projects frequently seek to satisfy only those stakeholders directly involved in the legal system: fellow lawyers, judges, and law professors. The purpose of commercial law reforms, however, is not to have better laws but to enhance socioeconomic development, which would suggest that the business sector should be involved in defining needs and priorities ("demand"). But private sector businesses are seldom an integral part of commercial law projects, except as a target group for education when lawyers and professors (who often have no business experience) complete their reforms of the business environment. Put another way, legal reformers do not learn what they ought to because they are talking to the wrong people about what they do. Just because lawyers or judges are pleased with the reforms does not mean that the heart of the economy is beating better. Unless economic actors become the focus of the reform efforts, practitioners are merely talking to themselves.

Third, beneficiaries do not determine success or failure: Donors do. Contractors fail when they do not meet various requirements for deliverables under their contracts with donor agencies. Deliverables are designed to produce certain results—drafting of new laws, for example—which in turn are supposed to produce positive socioeconomic change. A contractor can be completely successful and receive full payment even if full performance has resulted in negligible benefits. Lessons learned by contractors relate primarily to pleasing donors to ensure future contracts, which may not require significant performance adjustments. There are few, if any, direct incentives to adjust performance for greater economic impact.

This problem is exacerbated by the attenuated process of design, implementation, and evaluation of projects. Procurement regulations often prohibit those who design projects from bidding to implement those projects. Thus, potential for learning from mistakes in design is reduced. Service providers who eventually win a donor's request for proposals frequently employ professional proposal writers or home-office managers who do not participate meaningfully in the actual implementation. Implementers themselves tend to be mobile consultants who move from project to project, executing contracts for which they provided little if any input at the design stage. After their work is completed, the project will eventually be evaluated for impact by yet another team working for either the donor or a competing contractor. Measurable impact may take years to appear, by which point the designers and implementers have already moved on to other countries and projects. If any lessons are learned along the way, they may not influence future design or implementation. As already noted, such lessons are not actively captured or imparted through any system of structured learning.

Need for New Mind-Sets and Incentive Structures

The lessons of an earlier generation of rule-of-law aid practitioners were lost along the way to the most recent wave of efforts. Hasty transplants and short time frames, among others, were expressly identified in the 1970s as problems, yet practitioners have had to rediscover these findings anew, with substantial waste of resources. Improving the learning curve will require reduction of learning constraints. If the theories presented above about the nature of these constraints are correct, then most of the barriers can be reduced by correcting assumptions and adjusting incentives.

The starting point for change is in the assumptions made by rule-of-law practitioners, because assumptions define both approach and the critiques of that approach. The legal reform community must recognize that law is only a tool for reform and not its goal. This will allow practitioners to gear their efforts more effectively toward the actual goal: socioeconomic prosperity. Prosperity will require changes in law, but as an outgrowth of a policy development process that flows from popular demand for change. By recognizing that law reforms are only one step in a more complex process, the legal reform community can begin to develop a more complete and effective analytical framework, which will allow for the design and implementation of assistance programs that are better calculated to achieve the prosperity desired.

The rule-of-law aid community also needs to reconsider the incentive systems of the legal reform industry and how they affect learning. Currently, the system does not actively promote learning or distribution of knowledge. Practitioners will behave differently, however, if the incentives of the industry are redesigned to favor sharing over hoarding and reward investment in learning. The community must also institutionalize the learning process on an industry basis. Legal reform is a separate subspecialty of economic development (not law) requiring a specialized body of courses and materials available for practitioners.

Changes are under way. A small but increasing number of projects are being designed with serious commitment to interacting effectively with a broader range of relevant stakeholders. Some of these newer projects also commit substantial resources to public education to ensure broader understanding and acceptance of proposed reforms. Unfortunately, a greater number of projects continue to operate under old assumptions and incentives in which interaction is limited to small working groups and public education consists of a few brochures.

More changes are needed. Postcommunist countries continue to struggle with internal and external demand for competitive commercial environments. Little will be achieved, however, unless those involved in rule-of-law reform can actually learn the lessons available from past efforts. Such learning will require a candid assessment of current work and a commitment to reform. This may entail a temporary increase in financial expenditure by those paying for commercial reform, but such costs should be readily recoverable from the improvements that result from finally applying the lessons that should have already been learned.

Notes

An earlier version of this chapter was originally published as Carnegie Paper no. 57 (April 2005).

1. Richard E. Messick, "Judicial Reform and Economic Development: A Survey of the Issues," *World Bank Research Observer* 14, no. 1 (February 1999). See particularly the discussion of the law and development movement, pp. 125–8.
2. Clearly, bankruptcy laws are needed as part of the overall framework for commercial transactions. The high priority, however, seems to be based on the need for liquidation of defunct state-owned companies, not for an efficient market-exit mechanism when commercial enterprises fail. In the case of Serbia, bankruptcy law has been seen as a solution to the political problem of putting unpaid workers out of their jobs in failed state companies by shifting the responsibility for the layoffs from the state to the judges. Judges see this and resist by delaying cases for years.
3. The United States is not the only example of this "slow" reform. Even much smaller Western democracies, such as Austria and the Netherlands, can take years from inception to passage of new laws, using well-developed, existing mechanisms and processes.
4. The systemic approach should include reevaluation of the existing system in light of existing needs. Judicial systems of many transition countries were not designed to adjudicate commercial disputes between private parties. In the former Yugoslav republics, common problems of excessive delays indicate that such delays were deliberately designed into the system, especially as the state became one of the principal debtors subject to suit. Bosnia recently replaced its system with one designed to achieve more rapid, responsible resolution of claims. Reform can result in doing the wrong things more efficiently through improved court administration and management without necessarily addressing the more important problems of design.

CHAPTER SEVEN

The Legal Empowerment Alternative

STEPHEN GOLUB

LEGAL EMPOWERMENT is the use of legal services, often in combination with related development activities, to increase disadvantaged populations' control over their lives. It is both an alternative to the problematic, state-centric rule-of-law orthodoxy and a means of making rights-based development a reality by using law to support broader socioeconomic development initiatives.

This alternative paradigm, a manifestation of community-driven as well as rights-based development, is grounded in grass roots needs and activities but can translate community-level work into impact on national laws and institutions. It prioritizes civil society support because that is typically the best route to strengthening the legal capacities and power of the poor. But legal empowerment engages government wherever possible and does not preclude important roles for dedicated officials and ministries. It also addresses a central reality that the rule-of-law orthodoxy overlooks: In many developing countries, laws benefiting the poor exist on paper but not in practice unless the poor or their allies push for the laws' enforcement.

Legal empowerment differs from the rule-of-law orthodoxy in at least four additional ways: (1) attorneys support the poor as partners, instead of dominating them as proprietors of expertise; (2) the disadvantaged play a role in setting priorities, rather than government officials and donor personnel dictating the agenda; (3) addressing these priorities frequently involves nonjudicial strategies that transcend narrow notions of legal systems, justice sectors, and institution building; and (4) even more broadly, the use of law is often just part of integrated strategies that include other development activities.

This alternative approach is fundamentally more about power than about law. Although legal empowerment takes many forms, it typically *does not* involve legions of lawyers citing, using, and teaching laws to the exclusion or even detriment of other development activities and strategies. Rather, this approach generally places laws and lawyers in supportive roles for broader development strategies.

True, legal empowerment can involve lawyers pursuing sophisticated public interest litigation in some contexts—although even in such instances it best builds on community or societal mobilization that makes the court case a part of a larger effort and that makes implementation of a favorable ruling more likely. But legal empowerment can equally involve a group of women who become aware that they have rights without knowing the details of the law, or who learn what government office to approach for certain services and how to do so, and whose knowledge complements literacy, livelihood, or organizing efforts that enhance their power to battle domestic violence, assert inheritance rights, or otherwise pursue their priorities.

Thus, legal empowerment is not simply an alternative to the rule-of-law orthodoxy; it should be integrated into many mainstream socioeconomic development efforts that generally do not address the rule of law or the legal needs of the poor. Though still exceptions to the rule, there are increasing instances of this "mainstreaming" taking place in ways that benefit human rights, development, and project performance. Examples include initiatives addressing natural resources management in Ecuador, public health in South Africa, land reform in the Philippines, women's literacy and livelihood in Nepal, reproductive health in Senegal, and gender equity in Bangladesh.

This alternative approach puts community-driven and rights-based development into effect by offering concrete mechanisms involving, but not limited to, legal services. It can help alleviate poverty, advance the rights of the disadvantaged, and make the rule of law more of a reality for them. So far, however, legal empowerment efforts mainly consist of diverse civil society initiatives rather than deliberate donor programs. As a result, it is underappreciated and underused.

The upshot for rule-of-law development practitioners is that they need to think less like lawyers and more like agents of social change.

Conversely, development practitioners in other fields could benefit from thinking a bit more like lawyers and human rights advocates. The dual changes in perspective will open up vistas for using law to make a greater contribution to development, breaching the programmatic isolation represented by the rule-of-law orthodoxy. Both groups also should stop assuming that assistance to state institutions yields greater impact and more sustainable outcomes than does support for civil society. In key respects, the opposite is the case.

Legal empowerment is not necessarily the correct path to pursue under all circumstances. Nor is the dominant paradigm always inapplicable. Furthermore, the two are not mutually exclusive. But many development agencies that profess pro-poor priorities invest far more in building up government legal institutions and elites than in fortifying impoverished populations' legal capacities and power.[1] In the process, they often insufficiently heed the priorities of the poor, the experience of successful efforts to empower them, and the need to build up civil society if governments and their legal systems are to become responsive and accountable.

A growing array of qualitative and quantitative research suggests that where it has been pursued, legal empowerment has helped advance poverty alleviation, good governance, and other development goals. This alternative paradigm offers the added value of putting community-driven and rights-based development into effect by offering concrete mechanisms, involving legal services, for advancing the rights of the poor. Legal empowerment accordingly merits substantially increased financial and political support, whether directly or under the rubrics of rule-of-law development or mainstream socioeconomic development initiatives.

Legal empowerment both advances and transcends the rule of law. It advances the rule of law in the sense that where the poor have more power they are better able to make government officials implement the law and influential private parties abide by it. Such power also enables disadvantaged groups to play a greater role in local and national law reform. In these crucial respects, it builds good governance.

But legal empowerment is also about far more than the rule of law or governance; it is about poverty alleviation, broadly defined to include empowerment as well as material improvement. Many of its goals and results vindicate or expand the rights of the poor, whether framed in terms of local, national, or international law. But this is not always the same as their gaining greater control over their lives—sometimes dramatically, but often in subtle or apparently minor ways that never-theless mean a great deal to people scraping to get by. Thus, to reem-phasize the point, the key concept in legal empowerment is not law; it is power.

Nature of Legal Empowerment

Legal empowerment is consistent with a more general concept used by the World Bank: "In its broadest sense, empowerment is the expansion of freedom of choice and action."[2] The distinguishing feature of legal empowerment is that it involves the use of any of a diverse array of legal services for the poor to help advance those freedoms. At the same time, this legal work is often only a part (and not necessarily the most impor-tant part) of an integrated strategy that features other development ac-tivities—group formation, literacy training, or livelihood development, for instance.

In contrast with the rule-of-law orthodoxy, a strategy of fostering le-gal empowerment typically involves:

- An emphasis on strengthening the roles, capacities, and power of the disadvantaged and civil society;
- The selection of issues and strategies flowing from the evolving needs and preferences of the poor, rather than starting with a pre-determined, top-down focus on judiciaries or other state institu-tions;
- Attention to administrative agencies, local governments, informal justice systems, media, community organizing, group formation, or other processes and institutions that can be used to advance the poor's rights and well-being, rather than a focus on a narrowly de-fined justice sector;
- Civil society partnership with the state where there is genuine open-ness to reform on the part of governments, agencies, or state per-sonnel, and pressure on the state where that presents an effective alternative for the disadvantaged; and
- Greater attention to domestic ideas and initiatives, or experience from other developing countries, rather than Western imports.

Core Components

My definition of legal empowerment emphasizes the use of legal ser-vices and related development activities. By "legal services" I mean the following sorts of activities:

- counseling, mediation, negotiation, and other forms of nonjudicial representation;
- litigation, both on an individual basis and through public interest lawsuits designed to affect policies, effect precedents, or otherwise benefit large numbers of people;
- enhancing people's legal knowledge and skills through training, media, public education, advice, and other mechanisms;
- development of and services by paralegals (laypersons, often drawn from the groups they serve, who receive specialized legal training and who provide various forms of legal education, advice, and assistance to the disadvantaged); and
- advocating for, advising on, and building the poor's capacities regarding legal, regulatory, and policy reform.

In many country contexts, litigation is only one of numerous options used by legal services organizations and often constitutes a course of last resort. Most legal issues affecting the poor are handled not by judiciaries but by administrative law, local governments, alternative dispute resolution, and informal processes. And even where the courts are an option, the poor often prefer these alternatives because they are far more accessible (both geographically and financially) and comprehensible.

The "related activities" in my definition are any activities that complement legal services, but which themselves are not inherently law-oriented in nature. They include community organizing, group formation, political mobilization, and use of media. They may also involve development-oriented endeavors, such as livelihood development, microcredit provision, literacy training, reproductive health services, and natural resources management.

Legal services can in and of themselves constitute and produce legal empowerment, but experience indicates that greater impact frequently occurs when they are integrated with related development activities. Some links may be indirect, implicit, or initially unplanned, as in the case of a group formed for another purpose (such as microcredit) that later makes use of legal services.

Rights-Based Approach to Development

Legal empowerment should be seen as a practical strategy for implementing a rights-based approach to development. Although much good work and thinking are going into articulating the notion of rights-based development, the clarity of the concept still leaves much to be desired. Thus, as the UN Office of the High Commissioner for Human Rights (OHCHR) has noted, "There is no single, universally agreed rights-based approach, although there may be an emerging consensus on the basic constituent elements."[3] The OHCHR expands on this to suggest that "while a State is primarily responsible for realizing the human rights of the people living within its jurisdiction, other States and non-State actors are also obliged to contribute to, or at the very least not to violate, human rights."[4] It also highlights empowerment, participation, international human rights' universality, and numerous other concepts and activities as key elements of the approach.

In a crucial way, legal empowerment *is* a rights-based approach: It uses legal services to help the poor learn, act on, and enforce their rights in pursuit of development's poverty-alleviating goal. The realization of empowerment, freedom, and poverty alleviation typically equals enforcement of various human rights. Moreover, legal empowerment involves concrete, practical activities that directly feature the poor, in contrast with some more conceptual approaches to rights-based development.

Yet as emphasized above, legal empowerment is about power even more than it is about law. True, in practice, the goal of advancing the rights of the poor often is one and the same as alleviating their poverty. And much activity toward this end is rights-based in nature: teaching them relevant laws; building their capacities to use those laws themselves; providing legal representation where necessary; and drawing on such rights as freedom of speech, assembly, and association. But legal empowerment also often involves related development activities such as community organizing, group formation, livelihood development, and literacy training.

Thus, legal empowerment uses various mechanisms, many rights-based but some not, as means toward the *end* of making human rights a reality for the poor. It could accordingly be considered *rights-oriented* and not exclusively rights-based. But this distinction could risk splitting definitional hairs in ways that make no difference to the disadvantaged.

Nexus with Poverty Alleviation and Other Goals

Legal empowerment ultimately is about poverty alleviation, both in the narrow and broader meanings of the term. It contributes to poverty alleviation, narrowly defined, by improving material standards of living and accordingly addressing what is often called "income poverty." Thus, women may be less poor and have more control over their lives if they gain the right to work (and resulting employment) or a fair share of inheritances. The same applies to farmers and urban populations who respectively obtain land ownership and secure housing.

The UN Development Program (UNDP) and most of the development community also view poverty alleviation more broadly, however, often using the term *human poverty* and reflecting the fact that the poor "often define their own lot not so much in terms of 'lack of money' as an absence of empowerment."[5] Poverty alleviation accordingly includes increasing the capacities (such as legal knowledge and skills), participation, opportunities, and, most fundamentally, power of the poor concerning actions and decisions that affect their lives. Women are less poor and have more control to the extent that they affect government or family decisions, whether effecting gender equity or halting domestic violence. Minority groups similarly may benefit where their cultures are respected or they influence majority perspectives and policies. Legal empowerment helps achieve those goals.

Legal empowerment should also be viewed in the context of evolving thinking that illuminates how empowerment, human rights, freedom, development, and poverty alleviation blend in practice: Reaching one such goal often equals achieving another. In *Development as Freedom*, Sen addresses the processes through which people assume increasing control over their lives.[6] UNDP has similarly linked human development, human rights, and seven essential freedoms.[7] The World Bank advocates "facilitating empowerment" as a key means of attacking poverty.[8] Thus the notion of control contained in the definition of legal empowerment is equivalent to both freedom and power for the poor.

A number of donors have endorsed the kind of cross-sectoral integration represented by legal empowerment, although carrying it out in practice has been more problematic. A U.S. Agency for International Development (USAID) study found that the linkages of its democracy and governance sector (which includes law programs) "with other sectors are an emerging development success story."[9] The United Kingdom's Department for International Development (DFID) policy guidance highlights how its justice sector work can pursue entry points through public health, rural livelihood, or urban development projects.[10] The potential benefits of legal empowerment work are implied in various academic studies that point to the importance of civil society capacity building, organization, or political influence in improving the lives of the disadvantaged.[11] Other research identifies vibrant roles for nongovernmental organizations (NGOs) in successful development efforts, especially when they are able to engage or collaborate with government.[12] By building the poor's legal capacities, organization, and NGO links, legal empowerment may be particularly promising in connection with views of community-driven development articulated by Gupta et al.[13] For instance, it can help forge useful links with higher level government officials in situations where their local subordinates serve local vested interests. This can enhance project monitoring, accountability, and performance and of course serve broader development goals.

Central Role of Civil Society

Civil society usually plays a central role in legal empowerment. The most successful and creative legal services for the poor across the globe generally are carried out by NGOs, often in partnership with community-based organizations, or occasionally by law school programs that effectively function as NGOs.[14] This does not absolutely preclude a central role for the state: Sufficiently motivated government units also can carry out legal empowerment programs. However, civil society groups typically demonstrate more dedication, flexibility, and creativity than state institutions and personnel. Despite the best intentions of many such personnel, various actors and factors, not least their co-workers, may block them from doing their jobs properly. Related considerations that frustrate government responsiveness to the poor's legal and other needs include inappropriate resource allocation, excessive bureaucracy, corruption, patronage, gender bias, and general resistance to change.

I am not advocating the replacement of the rule-of-law orthodoxy with a similarly rigid civil society paradigm that naïvely glorifies NGOs as a panacea for poverty or presents them as universally altruistic and honest. It is crucial for donors to separate the wheat from the chaff in supporting civil society. Where civil society is weak, it is important to put in place long-term programs that help build it. Furthermore, legal empowerment is often about good governance, and so state institutions are extremely relevant. Legal empowerment can involve NGOs in building the capacities of state institutions and their personnel, through training and other devices.

What NGOs and their partner populations can do far more effectively than donors, simply by virtue of civil society efforts to extract cooperation from state institutions, is identify government agencies and personnel who manifest dedication, working with them and around their reform-resistant colleagues. In this way, civil society acts as a supportive force for cooperative elements in the state and as a countervailing force against anti-reform elements. Legal empowerment catalyzes this progress in the many contexts where legal knowledge and action are important parts of reformist strategies.

Again, this certainly is not to suggest that all development NGOs are effective, competent, and dedicated. Some are far more interested in developing their own resources than in helping the populations they purportedly serve. Others are so small as to limit their effectiveness (although we should not underestimate the ability of modestly staffed legal services NGOs to generate positive ripple effects through paralegal development, working in partnership with other civil society elements and contributing to policy and law reform advocacy coalitions). But where these constraints apply, they constitute arguments for steps such as involving responsible international NGOs, expanding the pool of persons who could sincerely engage in legal empowerment work (through law school programs, for example), and gradually building up civil society's reach and capacities.

In some war-torn, politically oppressed, or particularly impoverished societies, the presence, power, and capacities of NGOs that could engage in legal empowerment are especially limited. One would not expect assertive advocacy of women's rights, for instance, in areas controlled by many Afghan warlords. How development agencies might cautiously support legal empowerment under such circumstances is a matter I consider below. For now, suffice to say that the same obstacles constricting the work of legal services NGOs in problematic contexts similarly limit the prospects for building effective judiciaries and other legal institutions. Precluding support for the former while pushing ahead with the latter is a lopsided approach to justice and development.

Building a Legal Empowerment Program

Although detailing all elements and steps necessary to build a legal empowerment program is beyond the parameters of this chapter, some of the central parts of the process can be identified here. A wide range of potential elements can go into such a program but two—paralegal development and law school clinics—deserve special attention. In addition, the need for mainstreaming such efforts into the broader arena of donor assistance is crucial.

Wide Range of Potential Elements

A "model" program would comprise a mix of features: prioritizing the needs and concerns of the disadvantaged; emphasizing civil society, including legal services and development NGOs, as well as community-based groups; using whatever forums (often not the courts) the poor can best access in specific situations; encouraging a supportive rather than lead role for lawyers; cooperating with government wherever possible, but pressuring it where necessary; using community organizing or group formation; developing paralegal resources; integrating with mainstream socioeconomic development work; and building on community-level operations to enable the poor to inform or influence systemic change in laws, policies, and state institutions.

This model program inevitably gives way to the reality that legal empowerment work must vary from country to country, issue to issue, and even community to community. In the Philippines, this multifaceted work has featured community organizing and typically deals with administrative law and local governance; in Bangladesh, alternative dispute resolution and informal justice systems; in South Africa, public interest litigation and broad-based mobilization. Paralegal development and law reform cut across numerous legal empowerment initiatives, but there are many exceptions to this rule and many locally determined ways of undertaking these activities.

Legal empowerment programs should take a long-term perspective. It can take at least a few years to start producing impact and even longer for that impact to broaden and deepen. A long-term approach also involves building a public interest bar by supporting law school and NGO programs that engage law students and young attorneys in legal services and that teach them the skills and perspective of development lawyering: how to both teach and learn from the poor; how to view them as partners rather than (subservient) clients; how to analyze problems from a political, cultural, and gender perspective, rather than just a legal one; and how lawyers can advance social change. Conversely, exposing other development fields' young professionals to human rights and legal empowerment considerations could expand their capacities to integrate law and development into their work. In-country and international exchanges also can open up vistas for disadvantaged populations' leaders, NGO lawyers, law students, law professors, development practitioners, and government officials to learn from pertinent experience elsewhere.

Regardless of the exact shape of a legal empowerment program, it can be undertaken under at least three rubrics: (1) as aid specifically directed at legal empowerment; (2) as a part of a broader rule-of-law promotion strategy; or (3) as part of mainstream socioeconomic development work.

The program's effectiveness will hinge not just on *what* work is supported, but *how* it is supported. NGOs that show sufficient progress and potential merit ongoing core funding that enables them to pursue their own agendas in accordance with evolving circumstances and partner populations' priorities, rather than in response to sometimes rigid donor requirements. Similarly, it is best for funding agencies to take a flexible, foundation-like approach. This approach involves gradually identifying grantees, making grants, and building programs as situations evolve. It is in contrast to the project approach that tends to lock in activities at the outset. This is not to say that bilateral and multilateral donors can or should restructure to resemble foundations, but they should set up foundation-like assistance mechanisms for supporting legal empowerment.

This can involve channeling bilateral aid funds to local and international NGOs familiar with grant making, legal empowerment, civil society or grass roots development, as well as to those multilateral development agencies whose mandates and operating styles aim to serve the poor rather than their host governments. Funding for legal empowerment work should not be administered by aid agencies that are constrained by their policies or orientations to work through official channels rather than civil society, unless they can open appropriate funding windows or otherwise modify their operations. Although it would be a great step forward for multilateral banks to mainstream legal empowerment work into their socioeconomic development projects, the funds for that work should be grants rather than loans under most circumstances and should flow through organizations that can best take a foundation-like approach.

Paralegal Development as a Multifaceted Resource

Although this chapter cannot detail the myriad forms that legal empowerment takes, paralegal development merits special mention because it transcends many societies and sectors. As noted above, paralegals are laypersons, often drawn from the groups they serve, who receive specialized legal training and who provide various forms of legal education, advice, and assistance to the disadvantaged. Their education also includes learning through experience, often by soliciting advice from NGO lawyers or other NGO personnel (themselves paralegals) as concrete issues arise. Perhaps, then, the notion of paralegal training should give way to one of "ongoing paralegal development," including but not limited to training.

Depending on their level of sophistication and the needs of the populations they help, paralegal activities may range from providing basic information and advice on the one hand to representation in administrative processes and assisting litigation on the other. The training similarly is pitched to the paralegals' sophistication and levels of prior education.

Toward the more basic end of the paralegal skills spectrum, then, in India, the Karnataka Women's Legal Education Program provides an excellent example:

> [The program] mainly works through what are known as *sanghas* (collectives) to provide women with paralegal training. A *sangha*, typically composed of twenty to twenty-five community members, often is formed by a small local NGO in order to help it address livelihood, family planning, or credit needs. [The program] conducts paralegal workshops for both selected *sangha* members and NGO personnel.
>
> A fundamental feature of *sangha* training in India is the emphasis on attitudinal change. Given the deeply ingrained feelings of inferiority that the culture inculcates in both *dalits* (untouchables) and women, NGOs seek to broaden their perspectives. [The program] does this, in part, by emphasizing gender considerations such as the value of women's reproductive and household work.[15]

Drawing on this legal training and attitudinal change, the women report that they are able to band together against domestic violence in their communities. Armed with basic knowledge of minimum wage laws, they also negotiate better farm wages from local landlords—not necessarily as high as legally required, but better than what they previously were paid.

At the more sophisticated end of the spectrum, South Africa's Black Sash Trust, an NGO, uses professional paralegals to assist citizens with a diversity of problems, such as obtaining government benefits to which they are legally entitled and detecting illegal conduct by government personnel. It also trains volunteer, community-based paralegals. Black Sash builds on both kinds of experience to pursue policy advocacy and press for government accountability on national and state levels, often in partnership with other groups. Its work contributes, for example, to public interest litigation launched by another leading South African NGO, the Legal Resources Centre.

A recent review of Kenyan access to justice projects supported by DFID highlights that paralegal operations further the empowerment of disadvantaged individuals and groups in Kenya by facilitating local communities in the resolution of their own problems in a sustainable manner, playing an important role in civic education, and reaching creatively beyond the bounds of the formal legal system to integrate informal systems of justice.[16] Of course, not all paralegals can achieve such a wide array of results. Their effectiveness often hinges on their levels of education, the degrees to which their communities are organized, the extent to which government is responsive, and the overall political milieu within which they operate. But even modest initial achievements can set the stage for more dramatic impact down the line as conditions and capacities develop.

Law Students: Expanding Legal Empowerment's Pool of Attorneys

Although lawyers often play supportive rather than leading roles regarding legal empowerment, they of course are essential for a number of activities that strengthen disadvantaged populations' control over their lives. The best way to engage attorneys in this kind of work is to expose them to such activities and perspectives while they are in law school through clinical legal education and related activities.[17] Beyond expanding legal services to the poor, this approach expands the students' perspectives, experience, and contacts in ways that enable many to work with the disadvantaged over the long haul.

In South Africa, the Campus Law Clinic of the University of Natal–Durban, which operates much like an NGO, tackles many cases and issues that represent the interests of groups rather than individuals. Through both classroom instruction and actual practice, it familiarizes students with legal issues outside the ambit of the traditional curriculum.

Support by the Open Society Institute, the Ford Foundation, and USAID for clinical legal education in Central and Eastern Europe and the former Soviet Union appears to have contributed to the growth of public interest law in those transitional societies. In Poland and some other countries, this has included building up a nucleus of future attorneys dedicated to progressive legal practice.

The Philippines may be particularly noteworthy because many of the attorneys leading and staffing their very successful legal services NGOs, collectively known as Alternative Law Groups (ALGs), first received exposure to development work while in law school. The Ateneo Human Rights Center, an NGO based at a leading law school, has been particularly instrumental in this regard. But other law schools' programs, as well as ALGs' paid positions and internships for law students, have also contributed to sustaining this integration of development and law.

Coincidentally, the University of Dhaka Faculty of Law is now running a similar program for leading law students from across Bangladesh, immersing them in field research that exposes them to the lives and legal needs of disadvantaged populations. A number of alumni of this effort, and of a clinical legal education program that provides brief placements with NGOs, have gone on to staff legal services groups after graduation.

Finally, the integration of law and development in law schools is also taking hold in some programs in Latin America. As the Dean of Argentina's University of Palermo Law School notes, "the economic crisis in Argentina put us in a new situation where we could not just do public interest litigation, for we could not assume that the bankrupt state could respond to [the court decisions] . . . so we need to work with grassroots and poverty organizations in additional ways" that include paralegals and basing legal service lawyers in poor neighborhoods.[18]

Mainstreaming

Legal empowerment often operates best when it integrates various activities so that the whole is greater than the sum of the parts. This takes place in two ways. The first involves the integration of different kinds of legal services, so that public education, community training, paralegal development, negotiation, mediation, legal advice, litigation, and law reform reinforce one another.

For instance, paralegals engaged in negotiation or mediation can call on lawyers to take cases to court as a last resort; litigation is not usually used but increases the negotiating power of the parties being assisted by the paralegals. Even where a judicial system is terribly flawed, the possibility of going to court can alleviate the power imbalances that usually tip against women and the poor.

The other type of integration takes place where legal services blend with group formation, community organizing, and other activities pursued under the rubric of "mainstream" socioeconomic development fields—for example, rural development, public health, reproductive health, housing, natural resources—and address the goals and concerns of those fields. The work of the Philippines ALGs, for example, is sometimes called "development lawyering" or "developmental legal services" for this reason.

But it is not only legal services NGOs that take the lead in this work. Other NGOs conduct legal empowerment work, sometimes in combination with legal services groups but also on their own. Banchte Shekha, a women's movement based in rural Bangladesh, has improved its members' capacities and well-being through a combination of literacy training, rights education, livelihood development, consciousness raising, organizing, and alternative dispute resolution (ADR). By building on all of these other activities, the Banchte Shekha ADR—a reformed version of a traditional dispute resolution process called *shalish*—both addresses mistreatment of women and ameliorates the power imbalances that often tilt ADR against them. Survey research conducted by the Asia Foundation for the Asian Development Bank (ADB), discussed in more detail in the section below on impact, documents the NGO's positive impact on dowry, women's status, and other issues. A regrettably short-lived, USAID-supported initiative in the 1990s further illustrated the value of integrating law and mainstream development, in this instance legal and family planning services. Communities whose members were already familiar with reproductive health NGOs readily accepted the integrated programs. In introducing legal services, those NGOs drew on the goodwill established through many years of contact with the communities. An evaluation of the project confirmed the mutually beneficial relationship of the two kinds of work.[19]

One of the more significant forms of mainstreaming takes place where legal services facilitate agrarian reform and other land tenure improvements for the disadvantaged (for example, helping women with land claims stemming from divorce or inheritance). The Asia Foundation study mentioned above finds that research NGO lawyers and paralegals can contribute to the success of agrarian reform programs. The Rural Development Institute (RDI) similarly documents the positive contribution of legal services to such programs.[20] It also highlights the roles civil society can play more generally, urging aid donors to "provide technical assistance and financial support to indigenous non-governmental organizations, labor organizations, and other broad-based groups that are able to conduct essential grassroots education and organizing on the land reform issue."[21] The manifold benefits of agrarian reform include poverty-alleviating increases in crop production, nutritional welfare, and incomes; ripple effects on economic growth; and contributions to democratic development and stability.[22]

If legal services are to be mainstreamed into socioeconomic development, it will be necessary to overcome the sectoral divisions that hinder development effectiveness. One place to start would be the most basic sorts of workshops within development agencies. At these sessions, legal practitioners and those from other disciplines could share experiences about specific projects and resulting lessons. Those in the legal field would have more to learn than to teach about conducting impact-oriented research. However, they might bring to the table perspectives about ways of advancing rights and alleviating poverty simultaneously, perhaps fleshing out the concept of a rights-based approach to development.

Aid agencies should adopt structural changes to make mainstreaming possible. Their headquarters should launch cross-sectoral working groups to learn about existing civil society efforts and impact concerning legal empowerment, convert these lessons into guidance for field offices, and provide an impetus for those offices to consider launching legal empowerment initiatives.

A related process should take place in these agencies' country offices, with water or forest sector staff, for example, exploring how legal services might benefit their partner populations, as well as their current and potential projects. Conversely, justice sector staff (or governance sector colleagues who handle law-oriented programs in some organizations) could examine how a broader, cross-sectoral approach could benefit their work. To avoid a top-down approach, these efforts not only should involve consultation with partner groups but also should consider relevant efforts already under way in the country, particularly those of civil society, with a view toward possibly supporting or building on them. The end result of these processes would be initiatives that feature or include legal empowerment.

Reaching the Poorest of the Poor

What of the many situations in which civil society, legal services, and the basic capacities of the poor are torn by war, crushed by repression, stunted by severe poverty itself, or in the early stages of recovering from any of these situations? Admittedly, legal empowerment works best in the presence of a vibrant civil society. It may not be feasible for reaching the poorest of the poor. Legal empowerment (or, for that matter, state legal institutions) should not automatically be included in the initial mix of development efforts. Sometimes basic socioeconomic recovery should be the priority.

Still, despite these constraints, the building blocks of legal empowerment can be put in place. As discussed above, group formation around basic socioeconomic needs can provide an entry point for mainstreaming subsequent law-oriented work. A long-term strategy of building up a rights-oriented civil society can benefit both development and human rights.

Local conditions permitting, the long road toward the poorest of the poor achieving control over their lives can include introducing them to the very notion that they have rights and the ways in which those rights can benefit their daily existence. Training them regarding these matters should take account of their priorities, their levels of education, and the nature of the laws most relevant to them. This generally translates into the use of interactive, "popular education" methodologies rather than law lectures, and a focus on domestic laws rather than international human rights treaties (unless of course the domestic laws repress rather than serve the poor).

International NGOs may play leading roles in these efforts where local conditions or insufficient capacities bar domestic NGOs and community-based groups from doing so. A goal, of course, is to build those domestic capacities over time.

Filling the Informational Vacuum

Legal empowerment constitutes an appealing alternative to the rule-of-law orthodoxy, in that it has contributed to poverty alleviation, good governance, and other development goals. But the legal field remains far behind other development fields in documenting and learning from impact. Along with more general research on law and development, we need to better understand the dynamics underlying legal empowerment, the challenges it faces, and the impact it achieves.

A legal empowerment program, then, should include rigorous research that can help determine the most effective strategies and activities, as well as contribute knowledge to governance, rule-of-law, and socioeconomic development work. Quantitative and qualitative tools such as survey research and rapid rural appraisals should be used to scrutinize the dynamics that contribute to (or constrain) successful legal empowerment work, so as to derive lessons that will help human rights and development organizations build on that experience. At the same time, it is important to avoid becoming consumed by short-term indicators and other bureaucratic mechanisms that can counterproductively dominate monitoring and evaluation.

USAID (in Nepal), the Asia Foundation and ADB (in the Bangladesh and the Philippines), and the World Bank (in Ecuador) have begun to use research to fill the large informational vacuum. But we need more ambitious and varied studies across the globe if the international community is to most effectively integrate law and development so as to benefit the poor.

Impact and Activities

An expanding array of studies document legal empowerment's impact in both qualitative and quantitative terms. Most of that impact concerns poverty alleviation. But as noted above, in many instances it also can be framed in other general terms (such as justice, human rights, freedom, and, of course, empowerment) or more specific goals (such as improved governance, gender equity, or environmental protection).

Multicountry Documentation of Impact

In recent years, a few international studies have illuminated legal empowerment's manifold approaches and types of impact. A seven-nation, year-long examination of legal empowerment, conducted by the Asia Foundation for the ADB, concludes that this work "helps to advance good governance and to reduce poverty in both substantial and subtle ways."[23] The documented benefits range from Thai constitutional and consumer protection reforms to implementation of Pakistani women's voting rights and access to credit.

A multicountry review for the World Bank describes the poverty-alleviating impact of legal services NGOs and, by implication, of legal empowerment.[24] It highlights, inter alia, how such NGOs help enforce social and economic rights, facilitate the poor's engagement with local governance, assist women to reform laws that bar them from participating in development, and promote recovery in postconflict countries.

Finally, the Ford Foundation's eighteen-month review of legal services and related work by its grantees across the globe finds considerable positive impact on equitable and sustainable development, as well as on human rights, civic participation, and government accountability.[25] The resulting book describes the impact of university-based legal aid clinics, paralegals, public interest litigation, and law-related research, even in China, Eastern Europe, and other places where civil society is relatively weak.

National Impact

The picture I have so far sketched of legal empowerment mainly depicts community-oriented work, but legal empowerment can build on that work to have national impact (as well as impact on the state and province level, which in some countries is where important policy and legal decisions are made). The Asia Foundation/ADB, World Bank, and Ford Foundation reports, as well as other sources, document that impact to various degrees, describing numerous instances in which legal empowerment has helped generate such macrolevel reform.

For example, the Philippine ALGs have contributed to scores of national regulations and laws concerning agrarian reform, violence against women, indigenous peoples' rights, environmental protection, and a host of other issues.[26] Arguably, they have played roles in the bulk of such pro-poor reforms over the past decade, providing legal expertise and other assistance for coalitions of NGOs, national federations of poor people's organizations, and (sometimes) religious groups.

The ALGs derive their expertise and credibility from working on a grass roots level, where they make the most of existing laws while learning what reforms might make sense and, most crucially, what reforms the disadvantaged might want. They heavily engage in paralegal development, community training, and advocacy. Typically partnering with community-based organizations—and strengthening those groups' internal cohesiveness in the process—ALGs help farmers to avail themselves of land reform; fishing associations to guard their waters against outsiders' environmentally destructive practices that cut into their catch; community associations to understand and participate in local budgeting and governance; and other disadvantaged groups to act on local needs and priorities. So much of their work involves helping the disadvantaged interact with local elected and administrative officials that it is appropriate to think of the ALGs in terms of governance as well as law.

With the exception of a few fields, such as gender-oriented work, the ALGs largely have not worked through the Philippine courts for several reasons: judicial conservatism and corruption; the suitability of administrative, legislative, and other noncourt mechanisms to address partner populations' needs; and the fact that these populations are more legally self-sufficient when noncourt approaches are used.

Nevertheless, legal empowerment strategies can effectively use public interest litigation in those circumstances where there are prospects of winning and implementing favorable decisions, where it does not exclude the disadvantaged from decision making, and where its use does not preclude complementary approaches. This approach can be found in South Africa, where public interest litigation has built on a base of community and political activism. This has yielded a string of landmark court victories stretching over more than two decades, both vindicating South Africans' rights and increasing their control over their lives.

Under apartheid, the Legal Resources Centre, the university-based Centre for Applied Legal Studies, and their allies used public interest litigation to undermine restrictions on blacks' residence and travel rights, abuse of prisoners in detention, and the state policy of establishing black "homelands" in resource-poor parts of the country. In recent years, newer legal services NGOs have joined with those older centers to have significant impact on housing, land, and health rights and a host of other issues. Similarly oriented NGOs in neighboring countries, such as Namibia's Legal Assistance Centre, have also had notable success in this vein.

It is important to emphasize, however, the degree to which public interest litigation draws on and works with community concerns, not least in the identification of clients and cases. As explained by the head of the Legal Resources Centre's Constitutional Litigation Unit:

We work closely with community advice offices, which are sometimes an important focus for community organisation, public education and advocacy.

Our clients are often a community—for example in land restitution claims or a large eviction case.

We work in partnership with other NGOs which themselves are involved in supporting community organisation—most classically [under apartheid], when we supported communities resisting forced removal from their land, we worked very closely with . . . Black Sash [an NGO that provides grassroots paralegal assistance and training], which used community workers and field workers.

We represent organisations which are themselves the focus for a social movement—for example the Treatment Action Campaign, which is mobilising and leading the campaign for the provision of anti-retroviral drugs to prevent transmission of HIV, and to treat HIV/AIDS.[27]

Although activist, sophisticated civil society certainly facilitates both grass roots and national legal empowerment initiatives—witness South Africa and the Philippines—legal empowerment can have national impact even in less conducive settings. The Sustainable Use of Biological Resources Project in Ecuador, undertaken by the international NGO CARE in collaboration with local Afro-Ecuadorian groups in the remote northwest part of the country, has generated national reforms and local benefits. The government banned division of communal land into individual lots in response to these groups' identifying such changes as threatening their identity and way of life. The communities also successfully lobbied for Afro-Ecuadorian recognition in the national constitution, including protection for their collective rights as indigenous peoples.[28]

As in the Philippines and South Africa, the national impact of this legal empowerment initiative in Ecuador has built on a base of localized work and impact. These community-level results include the following:

- The paralegals have formed, and themselves joined, higher level organizations focused on conflict management, land titling, and community advisory services.
- Fifty communities have obtained legal status, a prerequisite to formal recognition of property rights.
- Some three dozen communities have secured title to approximately 50,000 hectares of their traditional lands.[29]

In a very different context, Senegal, the UN Children's Fund (UNICEF) provided financial and communications support that helped local NGOs and village women mobilize against female genital mutilation. The efforts facilitated the women learning about both their rights and the health implications of this practice. The result was the parliament's adoption of legislation banning it.[30]

Once again, the national reform was linked to local mobilization, in this case:

> . . . teaching women first about their human rights, followed by other modules related to problem solving, health, and hygiene . . . Although the project had originally targeted 30 villages . . . project organizers, facilitators and participants succeeded in expanding its reach. In November 1999 approximately 80,000 people from 105

villages participated in a ceremony during which they issued a public declaration ending the practice . . .[31]

To return to a general point about legal empowerment, even where foreign initiative has been involved in these cases, it seems to respond to local needs and priorities. In contrast, whatever the justifications for most endeavors carried out in accordance with the rule-of-law orthodoxy, it would not seem that the poor would see better courthouses or judicial administration as issues around which to rally.

The Ecuador and Senegal experiences indicate that where local civil society requires assistance, international organizations can play important facilitating roles regarding legal empowerment. In the end, this work must respond to community priorities, perhaps even more so when the implications are national rather than local. And preferably, the only foreign support that is needed is financial. But as with other development initiatives, there is room for other assistance (such as capacity building) where necessary.

At the same time, it is important not to become too enthralled with national impact, for the reasons I suggested in chapter 5 critiquing the rule-of-law orthodoxy: Changes in laws and policies mean little to the poor if they are not enforced, and enforcement is the exception rather than the rule in most developing countries. Both the Ford Foundation and Asia Foundation/ADB studies emphasize *implementation* of reform and not simply reform per se for this reason. A value of legal empowerment is that it can constitute a feedback loop, through which grass roots experience feeds legal and regulatory change, which further grass roots work in turn converts from reform on paper to reform in practice.

Quantitative Research Indicating Impact

With the caveat about national impact in mind, it is useful to turn to survey research, sometimes complemented by focus groups and other mechanisms, that documents legal empowerment's community-level results. A World Bank assessment of an NGO legal services program it supported for poor women in Ecuador found, inter alia, that as compared with demographically similar nonclient populations, clients experienced significantly less domestic violence, higher rates of child support payments, and enhanced self-esteem.[32] These results have powerful, positive implications for poor women and children. For instance, above and beyond its immediate damage, the poverty-exacerbating impact of violence against women has been well documented by the World Bank and other sources.[33] Reducing the violence yields numerous benefits.

The Asia Foundation/ADB study similarly used quantitative inquiries in two of the seven countries it covered, with similarly favorable results. Survey research, focus groups, and interviews with government officials in the Philippines all indicated that farmers who received NGO capacity-building and related legal services—from Kaisahan, one of the aforementioned ALGs—brought about more successful implementation of a government agrarian reform program than did farmers who did not receive such services. The research also suggested follow-on impact, in terms of greater productivity, income, farm investment, and housing quality among those recipients of legal services.[34]

In Bangladesh, the Asia Foundation/ADB study determined that two broad-based NGOs that integrate legal services with mainstream development work achieved manifold poverty-alleviating impact. Based on comparisons between their member populations and demographically similar control groups, these results included restraining the widespread but illegal practice of *dowry*;[35] successful citizen participation in joint actions and in influencing local government decisions; fostering positive community attitudes toward women's rights and participation in governance; use by the poor of government-managed lands that local elites otherwise seize; and dramatically less reliance on those elites for dispute resolution. The same research found that a third NGO, a legal services group that specializes in community-level mediation, achieved modest impact in some of these regards and an even greater impact on reducing elite dominance of dispute resolution.[36]

Finally, quantitative research on a USAID-funded Women's Empowerment Program in Nepal similarly suggests the value of integrating legal and socioeconomic development work. The program combined literacy classes, arithmetic education, microenterprise development and training, microcredit access, nonformal legal education, and advocacy-oriented group strengthening for 100,000 women. An impact study found that women involved with this project benefited in several ways when compared with control populations. They initiated eight times as many actions for "social change" (such as community development and health projects, and campaigns against domestic violence, alcohol, and gambling by men), participated 30 percent more in family and independent income allocation decisions, and better understood the importance of keeping their daughters in school.[37] A subsequent review concluded that literacy was a key element in the women's empowerment but reaffirmed the value of integrating legal and quasilegal (advocacy-oriented) components with the literacy training and other mainstream development activities.[38]

The findings of these various studies should be approached with some caution, because the methodologies may well benefit from refinement in the future. These inquiries, therefore, should be seen as modest initial forays into issues that merit far more scrutiny. Still, the results suggest the possibility of a powerful impact that affects poverty more directly and cost-effectively than does the dominant rule-of-law paradigm. Those results also indicate that legal empowerment holds great potential for mainstream socioeconomic development efforts.

Implications for Rule-of-Law Aid

Given the significant potential impact and value of a legal empowerment approach, it should be the sole focus of some rule-of-law programs and a core component of most others. This translates into substantial support for legal services and capacity building for the poor, toward the dual ends of both implementing and reforming laws. Where legal empowerment is the sole focus of a law program, it could be organized around general themes such as gender or agrarian issues, or could more comprehensively support pro-poor legal services. Regardless, a guiding principle is responsiveness to disadvantaged populations' legal needs, rather than a top-down focus on a narrow range of legal institutions. This emphasis is also guided by the fact that domestic civil society's homegrown analyses of problems and solutions are often better informed than those of foreign donors.

As a core component of law programs, legal empowerment can complement work with state institutions. This can take the form of collaboration with both upland populations and ministries of natural resources regarding environmental matters, for example. It can also involve strengthening the knowledge, capacities, and organization of those upland groups (or of farmers, or of women) regarding not just the legal issues specific to them but also the conventional justice sector. For instance, legal services for farmers who are originally organized around agrarian concerns may constitute an important complement to state-oriented efforts to improve police professionalism, where those farmers have sufficient legal knowledge and connections (with lawyers, higher level law enforcement personnel, other officials, politicians, NGO staff) to call police to account. Certainly, vibrant civil society is a valuable, even crucial, resource in promoting police accountability. Law enforcement personnel who are prone to abusive, corrupt conduct require outside, organized groups to ensure that state efforts to reorient them prove sustainable. Those groups typically exist for purposes other than police monitoring per se.

The bottom line, then, is not that government is always the problem and civil society the solution. Rather, part of the necessary paradigm shift is to view the justice sector more broadly, which necessarily results in greater support for civil society efforts that address a broader assortment of legal issues and that help or pressure government to do its job better. This can yield not only greater agrarian, gender, and environmental justice, but a greater likelihood of effecting safety, security, and access for the poor even within narrow notions of the sector.

Notes

This chapter was adapted from Stephen Golub's *Beyond Rule of Law Orthodoxy: The Legal Empowerment Alternative*, Carnegie Paper no. 41 (October 2003).

1. For instance, the World Bank's Africa Region Gender and Law Program has laudably implemented a program of matching grants for state and civil society institutions to implement legal services for women, but its funds are very limited and insecure in comparison with what the institution spends on judicial reform. The Bank's Legal and Judicial Reform Practice Group has commendably started to undertake support for legal services for the poor, but the effort is constrained by the relative paucity of funds devoted to such services—less than $400,000 of a $10.6 million judicial reform project in Ecuador, for instance, and even this project was an exception to the rule. See World Bank, *Impact of Legal Aid: Ecuador* (Washington, D.C.: World Bank, February 2003).
2. Available at www.worldbank.org/poverty/whatis/index.htm.
3. UN Office of the High Commissioner for Human Rights (OHCHR), "Rights-Based Approaches: Is There Only One Rights-Based Approach?" (Geneva: OHCHR, n.d.), available at www.unhchr.ch/development/approaches-05.html.
4. OHCHR, *Draft Guidelines: A Human Rights Approach to Poverty Reduction Strategies* (Geneva: OHCHR, 2003), para.13, available at www.unhchr.ch/development/povertyfinal.html.
5. Stephen Brown, "Governance and Human Poverty," *Choices* (September 2002).
6. See Amartya Sen, *Development as Freedom* (New York: Alfred A. Knopf, 2000).
7. See United Nations Development Program (UNDP), *Human Development Report 2000* (New York: Oxford University Press, 2000).
8. See World Bank, *World Development Report 2000/2001: Attacking Poverty* (New York: Oxford University Press, 2000), 7.
9. USAID Center for Development Information and Evaluation, *Linking Democracy and Development: An Idea for the Times*, USAID Evaluation Highlights no. 75 (Washington, D.C.: USAID, December 2001), 1.

10. DFID, Justice and Poverty Reduction: *Safety, Security, and Access to Justice for All* (London: DFID, 2000), 15.

11. See, for example, Michael Edwards, "NGO Performance—What Breeds Success? New Evidence from South Asia," *World Development* 27, no. 2 (1999): 371; P. Evans, "Development Strategies across the Public-Private Divide," *World Development* 24, no. 6 (1996): 1033–37; J. Fox, "How Does Civil Society Thicken? The Political Construction of Social Capital in Rural Mexico," *World Development* 24, no. 6 (1996): 1089–103.

12. See, for example, David Brown and Darcy Ashman, "Participation, Social Capital, Intersectoral Problem Solving: African and Asian Cases," *World Development* 24, no. 9 (1996): 1467–79; Kathryn Smith Pyle, "From Policy Advocate to Policy Maker: NGO in Recife," *Grassroots Development Journal* 21, no. 1 (1997); Maria Maia, "NGOs as Mediators: Their Role in Expertise, Language and Institutional Exemption in Urban Development Planning," Working Paper no. 77 (London: Development Planning, University College, May 1996), 12.

13. Monica Das Gupta, Helena Grandvoinnet, and Mattia Romani, *Fostering Community-Driven Development: What Role for the State?* World Bank Policy Research Working Paper no. 2969 (Washington, D.C.: World Bank, January 2003).

14. See, for example, Stephen Golub and Kim McQuay, "Legal Empowerment: Advancing Good Governance and Poverty Reduction," in *Law and Policy Reform at the Asian Development Bank*, 2001 edition (Manila: Asian Development Bank, 2001); Daniel Manning, *The Role of Legal Services Organizations in Attacking Poverty* (Washington, D.C.: World Bank, September 1999); Mary McClymont and Stephen Golub, eds., *Many Roads to Justice: The Law-Related Work of Ford Foundation Grantees around the World* (New York: Ford Foundation, February 2000).

15. Stephen Golub, "Nonlawyers as Legal Resources for Their Communities," in McClymont and Golub, *Many Roads to Justice*, 309.

16. South Consulting, "Kenya Civil Society Programme: Review of Access to Justice Projects," final draft (Nairobi: South Consulting, 2001), 28–29.

17. See, for example, Columbia University Budapest Law Center/Public Interest Law Initiative, Open Society Justice Initiative, and Fundacja Uniwesyteckich Poradni Prawnych, *Fifth Annual Colloquium on Clinical Legal Education, 15-16 November 2002* (Warsaw: 2002).

18. Dean of the University of Palermo Law School, Argentina, interview by author, July 15, 2003.

19. Karen L. Casper and Sultana Kamal, "Evaluation Report: Community Legal Services Conducted by Family Planning NGOs," a report prepared for the Asia Foundation's Bangladesh office (Dhaka: Asia Foundation, 1995).

20. See, for example, Leonard Rolfes Jr. and Gregory Mohrman, *Legal Aid Centers in Rural Russia: Helping People Improve Their Lives*, RDI Reports on Foreign Aid and Development no. 102 (Seattle: Rural Development Institute, February 2000).

21. See, for example, Roy L. Prosterman and Tim Hanstad, *Land Reform in the 21st Century: New Challenges, New Responses*, RDI Reports on Foreign Aid and Development no. 117 (Seattle: Rural Development Institute, March 2003), 24.

22. Prosterman and Hanstad, *Land Reform*, 4–7.

23. Golub and McQuay, "Legal Empowerment," 12.

24. Manning, *Role of Legal Services Organization*.

25. McClymont and Golub, *Many Roads to Justice*, 5.

26. The "alternative" in their name reflects their development-oriented perspectives and how their operations differ from private legal practice and traditional legal aid in the Philippines.

27. Geoff Budlender, e-mail correspondence with author, January 7, 2003.

28. CARE, "CARE Ecuador's Subir Project," unpublished summary produced by CARE International's Ecuador office, October 2000.

29. Ibid.

30. Available at www.unicef.org/newline/99prl.htm.

31. International Center for Research on Women (ICRW) and the Center for Development and Population Activities (CEDPA), "Report-in-Brief," Promoting Women in Development Program (Washington, D.C.: ICRW and CEDPA, 1999), 1–2.

32. World Bank, *Impact of Legal Aid: Ecuador* (Washington, D.C.: World Bank, February 2003), 11–12.

33. See, for example, Lori L. Heise with Jacqueline Pitanguy and Adrienne Germain, *Violence against Women: The Hidden Health Burden*, World Bank Discussion Paper no. 255 (Washington, D.C.: World Bank, 1994); and Andrew Morrison and María Beatriz Orlando, "Social and Economic Costs of Domestic Violence: Chile and Nicaragua," in *Too Close to Home: Domestic Violence in the Americas*, ed. Andrew Morrison and María Loreto Biehl (Washington, D.C.: Inter-American Development Bank, 1999).

34. See "Appendix 1: The Impact of Legal Empowerment Activities on Agrarian Reform Implementation in the Philippines," in Golub and McQuay, "Legal Empowerment," 135–49.

35. Dowry is the payment of money, livestock, or other material goods by the bride's family to the family of the groom in order to secure a marriage. After the agreed payments are made and marriage occurs, the dowry demands by the groom's family frequently escalate and are accompanied by violence or other abuse against the wife.

36. See "Appendix 2: The Impact of Legal Empowerment on Selected Aspects of Knowledge, Poverty, and Governance in Bangladesh: A Study of Three NGOs," in Golub and McQuay, "Legal Empowerment," 135–49.

37. Rajju Malla Dhakal and Misbah M. Sheikh, *Breaking Barriers—Building Bridges—A Case Study of USAID/Nepal's SO3 Women's Empowerment Program* (Washington, D.C.: Asia Foundation, 1997).

38. Gwen Thomas and Avra Shrestha, *Breaking New Ground: A Case Study of Women's Empowerment in Nepal, Women's Empowerment Program* (Katmandu: USAID/Nepal, 1998).

PART III

Regional Experiences

CHAPTER EIGHT

A Trojan Horse
in China?

MATTHEW STEPHENSON

CONSIDER THE FOLLOWING SCENARIO. Members of the U.S. government, academic, and nonprofit communities notice that in an important region of the developing world, legal institutions and substantive law appear inadequate. Laws seem opaque, unpredictable, and unfair. Legal institutions are inefficient, inaccessible to ordinary people, and subject to corruption and political interference. These legal deficiencies, it is believed, threaten sustained and equitable economic development, the protection of individual rights, and the possibility for greater democratic political reform. Thus, it seems logical to these U.S. observers that the United States, with its sophisticated laws and legal institutions and its years of experience developing a legal system, could provide useful expertise and assistance in promoting legal reform and development in this region.

The region in question is Latin America (and to a lesser extent Africa and Southeast Asia), and the time is the mid-1960s. Efforts to provide U.S. legal assistance in these countries—efforts that came to be known collectively as the law and development movement—began with great optimism. Yet the movement came to a virtual halt only a decade later, after a crisis of disillusionment not only with the specific projects, but with the whole vision of legal development that sustained them. The

The author thanks William Alford, Thomas Carothers, Richard Messick, Katharina Pistor, Matthew Price, Frederick Schauer, and his interviewees for their comments on and contributions to this chapter.

definitive critique of the law and development movement came from two of its most distinguished practitioners. In a 1974 article, David Trubek and Marc Galanter claimed that the law and development movement was based on a flawed theory of law and society, and a flawed ideal of "liberal legalism."[1] In many ways their criticisms echoed the prescient observations of Lawrence Friedman who noted as early as 1969 that among other failings Americans who went abroad to promote legal reform in developing countries lacked any "careful, thought out, explicit theory of law and society or law and development."[2] A more lengthy critique of the projects in Latin America came from a former Ford Foundation official, James Gardner, who claimed that these programs, though well-intentioned, amounted to "legal imperialism."[3] Under the weight of such intense internal and external criticism, the law and development movement withered. Funding dried up, programs were cancelled, and scholars turned their attention to other issues.[4]

It is important, when reflecting on the failure of the law and development movement, to keep in mind that many did not accept all of the critical arguments leveled against the enterprise. Several leading professionals in the law and development field at the time took issue with Trubek and Galanter's theoretical approach, as well as with their conclusions.[5] More recent scholars have pointed out that ten years was far too little time to declare such a complex endeavor a failure and have suggested that Trubek and Galanter's "self-estrangement" may have had more to do with a homegrown crisis of faith in U.S. institutions than experience in the developing world.[6] Nonetheless, it is undoubtedly true that the law and development movement collapsed in the late 1970s, and that much of this collapse can be traced to the weakness of the theoretical foundations of the enterprise. Even if Trubek and Galanter were too hasty in concluding that the movement was fatally flawed, the lack of a well-thought-out, cogent theory of how and why legal reform programs were supposed to work made the movement especially vulnerable to a crisis of confidence.

Given this history, anyone following the recent U.S. "rule-of-law initiative" to help China reform its laws and legal institutions has reason for concern. The opening paragraph of this chapter might apply equally well to the current rule-of-law initiative, focused on China, as to the previous law and development movement focused on Latin America and Africa. There are, of course, important differences, and I do not mean to suggest that legal reform efforts in China are bound to meet the same fate as those of the first law and development movement. Nevertheless, there are clearly parallels between the two. Therefore, given that weak theoretical foundations contributed to the failure—or at least the termination—of the earlier movement, it is worth examining more closely the theoretical foundations supporting the current U.S. push to promote the rule of law in China.[7]

How the "Rule of Law" Got on the U.S.–China Agenda

Since the late 1990s the rule of law has become a higher profile issue on the U.S.–China governmental agenda. Legal reform in China, however, is hardly a new issue for U.S. academics and nongovernmental organizations (NGOs). The China Legal Education and Exchange Committee (CLEEC), for example, has been in operation since 1984, funded initially by a grant from the Ford Foundation and then with additional assistance from the U.S. Information Agency. The Ford Foundation also sponsors numerous other projects in this field. The Asia Foundation has also been involved in sponsoring legal education programs in China for close to two decades, and recently it has started to initiate other types of legal reform projects as well. In addition, the American Bar Association has undertaken grant-funded legal reform and education projects in China. And these are only the largest and highest-profile NGOs.

Thus, when the Clinton administration announced its China rule-of-law initiative in 1997–1998, the U.S. government was not exactly moving into uncharted territory. It seemed, however, that the administration was staking out a place for greater government involvement and attempting to bring together diverse nongovernmental activities into a common framework, conceived of as promoting the rule of law.[8] Why did the Clinton administration suddenly start paying so much attention (at least rhetorically) to the rule of law in China? The answer has to do with the politics of U.S.–China policy, especially in the field of human rights.

Following the 1989 Tiananmen Square crackdown, there had been an annual effort in the U.S. Congress to deny most favored nation (MFN) trading status to China unless it improved its human rights record. Over time, the list of issues tied to MFN status expanded to include things such as nuclear and missile nonproliferation, but human rights remained the primary focus. The Clinton administration initially supported linking MFN status to human rights, but soon changed course when it became clear that such a policy was not viable. The threat to revoke MFN status was not credible given the U.S. stake in political and economic relations with China. Furthermore, the linkage between MFN status and human rights, and the yearly battle over MFN renewal, created substantial political difficulties for the administration and was widely criticized as corrosive to the overall Sino–U.S. relationship.

Therefore, in 1994 the Clinton administration—in keeping with its professed strategy of engagement with China—declared an end to the policy of linking MFN status with China's human rights performance. It was politically important, however, that the president articulate a constructive human rights strategy concurrently with the decision to delink human rights issues and MFN status, lest the administration be seen as abandoning the goal of promoting human rights in China. Therefore, President Clinton announced several instruments the United States would use to promote human rights in lieu of MFN pressure. Among these was "support for efforts underway in China to promote the rule of law, in particular for efforts to achieve legal reforms aimed at specific human rights abuses."[9]

Thus, the rule of law began to find its way onto the U.S.–China agenda, at least on the U.S. side, as a component of a broader human rights strategy intended to promote civil society in China. However, despite Clinton's 1994 announcement that the United States would sponsor programs to promote civil society—and, under that rubric, the rule of law—the proposed programs ran into all sorts of problems because of U.S. laws that prohibit the government from dealing with "gross human rights abusers." Influential members of Congress believed that the United States should not engage in any cooperative programs with the current Chinese government, and they successfully blocked funding for most of the initiatives that the administration proposed. In the end, the U.S. State Department had to retreat, settling for much more modest programs using development assistance money not covered by the problematic laws.

Nonetheless, interest within the State Department and elsewhere in the government for rule-of-law programs (not only in China, but throughout the world) persisted. In late 1996, the post of special coordinator for global rule of law was created within the State Department, and President Clinton brought Paul Gewirtz, a Yale Law School professor, on board to fill the position. Even though Gewirtz's portfolio was global, he was, in the words of one outside observer, "bitten by the China bug." Gewirtz was seen by many as instrumental for getting rule of law more prominently on the agenda for the 1997 summit between President Clinton and Chinese President Jiang Zemin. The Clinton–Jiang summit joint statement, issued on October 29, 1997, prominently mentioned "cooperation in the field of law" as an important way the two countries could promote their common interests.[10] During President Clinton's June 1998 visit to Beijing, the two sides issued another joint statement, this time making somewhat more specific declarations about the areas for cooperation in the field of law. The two sides announced their intention to cooperate in six specific areas: judicial and lawyer training, legal protection of human rights, administrative law, legal aid for the poor, commercial law and arbitration, and law enforcement.[11] The idea of promoting the rule of law, seemingly dormant since Clinton's 1994 speech, reemerged as a high-profile item on the Sino–U.S. agenda.

This rule-of-law initiative got off to something of a rocky start, encountering the same political obstacles that stymied President Clinton's 1994 interest in Sino–U.S. rule-of-law cooperation: Congressional opposition and U.S. laws regulating the types of programs the State Department can fund. As a result, in the years immediately following the Clinton–Jiang summit and the announcement of the rule-of-law initiative, there was little actual activity in this area other than a few off-the-record discussions between government officials and a conference convening law school deans in Beijing. Moreover, Gewirtz left the government shortly after the second Clinton–Jiang summit, and the global rule-of-law coordinator position remained vacant for more than six months. This lack of progress led some observers to criticize the administration for unveiling the rule-of-law initiative with little or no thought given to program specifics.

More recently, however, U.S.-sponsored rule-of-law projects in China have started to take off. In 2002 and 2003, the State Department's Bureau for Democracy, Human Rights, and Labor has provided nearly $9.1 million in grants to promote democracy in China, with approximately half of this amount going to legal reform programs. The State Department's Bureau for East Asia and Pacific Affairs has also sponsored a number of rule-of-law projects, including a $7 million grant to support Temple University Law School's legal education programs in China, as well as smaller grants administered by the U.S. Embassy in Beijing and by the American Bar Association. The State Department's Bureau for International Narcotics and Law Enforcement Affairs has also gotten involved in promoting rule-of-law reforms in China, appointing a resident legal advisor in Beijing to encourage and assist Chinese officials in reforming the Chinese justice system.[12] In light of this substantial investment in rule-of-law promotion, it is therefore worthwhile to inquire what the goals of such programs are—or should be—and whether they are likely to be realized.

Conflicting Objectives: What Is the Rule of Law?

One of the most fundamental questions one must ask about this or any law and development program concerns what, exactly, is being promoted. The United States has declared that it wants to see China build "the rule of law."[13] But *rule of law* is a notoriously plastic phrase. Sometimes it is used in an expansive, substantive sense, meant to describe a legal system that effectively protects specific individual rights and promotes specific substantive values. However, many scholars have criticized this use of the term as too broad. As Joseph Raz puts it,

> If the rule of law is the rule of good law then to explain its nature is to propound a complete social philosophy. But if so the term lacks any useful function. We have no need to be converted to the rule of law just in order to discover that to believe in it is to believe that good should triumph.[14]

Other scholars stress that the rule of law implies rules that are publicly known and predictable but do not necessarily embody specific substantive principles. Still others stress that the essence of the rule of law is the constraint of government discretion—here the "rule of law" is contrasted with the "rule of man." Thus, the definition of the phrase itself has been the subject of sustained academic debate for at least a century, and probably longer.

The ambiguity of the term is a disadvantage in academic discourse. However, the same ambiguity is an advantage in political discourse, which may go a long way to explaining why rule of law is used as the catchphrase for the China legal assistance projects. One academic China law expert put the point bluntly: "'Rule of Law' has no meaning. Everyone uses the phrase because everyone can get behind it and it might make it easier to get funding." Another scholar makes a similar observation on how the phrase is used in the policy discourse: "The 'rule of law' means whatever one wants it to mean. It's an empty vessel that everyone can fill up with their own vision." This ambiguity serves a very clear political purpose, stated explicitly by one State Department official: "The beauty of the 'rule of law' is that it's neutral. No one—the human rights community, the business community, the Chinese leadership—objects to it."

The political usefulness of this ambiguity is evident in how the term is used in official U.S. statements. When she was addressing U.S. business representatives, then-Secretary of State Madeleine Albright stressed that the rule of law will make China a good place to do business.[15] When responding to a reporter concerned with China's treatment of political dissidents, she trumpeted the rule-of-law initiative as a program that will address these concerns.[16] Indeed, in one speech, Albright listed all the virtues of a rule-of-law society. These included effective criminal law enforcement, lack of official corruption, protection of the environment, full political participation by all citizens, protection of individual rights, and peaceful participation in the global economy.[17] It is easy to see why such an expansive definition is politically advantageous. After all, if the rule of law includes all these things, who could object to promoting it? And if the government has an initiative to promote the rule of law, is not the government addressing all these concerns?

Not everyone in the field is thrilled with the way the U.S. government is using the phrase, however. One scholar finds it "troubling that the rule of law is packaged by the U.S. Chamber of Commerce as a good thing for the sale of U.S. products. This is not really what is traditionally meant by 'rule of law.'"[18] As Thomas Carothers has warned in the first chapter, rule-of-law promotion, while useful, "will not miraculously eliminate the hard choices between ideals and interests" that have plagued U.S.–China policy. Another academic observer is even more critical, arguing that we need to push beyond "the 'feel good' rhetoric of advocacy of the rule of law" in order to understand the real effects legal reforms are having in China—effects that are not well-understood, and by no means always necessarily desirable.[19] The U.S. government may be trying to avoid a clash between commercial and human rights interests by stressing the rule of law, but this harmony of interests may prove more rhetorical than real.

Another perhaps more important aspect of the ambiguity of the term concerns divergence in U.S. and Chinese law reform goals. To the U.S. government, *rule of law* is an attractive term not only because it may allow the U.S. business and human rights communities to rally around a common banner, but also because it is seen as an area in which the Chinese side has an interest. It is generally agreed, however, that the U.S. and Chinese governments have different things in mind when they talk about the rule of law. Indeed, it is not entirely true that the Chinese government is completely comfortable with the phrase. Prior to the 1997 Clinton–Jiang summit, the United States drafted a memorandum of understanding that identified rule-of-law as a potential area of Sino–U.S. cooperation. China strongly objected to the use of the phrase, which it considered politically sensitive. Thus, although the fact sheet released by the White House detailing the accomplishments of the October 1997 summit lists "promoting the rule of law" as an area where the two sides agreed to cooperate, the official joint statement uses the phrase "cooperation in the field of law" instead. Since then, the Chinese government seems to have become more comfortable using the term *rule of law*. However, the translation the Chinese government has started using is *yifazhiguo*, meaning "a country ruled according to law." This phrase has replaced *fazhi*, which was the original translation of the nineteenth-century concept of the German *Rechtstaat*. Although both are translated into English as "rule of law," the former term lacks the political connotations of the latter. Some have suggested that a more accurate translation of *yifazhiguo*, the preferred Chinese phrase, would be "rule *by* law."

The U.S. government may try to take advantage of the ambiguity of the term in order to "sell" legal reform to the Chinese, but ultimately the State Department conception of the rule of law has a clear substantive and political component. The State Department official who claimed that the beauty of the rule of law is that it is a neutral phrase also stated that to the United States, it means law that conforms to international standards, protects individual rights, and preserves justice. According to this official, rule-of-law traditionally has been, and has been seen at the State Department as, an aspect of U.S. human rights policy. Another State Department official said that the term as used by the department incorporates some substantive legal rights, although these rights need not be identical to those found in the United States. According to this official, rule of law means that all people are subject to and have access to a fair, equitable, transparent, and efficient legal system. Yet another official in the State Department argued instead that the essence of the rule of law was predictability, although this official also claimed that the legal system needed rules seen by the people as substantively right and just in order to be effective. Overall, there appears to be a general sense that the rule of law—that is, the vision of legal development that the United States wants to promote—has a clear and central substantive component related to the protection of individual rights. This belief seems to be shared in the nongovernmental community as well.

This is obviously not the vision of legal reform advocated by the Chinese government, and it is not what Beijing means when it articulates rule of law—or "a country ruled by law"—as a policy goal. The primary Chinese motivation for undertaking legal reform, according to most U.S. observers, is economic. The need to attract foreign investment and integrate with the global economy is cited by experts both in and out of the

U.S. government as an important motive for the Chinese to undertake legal reform. Other possible motives include China's desire not to be perceived as a rogue state, the need to control corruption, and the sense that a more rule-based system would help the central government improve control over the provinces. But the Chinese leadership wants to make sure legal reforms are limited to specific areas and that they remain under the control of the central government. Both U.S. government officials and nongovernmental experts maintain that although China wants legal reform in the commercial sphere, the leadership wants to prevent reforms from seeping into the political sphere and does not want any reforms that would undermine the central leadership's decision-making authority.

This divergence between the fundamental objectives of the two sides in this whole endeavor is the source of the most important strategic problem for the U.S.–China rule-of-law initiative, or indeed for any program that takes the U.S. vision of a substantive rule of law as the objective of Chinese legal reform. Given that Chinese leadership does not share this objective, how should legal reform proceed? It is here that underlying, implicit theories of legal and social change become important. For the U.S.–China rule-of-law initiative to be coherent—that is, for the adopted means to match the envisioned end—law must interact with society and with political institutions in a certain way. Specifically, legal reforms undertaken by the Chinese for commercial purposes must lead to a broader transformation in the legal, and ultimately the political, system. This vision of snowballing legal reform is the cornerstone of the U.S. rule-of-law promotion strategy.

Trojan Horse of Legal Reform

Given the divergence of U.S. and Chinese objectives, the United States appears to have adopted what I will call a "Trojan horse" strategy. The U.S. belief seems to be that the Chinese will adopt an initial set of legal reforms and legal education programs in order to achieve economic goals, and that those reforms, once adopted, will take on a life of their own. The growth of legal methods for dealing with commercial disputes will foster a culture of legality that will spread beyond economic transactions to other areas. The logic of controlling administrative discretion and corruption in the name of economics will evolve into stronger legal controls on government discretion at all levels. Because the same judicial institutions and legal profession that handle commercial issues also handle other types of legal issues, improving training and organization will lead to improvements in all areas, even if the original motive is strictly economic. And the success of legal reforms in the commercial area will strengthen the hand of reformers in China who want to push for legal reforms in other areas. A State Department official described the basic strategy as follows: "Once the Chinese open the door to legal reform, they won't be able to control it, and legal reform—and the principles of legality, predictability, and judicial independence—will seep into other areas." According to this official, because the underlying assumption is that the rule of law will spread as time goes on, the U.S. strategy is to "plant seeds in patches of sunlight." This official went on to draw an analogy to China's experience with the Internet. The Chinese knew they needed to adopt this new technology for economic reasons. They wanted to control it but ultimately could not. As with the Internet, the argument goes, so too with law.

The Trojan horse approach to Chinese legal reform appears pervasive in the NGO community as well as in the government. An official in one of the major NGOs doing work in this area stated that the organization subscribes to the view that once legal reform is introduced, there will be an inevitable transformation over time, even if the reform is initially introduced for commercial reasons. The interest in promoting complex market transactions, it was asserted, would lead to the protection of individual rights, although such a transformation might take a long time. An official in another U.S. NGO made a similar claim, arguing that the organization's fundamental view of law reform is that once you start, you will not be able to stop; once the Chinese have a law to cover one thing, they will find they need more laws to cover more things.

The Trojan horse view even affects those who are openly skeptical of the U.S. approach to this Chinese law reform. To take one striking example, an academic working on legal education, who was generally critical of the U.S. rule-of-law initiative, described legal education strategy in the following way:

> A lot of the things we do in legal education are not explicit. That's not to say we bring in a Trojan Horse. But we need to get into institutions first. Once we start up training programs, we can do all sorts of other stuff. The Ministries have no idea what we're doing—they just think we're running some neat training program.

Despite the disclaimer, it is hard to imagine a more explicit exposition of the Trojan horse strategy. This interviewee went on to explain that the idea is to teach Chinese students a more critical approach to law and policy analysis, concluding that training Chinese lawyers in critical thinking "is the most subversive thing we can get to happen. That starts to create subterranean fissures by changing the way people think, understand, and process issues. That's ultimately more effective than standing in Tiananmen Square." Another scholar, also involved with legal education efforts, envisions the appropriate U.S. strategy in similar though less secretive terms, noting that the U.S. government and NGOs have been trying to sell legal reform as a package deal. That is, they have been trying to convince the Chinese side that, in the long term, respect for the rule of law will be undermined if they try to be selective and partial in the areas where they allow legal reform.

In addition to the belief that legal reform, once introduced into China, will spread throughout the system, many on the U.S. side believe there is support for such reform within China. Most U.S. officials concede, however, that China's high-level leadership, although willing to take risks to achieve economic goals, is not enthusiastic about widespread legal reform outside the commercial and low-level administrative spheres. Thus the fundamental approach is still basically a Trojan horse strategy. The Chinese leadership is betting that it will be able to control the scope and extent of legal reform; the U.S. government and NGOs interested in building the rule of law are betting that it will not.

Problems with the Trojan Horse Strategy

What are the presumptions about the nature of law and the dynamics of legal reform that give rise to the Trojan horse strategy? It may, of course, be the case that it is less a well-thought-out strategy than a way to rationalize pursuing programs that are, of necessity, limited. But this is too cynical. Most of the people I interviewed in both the State Department and in major NGOs seemed sincere in their belief that limited, modest legal reforms would eventually—perhaps inevitably—lead to more fundamental reforms. The principles behind the strategy therefore ought to be examined more closely to see whether there is a sound basis for this conviction.

The assumption of the strategy is that legal reforms in certain narrow sectors will diffuse throughout the legal and political system, leading to widespread transformation in the direction of the U.S. rule-of-law vision. But the mechanism by which this diffusion will take place is rarely specified explicitly. At least three mechanisms are conceivable, and all three are evident in the thinking within governmental, academic, and NGO communities.

Mechanism One: The Interdependent, Unitary Legal System

Some advocates of the Trojan horse strategy presume that rule of law in one sphere will spread to other spheres, simply because that is the nature of law. Like the Internet, the analogy goes, the "technology" of legal modernization, by its nature, cannot be controlled. Specifically, it is thought that commercial law reform that builds an effectively independent judiciary—one that operates according to transparent, publicly known rules and is staffed by a well-trained bench and bar—will foster similar sorts of changes in those fields of law more closely related to human rights concerns. This, proponents assert, is the nature of law. However, the Chinese government has a strong incentive to limit rule-of-law reforms to the commercial sector and to branches of administrative law that increase central control of the bureaucracy and check abuses by low-level officials. The U.S. strategy implicitly—and sometimes explicitly—presumes that such limitation is impossible.

A theoretical or empirical basis for this belief, however, appears to be lacking. The dynamics of inevitably spreading legal reform are almost always couched in terms of assertions, analogies, or metaphors. I know of no social science research that provides a solid foundation for this hypothesis. Furthermore, there is some empirical evidence that setting up firewalls between sectors of the legal system—as the Chinese wish to do—is indeed possible. Consider the example of courts in authoritarian Spain under Franco, a case analyzed by Jose Toharia.[20] Toharia noted that in Spain, political authoritarianism co-existed with a great deal of judicial independence. Indeed, not only did the Spanish judiciary have a great deal of formal independence, but judges tended to be more liberal than the regime and frequently more liberal than the general population. Moreover, corruption and political interference in judges' activities appeared minimal.

How could a right-wing authoritarian regime tolerate such a liberal, independent judiciary? The simple answer is that, on sensitive issues, the judiciary had no power. The regular courts handled only those cases that were politically innocuous. Politically significant cases were handled by special tribunals—labor courts, military courts, and, most important, the State Security Tribunal—that were closely controlled by the executive. Not only did the Spanish government successfully control those areas of the law that might threaten its power and policies, but this system helped it economize on resources. After all, monitoring and disciplining the judiciary takes time and money. It was much easier to simply grant the judiciary a relatively high degree of independence in non-threatening areas and to maintain strict control over tribunals that handled sensitive disputes.

The analogy to the Chinese situation should be obvious. There is no particular reason that the Chinese government could not undertake extensive legal and judicial reform in certain areas—such as commercial and low-level administrative law—and maintain close control over politically sensitive issues that touch on matters of political dissent, labor unrest, and so forth. In fact, China already appears to be making efforts to set up institutional firewalls between areas where legal reform is seen as desirable and areas where it is considered suspect. China is developing a separate system of rules for foreign enterprises, and disputes concerning foreign businesses are frequently referred to a commercial arbitration body rather than the Chinese courts. The system does not work perfectly, and weaknesses of domestic Chinese legal institutions still create headaches for foreign investors, but it is hard to see why the basic strategy of keeping different areas of law institutionally separate cannot work in China. If the Franco regime could tolerate and control a judiciary with substantial formal independence, a high degree of autonomy, and relatively liberal political attitudes, then authoritarian China could certainly tolerate much more modest reforms.

A single counter-example does not disprove the prediction that legal reforms intended to improve economic performance will have spillover effects into other areas. And it may be that the types of laws needed for more efficient commercial activity—clear property rights, for example, or transparent administrative procedures related to taxation and regulation—are themselves beneficial for individual rights and well-being. But the Trojan horse strategy that U.S. advocates seem to have in mind presumes that legal reforms will spread throughout the system—that legality will prove, like the Internet, uncontrollable. Yet the Spanish case, and China's own efforts to keep legal issues separate, give us reason to doubt this strong spillover hypothesis. More general empirical research suggests that stable authoritarian regimes are frequently able to adopt systems that effectively protect property and contract rights without more extensive reforms in other parts of the legal system.[21] Therefore, if advocates of the Trojan horse strategy are to make the case that legalism or the rule of law will be able to jump the firewalls set up by the Chinese government, then the mechanism must be specified much more clearly. As of now, the theory behind this first mechanism is not well developed, and there is no particularly convincing empirical evidence for it either.

Mechanism Two: Changing China's "Legal Culture"

Even if different sections of the legal system can be kept institutionally separate, certain types of legal reform projects might still be able to smuggle in the seeds of a broader transformation in the Chinese legal system. One way this might be done is through programs intended to change China's "legal culture"—especially the culture of the bench, bar, and other professionals and government officials who work closely with the legal system. This is an explicit goal articulated by people inside and outside of the U.S. government. In this view, the Chinese government recognizes that it needs better-trained judges and lawyers and will therefore allow U.S.-sponsored legal education projects. These education programs, however, have the potential over time to transform the way the Chinese elite thinks about the law. Hence, much of the Trojan horse legal reform strategy stresses legal education and training of judges and lawyers, not only to improve their skills, but to change China's legal culture.

What exactly is China's legal culture, and how should it be changed? This is not an easy question to answer, in part because the term is about as clear and precise as the term *rule of law*. And, much as rule of law gets used as shorthand for "a desirable legal system," legal culture tends to be used as shorthand for "what people think about law," or sometimes even "those aspects of the legal system we can't observe or measure." Indeed, the phrase is so ill-defined that some have questioned whether there is any point in using it at all. Because of the vagueness of the term, I will focus on only one aspect of Chinese legal culture that often comes up in discussions of legal reform: the extent to which Chinese lawyers adopt a "formalistic" or "instrumental" approach to law. This focus is chosen, first, because it seems to capture one of the most important elements considered to be part of China's legal culture, and second, because the problems in this area illustrate broader difficulties with "changing legal culture" as a mechanism of fostering widespread systemic change.

Formalism and *instrumentalism* are terms used to describe the way lawyers and judges think about how laws should be interpreted and applied. The formalistic approach is characterized by relatively mechanical application of rules and an emphasis on statutory language. The instrumental approach places more stress on thinking about the goals a given law is meant to achieve and the likely real-world consequences of a particular legal decision. These are both ideal types, and no legal practitioner is ever purely formalistic or purely instrumental. But these ideal types do illustrate a potentially important difference in legal culture that is worth considering in the context of Chinese legal reform and the Trojan horse strategy.

The consensus on the U.S. side seems to be that the Chinese approach to law is too formalistic, and that Chinese students tend to approach law with the attitude of wanting to know "the right answer" rather than thinking critically about the issues involved in legal questions. Many of the Americans working in the Chinese legal education field want to encourage members of the Chinese legal community to take a more critical, policy-oriented, instrumental approach to the law. At least one leading academic working on legal education, quoted above, argues that this sort of change in mind-set will prove subversive and could lead to widespread reform throughout the system.

Setting aside for the moment whether such a change in mind-set is even possible, we should consider whether it is desirable. Much of the law and development movement was concerned with changing legal education in Latin America, and some of the most scathing attacks on the movement concerned its attempts to export an allegedly inappropriate U.S. model of legal education.[22] It is worth restating the basic elements of Trubek and Galanter's critique of these legal education projects. According to Trubek and Galanter, U.S. scholars believed that Latin American lawyers should be trained in a more instrumental, less formalistic approach to law. An instrumental perspective, it was believed, "would generate 'legal development,' which would in turn foster a system of governance by universal, purposive rules, and would accordingly contribute to the enhancement of liberty, equality, participation, and rationality."[23] The problem, according to Trubek and Galanter, was that this view neglected the social and political context in which this change in legal culture took place. An expanded and modernized legal profession tended to increase social inequality, because the social elite had greater access to the better-educated and professionalized legal personnel. Furthermore, these conservative elites could make use of better-trained lawyers to block changes that threatened their interests. In addition, the instrumental orientation actually weakened what legal guarantees of individual rights did exist. Formalism can provide a kind of protection for individuals from abusive government policies; instrumentalism makes it easier for individual "rights" to be circumvented in the name of some state-sponsored developmental goal.[24]

The point is not that there is something inherently anti-reform about instrumentalism, or that sophisticated, critical thinking about the principles behind law is necessarily pernicious. But there is no reason to presume that these modes of thought are necessarily conducive to reform either. Trubek and Galanter may have overstated the negative aspects of cultivating the instrumental approach to law, but the basic concern is still valid. Social and political realities—especially the material interests of the legal elite and those members of society able to purchase their services—probably have more to do with how laws are interpreted and applied than the particular style of legal reasoning taught in law schools. Legal instrumentalism in the service of conservative groups is no more likely to spread deeper, more progressive reform than strict legal formalism.

Perhaps legal culture does matter, and perhaps changes in legal education do make a difference in legal culture. But there is no strong evidence to suggest that this impact is more than marginal. In any event, there is enough indeterminacy about the relationship between the types of legal culture that can be influenced by legal education that this mechanism for the Trojan horse is problematic at best. Moreover, the criticisms of the first mechanism apply, for the most part, to this second mechanism as well. If the Chinese government is able to cordon off and control politically salient sections of the legal system, then changes in the legal culture of the overall legal community might not have much of an effect on the core human rights issues about which many in the United States are concerned.

In sum, this second mechanism for Trojan horse legal reform rests on three dubious assumptions: first, that it is possible to influence Chinese legal culture; second, that these cultural changes, if possible, would have desirable consequences for broader reform; and third, that a broad change in legal culture, even if generally conducive to greater reform, would be able to affect those sensitive areas of the law over which the Chinese government wants to maintain strict political control.

Mechanism Three: Building a Constituency for Further Reform

A third possible mechanism through which partial legal reforms might generate more widespread reform is the development of a public base of support for reform. The idea is that legal reforms in the economic sphere—especially those that guarantee property and contract rights and those that provide means of redress against government administrators—will make people better off, more secure, and willing and able to push for deeper reforms, not just in the economic realm, but overall. Thus, even if the spread of rule of law is not driven by the internal logic of the legal system, and even if it is not possible to change legal culture in ways that generate broader changes, partial reforms—to the extent that they are successful on their own terms—will create the social and political base for more reform.

The first obvious problem with this view has already been mentioned. Legal reform might well strengthen the position of conservative forces in society that oppose more widespread political, social, and economic reforms. This possibility has been discussed above, in reference to the efforts of the first law and development movement to cultivate a professionalized bench and bar and to promote a more "instrumental" or "realist" adjudicative approach. Second, also as previously discussed, some authoritarian regimes are able to provide relatively secure property and contract rights yet still resist broader political or social reforms. Even putting these problems aside, however, there are reasons to question the assumption that legal reforms in contract, property, and administrative law will necessarily generate widespread public support for further reform.

There are many reasons to question this assumption, but here I will focus on only one. We must consider the fact that greater legalization of economic relationships in China might have undesirable, unintended consequences if such legalization disrupts alternative informal institutions. According to one expert, a fair assessment of current law reform efforts must "try to take account of the ways in which the elaboration of the formal legal system is both by design and unwittingly eroding less formal institutions and customs."[25] This observer notes that such erosion is most apparent in the decline in mediation that has accompanied the rise in litigation. Changing patterns of dispute resolution may lead to a constricting of access for poorer people, especially in rural areas. Such a phenomenon clearly could have negative implications for a theory of spreading reform based on a growing constituency of previously marginalized Chinese. This mechanism for spreading reform assumes that reforms make people become both stronger and more pro-reform. Even if it can be established that the disruption in informal institutions is a temporary problem and that in the long term a shift to more formal, law-based institutions would make everyone better off, the erosion of informal institutions in the short term can make people politically weaker, more anti-reform, or both.

Again, an example from another part of the world may help illustrate how reforms in formal institutions, if not thought through carefully, can have serious negative consequences on the general population as informal institutions are undermined. This time, the example comes from legal reforms introduced by the British in rural areas around Bombay in the nineteenth century, as described by Rachel Kranton and Anand Swamy.[26] The British governors of the region observed, correctly, that the rural credit markets were characterized by local moneylenders who were able to charge interest rates in excess of those that could have been charged in a competitive market. They were able to do this because the lenders relied on informal mechanisms to enforce debt repayment, and these mechanisms in turn depended on ties between the lenders and other local elites. As a result, only a small number of lenders could operate in any given village. The British reasoned that effective formal contract enforcement would allow lenders to operate in many more villages, would create a competitive market, and would bring down interest rates for farmers.

The British were right about all of these things. What they did not anticipate was that the introduction of effective formal contract enforcement undermined what was effectively an informal insurance arrangement between lenders and borrowers. When lenders could charge monopolistic interest rates, they had a vested interest in their clientele remaining economically viable. Any given borrower represented a future stream of monopolistic interest rates to the lender, and that stream would disappear if the borrower lost everything and had to become a wage laborer. Why should the creditor kill a goose that lays golden eggs? If a borrower suffered an unexpected disaster—if a cow died, or a field was destroyed by flood, or crop prices collapsed—the lender had an incentive to forgive the debt or postpone repayment. But once effective civil courts created a competitive market in rural credit, creditors had no reason to expect that they would deal with any particular borrower again with any frequency. Therefore, creditors had less incentive to forgive debt or postpone repayment if the borrower suffered a disaster. Although borrowers under the new system were better off in good years, they could lose everything if disaster struck. This problem could be averted if borrowers were able to purchase insurance, but effective insurance markets simply did not exist in that part of India at the time.

Hence, the introduction of effective civil law created a competitive credit market, but it also destroyed the existing informal insurance arrangement without replacing it with any sort of compensating institution. In some villages, these changes—coupled with exogenous economic shocks—led to widespread rioting.

This example may at first seem far removed from Chinese rule-of-law reform. But it is entirely plausible that the Chinese system—lacking as it does both effective formal contract enforcement and widespread formal insurance markets—has evolved informal risk-sharing mechanisms that are closely integrated with the informal contracting structure and that could be disrupted by legal reform. More important, given that the Trojan horse strategy relies on pushing incremental reforms—"planting seeds in patches of sunlight"—and hoping that they will grow exponentially, the type of phenomenon the Bombay case illustrates is important even if the specific problem is not an issue.

In the absence—sometimes even in the presence—of formal legal institutions, complex informal institutions of contract, property, risk-sharing, and dispute resolution can develop. New legal reforms, especially those that prove effective, may disturb or undermine these informal institutions. This may be a good thing, but it may not be. Partial reforms—an inherent part of the Trojan horse strategy—are particularly likely candidates to disrupt an important informal institution without providing an adequate substitute. The above example of increasing litigation and the rising quality of legal professionals potentially undermining mediation and other dispute resolution mechanisms accessible to the rural poor is one example of this kind of problem.

The fact that partial reforms can disrupt existing informal institutions may undermine the third mechanism for the Trojan horse strategy. This mechanism assumes that incremental reforms protect and strengthen the interests and influence of pro-reform groups. But if legal reform undermines the informal institutions that these groups have evolved to protect their interests, this mechanism cannot work. Even worse, if the unintended consequences create especially serious social problems, there may be a backlash against reforms. The point is not that legal reform should never proceed because informal institutions will be disrupted, but that legal reformers ought to proceed with caution. Sometimes incremental reform can be worse than no reform at all. We cannot simply presume that incremental reforms will always lay the groundwork for more extensive changes.

Tensions and Conflicts between Fundamental Goals

These examples suggest that the three most obvious candidate mechanisms for the Trojan horse strategy, while not necessarily wrong, are problematic. At the very least, they need to be thought through much more thoroughly. But even if we could be confident that limited Chinese legal reforms would lead to more widespread evolution toward a rule-of-law system, and that the U.S. government or NGOs could in some way support or influence this process, there are several additional problems to consider.

First, legal reforms that allow citizens to challenge the legality of government action may actually hinder desirable economic reforms. Indeed, the rule of law envisioned by the U.S. government may actually create obstacles to other types of economic reforms it favors. After all, the same means that can be used to check arbitrary government abuses can be used to obstruct dramatic and desirable policy changes. Some scholars believe that the insulation of bureaucrats from politics was an important element of East Asian economic development, and this position would imply a tension between effective economic policy and the rule of law.

Costa Rica provides a concrete example of how rule-of-law reforms can have unintended consequences on economic liberalization. The Costa Rican government created a new chamber of its Supreme Court in the 1980s, with the mandate to review the constitutionality of government actions. The new chamber was created largely in response to declining public opinion of the judiciary. It soon became a popular avenue for groups to challenge government action. In fact, both the court's popularity and its activism came as a surprise to the government that had created it. Ultimately, the court's decisions seriously affected—and frequently hindered—the government's program of neoliberal economic reforms.[27]

Such a scenario is extremely unlikely in the Chinese case, but it is worth considering in light of the oft-repeated claim that rule-of-law legal reforms and market economy reforms are complements. This may be true. But to the extent that law reform succeeds in giving ordinary people the right to challenge central government decisions—and not merely the low-level decisions of individual bureaucrats—it may make it more difficult for the government to adopt difficult neoliberal market reforms. This may not be a bad thing, of course. But it is important that reform advocates consider these potential consequences, especially if one subscribes to the (controversial) hypothesis that political elites need a relatively high degree of autonomy to implement painful reforms.

Second, there exist potential tensions between strengthening adjudicative independence and controlling official corruption. Both of these goals come up in discussions of areas where the Chinese legal system needs improvement, although the U.S. side tends to emphasize the former and the Chinese the latter. To the extent that the United States considers both important goals, however, we must consider the difficulties in achieving both of them together. After all, the more adjudicators—be they judges or administrative officials—are subject to political controls, the more likely it is that their decisions will be influenced by political considerations rather than the application of supposedly impartial rules. The fewer controls placed on these adjudicators, the greater the difficulty of ensuring their accountability and checking corruption. Judge Clifford Wallace puts the point succinctly: "Although both judicial independence and judicial accountability are vital for maintaining the rule of law, they sometimes seem to conflict."[28] And a main conclusion of Mauro Cappelletti's comparative survey of judicial processes in Western countries is the necessity of balancing the "conflicting values, independence and accountability."[29] Both Wallace and Cappelletti conclude that independence and accountability are not mutually exclusive and that they can be balanced effectively given appropriate institutional choices. But the potential conflict is real—something that China rule-of-law reform advocates ought to consider more closely. There are other institutional tensions as well. Richard Messick and Linn Hammergren, for example, suggest that mechanisms to ensure judicial accountability may also create obstacles to judicial efficiency.[30] These analyses suggest that advocates of Chinese institutional reform need to think more carefully about these sources of tension. To the extent that reformers are successful in pushing one goal of institutional reform, they may undermine another.

A third issue is the possibility that there may be tensions not only at the level of institutional arrangements but also at the level of fundamental rule-of-law values. Consider, as one example, the tension between the rule-of-law goals of predictability and equity. Clear rules, systematically applied, are the best way to ensure predictability. But rules can never capture all the possible variations in individual cases, and sometimes a mechanical application of rules can lead to results that seem grossly unfair. Thus legal systems throughout history have tried to find ways to balance predictability with equity, making sure that individual cases are decided in accordance with principles of fairness and justice, even when the formal rules would dictate otherwise. According to one source in the U.S. government, U.S. NGOs do not see a tension between promoting equity and predictability in the Chinese case. The two values, it is argued, are not inconsistent, and the Chinese system is currently in such a state that these sorts of questions are not really relevant, at least not yet. This official has a point. If the current system is both unpredictable and unfair, it may seem like academic hair-splitting to worry about philosophical inconsistencies between the two goals of predictability and fairness. Nevertheless, if the rule-of-law reform strategy is based on the idea that principles adopted for one area of the legal system will spread, it is worth considering the possible tension between different facets of the U.S. rule-of-law vision.

A fourth concern is that U.S. support for rule-of-law reform in China is ultimately counterproductive for true systemic change in China, because these sorts of reforms merely help to legitimize the authoritarian Chinese state. This seems to be the view of some members of the U.S. Congress. State Department officials and NGOs alike express their frustration over congressmen who refuse to support any program that might be seen as helping the Chinese government do anything. But the association of this line of argument with members of Congress who are perceived as narrow minded and short sighted may have blinded some to the kernel of truth in the argument. As one academic observer put it, "One doesn't need to endorse Jesse Helms to believe that the legitimation issues are real." After all, one of the reasons China would want to talk openly about promoting the rule of law—albeit a reason secondary to attracting foreign investment—is that it may increase the regime's legitimacy. The extent to which it actually would, and whether the net effects for political reform would be positive or negative, is a question that has not been explored systematically. My view is that supporting rule-of-law programs would not contribute substantially to the legitimacy of the Chinese leadership, but this is a conjecture not grounded in any strong theory or evidence. Once we dissociate the legitimation argument from some of its more crude formulations and distasteful proponents, it becomes clear that it is an argument that needs to be taken seriously.

Conclusion

The U.S. government began advocating Chinese rule-of-law reform as an extension of U.S. human rights policy. It wants China to move in the direction of a substantive vision of the rule of law, one that protects certain basic rights and promotes a certain vision of justice. The Chinese government, however, has a very different idea of what is meant by the rule of law and wants to limit legal reform to those areas that are directly relevant to international economic integration and domestic economic reform. This creates obvious problems for U.S. backers of a legal reform initiative conceived of as an extension of U.S. human rights policy. Therefore, U.S. rule-of-law advocates have adopted what I have called a Trojan horse strategy. The belief is that limited law reforms will lead to more fundamental changes in the Chinese legal and political system, changes that the Chinese central government will not be able to control.

The mechanism by which this widespread change is to take place, however, is usually not specified clearly. Consideration of three possible mechanisms shows that each is problematic. There is no good theoretical reason to believe that legal systems have a kind of fundamental unity of principles and institutions, nor is there convincing empirical evidence that this is the case. Attempts to change China's legal culture—the way people, especially legal professionals, think about law—may not make much of an impact either. Not only is it difficult to bring about such change, but evidence suggests that the way people think about law itself is less important than social, economic, and political structures. The hope that limited legal reforms will stimulate growing public demand for further reforms may also be misplaced, given that incremental reforms are often disruptive and can generate anti-reform pressure. Moreover, there appear to be tensions between the goals espoused by rule-of-law reform advocates: legally constrained government versus decisive reform, independence versus accountability, predictability versus equity.

These considerations suggest that policy makers need to take a long, hard look at what they hope to achieve by promoting rule of law in China—and how they hope to achieve it. Again, I must stress that this does not mean that the various legal reform projects sponsored or advocated by the U.S. government and NGOs are bad ideas. If the dangers inherent in these sorts of projects can be avoided—and if the initiatives are successful in improving the functioning of Chinese courts, helping China attract foreign investment and engage in world trade, controlling corruption, and reining in abuses of discretion by the administrative bureaucracy—then they can be considered worthwhile even if they do not have any broader effects. I have not attempted to evaluate any of these individual programs; my subjective impression is that many of them are doing important, useful work. What I want to question is the larger claim that these programs will help promote a broader rule-of-law transformation in China, leading to widespread reforms even against the wishes of the current Chinese leadership. Rule of law made its way onto the U.S. governmental agenda, at least in part, because of this belief. But given the state of existing theory and empirical evidence, such a conviction seems unfounded. I say "unfounded" rather than "false" because we do not have enough evidence to conclude that the Trojan horse view is incorrect. But given the weakness of the theory and evidence behind this element of U.S. rule-of-law rhetoric and strategy, and in light of the sad history of the first law and development movement, there is ample reason to think more rigorously and realistically about the means and ends of law reform—and sooner, rather than later.

Notes

This chapter was adapted from Matthew Stephenson's "A Trojan Horse Behind Chinese Walls? Problems and Prospects of U.S.-Sponsored "Rule of Law" Reform Projects in the People's Republic of China," originally published in the *UCLA Pacific Basin Law Journal* (Fall 2000).

1. David M. Trubek and Marc Galanter, "Scholars in Self-Estrangement: Some Reflections on the Crisis in Law and Development Studies in the United States," *Wisconsin Law Review* 4 (1974): 1062.
2. Lawrence M. Friedman, "On Legal Development," *Rutgers Law Review* 24 (1969): 12.
3. James Gardner, *Legal Imperialism: American Lawyers and Foreign Aid in Latin America* (Madison: University of Wisconsin Press, 1980).
4. For contemporary postmortems of the movement, see John H. Merryman, "Comparative Law and Social Change: On the Origins, Style, Decline and Revival of the Law and Development Movement," *American Journal of Comparative Law* 25 (1977); and Elliot M. Burg, "Law and Development: A Review of the Literature and a Critique of 'Scholars in Self-Estrangement,'" *American Journal of Comparative Law* 25 (1977). For more recent reflections on the history of the movement and its lessons, see Brian Z. Tamanaha, "The Lessons of Law-and-Development Studies," *American Journal of International Law* 89, no. 2 (April 1995) (book review); and Richard E. Messick, "Judicial Reform and Economic Development: A Survey of the Issues," *World Bank Research Observer* 14, no. 1 (1999).
5. See, for example, Robert B. Seidman, "The Lessons of Self-Estrangement: On the Methodology of Law and Development," in *Yearbook of Research in Sociology of Law*, ed. Rita Simon (Greenwich, CT: JAI Press, 1978).
6. See Tamanaha, "Lessons of Law."
7. In addition to publicly available sources, in this chapter I also draw on a number of interviews I conducted in 1999 with several U.S. State Department officials, NGO officials, and scholarly observers. Interviewees generally preferred to remain confidential and so are identified only by general affiliation (government, academe, NGO) rather than by name or position.
8. This statement should not be taken as implying that the government sought a controlling role, or even that it intended to run a lot of programs directly. According to

one of the State Department officials working directly on the Initiative, none of the government's activities is intended to supplant existing NGO programs. Rather, the idea is to help raise the profile of issues, serve as a launching pad for new initiatives, and work through public-private partnerships. Nevertheless, the public rhetoric suggested a central role for U.S. government involvement.

9. President Clinton, Opening Address at News Conference, May 26, 1994.
10. See Press Release, Office of the Press Secretary, White House, November 17, 1997.
11. See Press Release, Office of the Press Secretary, White House, July 2, 1998.
12. U.S. General Accounting Office (GAO), "Foreign Assistance: U.S. Funding for Democracy Related Programs (China), GAO-04-445 (Washington, D.C.: GAO, 2004).
13. See, for example, President Clinton, "Address on China and the National Interest," October 24, 1997; Secretary of State Madeleine K. Albright, "Remarks at the National Judge's College," Beijing, April 30, 1998; and John Shattuck, "Statement before the House Committee on Appropriations, Subcommittee on Foreign Operations," Washington, D.C., April 1, 1998.
14. Joseph Raz, "The Rule of Law and its Virtue," *Law Quarterly Review* 93 (1977): 195–6.
15. See Secretary of State Madeleine K. Albright, "Remarks to U.S. Business Representatives," Sheraton International Club, Beijing, April 30, 1998.
16. See interview by Bob Schieffer with Secretary of State Madeleine K. Albright, *Face the Nation*, CBS television broadcast, June 28, 1998.
17. See Secretary of State Madeleine K. Albright, "Remarks and Q & A session at Delaware Theater Company," Wilmington, DE, May 19, 1997.
18. Author interview with U.S. academic, November 1999.
19. Author interview with U.S. academic, January 2000.
20. See Jose J. Toharia, "Judicial Independence in an Authoritarian Regime: The Case of Contemporary Spain," *Law and Society Review* 9, no. 3 (1975): 475–96.
21. See Christopher Clague et al., "Property and Contract Rights in Autocracies and Democracies," *Journal of Economic Growth* 1, no. 2 (1996): 243–76.
22. See Gardner, *Legal Imperialism*. Even some of those who argue against the critics concur that "what is needed in a developing country—to protect against the dangers of a purely instrumental view of law—is an established and functioning, formalistic-oriented rule-of-law system" (Tamanaha, "Lessons of Law," 475–6).
23. Trubek and Galanter, "Scholars in Self-Estrangement."
24. Ibid., p. 1076; see also Tamanaha, "Lessons of Law."
25. Author interview with U.S. academic, January 2000.
26. See Rachel E. Kranton and Anand V. Swamy, "The Hazards of Piecemeal Reform: British Civil Courts and the Credit Market in Colonial India," *Journal of Development Economics* 58, no. 1 (1999): 1–24.
27. See Bruce M. Wilson and Roger Handberg, "Opening Pandora's Box: The Unanticipated Consequences of Costa Rican Legal Reform," unpublished paper prepared for the Midwest Political Science Association, Chicago, IL, April 1998, 23–5.
28. J. Clifford Wallace, "Resolving Judicial Corruption While Preserving Judicial Independence: Comparative Perspectives," *California Western International Law Journal* 28. no. 2 (Spring 1998): 344.
29. Mauro Cappelletti, "Who Watches the Watchmen?" in *The Judicial Process in Comparative Perspective*, ed. Mauro Cappelletti, Paul J. Kollmer, and Joanne M. Olson (Oxford: Clarendon Press, 1989): 57–113.
30. See Richard E. Messick and Linn Hammergren, "The Challenge of Judicial Reform," in *Beyond the Washington Consensus: Institutions Matter*, ed. Shahid Javed Burki and Guillermo Perry (Washington, D.C.: World Bank, 1999), 109–19.

CHAPTER NINE

The Complexity of
Success in Russia

MATTHEW SPENCE

MIXED RESULTS FROM the proliferation of Western rule-of-law assistance efforts around the world over the past twenty years have taught us much about what does not work.[1] Criminal justice reform in Russia offers a different type of lesson; it is a rare success story of rule-of-law promotion.[2] In the 1990s, the U.S. government sought to promote the rule of law in many parts of the former Soviet Union and beyond, but few of these efforts outside Russia produced concrete results.[3] Instead, lawlessness became a primary symptom of the apparent failure of many attempted rule-of-law reforms in the former Soviet Union.[4]

Against this backdrop of disappointment, in 2001 Russia adopted a liberal new Criminal Procedure Code and introduced jury trials after nearly a decade of U.S. rule-of-law assistance that supported precisely these steps. U.S. policy makers considered these reforms a major success. Because problems with criminal procedure—arbitrary arrests, overzealous prosecutors, sham trials, and other due process violations—lay at the heart of some of Russia's worst human rights violations, the new code represented an important advance.[5] On paper and increasingly in practice, the code protects the accused from procedural abuses and defines and institutionalizes many of the civil rights expected of a liberal democracy.[6]

In addition, as the most liberal criminal procedure code in the former Soviet Union, the new Russian code can serve as a model for protecting human rights to the rest of the region.[7] That jury trials—a defining characteristic of the U.S. legal system—took root in an inhospitable Russian legal culture underscores the magnitude of the reform.[8] To top things off, the Russian legislator who sponsored the new Criminal Procedure Code even thanked U.S. government–funded advisors in a speech on the floor of the Russian parliament, thereby supporting the proposition that the U.S. government did, in fact, positively influence rule-of-law reform in a transition country.[9]

But how, if at all, did U.S. policy actually contribute to this legal reform? Why did these particular reforms succeed while others failed? The Russian story highlights the complex interaction of textual design, legal culture, and political coalitions in producing legal change. This is in part a story of the limits of U.S. influence. The Russian government drove the political process to pass the code, with U.S. policy makers contributing ideas only when asked. U.S. actors were only able to claim success once the Russian government independently decided to introduce legal reforms in 2000. Much of the substance of the reforms came from Russia's own legal history, and some criminal procedure reform would have likely happened regardless of what the U.S. actors did.

Yet this is also a story of U.S. influence in subtle but significant ways. U.S.-funded efforts shaped the Russian reform process in several meaningful respects: They expedited a process already under way to take advantage of the political window for reform, strengthened the political position of Russia's judicial reformers, and introduced several substantive and politically controversial changes that made the resulting law more liberal and more likely to be implemented in Russian daily life. Among the most significant of these changes, U.S. involvement introduced to Russia the concept of plea bargaining, a small but potentially critical logistical perquisite for widespread jury trials. Russia had other opportunities for legal reform in the 1990s, which reformers were unable to exploit. U.S. assistance helped Russian reformers take advantage of the political opening in 2000 to pass the new code. The Russian story thus teaches how the West can influence rule-of-law reform abroad by catalyzing domestic energy for legal change to shape the timing and substance of reforms.

Rocky Path to Russian Criminal Procedure Reform, 1989–2001

The path to criminal procedure reform in Russia was not a simple one. Initial impetus in the Gorbachev years stalled in the Yeltsin era. But reform gained backing from an unexpected source late in the 1990s.

Seeds of Criminal Procedure Reform in the Soviet Union

Although much has been said about the novelty of Russia holding Western-style jury trials, the ideas upon which the liberal 2001 Criminal Procedure Code was based were not actually alien to Russia. Rather, the key principles came from three domestic sources: Russia's own nineteenth-century legal reforms and the right to jury trials under Czar Alexander II; general ideas present in the Russian legal community about Western legal systems; and legal reforms from perestroika that build on czarist and Western traditions.[10]

Although Russia's legal reformers were not starting from scratch, they confronted a hostile legal landscape. Under the 1960 Soviet Criminal Procedure Code, prosecutors, not independent judges, dominated the process and ruled on the rights of the accused.[11] Coerced confessions, false and politically motivated prosecutions, and falsifications of evidence were commonplace. Defendants had few rights and were rarely acquitted. Until the passage of the new Criminal Procedure Code of 2001, Russia had long had the largest per capita prison population in the world. Rather than jury trials, a professional judge, or a judge and two lay assistants, decided verdicts—and they rarely sided against the prosecutor.[12] Nearly all of Russia's lawyers and judges had been trained and promoted within this system. Soviet-trained prosecutors controlled the administration of criminal justice in their regional fiefdoms stretching across Russia's eleven time zones and were reluctant to cede any power.

Despite Russia's weak legal culture, a strong movement for judicial reform gained strength in the late years of perestroika and the early years of Russia's independence—without direct U.S. involvement. As early as 1989, Mikhail Gorbachev called for the introduction of jury trials in a speech to the Soviet parliament. The Congress of People's Deputies and the parliament's upper chamber passed a resolution calling for jury trials as part of a package of criminal justice reforms.[13] Two months before the collapse of the Soviet Union, on October 21, 1991, the Russian parliament unanimously passed the "Concept of Judicial Reform," a resolution containing a statement of principles for rule-of-law reform. It was the most direct model for the new Criminal Procedure Code.

Western lawyers, who had no involvement in drafting the concept, later praised it as a model blueprint for legal reforms. It called for creating an independent judicial branch with lifetime tenure, introducing an adversarial process in the courts, and transferring authority from the prosecutor to judges over criminal investigations and intrusions into

violations of citizens' rights.[14] This resolution also cataloged specific provisions that Russians would later use to draft their new Criminal Procedure Code, including expanded rights for defense attorneys, reduction
of maximum length of pretrial detention, and jury trials for all crimes
punishable by "the deprivation of liberty" for one year or more.[15]

The domestic sources of Russian criminal justice reform were an important factor in the eventual passage of the code. Several of the authors
of the concept became intellectual driving forces behind Russian legal
reform throughout the 1990s, helping to draft legislation, providing general expertise, and keeping some movement for legal reform alive. The
basic idea for jury trials and legal reform was not implanted in Russia by
Western advisors; it grew from within.

An Early Victory: Liberal Criminal Procedure Protections in the Russian Constitution

The momentum for legal reform in the early 1990s delivered admirable
protections for the accused in Russia's constitution. On April 21, 1992,
the Russian parliament incorporated a declaration of rights into the 1978
Brezhnev-era constitution of Russia that required judicial approval for
arresting a suspect, searching a private home, intercepting mail, eaves-
dropping, or telephone tapping.[16] Likewise, Russia's post-Soviet constitution, passed in December 1993 (nearly two years after the Soviet Union
formally dissolved), provided for this same panoply of liberal rights.
Most were of the sort that would be familiar to Americans: the presumption of innocence;[17] protection against double jeopardy;[18] right to remain
silent;[19] right to exclude evidence gathered illegally;[20] right to defense
counsel upon arrest or detention;[21] prohibition against ex post facto laws;[22]
right to trial by jury to the extent provided by law; [23] and requirement of
a jury trial for death penalty cases.[24] In a sharp departure from the peripheral role courts played in the Soviet Union, the new constitution
provided that the Russian judiciary—and even international judicial
bodies—would guarantee protection of these far-reaching civil liberties.[25]

This victory was limited, however, because most of these legal reforms in the amended Brezhnev-era and new 1993 Russian constitutions
required additional federal legislation to come into effect. In 1991, the
Supreme Soviet passed a proviso suspending the enforcement of these
rights until the passage of implementing legislation.[26] In a similar vein,
the 1993 constitution delayed the enactment of jury trials and used other
Soviet-era procedures for criminal prosecutions—which, in particular,

did not require judicial authorization for pretrial detentions, searches, and wiretaps—until the passage of a new Criminal Procedure Code.[27] The reason for the delay was in part political compromise to opponents of the reforms. The constitutional provisions glossed over the controversies of what these rights would actually mean in practice, which reflected the limits of the momentum for legal change in Russia and the underlying weak support for these reforms.[28]

Delaying the enactment of these constitutional rights until the passage of implementing legislation also came from the recognition by the drafters of the constitution that the details of implementation were too lengthy and intricate to include in the actual text of the founding document. This illustrates a fundamental obstacle to rule-of-law reform. Even political agreement to guarantee constitutional rights does not answer the problems of resource constraints and logistical complexities.

Some provisions—such as the presumption of innocence, protection against double jeopardy, and prohibition against ex post facto laws—presumably were simple enough not to need detailed implementation plans, so the constitution nominally made these provisions immediately self-executing.[29] But even Russia's most zealous advocates for reform acknowledged that the Russian constitution could not simply by decree achieve a system of jury trials, free access to counsel, and other elements of the revolution in criminal procedure they sought.[30] For example, where would the money and enough trained attorneys come from for the state to provide "the right to qualified legal counsel" for those who could not afford it?[31] Jury trials alone would require millions of rubles to remodel courtrooms to add jury boxes, remove the bars behind which defendants sat, and pay jurors for their service.

Leaving these provisions vague in the constitution let reformers sidestep the unappealing debate over whether the new Russian government could afford such exotic legal reforms. At the precise moment that the International Monetary Fund (IMF) and Western governments were urging the Russian government to cut the bloated state budgets inherited from the Soviet Union to stave off economic collapse, Russian and Western legal reformers were urging the government to spend money on new reforms.[32] Even though the cost of these reforms was a pittance compared with the other budget issues the government faced, calling for the government to spend more money on anything other than unpaid pensions and salaries was still an unpopular demand. Russian legal reformers faced a Hobson's choice that few in the West understood. Requiring the Russian government to offer these legal protections immediately, when no resources yet existed to provide them, would put the government in a position of violating the constitution. That would be an inauspicious beginning to inculcate a new culture of constitutionalism in Russia.

Ironically, the decision by Russia's constitutional drafters to suspend the implementation of criminal procedure protections until resource questions were resolved may have ultimately strengthened these rights. Contrast these protections of criminal procedure to the constitutional guarantees of free provision of health care,[33] education,[34] housing,[35] and even "the right to rest and leisure"[36]—none of which the government could afford to provide to all Russian citizens. In practice, the government has ignored these positive rights and rendered these constitutional protections essentially meaningless.[37]

Momentum for Legal Reform Stalls

Soon after the passage of Russia's post-Soviet constitution, the heady perestroika-era momentum for rule-of-law reform stalled, starkly illustrating the disconnect between the political coalition required to put liberal provisions into a constitution and the wider coalition needed to put those liberal rights into practice. The slowdowns also underlined the time and budgetary constraints that reformers face even when "political will" exists for a given policy. And this window of opportunity for reform closed more quickly than reformers expected it would.

After reformers successfully wrote their provisions into the Russian constitution, advocates of democratic change breathed a temporary sigh of relief and devoted their efforts to other projects. They mistakenly failed to devote the same energy to the more difficult task of *implementing* constitutional rights as they did to ensuring those rights were constitutionalized. A small, dedicated group of legal reformers still focused on implementing legislation, but they became internally divided and increasingly marginalized, as Yeltsin's team focused on economic and other political reforms instead of legal change.

Although Yeltsin personally backed legal reforms, Russia's dispersed decision-making structures—namely, opposition in the Duma, the Ministry of Justice, and regional prosecutors and judges—undermined the passage of the needed implementing legislation. This gridlock was a direct consequence of Russia's democratic reforms. Namely, the same liberalizing forces that led to the collapse of Soviet rule also bequeathed Yeltsin weakened and chaotic administrative structures. Yeltsin's own democratic reforms empowered interest groups to stall policy. More-over, Russia's separation of powers between the parliament and presi-dent led to a stalemate over reform legislation.[38]

Implementation also proceeded slowly because legal reformers faced several bureaucratic obstacles that kept them from taking advantage of the quickly disappearing opportunity for legal reform. A pilot law led to the first jury trial in Russia since the Bolshevik revolution on December 15, 1993, in Saratov, in which the jury acquitted the defendant in a capi-tal murder case. In 1994 legislation expanded jury trials to nine regions in Russia, including Moscow. But legislation to extend jury trials be-yond these nine regions failed, and the regions that officially did have jury trials held them only sporadically.[39] Moscow, for example, did not hold its first jury trial until 2003. Implementation stalled because jury trials were expensive, exotic, and short on domestic support. Opinion polls showed that the public was uneducated about their benefits. Al-though some legal experts described jury trials as a key forum for citi-zen participation in the political process, few Russians viewed the intro-duction of jury trials as a "democratic" reform. Thus, Russian politicians spent their scarce resources on other reforms.

While Russian advocates of criminal procedure reform took care in drafting legislation to implement these complicated reforms, the politi-cal situation changed around them. Namely, skyrocketing inflation from Yeltsin's economic shock therapy engendered a backlash against Yeltsin and Western policy makers considered to be reformist allies. Yeltsin be-came increasingly unpopular, and the Russian parliament opposed his further reform agenda, which included criminal procedure reform. The political window that had allowed a radical change in the Russian con-stitution in favor of a liberal criminal justice system had closed, at least for the immediate future, faster than anyone expected. This setback would later serve as a reminder to the legal reformers of 2001 to seize the mo-ment for reform when it presented itself.

By the mid-1990s, criminal justice reform in Russia seemed dead. Yeltsin had fired his top advocate for legal reform, the Russian parlia-ment elected in 1995 was increasingly unsupportive of legal reforms, and no significant Russian political figures seemed to support criminal procedure reform or other types of rule-of-law reform. Rising crime and lawlessness in Russia created little public demand for giving more rights to accused criminals. Advocates of Russian criminal procedure reform split into warring camps, at one point working on at least three compet-ing drafts of a criminal code. The Duma held hearings on draft versions

of the Criminal Procedure Code, but few believed that it had any serious chance of passage. With legal reform stalled, many Russians felt
that little had changed since the end of the Soviet Union. Russia was still
using the 1960 Soviet Criminal Procedure Code, and protection of the
rights of the accused in the first decade of postcommunist Russia was
hardly any improvement over Soviet-era horror stories. A poll in late
1997 found that only 23 percent of Russians had confidence in the judicial system. Only one in ten believed there had been even a fair amount
of progress in establishing the rule of law since 1991.[40]

At the end of 1999, prospects for reform were so bleak that many in
the U.S. government argued for ending U.S. assistance to criminal procedure reform altogether. In early 2000, the Russian presidential administration would not even return phone calls from the Russian legislator
seeking to promote criminal procedure reform.[41]

An Unexpected Opening: Liberal Reform from an Illiberal Source

In early 2000, however, three changes at the top of Russian politics created space for legal reform, and Russia had a new Criminal Procedure
Code eighteen months later. First, President Vladimir Putin, who had
just been appointed to office by President Boris Yeltsin who resigned
unexpectedly, made legal reform a priority. Putin and his head of the
presidential administration, Dmitri Kozak, created a commission on judicial reform—the Russian Working Group on the Criminal Procedure
Code—to focus on criminal procedure. This working group benefited
from the fact that Putin was popular and threw his support behind the
process. Another positive element was that the forty-person working
group involved all stakeholders: Duma members, radical reformers, and
representatives from the Procuracy (the prosecutor's office), Interior
Ministry, Justice Ministry, internal security services, and presidential
administration. Unlike in previous efforts to pass reform legislation, the
working group included both those who supported and opposed judicial reform. Including potential spoilers on the committee undermined
their power to derail the process.[42] The logic was that if the reformers
could convince the working group, then Russia would have a new Criminal Procedure Code.

Surprisingly, democracy's traditional allies—namely, Russia's liberal
Yabloko Party—joined with the Communists in an odd alliance to water
down elements of the Criminal Procedure Code as it neared passage.[43]
The expected allies of criminal procedure reform—the public and

defense lawyers—played little role in the process. Thus, the Criminal Procedure Code stands as an example of the unexpected coalitions that supported Western reforms and the difficulty in identifying them.

Second, Putin's move to centralize decision-making power—which many criticized as undemocratic—ironically made democratic reform of the criminal justice system possible.[44] Namely, the December 1999 elections delivered a Duma that was not necessarily more inclined toward legal reform but was more loyal to the president than any other since the collapse of the Soviet Union.

The third ingredient was a "policy entrepreneur," in the form of Duma Deputy Elena Mizulina. Mizulina chaired the working group and made it her mission to pass the new Criminal Procedure Code at breakneck speed. She had written her doctoral thesis on modernizing the Russian criminal justice system, and U.S. advisors considered her very progressive and personally invested in legal reform. Other members of the working group cited Mizulina's influence as key to the code's passage.

The importance of Mizulina as a driving force to take advantage of a larger political opening for reform cannot be overstated. Under Mizulina's leadership, the working group completed more work on the code in seven months than other Duma committees had over the past seven years. Mizulina pushed the working group to review hundreds of amendments in a matter of weeks and made the code the primary item on her main legislative agenda.[45] After the working group produced a draft months ahead of schedule, some even criticized her for rushing a drafting process that, in comparison with other similar Russian legislation, should have taken at least another year to complete.[46]

As the code moved through its first and second readings in the Duma and neared its final reading required for passage in the fall of 2001, Mizulina and Kozak successfully fought off attempts by the Procuracy and other opponents to defeat it. Mizulina and her staff worked tirelessly to sort through the flood of amendments to the code and update the draft so that opponents could not use the logistical process of revising the draft as an excuse to delay its passage. At the level of political deal making, Kozak used the political power of the presidential administration to pressure and strike critical bargains with the code's opponents. Finally, on November 22, 2001, the Russian Duma ratified the code, and shortly thereafter Putin signed the bill into law.

Of course, good laws on the books in Russia are not always enforced. However, in a rare event in Russian legislation, the working group became an "implementation group" after the code passed. The group continued to work until January 2004, traveling throughout Russia to build consensus and introducing amendments to the code that would facilitate implementation.[47]

After over a decade of struggle, criminal procedure reforms were becoming a reality in Russian daily life.

Where U.S. Efforts Made a Difference

What impact did U.S. assistance efforts have in the abortive reform efforts during the 1990s and the ultimately successful passage of the Russian Criminal Procedure Code in 2001? The U.S. government primarily sought to influence the process by stimulating demand for criminal procedure reform in the hope that such demand would create a political opening for change and by providing administrative and design assistance to the drafters. U.S. government efforts had little effect on the alignment of political interests that created the possibility in Russia for some type of criminal procedure reform in 2000 or 2001. However, once the political conditions created a window for opportunity for reform in 2000, U.S. assistance contributed to a quicker passage of the law and the introduction of several substantive changes to the code. The U.S. government subsidized the code from behind the scenes, which made the reforms appear much more attractive to Russian politicians.

Little U.S. Influence on Creating the Political Conditions That Made Reform Possible

When efforts in the mid-1990s stalled and failed to implement the liberal protections contained in the Russian constitution, U.S. policy makers felt they could do little to get reform moving again, at least in the short term. Facing a nonresponsive central government, U.S. policy makers adopted the strategy that would become popular in democracy assistance in the late 1990s: Go grass roots. The U.S. government launched a "large-scale lobbying operation" to try to build a constituency for criminal procedure reform among the groups that would benefit most from a new code: lawyers, judges, and civil society groups.[48] As part of this effort, the U.S. government paid for Russian judges and lawyers to watch jury trials in the United States, printed and distributed manuals about how to preside over a jury trial, and hosted seminars for Russian judges and lawyers with U.S. law professors to explain how a modern criminal procedure code would save the courts and government time and money.

U.S. officials claimed that such efforts created a constituency of "hundreds, if not thousands, of judges and lawyers who became advocates of reform" and were essential to the passage of the new code.[49]

In reality, these U.S.-funded seminars and conferences had little demonstrable role in changing the political conditions for passing the new code. Some type of criminal procedure reform probably would have happened in 2000 or 2001 regardless of U.S. efforts. Further, most lawyers and judges opposed the new Criminal Procedure Code until its passage. And even if they supported the code, they had little political power to push for a new reform. Rather, they were part of the chorus that opposed reform.[50] Moreover, powerful interest groups arrayed in opposition to the code—prosecutors, the Ministry of Internal Affairs (MVD), the police, and many Russian lawyers—still opposed criminal procedure reform as firmly as they had earlier, and no public demand had emerged for criminal procedure reform.[51]

Instead, a second opportunity for reform only became possible in 2000 because of elite political dynamics—the dedication of Elena Mizulina, Putin's popularity and desire for legal reforms, and a strong propresidential majority in parliament—elements over which U.S. policy makers had little influence. Why did Putin—best known as a former KGB operative—prioritize legal reforms? It is difficult to attribute this to direct Western prodding, especially because Putin's crackdown on the media and brutal pursuit of the war in Chechnya (and unresponsiveness to Western entreaties to end both) had left top U.S. policy makers pessimistic about Putin's reformist colors and acceptance of Western democratic values.[52]

But it is difficult to rule out indirect Western influence in Putin's likely cost-benefit analysis. Putin calculated that allowing criminal justice reforms could signal his support for liberal Western ideas and contribute to his administrative reforms, both at little cost to his power. Putin could also present these reforms as part of his law-and-order platform, even though the nuance of providing *more* rights for the accused typically is not a familiar part of the pledge to crack down on criminals. To most Russians, jury trials symbolized little more than some exotic Western practice, not a fundamental democratic right. But to U.S. officials, jury trials were as central a feature of democracy as elections or a free press. The critical difference was that jury trials did not directly threaten Putin's power; they were a relatively low-cost form of citizen participation in the government. Thus, while Putin raised Western ire by waging a brutal war in Chechnya and indirectly closing down independent newspapers and television stations, he signaled his democratic bona fides—and came closer to receiving some of the benefits of joining the West—by adopting criminal procedure reforms. At the same time, such reforms could reinforce Putin's attempts to streamline the Russian administration and reverse the governmental chaos he inherited from Yeltsin.[53] Some Russians involved in the process attributed Putin's conception of legal reform as disciplining the Russian bureaucracy to Putin's own training as a lawyer. At the very least, introducing a new criminal procedure code could give Putin an opportunity to assert control over the fiefdoms that regional courts, police, and prosecutors had built.

Yet, although Putin calculated that it was in his interest to allow legal reforms, the benefits were likely neither powerful nor immediate enough for Putin to spend precious political capital on enacting them if they proved to be too costly. As discussed below, U.S. influence became important in keeping the costs of enacting this reform low to Putin, thereby changing the cost-benefit calculation in favor of criminal procedure reform.

Limited, Hands-Off U.S. Assistance in the Early 1990s

In the early- to mid-1990s, Western governments and aid organizations did not help Russia's legal reformers take advantage of the quickly closing window for reform or offer resources that might have made criminal procedure reform cheaper to enact and thus appear more attractive. Granted, the U.S. government offered some $15 million in assistance over three years, mostly for training seminars and logistical help for the courts. Yet U.S. officials did not offer help that some Russian drafters later claimed might have made a difference. Namely, U.S. advisors were not closely involved in the drafting process (in part due to the difficulties U.S. assistance projects faced in getting started in a new country); the U.S. government would not consider funding salaries for jurors (cited as a significant obstacle to reform, given the shortfalls in the Russian government budget, but U.S. policy did not allow paying the salaries of employees of foreign governments); and the U.S. government felt that lobbying Yeltsin to make criminal justice a greater priority was inappropriate interference in Russian domestic politics.[54]

Would deeper U.S. involvement in the drafting and passage of the Russian implementing legislation in the early 1990s have made a difference? It is difficult to say. To be sure, the window of opportunity in the early 1990s was smaller than in 2000. Putin was at the height of his popularity and dominated his parliament, whereas Yeltsin's political capital was quickly disappearing by mid-1992 in the face of an increasingly intransigent parliament and plunging approval ratings. Likewise, Elena Mizulina was an elected member of parliament, whereas the leaders of legal reform in the early 1990s were unelected judges and academics.

At the same time, however, contrast the U.S. government's hands-off approach to rule-of-law reform with its concerted effort to pass economic reforms in the early 1990s. U.S.-funded economic advisors famously sat in Russian government ministries drafting key portions of privatization and macroeconomic reform legislation. The IMF conditioned the receipt of massive economic assistance on the passage of specific key reforms.[55] Senior U.S. policy makers stressed the importance of specific economic reforms in private meetings and public statements. Whatever the limits of the U.S. government's success in prompting the Russian government to implement economic reform in the 1990s, these concerted U.S. government efforts kept economic reform on the Russian political agenda in a way that criminal justice reform was not.[56] U.S. policy makers felt that this type of aggressive assistance on legal reforms was improper and did not attempt it. We do not know whether Russia's legal reformers in the early 1990s would have been as receptive to the type of U.S. assistance that Mizulina accepted in 2000, but the U.S. government did offer the same help in the early 1990s.

Deeper U.S. Collaboration with the Drafters of the Code After 2000

The style of U.S. assistance in criminal procedure reform after 2000 was fundamentally different from earlier efforts and from other U.S. rule-of-law assistance efforts. U.S. efforts played a greater role in 2000 due in equal part to the good fortune of the arrival of a Russian policy entrepreneur who sought Western assistance and the willingness of U.S. policy makers to become deeply involved in the drafting and passage of the code, in the form of collaboration and involvement in the domestic politics of the transition country others in the U.S. assistance community considered improper.

To the surprise of U.S. officials who had previously encountered little receptiveness to criminal justice reform in the Russian government, Elena Mizulina welcomed direct U.S. help upon becoming the head of the Russian Working Group on the Criminal Procedure Code. Her group needed resources to pass the Criminal Procedure Code on her ambitious timeline, and the U.S. government was eager to provide them. The

U.S. Embassy Law Enforcement Section and the U.S.-funded American Bar Association's Central Eastern European Legal Initiative (ABA/CEELI) provided the two parts of U.S. assistance: logistical support to help the working group pass a code and expert advice on needed changes in the code.[57]

Beginning in the spring of 2000, U.S. advisors collaborated closely with Mizulina's working group. The Moscow-based U.S. Department of Justice representative spoke with Mizulina at least once a month. Two U.S.-funded American experts on comparative criminal procedure "effectively became ex-officio members of the working group," provided model language for parts of the code, and testified at Duma hearings.[58] Parts of the U.S. advisors' language made it into the final code.[59] In fact, before the second reading of the law in the Duma, U.S. Embassy officials retained the working group's only master working draft of the law.[60] The U.S. government also sponsored several conferences for the working group and trips to the United States to meet with American judges, which resulted in several substantive changes in the code, not just "technical" fixes.[61] After several of the U.S.-sponsored conferences, Mizulina went to her laptop and immediately incorporated the concrete suggestions from the conference into the draft law. Because the working group had little money of its own, it is unlikely that these conferences would have happened without U.S. assistance.

But U.S. policy makers stayed clear of offering their Russian counterparts any specific incentives—such as more foreign aid or meetings with the U.S. president or secretary of state—in exchange for passing the code. Significantly, U.S. advisors also intentionally remained in the background of the policy-making process to let Russia's politicians claim credit for the reform and to avoid any potential backlash from perceived U.S. interference in Russia's internal affairs. As the U.S. Embassy coordinator for the U.S. effort said:

> We're not here to lobby for Russian legislation. We're here to provide technical assistance. If we're asked for help, we'll give it. Usually the approach I tried to take is to offer things, such as model statutes and concepts, not to say 'You have to do this or we're leaving.' Ultimately, I don't think that would be politically effective in Russia.[62]

Even though U.S. advisors did not see all the reforms they would have wanted in the final law, in their eyes, they won their most important victory: the passage of the code itself and a concerted effort in the years after the code's passage to ensure it would be put into practice.

In fact, the United States exerted even more influence in the implementation stage than it did in the drafting stage. The U.S. government provided both funding ($1.2 million for criminal procedure work in 2002 alone) and logistical support to the implementation group's efforts.[63] Some Russians involved with drafting the code considered U.S. support to the implementation group its most important contribution. Because an implementation group for a newly passed law was an innovation in Russian policy making, domestic funding was not readily available. U.S. assistance allowed the group to avoid fighting the bureaucratic battle to secure funding and instead focus immediately on working with local courts and prosecutors to implement the law.

U.S. Influence on the Substance and Timing of the Code

Given that the Russian government drove the process to pass the code and U.S. support appeared to be primarily administrative and behind-the-scenes, would things have been different without U.S. involvement? Yes. One change was that some specific ideas—such as plea bargaining and five other concrete protections of defendant's rights, described in greater detail below—would not have made it into the final bill without U.S.-funded advisors.

To be sure, Western influence was more important to the design of legal texts at the stage of implementing legislation than it was in drafting the constitution itself. Although they praised the progressive provisions of the Russian constitution, Western lawyers had little involvement in drafting them. The immediate inspiration for the liberal provisions of the Russian constitution came from the Concept of Judicial Reform, which the Russian parliament passed before the collapse of the Soviet Union. The closest that Americans came to influencing the design of this early legal text, and thus the foundations for the 2001 Criminal Procedure Code, came from a general diffusion of Western ideas. For example, one of the authors of the concept had written her doctoral dissertation in the 1970s on the U.S. Criminal Procedure Code.[64] Yet in contrast to the presence of Western lawyers who rushed into Hungary, Poland, and elsewhere in Central Europe after the fall of the Berlin Wall, Russian drafters did not meet with any foreign advisors.[65] Only two of the seven co-authors of the concept spoke English, and even they were not known as America-philes (nor were they eager to work with Western advisors). Few Americans, both in and outside of the government, even knew about the resolution and the other legal reforms that the Soviet parliament was passing.[66] Russians drafted good laws on their own, but this alone did not legal reform make.

Drafting assistance did, however, make a difference at the stage of second-order implementing legislation, once Russian political coalitions had aligned to create a space for U.S. influence. Plea bargaining was the most significant provision that made it into the code *only after* U.S. involvement.[67] The introduction of this provision illustrates how U.S. assistance helped Russian reformers overcome specific practical and political obstacles that might have derailed the legislation. Plea bargaining is an essential requirement for American jury trials, to ensure that courts are not overwhelmed with trials. But Russian drafters had not seriously considered it before the American suggestion, and its introduction was a heated political fight.[68] Although jury trials without plea bargaining would have overwhelmed Russia's already overextended court system, many Russians felt that confessions before trial in plea bargaining smacked too much of the forced confessions of Stalin's show trials. U.S. experts helped explain the concept, offered ideas about how to make it happen, and eased fears about the confessions' Stalinist overtones. The plea bargaining system Russia finally adopted was very similar to the U.S. system. Plea bargaining also neutralized a critical argument of opponents of introducing jury trials—namely, that jury trials would either cause a greater backlog in Russia's criminal justice system or, worse, put criminals back on the streets.

Some members of the working group credited U.S. influence for the inclusion of other provisions about rules of evidence and other protections of the rights of the accused.[69] These provisions were in Russia's 1993 constitution but not in the actual drafts of the code before U.S. involvement began.[70]

More broadly, U.S. advisors helped Russian drafters update the czarist-era nineteenth-century concept of jury trials to twenty-first-century Russia. For example, the author of Russia's jury trial provisions, Sergei Pashin, recalled the influence of a U.S. government–funded trip to Harvard Law School that he took while drafting the law. Pashin drew on the American interpretation of the right of a citizen to obtain a writ of habeas corpus as a protection against illegal imprisonment and borrowed the selection and preemptive challenging of jurors from the U.S. federal court system.[71] Moreover, U.S. advisors convinced the drafters of the jury trial laws that certain practices of Russian courts—such as bringing defendants before a jury in shackles or seating them throughout the trial in a cage—had to change.[72] Russian judges even paraphrased certain parts of standard American jury instructions.[73]

In addition to introducing specific content into the code, U.S. efforts contributed in a second way by securing the code's timely passage. Whereas a political window for criminal procedure reform had opened and closed in the early 1990s due to bureaucratic delays, U.S. involvement in 2000 helped Russian politicians overcome these same obstacles to ensure that the opportunity for reform would not pass again. Such help included organizing the working group, maintaining various drafts, and keeping track of proposed changes. Russians working on the code said that it passed a year to eighteen months faster than it would have if the United States had not been involved.[74] Of course, it is highly probable that some reform would have passed eighteen months later. Yet it is worth remembering how quickly the political window of opportunity for reform closed in the early 1990s. While advocates of jury trials struggled in those years to overcome logistical obstacles to putting a good piece of legislation together, Russia elected a new parliament that was much more hostile to legal reforms. Yeltsin's popularity also fell, which made him a less effective patron of reform.

Likewise, consider the counterfactual of what would have happened if the Criminal Procedure Code had been delayed until 2003. In that year the Russian parliament faced reelection, and the code's champion, Elena Mizulina, might not have even kept her seat. Moreover, Putin faced reelection in 2004 and would have focused his energy on campaigning, not undertaking bold new reforms. With many Russians fearing that jury trials might lead to more criminals going free, introducing jury trials was hardly a populist move.

One of the coordinators of the U.S. effort from Moscow described the pathway of U.S. influence on the substance of the code and the timing of its passage as follows:

> It's kind of like the MacArthur Grants. You find people who are good, focused, and committed, and you support them. But the will needs to be indigenous. The ideas that underpinned what they were trying to do were already consistent with what the U.S. would support, and consistent with European norms. It was more that the Russians didn't have the resources to do what they wanted to do.[75]

U.S. assistance provided external validation for the proposed reforms and helped the Russian reformers defeat the arguments of their opponents. One of the Russian drafters explained how U.S. assistance was "more than a computer for information. America helped us defend our ideas. It let us say to our opponents, 'You can see the democratic system working abroad.'" Traveling to the United States and seeing the proposed reforms in practice converted some to support the new cause.[76] Mizulina said that U.S. commentaries on the draft laws "helped set the mindset for the drafters, so they started with a perspective of having a reformist law."[77]

In doing so, U.S. influence was part of, and supported by, a concert of other Western efforts. Experts funded by the British, German, Dutch, and French governments all offered ideas, and it is difficult to trace the parentage of many of the ideas that made it into the final code.[78] In fact, the most specific Western influence was not a U.S. document at all, but the European Convention on Human Rights.[79] U.S. advisors used Russia's desire to conform to the European Convention on Human Rights and the Council of Europe's standards to persuade Russians to change the Criminal Procedure Code.[80]

The European Convention was powerful in this case. It provided a set of concrete, enduring, and widely accepted standards of behavior. U.S. advisors felt this was a more legitimate vehicle through which to urge Russia to change its behavior, rather than simply asking the Russian government to follow U.S. advice. After the collapse of the Soviet Union, Russia had actually signed the European Convention as a requirement to join the Council of Europe. Although the council conferred on its members few of the concrete benefits that the European Union or the North Atlantic Treaty Organization did, membership still implied respect and recognition of Russia from the West, which Yeltsin and Putin sought to strengthen their legitimacy at home. Moreover, although Russia could and often did ignore provisions of the European Convention without facing any real sanctions from the council, disregarding the council's recommendations for the draft of the code would have undercut Putin's ability to use the code as a symbol of Russia's embrace of Western values.

Although European norms and the advice of Western governments helped shape particular provisions of the law, it was U.S. involvement that carried these European norms into the Russian policy-making process. The U.S. government funded the translation of Council of Europe recommendations for the code. In a more ongoing way, U.S. advisors used their close collaboration with the working group to bring principles from the European Convention into the drafting process. Members of the working group cited the U.S. government as the most directly engaged foreign government in the process. Offering logistical help to make reform cheaper to the Russian government was thus a way for U.S. advisors to exert influence over the substance of the final law.

Lessons for Rule-of-Law Promotion

Although it is important not to draw overly broad conclusions from a single case, the story of criminal procedure change in Russia suggests tempering expectations for what constitutes "successful" rule-of-law reform, calls into question conventional explanations for how legal reform happens, identifies an alternative approach for understanding how to promote the rule of law abroad, and suggests where practitioners might focus future efforts.

The Outcome: A Good, but Imperfect Law

This case shows that even a rule-of-law success does not imply that the final law completely reflects the preferences of Western advisors. To be sure, U.S. policy makers rightly considered the passage of the Criminal Procedure Code as one of the major successes of U.S. rule-of-law promotion in the former Soviet Union. Amnesty International praised the code,[81] and ABA/CEELI representatives called it the "most progressive Criminal Procedure Code in the NIS [Newly Independent States]."[82] U.S. Ambassador to Russia Alexander Vershbow proclaimed the code to be "the most important legal reform in Russia" in a century and a half.[83] Just six months after the code went into effect in July 2002, the number of criminal cases opened by the Procuracy declined by 25 percent, the number of suspects placed in pretrial detention declined by 30 percent, and the courts rejected 15 percent of requests for arrest warrants.[84] By February 2003, the number of arrests was down 33 percent, and the acquittal rate fell from one case per 270 to one in five for jury trials.[85] The code will also expand jury trials from a handful of "experimental" regions throughout the 1990s to all eighty-nine of Russia's regions by 2007.[86]

Yet this case also shows that few outcomes in democracy promotion can be placed unambiguously in the win or loss column. Several problems remain in the code. First, it does not address some important issues, such as falsification of evidence or police torture. Some Russian liberals criticized the code for not going far enough in protecting the rights of the accused,[87] but members of the working group countered that they did as much as Russian political realities allowed.[88] Second, even members of the working group admitted that the final code contains some technical mistakes and poorly explained procedures because it was passed so quickly.[89] U.S. policy makers readily admit that the law has shortcomings but argue that a new, flawed law is a better than no law at all. To the extent that Russia's criminal procedure reforms are a victory for post-Soviet legal reform, even successful reforms have significant flaws. Accordingly, both critics and crusaders of rule-of-law promotion should adjust their expectations of what constitutes success to the realities of what the political process produces.

New Approach to Rule-of-Law Promotion: Catalyzing Reform

More broadly, the story of Russian criminal procedure reform suggests a different strategy for supporting legal change abroad than the two prevailing approaches. One conventional view favors a "top-down" approach, in which building the rule of law is primarily about crafting the right laws and institutional arrangements, which can be informed by international best practices.[90] Critiques of this approach point to an alternative: a "bottom-up" strategy of providing foreign technical assistance to different players in a transition country's legal and political community—such as training lawyers and judges in Western practices—to build both a culture of respect for the law and a constituency that will demand legal reforms from their government.[91]

To be sure, these approaches are not mutually exclusive. Yet neither theory would have predicted the emergence of criminal procedure reform in Russia. First, Russia's successful criminal procedure reforms did not come from top-down design, the domain where rule-of-law promoters focus most of their efforts today. Constitutional design was, in itself, a relatively unimportant explanatory factor. The Russian constitution guaranteed extensive rights of criminal procedure and jury trials for over a decade before they became a functioning reality in Russian society. The design assistance that made a difference came in the second-order implementing legislation. The technical expertise that helped Russian drafters came at a level of detail that required an intimate knowledge of the practical problems facing the Russian government, not generic expertise that could be provided with model legislation or brief visits by foreign experts, the forms of assistance where much effort is directed today.

Nor did legal reforms come from the sources that the "bottom-up" approach expects. U.S. assistance providers sought to educate Russian lawyers and judges about the virtues of legal reform because they recognized that these key implementers fiercely opposed any changes that might take away their own power. Yet the lawyers and judges still largely opposed the code right up to its passage. The efforts of the U.S. government to reach out to these groups and build a constituency for reform—which some U.S. policy makers later identified as the *primary* channel of U.S. influence—had little impact on the substance or timing of the code. Even if these lawyers or judges had changed their minds, they were not major players in the passage of the new code. Not only did grass roots demand *not* produce the reforms Western policy makers expected, but, as described below, criminal procedure reforms were neither popular nor supported by Russia's traditional allies of democratic reform. Majoritarian democracy was in tension with deepening protections of civil liberties and the rule of law in Russia.

Instead, legal change came from a third source: a coalition of Russian political elites over whose initial emergence the U.S. government had little direct influence. Ironically, one of Russia's most significant liberal legal reforms was only possible under Russia's former KGB operator president, Vladimir Putin, who is known more for his illiberal tendencies than any democratic stripes.[92] Putin unexpectedly made legal reform a priority of his first administration, and his centralization of power in Russia opened a political window to pass controversial changes in the criminal justice system. An enterprising Russian legislator sought to take advantage of this opportunity for reform, without any prodding from the U.S. government. Legal change in Russia came from the top, not from grass roots demand.

Russian criminal procedure reform thus illustrates a third pathway for Western assistance to influence legal reform—what I term *catalyzing reform*—a strategy that has received comparatively little attention to date. This approach suggests that Western efforts can influence legal reform when two conditions are present: first, a policy entrepreneur who favors reform and some domestic political space to make her efforts a reality; and second, the need for legislation or a plan to implement reforms that are already part of the policy debate. When those conditions hold, the West can help bring about reforms by offering logistical and monetary support, without claiming credit.

Centrality of Domestic Policy Entrepreneurs

Although the U.S. government was deeply involved in Russian domestic politics, U.S. efforts had little influence over the presence of the first necessary condition for Russian legal reform. The driving political and intellectual forces behind Russia's criminal procedure reforms were domestic "policy entrepreneurs," who arose independent of any U.S. involvement. Policy entrepreneurs, in a combination of ideology and self-interest, want policy change as much as, if not more, than their Western supporters.

Russian domestic policy entrepreneurs supplied the core ideas for criminal procedure reform. One of the U.S. advisors to the drafters explained, "It's not like we drafted a law, and they picked it up and translated it."[93] Russian members of the working group resisted calling the U.S. role "influence."[94] The right to a jury trial, stronger defendants' rights, and the other landmark provisions of the Criminal Procedure Code had deep roots in Russia's perestroika reforms from before the collapse of the Soviet Union and in czarist legal reforms from a century before. Ideas from Western legal systems helped inspire those criminal justice reforms, but it was a much more diffuse Western influence than any direct U.S. involvement.[95] To claim parentage for these broader concepts would be to grossly overstate U.S. influence.

Having an existing group of domestic "policy entrepreneurs" who were dedicated to reforms, even if larger political obstacles frequently undermined their efforts, was critical in giving U.S. policy makers partners to work with and creating a channel for U.S. influence. The political opening for legal change in 2000 would have closed without notice if Elena Mizulina and her colleagues had not fought to take advantage of it.

It is through these domestic policy entrepreneurs that the foreign efforts are able to catalyze reform. Policy entrepreneurs who choose to undertake reforms still face budgetary constraints in the form of scarce time, money, and other bureaucratic resources that can delay and, as political conditions change, ultimately undermine a given reform. Western efforts can subsidize a country's policy-making process—namely, by providing infrastructure support and assistance in drafting legislation to implement constitutional provisions—to make a given reform cheaper for a transition government. As politicians choose which reforms to pursue once a political window opens, such third-party assistance can make politicians an offer they cannot refuse: lowering the costs of undertaking a given reform, while still letting the politicians claim the credit. As described below, this is the type of influence that the U.S. government successfully supplied in Russia to influence the timing and nature of the Criminal Procedure Code.

Question of Politics Not Just Assistance

The type of U.S. effort required to catalyze reform calls for deeper involvement in a country's domestic politics than conventional wisdom suggests. U.S. assistance after 2000 made a difference not because of its extent but because of its form: It was influence at a bargain. The U.S. government spent less than $1 million on this work from 1999 to 2002, the period when the United States had the most influence on the code. Compared with most other U.S. rule-of-law promotion efforts, however, the U.S. government was far more deeply involved in the Russian legislative process for the passage of the Criminal Procedure Code. In contradiction to the development community's technical assistance credo of avoiding interactions that support particular politicians or are otherwise partisan, such external support was necessarily political and at times even entailed surprisingly direct U.S. involvement in the politics of the host country. Some USAID officials even felt it was improper that the U.S. Department of Justice and ABA/CEELI played such a visible role in the passage of the code.[96]

This case suggests a middle ground between the "top-down" and "bottom-up" approaches to rule-of-law assistance. Constitutional engineers tend to devote inadequate attention to the extensive second-order legislation required to implement even the most detailed and well-designed constitutional provisions. Harnessing the energy for reform demands much deeper, longer (in years, not just months), and more subtle involvement than the focus of the top-down approach on the founding document. Likewise, the "bottom-up" approach of providing general support to constituencies across society is unlikely, at least in the short term, to affect those who are driving a particular reform. Supporters of the bottom-up approach respond that such criticisms are premature; the grass roots strategy is intended to produce results in decades, not years. Even assuming that such a strategy will eventually produce results, it still falls to its defenders to be much more explicit about just how long transition countries can expect to wait for change. Moreover, the short-term electoral incentives of U.S. politics make it difficult to sustain a domestic political constituency for foreign aid. In seeking to build domestic support in the United States for rule-of-law promotion abroad, is it wise to rely primarily on a rule-of-law promotion strategy that will only produce results in decades?

Fundamentally, the Russian example shows that the passage of important legal reforms is a *political* process. To exert influence, Western assistance providers must work with the political actors driving the process. U.S. influence was only possible because U.S. advisors built unusually close relationships with key Russian decision makers. Such "collusion" was a necessary condition for U.S. influence, not a form of corruption as some critics of Western assistance have alleged.[97]

Reform from Unexpected Sources

Finally, this case illustrates the difficulty of identifying the opportunities for Western political influence, because legal reform often comes from unexpected sources. "Democratic reforms" do not necessarily come from "democrats." Russian legal reform came neither from a "democratic" leader and open policy-making procedures, nor from demand from the public, defense lawyers, or other expected constituencies for legal reform. To the contrary, leaders who have centralized power, even to an undemocratic degree, may have greater ability to carry out legal reforms. That rule-of-law reform stalled under Yeltsin and proceeded under Putin suggests tensions between rule-of-law and democratic reforms. A more optimistic conclusion is that at least some meaningful legal reforms may be possible under seemingly illiberal governments.

This paradox challenges the model used by Western policy makers, who often speak of democracy and rule of law as a single, mutually reinforcing package.[98] But the tension between majoritarian democracy and the protection of civil rights is less surprising to students of constitutionalism. Campaigning to limit the government's power to arrest and convict criminals was unlikely to find widespread support in a Russian society confronting rising crime. Interest groups in Russia were already weak and unlikely to develop first for "criminals." It is precisely for this reason that democracies turn to antimajoritarian courts to protect civil liberties. This case suggests not only that democracy and the rule of law must be thought of as related but intellectually distinct concepts, but also that *strategies* for promoting democracy and the rule of law cannot be assumed to be the same.

The unexpected sources of Russian criminal procedure reform offer another sobering conclusion about the idiosyncratic factors of legal change that make external influence possible at all. At the end of 1999, prospects for reform were so bleak that many in the U.S. government argued for ending U.S. assistance to criminal procedure reform altogether. In fact, many of the "lessons learned" from Western rule-of-law assistance would have prescribed precisely that: Western assistance projects should only continue when the central government shows clear interest in undertaking reforms.[99] That recommendation seemed unassailable, because no one with any influence in the Russian government seemed to have any interest in criminal procedure reform.[100] Yet, had the U.S. government diverted its resources to support reform that seemed more likely at the time, it would have missed an opportunity to influence the passage of the Criminal Procedure Code. In short, the idiosyncratic and unpredictable domestic political coalitions that make reforms possible pose a dilemma for U.S. policy makers seeking to allocate scarce resources in support of reforms.

Top U.S. policy makers now point to Russian adoption of jury trials as the result of successful U.S. influence, and it is true that U.S. efforts contributed to a meaningful rule-of-law reform.[101] However, the method of U.S. influence—harnessing the energy for reform—requires either luck or very intimate knowledge of potential political openings in the host government to identify those with whom to work.

Practitioners have imperfectly dubbed the conditions under which Western assistance can make a difference as "political will." Yet this term is analytically imprecise and operationally unhelpful. Political will is too often defined tautologically: It is assumed to have existed once a reform passed. Further research should seek to understand more precisely what political will means. This case study indicates that political will does not necessarily depend on the presence of a "democratic" leader (itself a problematic term). Assessing political will requires a more sophisticated understanding of local decision-making structures that make implementing reforms possible. Although this understanding is difficult, criminal justice reform in Russia illustrates that catalyzing reform is possible.

Notes

An earlier version of this chapter was originally published as Carnegie Paper no. 60 (July 2005).

1. As one commentator put it, "One cannot get through a foreign policy debate these days without someone proposing the rule of law as a solution to the world's troubles. . . . It promises to remove all the chief obstacles on the path to democracy and market economies." See Thomas Carothers, chapter 1 in this volume. Yet the *rule of law* is itself a vague concept, conceived of today as more of a mantra than a precise analytical definition. Parsing this concept in detail is beyond the scope of this chapter. Here I consider rule of law in terms of what U.S. policy makers were seeking to promote. In the former Soviet Union, these objectives included strengthening an independent judiciary, improving law enforcement practices, developing the

foundations for reform, increasing citizens' access to justice, and improving legal education and the quality of legal professionals. U.S. General Accounting Office (GAO), "Former Soviet Union: U.S. Rule of Law Assistance Has Had Limited Impact," GAO-01-354 (Washington, D.C.: GAO, April 2001).

2. For this study I carried out research in Russia and Washington from 2001 to 2003, including interviews with the U.S. Embassy, State Department, and White House officials; members of the Russian Working Group on the Criminal Procedure Code; Russian judges and lawyers; authors of Russian legislation; and Western-funded organizations providing legal assistance in the former Soviet Union.

3. From fiscal 1992 to 2000, the U.S. government spent $216 million on rule-of-law projects in the former Soviet Union, of which Russia received $77 million. GAO, "Former Soviet Union," p. 6. The very title of General Accounting Office's report evaluating U.S. rule-of-law assistance in April 2001 was telling: "Former Soviet Union: U.S. Rule of Law Assistance Has Had Limited Impacts." U.S. rule-of-law promotion projects in the former communist bloc ranged widely from introducing civil codes and securities laws to support a market economy, to supporting the independence of the courts. Many of these projects were designed as a long-term strategy, so practitioners argued that results could not be expected in less than one-seventh of the years in which Soviet communism dominated the region. Other efforts resulted in the passage of civil codes and other pieces of legislation. Yet these laws have often not been implemented, and policy makers have not claimed success for them in the same way as criminal procedure reform in Russia. See also Stephen Golub, chapter 5 in this volume.

4. See, for example, Stephen F. Cohen, *Failed Crusade: America and the Tragedy of Post Communist Russia* (New York: W.W. Norton, 2000); and Janine Wedel, *Collision and Collusion: The Strange Case of Western Aid to Eastern Europe, 1989–1998* (New York: St. Martin's Press, 1998).

5. During the 1990s some 11,000 detainees and prisoners died in custody each year in Russia, some from beatings, but most from overcrowding. The *2001 U.S. State Department Human Rights Report* singled out the conditions of pretrial detention and torture of prisoners as among Russia's worst human rights violations. U.S. Bureau of Democracy, Human Rights, and Labor, *Country Reports on Human Rights Practices for 2001* (Washington, D.C.: U.S. Department of State, 2002). See also Amnesty International, "Denial of Justice" (New York: Amnesty International, 2002), available at: http://web.amnesty.org/ai.nsf/Index/EUR460272002; and Human Rights Watch, *Confessions at Any Cost: Police Torture in Russia* (New York: Human Rights Watch, 1999).

6. Juan J. Linz and Alfred Stepan, *Problems of Democratic Transition and Consolidation* (Baltimore, MD: Johns Hopkins University Press, 1996); and Fareed Zakaria, "The Rise of Illiberal Democracy," *Foreign Affairs* 76 (November/December 1997).

7. Amnesty International, "Denial of Justice."

8. For more on jury trials in the U.S. legal system, see U.S. Constitution, amends. 6 and 7. On the consequences of the Soviet legacy for Russian legal reform, see, for example, Peter Solomon and Todd Fogelsong, *Courts and Transition in Russia: The Challenge of Judicial Reform* (Boulder, CO: Westview Press, 2000). Moreover, civil law–based countries, which Russia is usually considered, do not typically have jury trials.

9. Elena Mizulina, interview by author, Golitsna, Russia, May 14, 2003.

10. Czar Alexander II provided the right to jury trial through the Judicial Reform Act of 1864. It was virtually the only way citizens of imperial Russia could have uncensored speech and a voice in their government. When discussing the Criminal Procedure Code, one of the authors of the Concept of Judicial Reform even referred to the section on jury trials in a well-worn copy of Russia's 1868 Criminal Procedure

Code. Inga Mikhailovskaya, co-author of the Concept of Judicial Reform and member of the Russian Working Group on the Criminal Procedure Code, interview by author, Moscow, November 26, 2002.

11. Russia used an "inquisitorial" process, more common in European civil law countries, in which prosecutors had the most responsibility to find the truth. Contrast this with the U.S. adversarial system. In practice, however, the Soviet Union's inquisitorial system meant prosecution dominance with few checks. See Stephen C. Thaman, "The Resurrection of Trial by Jury in Russia," *Stanford Journal of International Law* 31 (1995).

12. These two "people's assessors" technically had the power to override the decisions of judges but were known in practice as "nodders," because they always agreed with the judges' decisions. Even the judges were appointed and completely beholden to the Communist Party. Party officials routinely called judges to instruct them how to rule, regardless of the case's facts, a practice known as "telephone justice." See Solomon and Fogelsong, *Courts and Transition in Russia.*

13. Thaman, "Resurrection of Trial," 70.

14. The 1993 Russian constitution was ultimately silent on "lifetime tenure." It only provided that citizens must be at least twenty-five years old, hold a law degree, and must have worked in the law profession for at least five years. The constitution left federal law to define further qualifications (Russian Constitution, art. 119). The tenure of justices on the Russian Constitutional Court received the most attention. The legislature set the minimum age at forty-five and mandatory retirement at sixty-five, in effect creating twenty-year maximum terms to serve on the court.

15. Sergei Pashin, author of a book on Russian jury trials and head of the Judicial Reform Department of the President's Administration of the Russian Federation, 1992–1995, interview by author, Moscow, December 9, 2002. The concept reduced the length of pretrial detention from eighteen months to six to nine months. The 1999 code had reduced the time to three days.

16. Thaman, "Resurrection of Trial," 76–7.

17. Russian Constitution, art. 49.

18. Ibid., art. 50, sec. 1.

19. Ibid., art. 51.

20. Ibid., art. 50, sec. 2.

21. Ibid., art. 48.

22. Ibid., art. 54.

23. Two provisions in the Russian constitution provided for the right to jury trials. Article 20 provided that "Capital punishment may, until its abolition, be instituted by federal law as exceptional punishment for especially grave crimes against life, with the accused having the right to have his case considered in a law court by jury." Article 47 stated that "Anyone charged with a crime has the right to have his or her case reviewed by a court of law with the participation of jurors in cases stipulated by federal law."

24. The constitution also required the courts to monitor restrictions upon basic civil liberties, such as telephone and other electronic surveillance, taking of private property, and searches of homes (Russian Constitution, arts. 22 and 25).

25. Article 46 of the constitution provided that "Everyone shall be guaranteed protection of his or her rights and liberties in a court of law." The "decisions and actions (or inaction)" of any state body were subject to appeal in court. Should domestic remedies fail, the constitution further specified: "In conformity with international treaties of the Russian Federation, everyone shall have the right to turn to interstate organs concerned with the protection of human rights and liberties when all the means of legal protection available within the state have been exhausted." Human rights

groups in Russia have used this provision to bring cases before the Council of Europe. Such efforts led to the abolition of the death penalty in Russia. The elimination was contemplated in article 20 of the constitution but proved unpopular in Russian opinion polls. Ultimately, the Russian government agreed to eliminate the death penalty as a condition for joining the Council of Europe. However, the efforts of human rights groups to appeal to international judicial bodies over human rights cases in Chechnya have produced little change in Russia. International judicial bodies played little role in the introduction of the new Criminal Procedure Code and jury trials in Russia.

26. Thaman, "Resurrection of Trial," 76–7.

27. In the "Concluding and Transitional Part" of the Russian constitution, article 5 set out: "Courts in the Russian Federation exercise the right to administer justice in accordance with their powers set down in this Constitution." But the next article explicitly restricted what this would mean: Until the adoption of a federal law setting forth the procedures for trial by jury, the prior procedure for conducting trials shall be retained. Until the enforcement of criminal-procedural legislation of the Russian Federation in accordance with the provisions of this Constitution, *the prior procedures of the arrest, custody and detention of individuals suspected of committing crimes shall be maintained* (art. 6, emphasis added).

28. Opponents used implementing legislation to fight against the reforms by various means. The "Transition" section of the 1993 constitution suspended the enactment of criminal procedure reforms until the passage of additional legislation. In the sections articulating the substance of the rights, the constitution still intentionally limited the two most controversial and supposedly "exotic" reforms—jury trials and state-funded defense counsel—to "cases stipulated by law" (arts. 47 and 48). Even though the constitution mandated that the rights articulated therein "shall determine the meaning, content and application of the laws, and the activities of the legislative and executive branches and local self-government," a close reading of the text shows that the constitution, in reality, established two tiers of rights (art. 18). In fact, jury trials and state-funded defense counsel are the few rights listed in the constitution's 137 articles (leaving aside temporary suspensions of rights in emergency powers) that the legislature had the explicit right to define and thus restrict in ordinary circumstances.

29. Russian Constitution, art. 18. Yet these provisions still required rewriting instructions for judges in deciding cases. In practice, even these protections often had little meaning in courts that still used Soviet-era criminal procedure practices. For example, despite the presumption of innocence, Russia had one of the highest conviction rates in the world. For much of the 1990s, only one out of every 270 Russian defendants was acquitted. See Mark McDonald, "Russia Begins New Twist on Trials: Juries," *Knight-Ridder*, February 17, 2003.

30. Pashin, interview.

31. For that reason the Russian constitution only provided for access to legal counsel "in cases stipulated by the law" (art. 48).

32. See, for example, Randall Stone, *Lending Credibility* (Princeton, NJ: Princeton University Press, 2002).

33. Russian Constitution, art. 41.

34. The constitution requires "general education" for all Russians and requires the state to provide free higher education (art. 43). As of 2004, these rights have glaringly not been provided in Russia.

35. Russian Constitution, art. 40.

36. Ibid., art. 37.

37. Although individuals have successfully sued the government for the violation of these rights, the government has not complied with these decisions.

38. For more on the dispersion of Russian decision-making structures in Yeltsin's first term, see, for example, Michael McFaul, *Russia's Unfinished Revolution: Political Change from Gorbachev to Putin* (Ithica, NY: Cornell University Press, 2001).

39. By January 1, 1995, 173 jury trials took place in nine Russian regions. Irina Dline and Olga Schwartz, "The Jury Is Still Out on the Future of Jury Trials in Russia," *East European Constitutional Review* 11 (2002), at 104–10; Stephen C. Thaman, "The Resurrection of Trial by Jury in Russia," *Stanford Journal of International Law* 31 (1995).

40. Richard B. Dobson, "Russians Favor Religious Freedom, See Few Signs of the Rule of Law" (Washington, D.C.: U.S. Information Agency, Office of Research and Media Relations, 1998).

41. This legislator was Duma Deputy Elena Mizulina. Christopher Lehmann, U.S. Department of Justice Representative, U.S. Embassy Moscow, interview by author, Moscow, November 14, 2002.

42. Members of the Russian Working Group on the Criminal Procedure Code, interview by author, Moscow, May 14, 2003.

43. Both Yabloko and Communist deputies feared that plea bargaining—what U.S. policy makers argued was needed for jury trials—would lead to forced self-incrimination and sought to reduce its reach. In another odd alliance, the author of Yeltsin's initial criminal procedure reforms and his allies opposed the code, claiming its reforms were not far-reaching enough. Pashin, interview.

44. See Lilia Shevtsova, *Putin's Russia* (Washington, D.C.: Carnegie Endowment for International Peace, 2003).

45. Christopher Scott, from the American Bar Association's Central Eastern European Legal Initiative (ABA/CEELI), interview by author, Moscow, October 22, 2002. "Only because of Mizulina and her tenacity was this law passed in such a short time," said one member of the working group. Olga Schwartz, advisor to the Russian Working Group on the Criminal Procedure Code, interview by author, Moscow, November 7, 2002.

46. Critics of the working group, who felt Mizulina was too ready to compromise and water down liberal provisions of the code, claimed that the unprecedented speed of the process meant that the code that passed was riddled with errors and inaccuracies. Pashin, interview. The working group acknowledged these errors but corrected them during the implementing process with amendments to the code. Members of the Russian Working Group on the Criminal Procedure Code, interview.

47. In attending a working group meeting outside Moscow, the author observed that the regional meetings were heated, with some shouting and opposition to the code, but also that real work was done. Some regional law enforcement began the working group meetings very hostile to the code. But they were often placated by the fact that legislators from Moscow traveled to the far reaches of Russia to ensure that the code was implemented, rather than the usual practice of Moscow handing down impractical decrees. Based on key suggestions from each of the six working group meetings during 2002–2003, Mizulina drafted amendments to the Criminal Procedure Code, which the Duma appeared likely to approve.

48. U.S. government official, telephone interview with author, 2002 (anonymous at the request of the interviewee; interview notes on file with the author).

49. U.S. government official, telephone interview.

50. Members of the Russian Working Group on the Criminal Procedure Code, interview.

51. Mikhailovskaya, interview.

52. Strobe Talbott, *The Russia Hand: A Memoir of Presidential Diplomacy* (New York: Random House, 2002).

53. Other reforms included redistricting Russia's regions and redesigning the upper chamber of the parliament. See Shevtsova, *Putin's Russia*.

54. U.S. Embassy officials, interview by author, Moscow, Russia, and Washington, D.C., 2003. However, U.S. officials did not see coupling foreign assistance with diplomatic pressure as inappropriate interference in pushing neoliberal economic reforms. The political economy explanation of reform as budgeting scarce resources explains why Western governments supported some reforms more intensely than others. Namely, U.S. politicians—reacting to voters seeking a peace dividend at the end of the Cold War—felt they had little domestic support for an aggressive assistance package. Thus, they focused their assistance on promoting market economic reforms in Russia, which was seen as providing a more immediate and tangible benefit to the United States than democratic reforms. For more on the tension of U.S. policy promoting market reforms more vigorously than democratic changes, see Matthew Spence, *The Impact of U.S. Democracy Promotion in Post-Soviet Russia, Ukraine, and Kyrgyzstan*, unpublished D.Phil. dissertation, Oxford University, Oxford, U.K., 2004.

55. Even given the mixed record of the IMF in holding the Russian government to these economic conditionalities, no aid was conditioned on the Russian government adopting any criminal procedure reforms. For more on the impact of IMF conditionalities in Russia, see Randall Stone, *Lending Credibility* (Princeton, NJ: Princeton University Press, 2002).

56. See, for example, Anders Åslund, *Building Capitalism* (New York: Cambridge University Press, 2002).

57. This was part of the U.S. Department of Justice's Office of Overseas Prosecutorial Development Assistance and Training (OPDAT). OPDAT, in its current incarnation, was created in April 1995 in an effort to bring international criminal justice reform efforts worldwide up to common standards. In the U.S. government, the Department of Justice handled criminal justice reform, while the U.S. Agency for International Development (USAID) was responsible for all other areas of rule-of-law reform.

58. U.S. advisors played significant roles in the process, even after Mizulina cut the working group from forty-two to about fifteen people (that U.S. advisors remained involved in the smaller working group further increased U.S. influence). One of the U.S.-funded advisors, Saint Louis University law professor Stephen Thaman, testified at a Duma hearing on abbreviated, expedited, and consensual pretrial procedures that were intended to ensure speeder trials and less time in pretrail detention. Thaman spoke fluent Russian, which helped him work seamlessly with the working group. The other U.S.-funded advisor was Professor William Burnham of Wayne State University School of Law. Lehmann, interview; U.S. government official, telephone interview.

59. Thaman wrote a draft chapter of the law on alternate procedures, which included expedited, abbreviated, and consensual procedures based heavily on models existing in Western Europe (primarily Italy). One of the five suggested procedures based on the Italian *patteggiamento* made it into the final law. Stephen C. Thaman, U.S.-funded advisor to the Russian government for criminal procedure reform, telephone interview with author, November 21, 2002.

60. At one point, the Duma lost their copy of the final draft that reflected all of the most recent changes and called the U.S. Embassy to get a draft. After giving the Duma the draft, U.S. Embassy officials joked that they had missed their real chance to shape the Russian criminal procedure code. Natalia Chazova, U.S. advisor to the Russian Working Group on the Criminal Procedure Code, interview by author, Moscow, June 4, 2003.

61. Lehmann, interview.

62. Ibid.

63. About $300,000 of the U.S. Embassy's budget for criminal procedure reform in 2002 went to the implementation project. The funds covered travel throughout Russia, a

visit to the United States by members of the working group to study issues related to amendments to the Criminal Procedure Code, and other logistical support. Lehmann, interview.

64. Mikhailovskaya, interview.
65. American Bar Association representatives and former U.S. attorney general Richard Thornburg met with Russians who were not drafting these reforms to discuss judicial and criminal procedure reform. Those visits appeared to have no impact on the early reform documents. U.S. government official, telephone interview; Pashin, interview.
66. Thaman, telephone interview.
67. The Russian Criminal Procedure Code refers to these as "abbreviated procedures."
68. An estimated less than 5 percent of U.S. criminal cases go to jury trial. Dline and Schwartz, "Jury Is Still Out," 106.
69. This included influence on motions to suppress evidence and strengthening the exclusionary rule in relation to custodial investigations. But U.S. advisors emphasize that they only had influence on selected parts of the code. Thaman, telephone interview.
70. Some of these provisions included:
    1. Amending the rules of evidence to allow defendants to challenge the state more easily, including adding a motion to suppress evidence and one of the strongest exclusionary rules in Europe (even stronger than in the United States): a confession obtained without a suspect's defense attorney present could be thrown out.
    2. Transferring supervision of pretrial detention from the Procuracy (prosecutor's office) to judges, and judicial approval for search and seizures.
    3. Eliminating Procuracy reinvestigation of a case after the court rules on it.
    4. Decreasing the maximum allowable period for pretrial detention (detaining suspects before presenting charges) from 72 to 48 hours.
    Lehmann, interview; Schwartz, interview; Scott, interview; and U.S. government official, telephone interview. Provisions 2 and 3 exemplified how U.S. involvement helped the working group defeat objectionable provisions that the Procuracy and other opponents of the code sought to introduce. Mizulina, interview.
71. Pashin selected jurors based on voters' lists, as done in the United States. Whereas the old juror system gave only the prosecutor the right to exclude up to six jurors without cause, Pashin extended that right to the defense counsel as well. Pashin, interview.
72. Marian Dent, Director of ABA/CEELI Moscow, 1992–1995, interview by author, Moscow, November 12, 2002. Although the working group members were indeed convinced that the shackles and cages were prejudicial, by 2004 they had not yet been removed, by law or practice, from Russian courtrooms. Lehmann, interview.
73. Thaman, "Resurrection of Trial," 124.
74. Schwartz, interview.
75. Lehmann, interview.
76. Vitsin cited the importance of trips to the United States in making effective arguments about reform at home. "We had already many books on the Anglo-Saxon system of the judiciary, but we had to look at it face to face." Sergei Vitsin, co-author of the *Concept of Judicial Reform* and member of the Russian Working Group on the Criminal Procedure Code, interview by author, Moscow, November 26, 2002. However, Mizulina felt that U.S. experts had at best a mixed influence, winning over as many Duma members as their presence alienated. Mizulina, interview.
77. Mizulina, interview.
78. For example, while working on the code, the working group visited Leiden University in the Netherlands three times, courts in the United Kingdom and France, and

the French Institute for Comparative Law. Working group members did not visit German courts. The U.S. government even paid non-American experts to work with the working group. Lehmann, interview; Vitsin, interview.

79. Vitsin, interview.

80. Thaman, telephone interview; Vitsin, interview.

81. Amnesty International, "Denial of Justice."

82. Scott, interview.

83. U.S. Ambassador Alexander Vershbow, address presented at the All Russia Academic Conference on Implementation of the Criminal Procedure Code of the Russian Federation, February 2, 2002, available at http://moscow.usembassy.gov/embassy/statement.php?record_id=1.

84. Bureau of Democracy, Human Rights, and Labor, *Russia: Country Reports on Human Rights Practices 2002* (Washington, D.C.: U.S. Department of State, 2003).

85. McDonald, "Russia Begins New Twist." However, statistics from the first part of 2003 showed that the number of detentions rose again, on pace to include more detentions than the last six months of 2002. It is unclear if this was due to police abuses, a rise in crime, or a population increase in Russia. Still, the overall acquittal rate for all of Russia remained at 0.8 percent (double the rate from the previous year), a far cry from that found in Europe or the United States, where acquittal rates fell between 17 and 30 percent. More disturbing for legal reform, Russia's upper courts still threw out approximately 40 percent of the acquittals by lower courts—where most jury trials are conducted. Alexei Nikolsky, "Number of People Detained Is on Rise," *Moscow Times*, May 15, 2003.

86. In 2007, jury trials were scheduled to go into effect in Chechnya, the last of Russia's eighty-nine regions to have jury trials. Fred Weir, "Russia Embraces Trial by Peers," *Christian Science Monitor*, March 5, 2003; Lehmann, interview.

87. Pashin, interview.

88. Some remaining problems with the code were that judges had wide latitude in overturning jury trial verdicts and that defense attorneys still needed the approval of prosecutors to call witnesses in a criminal case.

89. Members of the Russian Working Group on the Criminal Procedure Code, interview.

90. The vast literature on "constitutional engineering" in both legal scholarship and political science nominally acknowledges the importance of political culture and local political interactions yet devotes most attention to institutional design. See, for example, Juan J. Linz and Arturo Valenzuela, eds., *The Failure of Presidential Democracy: Comparative Perspectives* (Baltimore, MD: Johns Hopkins University Press, 1994); Giovanni Sartori, *Comparative Constitutional Engineering* (New York: New York University Press, 1997); and Matthew Shugart and John Carey, *Presidents and Assemblies: Constitutional Design and Electoral Dynamics* (New York: Cambridge University Press, 1992).

91. This approach is popular among practitioners. See, for example, U.S. Agency for International Development (USAID), *Russia Strategy Amendment, 1999–2005* (Washington, D.C.: USAID, 2002); U.S. State Department's Office of the Coordinator of U.S. Assistance to the Newly Independent States, *U.S. Government Assistance to and Cooperative Activities with the New Independent States of the Former Soviet Union: FY2002* (Washington, D.C.: U.S. Department of State, 2003), which describes changing U.S. assistance strategy to focus on building grass roots constituencies to demand rule-of-law and democratic reforms.

92. Putin's illiberal assault on media freedoms, restrictions on civil society, and human rights abuses in Chechnya have been well documented. See, for example, Freedom House, *Nations in Transit* (Washington, D.C.: Freedom House, 2004), 462–89, which describes in detail the decline in political freedoms in several areas in Russia under Putin; and Shevtsova, *Putin's Russia*.

93. U.S. advisors stress that they "really only had influence in selected areas and never even came close to presenting any draft code." Thaman, telephone interview.

94. USAID rule-of-law programs typically worked only indirectly by training Russian lawyers, judges, and other potentially influential groups. Members of the Russian Working Group on the Criminal Procedure Code, interview.

95. For an interesting argument about how global "scripts" of legal systems produce remarkably similar legal institutions across cultures, see John Meyer and Elizabeth Boyle, "Modern Law as a Secularized and Global Model: Implications for the Sociology of Law," in *Global Prescriptions: The Production, Exportation, and Importation of a New Legal Orthodoxy*, ed. Yves Dezalay and Bryant G. Garth (Ann Arbor: University of Michigan Press, 2002). Several members of the working group claimed that the 1991 Concept of Judicial Reform and nineteenth-century Russian legal reforms were the strongest influence in drafting the Criminal Procedure Code. Mikhailovskaya, interview; Mizulina, interview; Vitsin, interview.

96. USAID officials, interview by author, Moscow, 2003 (listed anonymously at the request of interviewees; interview names and notes on file with the author).

97. Wedel, *Collision and Collusion*.

98. Urging Russians to embrace democracy, the rule of law, and market reforms as a single package—with little sense of the tensions between or sequencing among these reforms—became a mantra of U.S. speeches in the region. See, for example, U.S. Secretary of State Warren Christopher, "U.S. Support for Russian Reform: An Investment in America's Security," address at the Hubert H. Humphrey Institute of Public Affairs, University of Minnesota, Minneapolis, MN, May 27, 1993, reprinted in Warren Christopher, *In the Stream of History* (Stanford, CA: Stanford University Press, 1998), 51–60.

99. See, for example, USAID, *Foreign Aid in the National Interest* (Washington, D.C.: USAID, 2003).

100. Mizulina, interview; Lehmann, interview.

101. Thomas Pickering, U.S. Ambassador to Russia, 1993–1996, interview by author, Arlington, VA, July 16, 2002.

CHAPTER TEN

Middle East Dilemmas

DAVID MEDNICOFF

THE PROBLEM OF KNOWLEDGE in rule-of-law promotion, above all the basic question of whether Western rule-of-law aid programs are on the right track to help build the rule of law in recipient countries, is especially acute in the Arab world. Arab states generally share two features that render external rule-of-law aid particularly difficult—longstanding nondemocratic governments, and legal systems that graft Ottoman, European, and contemporary sources onto Islamic norms. We cannot presume that U.S. common-law practitioners can build the rule of law by transporting or transplanting their technocratic techniques into such different legal soil. Indeed, the very idea that people in Arab societies would be receptive to American guidance in legal reform is dubious in the current climate of broad, popular mistrust of the United States.

The author gratefully acknowledges the research support of the College of Social and Behavioral Sciences, the Center of Public Policy and Administration, the Healey Endowment/Faculty Research Grant program, Maura Devlin, Susan Macek, and Brahim Oulbeid at the University of Massachusetts–Amherst. Several U.S. rule-of-law specialists and Arab lawyers were generous with their time; their insights are reflected directly and indirectly in this chapter. The author also thanks Jon Alterman at the Center for Strategic and International Studies, Nathan Brown and Thomas Carothers at the Carnegie Endowment for International Peace, Joya Misra at the University of Massachusetts–Amherst, and the members of the Department of Legal Studies Faculty Seminar 2004–2005 for their suggestions.

Thus, expectations must be low for the prospects for U.S. law specialists to improve the rule of law for Arabs. Nonetheless, the desire of many Arabs for more predictable, responsive, and fair laws is indisputable, a desire that is growing as pressure for liberalizing political change in the region mounts. The 2004 *Arab Human Development Report* is only the latest and most prominent statement by Arabs of the central importance of the rule of law to social improvement. Moreover, although U.S. rule-of-law aid to Arab countries during the last decade was a rather modest endeavor, receiving little backing from senior U.S. officials, rule-of-law reform is now a subject of much greater attention and funding, as part of the George W. Bush administration's broader push for democratic change in the region. Therefore, this is a propitious time to examine how the United States can work to enhance the rule of law in ways that are useful to Arabs.

U.S. rule-of-law advisors face a daunting impediment right from the start: widespread, twofold Arab skepticism about the United States as the messenger for the rule of law in the Middle East. Many Arabs believe that U.S. policy makers neither know nor care to know basic aspects of law, politics, and society in Arab countries. And there is an even stronger and equally widespread perception that the United States does not in fact practice what it preaches about the rule of law in its own policies, particularly those in the Middle East.

As a result, however well-intentioned, U.S. efforts to export ideas and techniques about the rule of law to Arabs are likely to be handicapped unless and until the United States is seen as less hypocritical in its own embrace of the rule of law at home and abroad. Even should this change, U.S. rule-of-law development programs as currently configured will be problematic for two reasons. First, the typical emphasis of these programs on the performance of courts rests on the questionable assumption that judicial reform is central to bolstering the rule of law more generally, despite the fact that a broad social understanding of legal rights and respect for law's authority is not necessarily achieved by improving the efficiency of courts. Second, the rule of law in Arab states cannot be decoupled readily from its general authoritarian political context. Programs that aim to improve the rule of law without taking account of the possibility that increasing legal efficiency will merely heighten political centralization will do little to foster democratization.

With these basic points in mind, after looking briefly at several key tensions within the concept of the rule of law itself, I examine in this chapter how conceptions of law are similar and different in the United

States and in Arab societies. I then analyze the approaches of U.S.-based rule-of-law programs in the Middle East to assess their prospects and problems for contributing to actual Arab legal and political reform. I conclude by recommending areas that hold the best hope for U.S.-based rule-of-law work in Arab contexts—areas that have the potential to decrease the gap between the concept's ideal and reality in the subordination of government elites to laws.

What Is the Rule of Law?

The rule of law often appears as a vague or undefined idea in both general speech and technical policy documents. As one scholar put it, "the rule of law thus stands in the peculiar state of being *the* preeminent legitimizing ideal in the world today, without agreement on precisely what it means."[1] The concept generally refers to two different things. On the one hand, it stands for the ideal that legal norms should prevail over personal political authority, or, as often formulated, a government of laws, not men. On the other hand, it can describe a specific set or constellation of functioning legal institutions.

When used to denote an ideal, the term *rule of law* is often deployed in diverse and imprecise ways.[2] Nevertheless, these uses typically assume a separation between a society's politics and law.[3] Specifically, the rule of law is meant to protect people from political anarchy and arbitrariness. It suggests a promise that legal supremacy, stability, and accountability will prevail over leaders' caprices.

Yet, the ideal embodies a tension between the importance of law in providing order, and the promise of law to guarantee citizens' rights, justice, and equality. Despite the ideal that laws will stand above the self-interested actions of specific people, the reality is that the drafters, executors, or interpreters of law can flout this ideal unless meaningful accountability, popular awareness, and transparency exist in the political system. In other words, the rule of law can bolster democracy or it can slide into rule *by* law and reinforce strong-handed political control.

Indeed, one vein of recent social scientific scholarship on the rule of law insists that the ideal is unrealizable and that the concept is inseparable from specific political practices.[4] This is in line with the way in which lawyers and development specialists often use the term, as shorthand for well-functioning courts and other legal institutions. Ideas about implementing the rule of law in non-Western countries focus on the dimension of institutional reform, especially of courts, with little overt rationalization as to how or even whether such reform connects to the ideal. In Arab countries, U.S. rule-of-law aid has primarily followed this line, seeking to promote judicial modernization through judicial training or other forms of technical assistance for the courts.

Yet how the practices of legal institutions link to the ideal of the rule of law is important for understanding the context and consequences of institutional reform. When reform efforts are confined to legal institutional performance with little reference to the issues of broader justice, a society may be ruled by law without approximating the democratizing dimension of the ideal of the rule of law.[5] For this reason, the most promising general approaches to conceptualizing the rule of law, such as those put forward by Rachel Kleinfeld, tie ideals to practices by developing detailed criteria for how political and legal systems approximate rule-of-law values in areas such as legal restraints on government, neutrality, and popular respect for law and human rights.[6] Such criteria can certainly be applied and evaluated in contemporary Arab contexts.

Yet, there is little empirical research as to how legalist ideals and practices are connected in specific Arab societies. Existing work tends to focus on judicial opinions and the function of courts, rather than whether or how popular understanding of or respect for law may matter to legal and political systems more generally.[7] As insightful and important as this research is, both its sparseness and lack of specific argument as to how elite legal functionaries connect to broader social rule-of-law ideals serve to underscore the problem of knowledge for rule-of-law programs in places like the Middle East.[8] My overview below of the ideal and practice of the rule of law in Arab societies is meant as a very modest step in the direction of addressing the knowledge problem in a particularly important specific current context.

Rule of Law in Arab and American Settings: Points in Common

As in the United States, the rule of law has long been an influential doctrine in the Arab world. Indeed, the Islamic and Ottoman socio-legal traditions that contribute to contemporary Arab law predate the Anglo-American common law by many centuries. Moreover, the Middle Eastern origin of two of the most renowned, ancient legal codes—the Code of Hammurabi and the Judeo-Christian Bible—should not be forgotten. Thus, discussion about the potential for U.S. rule-of-law specialists to bolster the rule of law in Arab states cannot proceed without acknowledgment that the general concept has deep Middle Eastern roots.

Although Arab legal systems combine a variety of traditions, including Islam, I focus in this section on common points between Islamic law and U.S. law with regard to the overall idea of the rule of law. This is sensible in light of several facts. First, Islam has dominated the development and practice of law in the Arab world from the seventh century until the present. It remains at the rhetorical and actual center of discussions of law in contemporary Arab states. In particular, many Arab constitutions clearly endorse traditional Islamic law as the primary source for legislation.[9] Second, the dominant current trope of political discourse and opposition in Arab countries at present is also Islam. Thus, the notion that Islamic law may resemble law in the United States in significant respects has implications for contemporary rule-of-law work. Third, given the above points, Islamic ideals play the same broad, basic foundational role in Arab legal orders that the combination of Judeo-Christian values and original constitutional principles do in the United States.

The legal sources and historical patterns of Islamic law are too diverse to allow for simple description or derivation from the founding documents of the religion, the Quran and the *hadith* (sayings attributed to the prophet Mohammed).[10] Despite this, it is possible to delineate three sociopolitical effects of Islam from its seventh-century inception of obvious relevance to the rule of law and to comparisons with U.S. legal ideas. First is the general understanding of Muslims that Islamic theory specifically stressed political accountability by insisting that rulers' legitimacy was grounded in their status as defenders of the Islamic faith and its principles, whether this status is based on descent from the prophet Mohammed's bloodline or some other distinction. In particular, rulers were to be judged by qualified Islamic scholars and Muslims more generally on their record of executing and enforcing Islamic law.

To be sure, leaders historically used their military might more frequently to subjugate than to empower Muslim jurists, although the latter were supposed to determine when Islamic law was being upheld. In fact, the gradual restriction of the functions of legal promulgation and interpretation to those jurists who were part of ruling elites in Islamic history is a reflection of the very tension between the ideal of the rule of law as constraining rulers and the ordering tendencies of rule by law described above. Thus, the subordination of laws to authority stood alongside the ideological link between law and political legitimacy as a core trend in Islamic history. Because the very purpose of an Islamic political order is to execute law, the rule of law is an ideal integral to Muslim society; institutional practice is what has often fallen short.[11]

A second point of importance for the rule of law is the manner in which concerns about justice have been centrally and popularly embedded in Islam. Justice as a concept and a discourse is ubiquitous in the Quran. Moreover, as is true with American legal ideals, Islam's emphasis on justice includes significant attention to social equity and individual rights. Thus, discussions of many of the general and specific issues that frame legal discourse are engrained in the religious identity of a large majority of the people in Arab societies. The importance of justice within Islam also contributed to the fact that Islamic jurisprudence never fully developed a concept of natural law. This has meant that there is no clear theory to ground a completely secular legal order, as natural law helped do over time in the West.[12]

A third, if more debatable, point is that Islamic political theory can be read as presupposing two central tenets that have clear relevance to contemporary Western ideas about the rule of law: first, that despite the ideal that political authority exists for the benefit of Islam, authority in practice will tend toward absolutism, rather than subordinating itself to communal legitimacy or justice; and second, that resources autonomous from the state (civil society) are needed to check leaders' actions. In essence, a significant tendency of classical Islamic legal theory is a distrust of government and an emphasis on finding legal ways to constrain authority that would sound quite familiar to many Americans.[13]

One scholar argues that Islamic law shares a fourth and crucial feature of Anglo-American law—it is a common law system. Anthropologist Lawrence Rosen makes a good case for considering as fundamentally similar American and Islamic laws' reliance on local courts and local cultural information as characteristics that distinguish both from the legal centralization of a civil law system.[14] Thus, American and Arab lawyers may share a similar understanding of the importance of locally based legal processes, among other things.

Points in Contention

I have argued so far that, due to the influence of Islamic legal ideals and development, the rule of law exists as a political touchstone in Arab societies in a manner similar to its status in the United States. Yet particular differences in the sociopolitical history of the Middle East and North America shape local understandings and implementation of the rule of law in significant ways. An appreciation that legal systems in the United

States and the Middle East may share important features should not carry with it the assumption that differences can or should be minimized.

Prime among these differences—and an important if sometimes overstated source of many contemporary Arabs' concerns about Western countries' politics—is the multifaceted impact of Ottoman and European colonial domination. The impact of foreign great power rule on the rule of law in the Middle East and North Africa was threefold. First, it led to a patchwork of legal orders in a given society, rather than the relatively long-standing growth of a unitary national legal system such as occurred in the United States. Second, it set up an authoritarian norm that law would in fact be subordinated to imperial political power. And, third, it fostered a tendency for constitutions to exist without a significant history of judicial interpretation. In some states, such as Morocco, this led to frequent postcolonial redrafts of the constitution to reflect changes in the power or preoccupations of political authority, in contrast with the U.S. norm of a single basic constitutional document that can only be modified with difficulty.

The legal system of every contemporary Arab nation is a unique mixture of Islamic, Ottoman, European, and postindependence laws.[15] To be sure, a number of territories escaped direct foreign domination, most notably in the Persian Gulf. Yet even in these places, Western legal ideas and practices have supplemented indigenous combinations of Islamic and customary law. The mélange of legal sources in most Arab societies does not in itself preclude legal clarity or checks on authority. However, along with the lapses in territorial and ethnic logic that European colonial powers frequently employed in setting borders for many of the contemporary nations of the Middle East, the lack of legal systemic unity in Arab states has two consequences for recent U.S.-fostered efforts to enhance the rule of law.[16] It means that the jurisprudential reference points of lawyers in the United States are not likely to be of direct use to Arab societies. And it has contributed to political situations in which postcolonial Arab leaders have had many incentives to centralize their authority and no real legal impediments to doing so.

This second point is even more obviously related to the primary legacy of colonialism in the Middle East—an emphasis on control backed by force that was not meant primarily to serve the best interests of indigenous citizens. The political example that socialized Arab nationalist elites was the colonial regimes' resort to invented political forms like mandates and protectorates to conceal their exercise of raw power. Legal norms and institutions existed under colonialism in which the contradictions between stated and true purposes were readily apparent.

At the same time, these norms and institutions were somewhat successful at centralizing political and economic administration. However much Arab nationalists rebelled against colonial rule, they also learned that the lofty promises of colonial political ideas were generally subservient, or even in direct contrast, to the reality of police control. It is small wonder, facing severe economic and other challenges, that these nationalists built on, instead of dismantled, the legacies of authoritarian rule that they inherited.

To be sure, the ideal of the rule of law will often be at odds with the centralizing tendency of governments. I argue that Arab states in the Middle East in general had an especially wide gap between the ideal and the reality because of the combination of the relative lack of autonomous precolonial unified legal order in these states and the particular repressive nature of colonial governments. More subtly, I am suggesting that the level of discontinuity between the rational, legalistic values preached by European administrators and their practice of resource extraction and police rule tainted the very ideal of the rule of law in a way that is unlikely to resonate with the socialization of many American lawyers.

In short, many Arabs view the rule of law in a manner similar to American legal scholars on the left, as an ideology of political control, not as a check on political abuse. This is important because it implies that efforts by internal and external reformers to strengthen the rule of law will not necessarily be associated with political opening within Arab societies. A striking example of how well-formulated ideas of the rule of law can exist alongside repressive political tendencies is the publication of a thoughtful tract on the ideal of legalism in Iraq at the very same time that Saddam Hussein was beginning his final consolidation of his particular style of brutal authoritarian rule.[17]

Despite this authoritarianism, Arab regimes have not lacked defined legal structures. In fact, most Arab states have basic laws or constitutions. Thus, a third major distinction between Arab and American political experiences with the rule of law is that Arab constitutions exist and may matter, but they have had much less of a history of institutionalization and independent judicial interpretation than has the U.S. Constitution.

This difference is neither surprising nor unknown to U.S. rule-of-law experts. In fact, given Arab political centralization, the very existence of constitutions is at least as interesting a political phenomenon as the dearth of independent judicial interpretative traditions for these documents.[18] For my purposes here, however, it is worth underscoring the challenge that the juxtaposition of constitutions and political regimes with few genuine legal checks poses for building broad social support, or even judicial competence, for the rule of law.

A fourth difference of approach to the rule of law between U.S. and Arab societies does not connect directly to the Middle East's history of outside great power influence. It is the relationship of law and religion. Within the United States, religious pluralism has led to the ideal that law should facilitate the separation of church and state. However, most Arab societies have predominantly Muslim populations, with political orders that often establish Islam as a state religion. Thus, laws and legal institutions in many Arab states, even those with secularized leaders, privilege Islam and its traditions.

Of course, most scholars of U.S. constitutional law would assert that the separation of church and state in the United States is far from perfect or unproblematic and has often favored Christian ideas.[19] Ironically, as suggested above, the way in which religious influences have grounded the rule of law in Arab countries has much in common with the United States. Nonetheless, the assumption that Islam *should* inform the political and social order has caused and is likely to continue to cause misunderstandings and difficulties for would-be U.S. political reformers in the region.

The extent to which Islam in general and the Sharia in particular should inform the rule of law and what forms this should take is currently a complicated area of great debate and discussion among Arab and non-Arab Muslim scholars. Adding to the complexity of this issue is the theoretical contradiction between the Islamic ideal of *siyyasa al-shari'a* (the government of God's law) and *siyadat al-qanun* (the sovereignty of man-made law). The latter term, the general way in which the Western idea of the rule of law is translated into Arabic, conveys with it a patina of illegitimacy to some, although by no means all, Muslims.[20]

There is no obvious reason that the ideal political effects of the rule of law of constraining governmental abuse and providing procedural fairness are impossible to achieve in a society with an established religion, so long as religious dissenters and minorities receive legal protection. Yet understanding, navigating, and being sensitive to the ways that religion and politics are intertwined in most Arab societies is a daunting task for U.S. rule-of-law experts, and one that their own socialization and training in the First Amendment of the U.S. Constitution is unlikely to facilitate. This is especially the case because the ways in which Islamic norms and theory are used in Arab politics are many and varied, often having in common only a shared rejection of the theoretical ideal of a wall between religion and secular state.

Within the broad point that the Islamic legal tradition is bound up in contemporary Arab reform, four trends can be identified, which I refer to as orthodox, conservative, reconstructionist, and reform:

- **Orthodox:** This tendency is what Americans often refer to as Islamic fundamentalism. Corresponding no less to the Saudi Arabian government than to Al Qaeda and the former Taliban regime, reformers within this category think of Islam in rather rigid terms that embrace many of the social norms and practices of Islamic history, including the subordination of women. Such a tendency can continue the historical practice of authoritarian control, so long as a ruling government is enforcing a well-defined tradition of Islamic law.

- **Conservative:** I use this term in its most obvious and literal sense, that of resisting change. This tendency simply refers to a lack of strong interest in reforming the patchwork of Islamic, colonial, and other laws out of comfort with or belief in the importance of maintaining the status quo. Alexis de Tocqueville's observation that lawyers in the United States tend to have affinities for order and power may be no less true for legal professionals in Arab societies, who frequently see the major problem with their own legal systems as citizens' lack of respect for law, as opposed to issues about the accountability or effectiveness of law itself.

- **Reconstructionist:** Islamic jurisprudence has nearly always been characterized by a strong tendency to reinterpret specific and important principles in a manner that addresses the needs of a particular situation. Although the use of classical terminology often leads some contemporary Islamic reconstructionists to be labeled as "fundamentalists," the varied Western and Arab proponents of this approach display a variety of exciting, articulate approaches to reinventing, rather than reverting to, traditional practices based on the relationship of Islam and society. The common point here is a belief that Islamic ideas with historical resonance can be rethought to be compatible with analogues in Western and other democratic theory. Influential theorists such as the Sudanese-American scholar

Abdellahi An-Naim and the Syrian Mohammed Shahrur exemplify this approach.[21]

- **Reform:** This tendency cautions against having too much faith in the prospects for traditional Islamic political and legal theory to contain or embrace many core ideas in contemporary Western or other democratic theory. Reflected in the work of the authors of the *Arab Human Development Reports*, this posture is not a rejection of the importance of Islamic identity or law per se. Rather, it is a preference, or at least a willingness, to articulate theories of legal and political reform in terms translated directly from global usage such as *dimaqatriyya* (democracy), *huquq-el-insan* (human rights), and *siyadat al-qanun*. This tendency can be grounded in skepticism about the possibility of traditional Islamic terms to adapt to modern political debates, a desire to avoid overburdening religious concepts with excess contemporary meaning, or both.

Given that all four of the different trends above assume some connection between Islam and the rule of law, it would be easy for American-trained lawyers who think of the religion-state link as ideally one of separation to miss the important distinctions among them. As a general matter, Western advocates of Arab legal change often favor ideas that fall within the "reform" category above, while indigenous activists more typically fit within the "reconstuctionist" and "orthodox" trends. The U.S. government has often supported "conservatives" and has even aided "orthodox" Arab governments and nonstate movements, most obviously in the respective cases of Saudi Arabia and the Islamist militias who fought Soviet control of Afghanistan in the 1980s. Yet, if Western rule-of-law or other democratization specialists are unprepared for the extent to which and the diversity in which indigenous Arab language of legal change is saturated with Islamic terminology, even within the reform trend, their ability to see nuances and connect with actual legal change will be hobbled.

It is important to reiterate that the above four major differences between Arab and American experiences with the rule of law do not preclude either that Arab governments can have more robust legal checks or that many Arabs value the rule of law. My point is instead that the experiential differences discussed above pose intellectual barriers for U.S. law specialists who seek to strengthen the rule of law in the Middle East. Moreover, these differences raise some Arabs' suspicions that American lawyers are functioning in the manner of previous agents of

Western foreign powers, whose attractive political words concealed their complicity in imperial coercion.

In sum, U.S. and other Western rule-of-law experts face a variety of general and specific cognitive handicaps in trying to bring legal reform to Arab societies. The diverse sources and systems of law, the repressive legacy of colonialism, the lack of authority and tradition of judicial review, and the connection of mosque and state are all features of the Middle Eastern legal landscape that hinder easy access for lawyers whose primary grounding is in U.S. common law and politics. Furthermore, a general wariness toward Western incursion alongside a particular negative reaction to U.S. foreign policy since September 11, 2001, creates in many Arab quarters a particularly unreceptive current environment for rule-of-law reformers with even the best of techniques and intentions.

What U.S. Rule-of-Law Reformers Do in Arab Countries

I have argued above that there is a likely mismatch between the training of American lawyers in general and the specific context for rule-of-law work in Arab countries, despite the importance of the rule of law in both the United States and the Arab world. Compounding this are at least two additional barriers to effective U.S.-based rule-of-law assistance in the region. First, the general lack of international and Middle Eastern expertise by many Americans in general and American lawyers in particular makes it difficult to find knowledgeable and experienced specialists to staff particular programs. A second barrier is literal; as several Americans with rule-of-law mission experience have mentioned to me, U.S. citizens' concern for their safety in Arab countries often keeps them within isolated quarters or compounds, thereby further decreasing their opportunities to develop a deep understanding of the everyday realities of Arab societies.

Rule-of-law work is thus likely to be done by well-meaning Americans with limited detailed knowledge of the people and legal systems which they hope to aid. This makes it tempting for practitioners to carry assumptions based on their own national experiences into Arab contexts. Rule-of-law specialists are aware of this problem and of the general difficulty of resolving mismatches between their experiences of law and the needs of Arab countries. Yet, these translation problems can still be daunting and easy to underestimate.

In fact, it can be tough for American lawyers to realize how unusual (and not necessarily portable) U.S. ideas and practices about law truly are. One experienced professional conveyed his conviction that Arab judges found strange and irrelevant the extent to which rule-of-law programs focused on teaching U.S. notions of intellectual property law and alternative dispute resolution, neither of which seem to have much of anything to do with current questions of greatest import in Middle Eastern courts or societies.[22] Coupled with the lack of specific information as to what supports the rule of law, and whether and how the rule of law encourages democracy, barriers to knowledge and understanding in this area of foreign policy appear particularly challenging.

How have U.S. practitioners dealt with this challenging environment? In many respects, it is too early to generalize, given that rule-of-law programs in Arab countries are in their early stages of development. One clear conclusion is that U.S. rule-of-law work has so far been focused almost exclusively on Arab judges and courts. This corresponds to the more general experience and efforts to analyze and apply the experience that U.S. development agencies have accrued in judicial reform in parts of the world other than the Middle East.[23]

The slant of U.S. rule-of-law programs toward judiciaries is readily understandable for a number of reasons. Judges are a small, elite subset of Arab societies, often with strong Western educational training and language facility, making them easy collaborators for American lawyers. Judges' work, in the form of case decisions, can often be monitored, quantified, and even read, meaning that methods exist to measure program results, which is naturally important to development aid administrators in Washington. The general nature of common law and the particular significance of judicial review in the United States may also predispose American lawyers and political figures to conflate the rule of law and the primacy of judges.

Moreover, centering rule-of-law work on Arab judiciaries has a defensible rationale; a truly independent judicial authority can indeed be a potent force for subordinating political officials to law. Yet arguing that an established judiciary with significant autonomy from other parts of government helps laws trump rulers says nothing as to whether U.S. programs geared toward judiciaries can actually lead to this goal in particular Arab contexts. It is difficult in terms of both theorizing and data collection to be sure about how judicial independence in a society is developed and maintained.[24] Because U.S. programs in the Arab region to date have most often emphasized issues such as court administration and training judges in the application of commercial law, these programs may not have any logical connection to political liberalization.[25]

In fact, there are grounds to suspect that U.S.-sponsored programs that are mostly limited to Arab judiciaries might even work against the very goal of increasing judicial authority. Court efficiency can be a tool of political centralization and repression, just as it can serve to protect people against government excess. If little empirical research exists to suggest when U.S. technical assistance to Arab judges might serve political liberalization, there are several logical reasons to suspect that such work may be more likely to contribute to entrenching authoritarianism.

First, the level of political cooperation between Arab governmental entities and U.S. aid contractors necessary to implement projects may subordinate U.S. rule-of-law work to the agendas of local political authorities, which have extensive experience at thwarting pressures for liberalization. The entrenchment of illiberal political systems in Arab countries makes the problem of authoritarian control especially significant. As one expert told me, in democratizing contexts like Eastern Europe, because of the potential for rapid integration with the West that has come along with economic and political reforms, rule-of-law reformers have a much wider variety of carrots and sticks to use with political actors than in the authoritarian setting of Arab countries.[26]

Second, in the context of widespread anti-American rhetoric in many Arab societies, judges may not be particularly receptive to efforts by U.S.-based legal professionals to train them. In fact, judges may have little stake in broad political change or may see their judicial system as in need of nothing more than modest gains in efficiency. Third, and as a consequence, both judges and U.S. rule-of-law specialists may find themselves identified more with unpopular political elites than with forces within Arab societies striving for greater political autonomy. Even in Egypt, the Arab country in which the principle and the practice of judicial review are the most developed,[27] it is easy to see courts as dependent on the government.[28] When judges in a country such as Egypt do confront the authoritarian leadership, they may limit their efforts to legal issues and to strategies that do not undermine the advantages they enjoy through a conciliatory attitude toward central power.[29]

Concerns about becoming embroiled in local politics are precisely why most U.S.-based rule-of-law programs are conceived in technical terms that avoid political sensitivity. It is easy to argue that narrowly focused work is most practical in the context of pervasive Arab political centralization and vigilance. Yet it does not stand to reason that such work can foster judicial independence, which seems to be the key hope for connecting rule-of-law work to democratization.

Because Arab governments have used and will continue to use their talent for the co-optation of potential political opposition to consolidate their authority, efforts to buttress the power of the judiciary or the autonomy of law would seem most likely to succeed when they are linked to nongovernmental or popular Arab social forces. Yet U.S. rule-of-law programs have not generally taken this direction, and not merely because of concerns about politicization. In a field in which there are few data about results, donor organizations and U.S. governmental agencies expect rule-of-law specialists to be able to demonstrate specific results. This means that programs on broad issues of improving legal education, fostering social support for law, and building citizen knowledge of legal protections are only a tiny piece of the U.S. rule-of-law industry; such programs are generally quite unlikely to produce obvious or quick results.

Nonetheless, Arab lawyers and U.S. experts with whom I have spoken tend to agree that programs geared toward civic and professional education are precisely what is needed to achieve real progress on improving the rule of law, judicial independence, and democratization. Because governments have the coercive capacity to repress courts, judicial independence is to some extent dependent on acceptance by a significant segment of a country's population that citizens have rights, as well as obligations, under law, and that judges can and should help citizens realize their rights. The 2004 *Arab Human Development Report* stresses that local civic education in human rights is a severely underdeveloped prerequisite for political freedom in Arab societies.[30] Arab legal education for the most part does not include critical analytical skills or broad thinking about justice; indeed, most Arab university law faculties lack prestige, sufficient teaching and economic resources, and pedagogical accountability to students.

If Arab citizens and lawyers are taught that their legal system has little respectability and reliability, then judges can find few allies or pressures to challenge their subordination and the subordination of law more generally to the authoritarian political systems in which they operate. Making courts function more efficiently in such a context may serve to further centralize antidemocratic governments and even increase Arabs' cynicism about what the rule of law means in practice. In short, U.S.-based rule-of-law programs in countries that are focused almost entirely on judicial efficiency at best have an indeterminate effect on Arab democratization and at worst can damage it.

Of course, this discussion is premised on the assumption that Washington means what it says when it links the rule of law to democratization. Perhaps rule-of-law programs in Arab societies really reflect the ambivalent cooperation of the United States with repressive regimes or the desire of American lawyers to feel useful in the world. If so, then it is less significant that neither empirical data nor analytical logic support is a link between the programs we have run and the prospects for Arab laws to constrain leaders. However, if the point of U.S.-based rule-of-law programs is truly to strengthen the authority, accountability, and autonomy of Arab law, then both the contours of Arab debates about the rule of law and the context of enduring Arab authoritarianism must be central to informing and shaping Washington's efforts.

Reforming What the Reformers Do

One response to the formidable challenges to U.S.-based rule-of-law work in Arab countries is to cede the terrain of reform to indigenous Arab activists and experts, who are best-suited to understand their sociopolitical environments. Because U.S. foreign policy hubris and naïveté may have weakened U.S. ability to influence certain types of change in the region, American humility and introspection may prove to be the best strategy to foster legal reform in the long run.

Nonetheless, given that even prominent Arab reform specialists believe that foreign governments can be useful, I do not contend that abandoning the possibility of a meaningful role for the United States in Arab legal reform is a necessary conclusion from my analysis above.[31] Working to improve the prospects for legal systems to moderate governmental excess continues to be one possible way of improving Arabs' lives, and remains a potential channel for the real idealism and commitment for this task that motivates the Americans involved in this work. The key to rule-of-law work in the Middle East is the realization that it cannot get very far if it is decoupled from broader strategies that address the repressive tendencies of authoritarian regimes in the region, along with the popular perceptions of many Arabs that the U.S. government is complicit in this repression.

Explanations abound for why Arab governments consistently rank among the worst cases in the world in their refusal to uphold their citizens' political freedoms, human rights, and civil liberties.[32] Part of the story is Washington's understandable, if short-sighted, historical practice of preferring governments in the Middle East that it might characterize as stable, even when stability comes at the point of a gun. For example, Egypt, the second-largest recipient of U.S. foreign aid in almost every year since the late 1970s, has used its funds to increase the coercive capacity of the unpopular authoritarian leader Hosni Mubarak. Washington's predilection for maintaining extant regimes has generally outweighed its commitment to popular accountability and democratization. In fact, it may be no accident that U.S. rule-of-law programs in Arab contexts have focused more on law as order than on law as empowering citizens against unpopular leaders.

However, the aftermath of the September 11 attacks against the United States has changed this picture. Although the Bush administration continues to maintain close relations with autocratic Arab regimes, President Bush is making the promotion of democracy in the Middle East one of the rhetorical centerpieces of his foreign policy. And the administration has begun to exert diplomatic pressure for political change against some Arab leaders, notably, Egyptian President Hosni Mubarak, and has launched new aid initiatives aimed at supporting political and other reforms in the region. Washington's new apparent emphasis on the problem of Arab authoritarianism is an opportunity to rethink and reformulate U.S. rule-of-law programs in the Middle East.

The bad feelings that Arabs retain for the experience of Western imposition of laws and politics on their societies should serve as a general caution that the United States cannot and should not expect that it can create new legal orders in the Middle East. However, experienced rule-of-law practitioners, who would doubtlessly share this general caution, can take other steps to help Arab legal systems function more credibly. One obvious first step is for reform efforts to be more specific about recognizing the common and contentious points discussed above with respect to the nature and cultural reception of the law. Each Arab society's own unique discourse on Islam and politics, mixture of legal systems, and pattern of popular understanding of law and its relation to authority need to be mapped with an eye to exactly how country-specific reform might be possible. Rule-of-law specialists whom I interviewed would embrace this suggestion wholeheartedly; realizing this, however, would require much more research and on-the-ground knowledge about the detailed patterns of legal culture in individual Arab contexts, as well as data on how rule-of-law work connects to particular rule-of-law ideals.

A second more challenging step is for rule-of-law reformers to tailor their efforts to reflect clearly that entrenched authoritarian practices are the major impediment to expanding the role that legal norms and institutions can play in Arab political liberalization. Doing this is not necessarily easy; it runs counter to the argument that rule-of-law work is most effective when it is politically uncontroversial and technical. Moreover, steering rule-of-law projects toward addressing broad anti-democratic social patterns is less amenable to short-term assessment than focused, technocratic initiatives. For this reason, such projects are not necessarily appealing to donor agencies.

Despite these concerns, I believe that rule-of-law work that aims to build a broad social understanding of law offers more potential to enhance legalism in Arab societies in the long run than work geared mostly to the reform of judges and courts. Examples of projects that would fit this approach would include law school curriculum enhancement, funding of independent or populist local media projects that provide independent information about law, and collaborations with indigenous human rights movements. Programs such as these tend to require a longer-term commitment and ongoing, relatively equal partnership on the part of U.S. specialists. Such programs also are likely to expose U.S.-based practitioners to a wider range and deeper level of local knowledge and contacts. This, in turn, has the potential to increase social trust of Washington-sponsored rule-of-law work among a more varied sample of Arabs than typical judicial reform programs, as well as to increase the expertise of U.S. specialists. Given these advantages, it is not surprising that both Arab lawyers and senior U.S. experts with whom I spoke agree that rule-of-law programs should attempt to connect directly with a wider range of people than judges over a sustained period of time if possible.[33]

Indeed, teaching Arab legal functionaries about management and specialized topics of law is likely to be useful in genuinely broadening the impact of the rule of law only if the judges wish to or have political space to decide cases or write opinions independent of governmental control. However, strengthening the capacity of marginalized groups with liberalizing agendas to make claims grounded in law that challenge the repressive excesses of Arab regimes may foster broader respect for legal tools and ideas among Arab citizens. This is why grassroots programs to improve legal education and popular legal knowledge are potentially at least as important as projects aimed at judges and officials. The kinds of legal empowerment approaches that Stephen Golub has advocated for the Asian context are very relevant for the Middle East as well.[34]

Of course, current Arab governments may be reluctant to endorse or facilitate rule-of-law projects that foster real political liberalization. Nonetheless, legalism can only flourish in postcolonial Arab societies where there is widespread belief that it is genuine, rather than window dressing for a repressive regime. Given this, if rule-of-law specialists are unable to gain Arab governmental cooperation for work targeted toward broader popular support and respect for law, it may be preferable for them to hold off on their efforts. Programs that are limited to a narrow stratum of judges and approved by autocratic officials may actually have the effect of further isolating the judiciary from sources of political support and, thereby, strengthening these autocrats' political control.

Even where a narrowly construed judicial reform project achieves some success, it can be partially undermined by its dependence on the changing priorities of political elites. The World Bank team responsible for developing discrete commercial courts in Morocco experienced this problem, leading team leaders to assert the importance of identifying as early as possible a wide variety of local stakeholders as a key lesson for future rule-of-law projects.[35] The World Bank's report from this project thus implies what I am arguing directly—rule-of-law work in Arab societies should prioritize ways to build diverse constituencies within a target country that have a stake in legalist reform.

A general approach to rule-of-law work in Arab countries that moves beyond court reform to attempt to build broader social support for law should follow four operational principles:

1. Link to and build on Arab-led activities and initiatives;
2. Look for more multilateral program development opportunities, especially with European groups that may have complementary experience and expertise;
3. Focus reform on issues or sectors that increase legal pressures for political accountability; and
4. Emphasize issues such as education, freedom of the press, and popular access to diverse, international media and opinions that may be prerequisites, rather than obvious components, of respect for the rule of law.

Successful examples exist of work that builds on these principles to improve social respect for law and legal constraints on government. Arab human rights reform provides one interesting set of case studies.[36] As I have argued elsewhere, a variety of politicized groups in several Arab countries in the 1980s and early 1990s found human rights activism particularly useful, because it manifested the potential to chip away at state authoritarianism.[37] More specifically, international human rights activism in Morocco and Tunisia was able to link particularly well with local

initiatives to the extent that it seemed in tune with pressuring governments to liberalize politically.

In Morocco, the ongoing synergy between rights activism and gradual
political opening has meant a continuation and diversification of human rights politics. This culminated notably in work that bridged the
efforts of international and indigenous women's rights supporters to
reform the country's *mudawana* (family code) in early 2004. The new
mudawana encompasses the most extensive set of changes of any Arab
country to family law provisions that are anchored in Islamic norms.
The variety of Moroccans involved in this legal reform, in turn, has caused
this issue to enjoy a high profile sufficient to encourage broader discussions in the news media on the importance of law in society more generally.[38]

The 2003 release of prominent Egyptian sociologist Saad Eddin
Ibrahim, who was imprisoned in Egypt for his criticism of Hosni
Mubarak's government, is another notable example of the involvement
of a coalition of Arab and Western lawyers, intellectuals, and other activists on an issue with potentially important implications for the rule of
law. This coalition managed to get the Bush administration to put high-
level pressure on the Egyptian government, which in turn publicized
the extent to which the Mubarak regime's trial and sentencing of an out-
spoken critic flouted legalist ideals, despite the existence of an efficient
court system and judicial review. Even though Ibrahim's release might
appear to be a more modest accomplishment than the training of a cadre
of judges in Anglo-American jurisprudence, it serves the growth of the
rule of law precisely because it highlights the general manner in which a
well-developed Arab legal system can nonetheless be subordinated to
authoritarian politics. Moreover, the case demonstrates that creative
coalitions of activism can produce cracks in the authoritarian barriers to
the prospects for law to serve political liberalization.

My suggested strategic approach to rule-of-law work builds on four
major points from this essay. First, the rule of law as an ideal is relevant
to and understandable within Arab societies. Second, the legacy and
endurance of authoritarianism in Arab countries engenders understandable cynicism about governments' and outsiders' use of the term. Third,
rule-of-law work cannot therefore be decoupled from addressing the
resilience of political elites who see law as serving rather than constraining them. Fourth, the particular differences between the Arab and U.S.
contexts for the rule of law and the particular distrust which many Arabs have for the U.S. government require circumspection, caution, and

coalition with Arab activists if rule-of-law work is to have even a modest hope of success.

This sketch of the broad contours of politics of rule-of-law work in contemporary Arab societies and the conclusions that follow should not be read as an attack on U.S. specialists who believe in the importance of strengthening the promise of equality, rights, and political accountability for the betterment of Arabs in general. I am simply arguing something that is likely to be known by the most experienced and proficient of these activists—that a change of tactics, a scaling-down of expectations, and a scaling-up of patience represent the best prospects to counteract the sustained subjugation of law by some Arab leaders.

The above may sound like a bromide, yet calls for caution, cross-national cooperation, and circumspection are essential in a U.S. policy environment where major initiatives like forced Iraqi regime change are undertaken that may seem rushed or unsound in their long-term reasoning. Echoing Tocqueville's belief that American lawyers are less inclined than most Americans to political rashness, I would like to think that the U.S.-based practitioners of rule-of-law projects in Arab societies would allow this particular policy area to be characterized by diligence, deliberation, and diplomacy, rather than unsubstantiated strategies that have little to do with regional realities.

Notes

An earlier version of this chapter was originally published as Carnegie Paper no. 61 (September 2005).

1. Brian Z. Tamanaha, *On the Rule of Law: History, Politics, Theory* (Cambridge: Cambridge University Press, 2004), 4.
2. See Richard Fallon, "'The Rule of Law' as a Concept in Constitutional Discourse," *Columbia Law Review* 97 (1997), 1–40; and Frank Upham, "Mythmaking in the Rule-of-Law Orthodoxy," chapter 4 in this volume.
3. Gerhard Robbers, "The Rule of Law and Its Ethical Foundations," in *The Rule of Law*, ed. Joseph Thesing (Sankt Augustin, Germany: Konrad Adenauer Stiftung, 1997).
4. José María Maravall and Adam Przeworski, eds., *Democracy and the Rule of Law* (Cambridge: Cambridge University Press, 2003), 15.
5. Guillermo O'Donnell, "Why the Rule of Law Matters," *Journal of Democracy* 15, no. 4 (2004), 33–4.
6. Rachel Kleinfeld, "Competing Definitions of the Rule of Law," chapter 3 in this volume.
7. See, for example, Eugene Cotran and Mai Yamani, eds., *The Rule of Law in the Middle East and the Islamic World: Human Rights and the Judicial Process* (New York: I. B. Tauris, 2000); and Erik G. Jensen and Thomas C. Heller, eds., *Beyond Common Knowledge: Empirical Approaches to the Rule of Law* (Stanford, CA: Stanford University Press, 2003). The latter useful study notes both the conflation of the rule of law to institutional

programs by reform specialists, as well as the limited impact of such reform programs, pp. 1–3.

8. But, see Nathan Brown, *The Rule of Law in the Arab World* (Cambridge: Cambridge University Press, 1997), for work on courts in Arab countries that provides insights regarding embedded Arab authoritarian politics.

9. Even a country with as developed secular legal and social traditions as Egypt makes Islam its basic source for legislation in article 2 of its constitution. For discussion of this, see Baudouin Dupret, "La Chari'a est la Source de la Législation: Interprétations Jurisprudentielles et Théories Juridiques," in *l'État de Droit dans le Monde Arabe*, ed. Ahmed Mahiou (Paris: CNRS Éditions, 1997), 125–42.

10. Chibli Mallat, "From Islamic to Middle Eastern Law: A Restatement of the Field (Part II)," *American Journal of Comparative Law* 52, no. 1 (2004) 285.

11. For a general account of the tension between the ideal and practice of the rule of law in Islam, see Khaled Abou el Fadl, *Islam and the Challenge of Democracy* (Princeton, NJ: Princeton University Press, 2004), 12–4.

12. George N. Sfeir, *The Modernization of Arab Law: An Investigation into Current Civil, Criminal, and Constitutional Law in the Arab World* (San Francisco: Austin and Winfield, 1998), 11–2.

13. Ellis Goldberg, "Private Goods, Public Wrongs and Civil Society in Some Medieval Arab Theory and Practice," in *Rules and Rights in the Middle East: Democracy, Law, and Society*, ed. Ellis Goldberg, Resat Kasaba, and Joel S. Migdal (Seattle: University of Washington Press, 1993), 251, 255, and 263.

14. Lawrence Rosen, *The Justice of Islam* (Oxford: Oxford University Press, 2000), 48–9.

15. For a succinct summary of the combination of sources of law in each Arab area, see Brown, *Rule of Law*, 3–5.

16. Roger Owen, *State, Power and Politics in the Making of the Modern Middle East* (London: Routledge, 2000), 11.

17. Samir Khairi Tawfiq, *Mabda Siyadat al-Qa'nun* [The Principle of the Rule of Law] (Baghdad: 1978). Considering that it was published a year before Saddam Hussein moved from partial to undisputed political control of Iraq, this thoughtful, philosophical discussion of the rule of law in terms that would sound familiar to Western legal scholars is a particularly interesting treatise on the subject in the Arabic language.

18. For a detailed discussion of the political roles for Arab constitutions, see Nathan Brown, *Constitutions in a Non-Constitutional World* (Albany: State University of New York Press, 2002).

19. Indeed, one might question American exceptionalism with respect to religion and politics generally as is done thoughtfully based on a multination comparison by N. J. Demarath III in *Crossing the Gods: World Religions and Worldly Politics* (New Brunswick, NJ: Rutgers University Press, 2001), 215–46.

20. One of the signs of both legal pluralism and the relative novelty of the Western notion of the rule of law in Arab countries is that there is no single phrase that is used in every country to translate the term. For example, in Morocco, the concept is often referred to as *dawla el-haq w'al-qa'nun* (the rule of right and law), instead of *siyadat al-qa'nun*. This term gained currency through the Moroccan monarchy's efforts to employ it as a slogan for its own purported fealty to the ideal of the rule of law.

21. A thorough and excellent discussion of many of the varied ideas that fit into contemporary Arab debates on democracy and that generally assume the possibility of what I am calling the reconstructionist tendency can be found in Larbi Sadiki, *The Search for Arab Democracy: Discourse and Counter-Discourses* (New York: Columbia University Press, 2004), especially 198–252.

22. John Stuart Blackton, interview with author, April 8, 2005.

23. Perhaps the best publicly available document that tries to accrue lessons from judicial rule-of-law programs is a study that was published by the U.S. Agency for International Development (USAID) in 2002, *Guidance for Promoting Judicial Independence and Impartiality* (Washington, D.C.: Office of Democracy and Governance, USAID, 2002). This remarkable document, which brings together the perspectives of leading scholars and experienced practitioners, does not include data or assessments from Arab countries because of the relative youth of dedicated U.S.-based rule-of-law programs in these countries.

24. Matthew Stephenson, "Judicial Independence: What It Is, How It Can Be Measured, Why It Occurs," World Bank Policy Brief (Washington, D.C.: World Bank), available at www1.worldbank.org/publicsector/legal/judicialindependence.htm.

25. John Stuart Blackton, "Neo-Wilsonianism in the Middle East: Democracy-Lite," *National Interest* 2, no. 43 (November 5, 2003), 2.

26. Keith Schulz, interview with author, April 7, 2005.

27. For a valuable inside appraisal of Egypt's recent experience with judicial review, see Adel Omar Sherif, "The Rule of Law in Egypt from a Judicial Perspective," in Cotran and Yamani, *Rule of Law*, 1–34.

28. Yustina Saleh, "Law, the Rule of Law and Religious Minorities in Egypt," *Middle East Review of International Affairs* 8, no. 4 (December 2004), 83.

29. Nathan J. Brown and Hesham Nasr, *Egypt's Judges Step Forward: The Judicial Election Boycott and Egyptian Reform*, policy outlook (Washington, D.C.: Carnegie Endowment for International Peace, May 2005), 1, 4.

30. United Nations Development Programme (UNDP), *The Arab Human Development Report 2004* (New York: United Nations, 2005), 149.

31. UNDP, *Arab Human Development Report 2004*, 20.

32. See, for example, the special issue of *Comparative Politics* from January 2004 devoted entirely to explaining Arab authoritarianism and Daniel Brumberg, "Liberalization versus Democracy: Understanding Arab Political Reform," Carnegie Endowment Working Paper no. 37 (Washington, D.C.: Carnegie Endowment for International Peace, April 2003).

33. For example, John Stuart Blackton, interview, and Attorney Myriam Bennani, interview with author, March 12, 2005, Casablanca, Morocco.

34. Stephen Golub, "The Legal Empowerment Alternative," chapter 7 in this volume.

35. World Bank, Implementation Completion Report (Scl-45630) on a Loan in the Amount of US $5.3 Million to the Kingdom of Morocco for a Legal and Judicial Development Project (Washington, D.C.: World Bank, December 30, 2004), 12–7.

36. See, generally, Ann Elizabeth Mayer, *Islam and Human Rights*, 3rd edition (Boulder, CO: Westview Press, 1998); and Susan Waltz, *Human Rights and Reform: Changing the Face of North African Politics* (Berkeley: University of California Press, 1995).

37. David M. Mednicoff, "Think Locally, Act Globally? Cultural Framing and Human Rights Movements in Tunisia and Morocco," *International Journal of Human Rights* 7, no. 3 (2003), 72–102.

38. See, for example, the article "Un An Après: la Moudawana à l'Ëpreuve du Réel," which covered the general legal enforcement and understanding of the new family code in urban courts and the countryside and appeared in a weekly Moroccan news magazine with a growing reputation for accuracy and independence, *Tel Quel* (March 5–11, 2005), 22–9.

CHAPTER ELEVEN

Time to Learn,
Time to Act in Africa

LAURE-HÉLÈNE PIRON

DONOR ASSISTANCE TO JUSTICE sector reform in sub-Saharan Africa has increased massively over the last decade. Official development assistance data for legal and judicial initiatives indicate a rise from $17.7 million in 1994 to over $110 million in 2002, while total aid commitments to the region remained stable at $12 billion. During this period, the United Kingdom overtook the United States as the largest bilateral justice aid provider to Africa.[1] These figures, however, need to be treated with caution and probably underestimate real aid volumes. Nonetheless, they point to a potentially significant change in donor priorities.

This increase can be explained by donors responding to Africa-specific events during the 1990s, such as democratization and the need for constitutional reforms or reconstructing basic state functions in the aftermath of violent conflicts. It also reflects more global trends, in particular the growing awareness that "governance" is key to effective development and poverty reduction. But are donors grounding their assistance in a proper understanding of Africa? Are they putting into practice

This chapter builds on an earlier essay for the Open Society Institute Justice Initiative, commissioned by Stephen Humphreys. The author thanks Thomas Carothers, Joanna Bosworth, Richard Messick, Martin Pierce, and Erika Schläppi for their comments on this longer version. The views expressed here are solely that of the author and do not represent the organizations for which she currently works or has worked.

their numerous commitments to improving how aid to the justice sector is to be provided?

This chapter is a personal reflection based on five years of working on a number of justice sector–related assignments as part of the "aid industry." It is not grounded on a systematic review of the evidence— which as correctly noted in several chapters in this book is seriously lacking. Its aim is more humble: to describe the growing consensus surrounding justice sector aid to Africa, to identify some of the key challenges that aid practitioners and their recipients face in trying to make such work effective, and to urge aid agencies and African governments to make greater efforts to change their practices.

The term *justice sector* is used here as a shorthand to refer not just to the judiciary, ministries of justice, and lawyers but also to the police, prosecutors, prisons, ministries of interior, human rights bodies, nonstate mechanisms (such as traditional rulers), and civil society organizations that contribute to domestic dispute resolution and the provision of security and stability. This sector is more commonly referred to as the *rule of law*, which has a more value-laden meaning, or to *law and order* with a more repressive undertone. This definition is purposefully broad. It draws attention to the need for these agencies to work together as well as with other official bodies not directly related to criminal, civil, or commercial justice (such as social work agencies or local governments), and to engage with a wider set of social norms and structures. The goal is not just to build state capacity but also to deliver services to citizens.

Changing Donor Priorities

The current donor attention to justice sector reform in Africa reflects an evolution of donor priorities in the legal domain, from an early emphasis on legal education and legal reform to the more general concept of the rule of law. In recent years the broader donor emphasis on poverty reduction has further modified approaches to legal assistance issues in the region.

From Law Reform to the Rule of Law

Donor policy and practice today regarding justice sector reform in Africa can be contrasted with narrower past approaches in the law domain. It is different, for example, from that of the law and development movement of the 1960s and 1970s, in which U.S. aid focused on improving legal education. It also differs from the wave of law reform work sponsored by the World Bank and other multilateral development banks in the 1980s, the early era of structural adjustment programs, as a means of helping develop legal environments favorable to investment.

In the late 1980s, the World Bank added to its law reform portfolio in Africa and started to engage in judicial reform. This reflected a shift in the bank particularly and in donors' policies more generally. The new concept of governance was gaining prominence, reflecting a concern for building effective state institutions. The World Bank's 1997 *World Development Report* recognized that minimal state functions included providing pure public goods, such as law and order and property rights.[2] The *rule of law* was emphasized, seen as essential for establishing a stable, predictable environment conforming to formal rules rather than patronage, with the judiciary acting as a check on arbitrary state action. By 2000, the World Bank could write about Africa: "legal reform has become a priority in many countries, and one that Africa's development partners are beginning to assist."[3] The focus of external assistance went beyond sound legal frameworks; at its core was the judiciary, and a new panoply of loans and projects to strengthen its independence and organizational effectiveness.

In Africa, rule-of-law interventions gained in importance after the end of the Cold War, during the growing trend toward multiparty democracy across the continent in the early 1990s. For example, Swiss support for the rule of law in Africa began as a late response to apartheid in South Africa and to increased political repression in Rwanda in the years prior to the 1994 genocide.[4] The U.S. Agency for International Development (USAID) came to Africa with a "democratization" lens, inherited from its work in Latin America, and began attempting to strengthen the independence of judiciaries in the face of overpowering executives and to provide assistance in drafting democratic constitutions.

The new approach also included support for domestic civil society organizations—as a means to increase demand for better justice, monitor human rights, and provide legal assistance. For example, Ford Foundation grantees in South Africa undertook public interest litigation, exploiting loopholes in the apartheid system's rhetorical commitment to the rule of law. These groups later played a major role in informing the country's new constitutional structure and have since established networks across civil society to make legal services more accessible to all.[5]

Over the course of the 1990s donor-supported work on justice sector reform in Africa added more and more elements beyond the courts and the administration of justice, such as improving physical infrastructure, supporting legal and judicial training, making legal information accessible or upgrading management systems in ministries. Despite the expanding range of activities, the focus remained on building more effective institutions. In Mozambique, for example, following a diagnostic process in the late 1990s, USAID helped establish a National Judicial Training Center and provided support to improve the efficiency of the Maputo City Court through the provision of equipment, benchbooks, a computerized case-tracking system, and a court administrator.[6]

The 1994 genocide in Rwanda and the ensuing donor commitment to aiding the reconstruction of its justice sector marked a turning point in the sheer scale of assistance and the range of multilateral and bilateral donor agencies involved. Activities in Rwanda ranged from building courthouses, improving prison conditions, preparing genocide case files, establishing a bar association and a body of paralegals to working with the Ministry of Justice, and reforming the police. To help manage this rush of aid, donors established pooling mechanisms, the UN Development Program (UNDP) trust fund, for example. Nonetheless, bilateral donors, such as the Americans, Belgians, Canadians, Dutch, Germans, Swiss, and many others, have continued to also sponsor their own projects, at times poorly coordinated. The European Commission provided assistance to international nongovernmental organizations (NGOs) specializing in legal, judicial, and penal reforms (including Avocats sans Frontières, Réseau des Citoyens, Danish Centre for Human Rights, and Penal Reform International).

Incorporating the New Poverty Reduction Agenda

The current justice sector aid paradigm starts from this inherited institutional perspective. In line with the rest of the industry, it is attempting to adjust itself to another shift in global aid thinking. Poverty reduction became the official objective of development in the late 1990s, as articulated in particular in the United Nations Millennium Declaration and its results-oriented Millennium Development Goals (MDGs).[7] This has been associated with a commitment to change how official aid is to be provided, based on a "partnership approach" and the "ownership" of reform by local actors, aiming to improve coordination of aid and moving toward a harmonization of donor procedures and eventual alignment of donor assistance with national partners' policies and systems.[8]

The relevance of justice reform was not explicitly stated in this new aid discourse. For example, although there is a commitment to human rights, democracy, and the rule of law in the Millennium Declaration, a political statement adopted by heads of state and government, there is no MDG or indicator related to justice or security. Given that the MDGs influence donor programming to a much greater extent than the Millennium Declaration, justice programs have not benefited from the same rhetorical push that the MDGs have provided for other sectors such as health or education.

Donors have been challenged to justify how support to justice could contribute to poverty reduction, and, as a result, some have felt compelled to amend their approach to assisting this sector. They have put forward various studies to demonstrate the importance of functioning, fair, and accessible justice institutions to ensure social cohesion and combat poverty. The World Bank's 2000 *Voices of the Poor* report, for example, highlighted lawlessness and fear of crime in poor people's own descriptions of the experience of poverty. The negative role played by the police in these accounts was striking—often considered corrupt and politically repressive, harassing small traders and targeting minorities.[9]

Lesson-learning exercises showed the failings of donors' approaches to date, such as the need to better understand whether minimal conditions were in place before a program of support could be envisaged in the case of USAID[10] or to move beyond stand-alone police projects in the case of the United Kingdom.[11] A comparative study by the International Council on Human Rights Policy in 2000 set out a more strategic, pro-poor approach, with clear messages:[12]

- *Start from the beneficiary perspective*, fostering local ownership of reform, using participatory needs assessments;
- *Adopt a rights-based approach*, emphasizing the legal enforcement of human rights claims, the role of institutions in respecting standards, and the positive duties of the police, prosecutors, courts, and others to respect and protect the rights of victims, prisoners, and the general public;
- *Recognize that justice is a sector* and not a set of separate institutions—which requires strengthening links and improving coordination, including with civil society bodies;
- *Give priority to the needs of poor, vulnerable, and marginalized groups*, by enhancing their access to justice, tackling discrimination, ensuring

minority participation, recognizing indigenous systems, and paying attention to women's rights; and

- *Improve the effectiveness of the aid relationship*, including transparency
  in donor agendas, recognizing the long-term process of justice reform, providing flexible responses, respecting local priorities, and
  avoiding imported solutions.

In response to these and similar suggestions, most donors have been
amending their policy orientations. The United Kingdom's Department
for International Development (DFID) provides a good illustration. Building on an established tradition of providing support for policing projects,
it radically transformed its policy, putting at the center of the analysis
how poor people themselves experience insecurity and injustice, and
highlighting the need for a sectorwide perspective, referred to as "safety,
security, and access to justice" (SSAJ).[13] Two large-scale programs in
Africa were designed to conform to this new policy and have now been
in place for a few years. The Malawi Safety, Security, and Access to Justice Program (which started implementation in 2002 with £35 million
approved for the first five years) and the Nigeria Access to Justice Program (with £30 million approved in 2001 for a period of seven years)
both had the mandate to move away from a purely institutional approach
by emphasizing sectorwide policies and coordination and paying particular attention to research and the perspective of the poor. Five years
on, DFID's new approach is taking shape in Africa, with SSAJ programs
in most of the countries where DFID provides significant assistance, such
as the Sierra Leone Justice Sector Development Program, which began
in early 2005 with £25 million allocated over five years. According to
unpublished data, almost 70 percent of DFID programming on SSAJ is
spent in Africa, a minimum of £160 million since 2000.

Incorporation of these new aid imperatives is also evident in the approaches of other donors, such as in the UNDP's new Access to Justice
for All policy, which prioritizes people's equal ability to use justice services—regardless of their gender, ethnicity, religion, political views, age,
class, disability, or other sources of distinction.[14] The UN Secretary-
General's report, *The Rule of Law and Transitional Justice in Conflict and
Post-Conflict Societies*, also recognizes the importance of international
human rights norms, national leadership, supporting domestic constituencies, and embracing an integrated approach.[15] The World Bank too
has adopted "access to justice," as one of three strategic objectives, in
addition to legal and judicial reform. This covers improving access to

existing services, expanding access through encouraging nontraditional users or new dispute resolution mechanisms, or creating new legal standing. At least on paper, the World Bank now explicitly recognizes that member states have human rights obligations and that they can be assisted in fulfilling them—a major change from earlier attitudes toward human rights described as lying outside the bank's mandate.[16] In programming terms, this new World Bank approach is illustrated by grants in fourteen African countries to support gender-responsive legal reform processes, such as civil society provision of legal assistance to women in Rwanda. However, not all donors have adopted an explicitly pro-poor approach. USAID, for example, retains a focus on rule-of-law programming aimed at the twin goals of economic growth and democracy.

New Agenda in Practice

With both Jeffrey Sachs' UN Millennium Project and British Prime Minister Tony Blair's Commission for Africa advocating for a massive increase in aid to Africa with a renewed focus on governance, 2005 is being presented as a year pregnant with opportunities to achieve development and poverty eradication on the continent.[17] Although additional financial and technical resources are certainly needed, *how* aid is provided remains one of the biggest hurdles. There are five challenges that both donors and African governments need to overcome if they are to turn the anticipated 2005 increases in aid volume into visible results that benefit not just states but also their populations: enhancing resources, adopting a sectoral approach, understanding the political context, involving nonstate actors, and improving donor habits and incentives.

Enhancing Resources

The first challenge is an obvious starting point: Africa's justice systems tend to be chronically underresourced, with a decaying infrastructure, outdated legal frameworks (often dating from authoritarian colonial times), insufficient numbers of trained professionals, absence of legal and other basic materials, and low salaries. This not only creates difficult working conditions but also affects the performance and credibility of the systems. In Nigeria, for example, DFID found that judges often had to rely on private lawyers appearing before them to gain access to law reports, which impaired their standing and created the impression in the legal community that private practitioners were better versed in the law. Judges, particularly in the lower courts, would often be forced to acquire pens and paper from court users to perform their judicial functions.[18]

Rwanda in the aftermath of the genocide offers an extreme case of underresourcing. For a population of 7.5 million, it only had about fifty newly recruited judges or young graduates, twenty prosecutors, and fifty lawyers when the first Bar Association was created in 1997. Prisons and other places of detention soon became overcrowded with over 130,000 persons accused of involvement in the genocide, and experts estimated that it would take over a century to deal with their cases. By 2002, there were significantly more lawyers, paralegal defenders, prosecutors, and judges; the police had undergone a massive transformation; and *gacacas* (special participatory grass roots justice mechanisms) were being piloted to deal with the genocide. However, only about 9 percent of judges had a first degree in law and only just over 7,000 genocide court cases had been closed. By 2005, following some releases, 80,000 persons remained in prison on genocide charges—detained without trial for over ten years—and the nongenocide prison population had risen to 8,000. Estimates that up to one million new persons could eventually be implicated in the genocide as a result of the *gacaca* jurisdictions (which are only starting on a nationwide scale in 2005) may lead to renewed overcrowding of prisons and courts backlogs for those accused of the most serious crimes. Massive investments to date are likely to remain insufficient to deal not only with the genocide, but ongoing societal, administrative, and commercial disputes.

Underresourcing and low performance are general characteristics of African public sectors. Security institutions (such as the police or paramilitary) may get a decent allocation, given their role in maintaining state control over the population, but courts, prisons, and oversight bodies are usually ignored. Somaliland provides an interesting example of the priority-setting process of an embryonic state authority: In 2004, out of a budget estimated at $25 million (collected through local taxes and ports), 80 percent was devoted to security, including the military. Financial allocation, however, does not mean that resources are used in the interest of the public. Police forces across the continent still have to overcome a legacy of being used as a tool for repression and societal control, by colonial and postcolonial regimes alike.

Both Jeffrey Sachs and the Commission for Africa are correct in suggesting the need for massive investments in Africa. How to increase aid so that it can be absorbed and not overwhelm domestic capacity is the challenge. The fundamental principle of the current aid effectiveness agenda is that donors should promote domestic leadership and ownership of reforms. This is not easy to achieve in the current African context. High levels of aid dependency have given donors a huge influence over policies and programs. The gap between the resources available to donors and those of their national partners means that donors easily become excessively influential in deciding what to support—and governments can just as easily forgo their own responsibilities.

Many donor interventions continue to be far from sustainable. Some of the pitfalls of current donor projects are illustrated by European and British support for an initiative to address the backlog in homicide cases in Malawi. Backlog had increased considerably following the introduction of a jury trial system in 1995. In 1999, donors provided resources to cover the costs of accommodation, allowances, and transport for all those involved in tackling the backlog—judiciary, police, prosecution, legal aid, jury members, witnesses, and a doctor. This support was meant to be temporary, but an independent evaluation of the project in 2003 identified excessive reliance on external resources. Government funding for the processing of homicide cases had effectively ceased and the donor initiative had not, by then, led to the creation of an improved and sustainable mechanism for homicide cases after the project's end.

A new approach to priority setting is meant to create a "virtuous circle" of donors backing nationally developed and owned reforms. The Poverty Reduction Strategy Paper (PRSP) approach adopted by the international financial institutions in the late 1990s as part of debt-relief conditionality is now being adopted by a significant part of the donor community. It requires recipient countries to go through a broadly consultative process to set national priorities, link them more realistically to spending plans, and make greater efforts to monitor results. Donors are meant to engage in dialogue rather than impose their policy preferences. A number of them are increasingly providing their assistance directly through the national budget or through pooled support to a specific sector rather than through stand-alone projects.

The extent to which this is happening in practice is contested. Uganda is often promoted as the country having made the most progress in linking aid resources to nationally owned priorities and the budget process. Yet, even in this situation, justice institutions have failed to financially gain from their reform efforts and their participation in Uganda's PRSP. Resources allocated to the sector have continued to decline, from 6.3 percent of government expenditure in the 2000–2001 budget down to a projected 5.9 percent in the 2003–2004 Medium-Term Expenditure Framework. Justice remains a "nonpriority" sector, regularly receiving less than what it had been allocated because it does not benefit from the same protection from in-year cuts as sectors clearly identified as pro-poor, such as health and education, or with presidential political backing, such as defense.[19] Projections for the 2006–2007 budget allocate 186 billion Ugandan shillings for the ten justice sector institutions, including 76 billion Ugandan shillings for the police, compared with 386 billion shillings for security (defense and intelligence services).[20]

Increasing investments in justice institutions require sound technical arguments to win over ministries of finance in charge of PRSP processes. Starting from institutional beneficiaries' own priorities may not lead to making the case effectively, and consulting justice sector officials will often not result in identifying pro-poor priorities. In Nigeria, the judges I interviewed as part of a DFID assessment exercise prioritized longer summer vacations for themselves, or the construction of a fence to keep goats out of the court's perimeter. These answers do point to the need to better communicate what pro-poor investments require, and to establish or consolidate basic systems, including working conditions, rather than necessarily fund major reform efforts.

Rwanda illustrates well the consequences of poor financial planning. Its ambitious attempts during 2002–2005 to increase the status and performance of judges and prosecutors through higher educational standards and salary increases and benefits failed to engage the Ministry of Economic Planning and Finance and other actors key to national budgeting early enough in the process. Not only have officials failed to appoint about half of the posts, but they are unlikely to attract and retain qualified staff without the promised increases.

Given the generic underresourcing of African states, investments in justice systems need professionals able to make a strong political and technical case to their national authorities and identify how best to use aid. Unless the case is better made, with evidence to back up the relevance of justice for poverty reduction and mechanisms to monitor the use of funds, including to tackle corruption, underresourcing will continue.

Adopting a Sectoral Approach

A second key challenge in making justice sector aid more effective is learning how to develop coherent sectoral approaches in the face of the sheer complexity of justice systems. In such systems, both state and civil society institutions are keen to preserve their independence and benefit individually from resources that may become available: The police want more radios and weapons; judges better court houses and law books; and legal aid funds actually need funds. The number of donor agencies with their own diverse policy priorities, procedures, and implementing arrangements—ranging from private sector companies to individual experts—only aggravates this complex picture, making efficient allocation and use of resources next to impossible.

Initiatives in Uganda have shown the benefits of a sectoral approach to justice work. In the Masaka District, piloting mechanisms for interagency coordination between local criminal justice agencies—such as monthly meetings of a "case management committee"—has yielded low-cost improvements, which are now inspiring reform in other countries.[21] A range of Ugandan institutions came together in 1999 to create a Justice, Law, and Order Sector (JLOS) with a joint strategy and investment plan approved as part of the country's PRSP. Donor assistance is provided in a manner that aims to respect this national leadership: through the national budget to which some donors directly contribute, or by funding only projects that fall within the national strategy. More recently, in Kenya, a "Donor Group" was established by eleven donors aiming to adopt a similar coordinated approach.

The adoption of a sectoral approach is proving to be one of the most daunting but important innovations in DFID's policy. It is intuitively highly sensible: Improvements in one part of the justice system are likely to stall if related institutions continue to underperform. For example, prisons are usually at the receiving end of a failed criminal justice chain. I was able to observe the appalling prison conditions in Somaliland during a mission in 2004. To its credit, the UNDP Rule of Law and Security Program had recognized the importance of working with all the main security and justice actors. It was trying hard to get the authorities to invest in improving prison infrastructure—a low political priority in a context of widespread poverty, insecurity, and protostate structures. Yet, parallel efforts to establish functioning police and courts could only, in the near future, lead to a worse situation in the prisons, with more arrests and prolonged detentions. New procedures or training of correctional staff, supported by UNDP, would not improve the immediate situation. We asked ourselves: Was the international community funding this UN initiative complicit in furthering basic human rights violations of detainees?

In practice, a sectoral approach has been understood to require, as a starting point, a sectorwide assessment to identify priorities and allow specific interventions to be designed. It should not mean that a single donor program attempts to address all weaknesses simultaneously but that governmental and donor interventions start from a shared comprehensive "diagnostic." This initial first step can be a major hurdle and create significant delays. For example, donors have attempted to work together in the Democratic Republic of the Congo. Following peace accords and agreement on a political transition and national dialogue in 2002–2003, donors identified the reestablishment of the rule of law as a priority. During the second part of 2003, a joint donor assessment mission began a detailed review of the justice sector. The process was led by the European Commission, supported by the UN Office of the High Commissioner for Human Rights, the UNDP, and the Governments of Belgium, France, and the United Kingdom, liaising with the UN peacekeeping mission. The team comprised over sixteen experts (both national and international) reviewing the legal framework, the operation of the courts, the legal profession, the police and prosecution, the penal system, judicial statistics, training institutions, nonstate mechanisms (mediators, traditional justice), donor and NGO interventions, relations between citizens and the justice system, as well as transitional justice and national reconciliation. By May 2004, a report of almost ninety pages had failed to identify a feasible and costed set of priority interventions that donors could fund. It is only after several more workshops and negotiations that aid interventions could get started.

A sectoral approach aims to encourage strategic planning and greater coordination not just between donors, but also between national institutions. However, donor programs encounter technical and political resistance from national authorities who are not keen, or are unable, to coordinate policy and implementation across several ministries and agencies, let alone with civil society. This is especially so because judiciaries and horizontal accountability bodies need to defend the little constitutional independence they may have. In most countries, it is extremely difficult to support the Ministry of Justice and Supreme Court to work together toward agreeing on a joint reform strategy. In Nigeria, the federal attorney general and the chief justice could not be invited to the same event, let alone to a joint reform steering committee to guide donor programs. In such a situation, it is only at the presidential or prime ministerial level that these bodies can be brought together with the Ministry of Interior, police, and others from civil society. What seems rational is simply often not politically feasible and may turn out to be excessively bureaucratic.

An additional constraint has been the lack of appropriate mechanisms to deliver such complex programs aiming to work across a number of institutions, from both the state and civil society. Putting into practice the new aid paradigm would entail providing assistance directly to governments themselves for managing their own comprehensive reform efforts. When this is not feasible, in particular when governmental financial management is not seen as sufficiently sound, separate technical assistance units may be established. In Malawi, international experts have worked from within a DFID office, reporting to a Malawi steering committee but operating outside state structures. In many other African countries, DFID has "contracted out" implementation to the British Council or private companies. Although this allows DFID and other donors to keep a hands-off approach to program implementation, it creates a series of principal-agent problems, including balancing the commercial interests or visibility of the implementers with the priorities of governmental and civil society partners.

Sectoral approaches, however, should not be jettisoned because of these difficulties. Donors who understand the value of seeing justice as an integrated sector need to be less ambitious in how they try to impart the message and structure their aid. But they should avoid focusing only on the one institution which they feel can work, pay attention to systemwide consequences, and not forget about social and poverty outcomes.

Understanding the Political Context

A third challenge is that even if assistance is designed in a manner that backs sectorwide initiatives, rather than financially unsustainable institution-based activities, donors still need to learn to go beyond "technical" solutions and understand the political *context* for intended reforms. A particular difficulty lies in the inherent conservatism of justice systems and the politically sensitive changes that might be needed to effect reforms.

In many African countries, executives remain dominant, with relatively weaker parliaments or judiciaries charged with upholding checks and balances. Justice sector reform aimed at increasing judicial independence and impartiality or police accountability can pose a threat to the powerful. Independent court decisions are not welcomed when presidents attempt constitutional change to lengthen their terms in office. In Malawi, for example, judges were reportedly sacked when they stood in the way of President Muluzi's efforts to stand for a third term.

The police are often called on at election time to serve their political masters rather than the public. Human Rights Watch, for example, has criticized the behavior of the Nigerian security forces, in particular the paramilitary mobile police seen as acting in collusion with ruling party officials during the 2003 general elections, which were marred by high levels of political violence.[22] Such violence was not uncommon prior to the elections: Vigilante groups associated with governors were known to be using whatever means at their disposal to secure their power. For example, in 2000 and 2001, the "Bakassi Boys," set up by the governor with legal backing as the Anambra state's vigilantes, were allegedly involved in the execution of businessmen and of an opposition local government official.

Yet too often donors still fail to account for the political aspects of this work, and talk of national "ownership" of democratic reform can sound naïve in such environments. Thomas Carothers cites the "politically treacherous" example of constitutional reform assistance in Zambia. Rather than following the recommendations of the (donor-supported) Constitutional Review Commission, President Frederick Chiluba imposed a provision to disqualify his main rival, Kenneth Kaunda, from the 1996 elections, and had the constitution approved by the National Assembly, which he controlled, thus avoiding the commission and the need for a referendum.[23]

My own experience in Nigeria shows how donor agencies can get entangled in local power relations, attempting to push through "rational" strategic approaches in an environment of short-term political gains and missing out on opportunities available outside their predesigned frameworks. The DFID Nigeria country program had been reshaped around a limited number of interventions at the federal level and more intensive investments in four focal states. The approach, which made sense in large federal countries such as India, turned out to be highly problematic in Nigeria, because some nonviable and thinly populated states, such as Ekiti in the southwest Yoruba region, were slated to receive potentially large amounts of aid, while centers of legal and judicial activity and expertise, such as Lagos or Kaduna, were largely ignored. DFID thus attempted to identify reform-minded governors with whom partnerships could be built—only to have some of them lose their seats during the following elections. Having agreed that SSAJ would be a DFID

Nigeria priority, the challenge became to try to support reforms in the selected states, linking them with federal initiatives. A happy coincidence meant that Ekiti's attorney general showed interest in the SSAJ program during its design. However, he had been expecting immediate, visible support that could have furthered his reputation and political career. The delays in moving from design (in 2000) to implementation (in 2002) meant that DFID was not able to deliver on its part of the bargain. Once in place, implementers had to contend with a dizzying turnover of counterparts: three attorneys general in Ekiti, the assassination of the federal attorney general, the sacking of the inspector general of police, and the retirement of the controller general of prisons, and all this before the 2003 elections.

Donors need to be politically astute. A fine balance has to be found between identifying nationally owned objectives with influential backers that aid can support, and the danger of excessive politicization of assistance. Although they desperately need the support of current politicians, donor programs also need to find entry points to strengthen systems or support reforms in a manner that can outlast elected governments and benefit populations, building on consensus that can reach across parties and other power divisions. This conclusion is illustrated by the DFID Malawi program's experience with its steering committee. The National Council for Safety and Justice, coordinating aid and policy initiatives for fourteen institutions, was designed to have high-political backing, and Malawi's vice president was appointed to lead it. However, this approach backfired: As the 2004 elections approached, and the vice president became the president's main opponent, the program fell victim to electoral and postelectoral politics. A technical-level committee would have allowed a smoother functioning, though possibly with less visibility and senior leadership.

The examples cited here cover only one aspect of the formal political context that donors need to better understand. Informal networks, patterns of corruption, institutional rivalries, prior reform attempts, and geopolitical allegiances all play a part in defining what is desirable and feasible. Experience often shows, however, that the powers that be are unlikely to be concerned about the very poorest, and more often than not will only pay lip service to donors' new poverty reduction agendas.

Despite the pretty depressing picture painted in this review, justice sector reform has happened on the continent. Rwanda provides such an example. The question is whether this reform can genuinely be described as directly aiming at pro-poor impacts, rather than continuing to build

state security and capacity in the aftermath of the civil war and genocide. After a major restructuring of its police force (merging together the
paramilitary gendarmerie and communal and judicial police forces),
Rwanda is now undergoing a wholesale transformation of its judicial
and prosecutorial system, which a high-profile Law Reform Commission was able to design and (in the main) successfully push through.
This effort has included securing in the 2003 constitution the independence of the judiciary, a functioning Supreme Court, reorganized court
structures, and rationalized public prosecution services. This was not
easy. The commission's proposals were opposed by the Ministry of Justice, which saw its powers diminishing. The commission had to reverse
provisions in the first draft of the constitution that would not have guaranteed the separation of powers. Efforts to enhance salaries and benefits
were not adequately negotiated with the Ministry of Finance and failed.
And the commission was not institutionalized as a permanent body.
However, the reasons why the regime's strongmen seem interested in
reforms, which if truly put into practice would limit executive authority, remain unclear. Donor pressures, for example from the Americans
or Dutch, cannot by themselves explain the changes that have happened.
Although some reforms, such as the introduction of local-level mediators, could potentially enhance access to justice for rural communities,
the driving force does not appear to have been poverty reduction.

Donor agencies can certainly become better at understanding the political context within which they operate and at adjusting their assistance accordingly, although this will not necessarily guarantee greater
success. It needs to be remembered that challenges to executive authority can come from unexpected quarters. In Europe, it took a Norwegian
judge facing death threats to tackle corruption at the heart of the French
state (the Elf affair) and an unelected upper chamber to counter executive assault on civil liberties in the name of terrorism in the United Kingdom (detention orders).

Involving Nonstate Actors

A fourth challenge is that national ownership of reform is still often understood to refer to *government* ownership—and the considerable funding required to make significant changes often leads to state-centric assistance. Yet any examination of the experiences of poor and marginalized
persons in Africa trying to access justice or guarantee their own security
must conclude that formal state institutions are often not the most

relevant for them. Stephen Golub's call in chapter 7 for donors to adopt a legal empowerment alternative is a response to this finding:

> Many development agencies that profess pro-poor priorities invest far more in building up government legal institutions and elites than in fortifying impoverished populations' legal capacities and power. In the process, they often insufficiently heed the priorities of the poor, the experience of successful efforts to empower them, and the need to build up civil society if governments and their legal systems are to become responsive and accountable.

Within civil society, donor agencies need to better understand and develop more effective working relations with two sets of institutions: first, traditional, customary, and informal mechanisms that offer community-based justice or security; and second, NGOs and other more formal bodies.

More than 80 to 90 percent of day-to-day disputes in Africa are said to be resolved through nonstate systems such as traditional authorities, but only a few donors (such as Germany's Gesellschaft fur Technische Zusammenarbeit, or GTZ, and the United Kingdom's DFID) have taken this important fact seriously.[24] The lack of research and policy-relevant evidence in this domain is a real constraint and also reflects the more general absence of aid agency awareness of these issues. In Somaliland, UNDP data show that traditional systems of justice are perceived to be the most accessible: Clan and community elders were used by 98 percent of people in rural or nomadic areas and by 94 percent of those in urban areas, followed by council elders and Sharia. Only 35 percent of people in urban areas and 26 percent in rural or nomadic areas used the judiciary.[25] Malawi has a predominantly rural population of nine million, yet there are only about 300 lawyers, mostly in the urban centers, and only nine of the country's magistrates have had professional training. By contrast, there are at least 24,000 customary justice forums.[26] DFID's Malawi program is now piloting "primary justice" initiatives—improving linkages between the formal and informal systems and enhancing skills and accountability of nonstate structures. DFID's Nigeria program is also trying to work with traditional institutions, aiming in particular to improve the recording of cases resolved by chiefs or emirs.[27]

Donors wrongly tend to avoid working with these traditional or community bodies—sometimes simply because a lack of social or anthropological knowledge makes them blind to their existence and relevance for the poorest. When they do, however, they are rightly cautious about the risks involved. During the design process for the Nigeria program, for example, the boundary between "legitimate" community mechanisms providing the only form of policing and security for rural populations, and illegitimate vigilantes (such as the O'odua Peoples Congress in southwestern Nigeria or the Bakassi Boys in southeastern Nigeria) was hard to define. In Rwanda, "local defence forces" are presented by the government as local volunteers assisting the police. They are in fact much closer to state authorities and at times involved in arbitrary killings and excessive use of force.[28] In Malawi, users of nonstate systems regularly express concerns about the corruption and bias of customary authorities; they prefer having a range of options to choose from, using the paramount chief, local government authorities, or lowest courts when appropriate to meet their various needs.

Serious concerns about these systems also include harsh physical punishments, banishment, discriminatory practices against women or those considered from "outside" the community. It is often on such human rights grounds that donors shy away from finding approaches to strengthen or reform them. Ignoring them altogether is, however, not a viable option: It leads to a denial of the potential for enhanced access to a fairer local justice or improved safety and security for the poorest and most marginalized. It is a similar mix of blindness that makes many aid agencies reluctant to identify how best to work with Sharia systems. In some countries aid agencies do not authorize their assistance to be involved in Sharia systems, but in Somalia or northern Nigeria, this is simply unrealistic.

By contrast, donors do work with international and local NGOs, but here too practice could improve. When they have the right approach, international NGOs working on human rights, anticorruption, or other public interest issues can play an important role in building local capacity or providing a counterbalance to governmental aid agencies priorities. In Rwanda, for example, Penal Reform International (PRI) is undertaking an independent monitoring of the *gacaca* process.[29] While aiming at achieving the potentially contradictory goals of truth, justice, and reconciliation, the *gacaca* process has suspended many due process aspects (such as the right to a defense lawyer) and risks reigniting ethnically based feelings. PRI's work here is an example of sensitive research that domestic actors simply could not undertake with the same degree of impartiality and independence in the current political environment. Questions can however be asked when international NGOs redefine their objectives so as to be able to remain in a country when there is no longer a clear need for them, or simply move on to the next crisis where new international funding is likely to come on stream.

State-centric aid needs to value the importance of "local demand for reform" and creating improved channels of accountability of African states to their populations. One should not naïvely assume that African NGOs represent "the voices of the poor" or the full range of domestic constituencies for change. If they are able to engage with donors and government officials, it is likely that they themselves represent elite groups with their own economic and political interests. In Rwanda, for example, the Bar Association has been a staunch opponent of the Corps of Judicial Defenders—a body of paralegals created to provide advice to those accused of the genocide at a time when there was a shortage of trained lawyers. The corps, which could have provided the basis of a strategy for paralegal assistance, has now been dissolved. There are only about a hundred qualified lawyers, who rarely work outside of Kigali, leaving the 90 percent rural population with very limited access to legal aid.

Yet, such organizations can be highly valuable as a counterbalance to both donor agendas and entrenched state interests. In Nigeria, I came across a range of remarkable individuals who had survived the Abacha era and had set up human rights organizations. The transition from human rights defender to encouraging government reform under President Obasanjo was not easy, and some groups had little capacity beyond one strong charismatic leader. They were, however, still part of the (small) domestic reform constituency, with much better entry points and knowledge than external donor agencies. A few specific groups still come to mind: the Prisoners Rehabilitation and Welfare Action, with unparalleled access to places of detention and the controller general of prisons; the Centre for Law Enforcement Education in Nigeria, whose "Constable Joe" radio program promoted more accountable policing; or the Legal Resources Centre, with contacts ranging from the federal ministry down to legal clinics in rural areas. One of the most effective forms of assistance was that provided by the Ford Foundation, through substantial direct institutional grants rather than project support. This is a high-risk strategy given widespread financial misappropriation or simply poor accounting practices, but where it worked it delivered impressive results. The European Commission's approach of channeling its support through international NGOs seemed at times to be creating rivalries between international and local organizations and dependence on access through Brussels contacts.

Improving Donor Habits and Incentives

The fifth challenge is that, ultimately, few efforts are likely to succeed unless donors pay closer scrutiny to the way in which aid is delivered. In the words of Thomas Carothers, rule-of-law aid providers "tend to underestimate the challenges" and "seem determined to repeat mistakes made in other places."[30] I have repeatedly come across examples of bad practice in the field that easily could have been avoided. For example, it is well known that training cannot be the answer to poor performance without accompanying measures, such as ensuring that those trained will remain in their posts, that they are given incentives to use their new skills, and that other aspects of the organization—in particular, strategic vision, budgeting, and management—are also strengthened. In Nigeria, and a few years later in Ghana, I have come across reports of donors funding training for court stenographers, with the aim of speeding up court processes by relieving judges from having to take notes by hand. However, in both countries, this had been done before systems had been established to guarantee stenographers' positions and salaries. As a result, once trained, they moved on to better jobs, and little was achieved.

Why is this so often the case? A recent review of Swedish justice aid concluded that: "Many actors in the legal arena are unwilling to accept general development co-operation experiences."[31] Even if the tendency to copy laws or attempt the wholesale importation of legal systems from abroad is on the decline, many of the lessons and policy imperatives learned along the way are still undermined in the actual implementation. How best to provide technical expertise is a challenge faced across the sectors where the aid industry operates. Yet there seems to be an added constraint in justice programs, with the dominance of legal or other experts from North America or Western Europe who do not necessarily possess either a background in development or experience of Africa. Senior judges, ambitious young lawyers, or retired police officers are often placed in positions of designing or managing projects, providing advice to local counterparts, or delivering training. Most are well intentioned, but being a successful professional in the United Kingdom or the United States does not guarantee having project management or capacity-building skills.

As Stephen Golub correctly notes, the background of these technical experts affects how they design and implement programs:

> the main actors involved in designing and carrying out the aid are lawyers and judges. Unlike the development professionals who

dominate many other areas of development aid, many Western rule-of-law aid practitioners have little or no prior experience in developing and transitional societies before they enter the aid domain. They naturally see the problems and prospects for legal systems development in terms of their experience in their own countries, experience that typically features the courts and other forums through which they work with legal colleagues. The single greatest category of funding, then, focuses on assistance for judiciaries.[32]

Donor agencies need to train specialized justice sector experts in basic development skills, and, conversely, general development professionals need to be trained in justice sector reform so that they become less daunted by the challenge of working with often conservative, corrupt, discriminatory, and repressive institutions. Even better would be much greater reliance on African experts in design and implementation, who also need to be inducted into how to engage with complex donor procedures and their internal politics. Starting from locally developed initiatives, even when they do not fully conform to the latest policy statements, is also probably more likely to result in successful small step changes rather than failed wholesale reform attempts.

Incentive structures within donor agencies too can affect the quality and timeliness of aid. There is often pressure to spend money quickly—on large conferences or other events viewed as prestigious for senior colleagues at headquarters or on study tours to Western capitals for diplomatic or other political reasons, even when experience from other African countries might be more relevant. The perks associated with such tours (subsistence allowances, opportunity to shop overseas, and so on) often mean that the most senior persons—rather than the most appropriate ones—get to go, and they do not necessarily impart their newly acquired insights on their return. A clash of culture and objectives between development agencies and ministries of foreign affairs can also weaken the quality of aid. For example, in the United Kingdom, the Foreign and Commonwealth Office is often keen on sending senior police officers from recipient countries to training courses in elite British institutions as part of building contacts and gaining political clout. DFID, however, would much prefer investing in building domestic capacity to design and deliver institutionalized training programs in a country's police academy, a process that takes many more years and can of course fail.

Delays are caused for internal bureaucratic reasons, for example, when donor agency staff move on to new assignments at key stages in project development, or when country program management gets decentralized from headquarters to the partner country, putting new initiatives on hold. As a result, a justice program may lose internal agency champions, and local counterparts have to reestablish contacts. When I left Nigeria, after fifteen months of investing in building trust and partnerships, it took over a year for the program implementation structures to be put in place, given the necessity of new understandings of partners and opportunities for reform to be developed. It took two years for the Malawi program to be approved and start implementing. Such timelines appear standard. Donor policies now officially recognize that justice reform efforts require a very long time frame, as reflected in the duration of the new DFID programs. However, they are not always given the chance to succeed: Staffing rotations and new donor priorities mean that such programs will often change focus. In Nigeria, growth has been added to the DFID policy objectives of security and accessible justice, and DFID is moving out of some of its focal states. Although this is meant to be correcting shortcomings of the original design that was faithfully trying to follow existing policy prescriptions, it risks pulling the program in different directions by viewing both international investors and rural populations as stakeholders.

Donor coordination is one of the basic steps to improve aid effectiveness. However, the simple regular sharing of information regarding funded activities with government and other donors does not always happen. As a result of the 2003 Rome and 2005 Paris Declarations, aid alignment and harmonization are rising to the top of donors' agendas, and more efforts are under way to ensure that donors do share information and coordinate their efforts, at least among themselves—but this is hard work. During 2000 in Nigeria, a USAID design mission became a joint donor process, bringing together the major agencies (DFID, World Bank, EU, USAID, and UNDP), which required a personal investment of time and commitment to joint working from all involved, in particular from a team of relatively young staff across the main agencies. This aid coordination process, however, was hard to sustain over a long period of time, when staff moved on and the timetables and administrative procedures of different donor agencies clashed with each other.

Rivalries still arise between different models offered by donors based on their own domestic legal and judicial systems. In the Balkans, debates over conflicting donor models take on almost a geopolitical edge, with American lawyers unversed in civil law desperately trying to introduce common law principles, or different European police forces putting forward as the best model their own approaches to community policing. The result can be inconsistent legal frameworks and institutional cultures, which domestic actors need to learn to navigate. The widely accepted principle that aid providers do best when they offer access to a range of options and assist partners in choosing what would work best for them, rather than imposing their systems, is still often not being put into practice.

In Africa, relationships between former colonial masters and their ex-colonies can lead to embarrassing situations vested with political meaning. In Somaliland, for example, pictures of the last British chief justice still adorn the offices of senior members of the judiciary, and the head of the police praises the days of British rule under which he had served. It is not a fondness for the British Empire per se that prompts such comments; rather, the longing for international recognition of Somaliland with the borders it had as a British protectorate. Rwanda for its part is moving toward a hybrid system, introducing common law features into a system based on German and Belgian antecedents. Although international experts at the various conferences organized by the Law Reform Commission could highlight the advantages and drawbacks of various systems, the political backdrop of this transformation cannot be hidden, in particular the various drivers for greater integration with (Anglophone) East African states of a predominantly Francophone country. Domestic and international opposition to reforms—for example, the Ministry of Justice losing some of its powers to a strengthened judiciary or the replacement of a panel of three judges by a single judge in the lowest courts—needs to be understood as both technical and political.

In general, aid agency staff need to become much more aware of the impact of colonial histories. Colonial links can be valuable if they create trust and genuinely enable better technical advice; they can also blind aid providers to the social and political realities of current-day Africa and to the possible resentment of seeing Belgian, British, French, or Italian experts once again in positions of authority.

Time to Learn, Time to Act

In the face of the challenges identified above, there is a danger that agencies will simply give up, either sticking with institution-based projects using international contractors or shifting into budget-support mode and bypassing the need to engage with the justice sector, including through politically sensitive political or human rights dialogue. New fads will probably soon be developed, as individual Western policy makers try to make their own mark and reinvent the wheel. However, the main thrusts of the current justice aid agenda—putting social outcomes and not just institutions at the center of the analysis—do not seem misguided. The multiplicity of goals needs to be recognized: from growth and democracy, to poverty reduction and human rights. The growing emphasis toward international security and state fragility as a result of the post–9/11 policy shift in aid agencies needs to be carefully watched.[33] Yet, this reflects the various roles that justice institutions play in developed and developing countries alike.

Thomas Carothers in chapter 2 of this volume has noted "the problem of knowledge" surrounding rule-of-law interventions. My personal experience confirms the repeated lack of interest in serious research, monitoring, and evaluation on the part of donors, implementers, and recipients alike. In particular, in postconflict situations, attention is placed on "getting things done," with little reflection on whether these are suitable objectives or whether impacts are sustainable. Similar lessons get learned across programs, but not much changes from country to country.

What seems needed is a serious look at what basic principles of good aid are not being put into practice, why that is the case, and how the situation can be improved. Structural constraints lie in the nature of the aid industry itself. This is why practitioners cannot simply be security or legal experts; they need to learn to be aid experts as well and to understand how to make aid more effective, so that it benefits populations but does not undermine state capacity. Constraints also reside in the nature of African states and societies, the consequences of colonialism, authoritarian rule, strong executives, legal pluralism, and cultural diversity. This is the reason that Africans are best placed to lead those reform processes, drawing on foreign expertise when needed.

Public accountability—to African citizens at the receiving end of those programs as well as to citizens of donor countries who pay for those reforms through their taxes—requires that shared objectives and minimum standards be set, options debated, and progress measured. There needs to be common agreement that justice sector aid is a long-term developmental endeavor that contributes to the realization of human rights and poverty reduction. Aid to the justice sector represents only about 1 percent of total aid to Africa. Planned aid increases will probably focus on infrastructure, human development, or strengthening executive capacity. Both Sachs and the Africa Commission only see the tip of the iceberg when they briefly reflect on the role of the judiciary as part of a good governance agenda.

Notes

1. Development assistance committee country commitments for legal and judicial development in Sub-Saharan Africa. OECD (2005). International Development Statistics. Online edition, Organisation for Economic Cooperation and Development, Paris.
2. World Bank, *World Development Report 1997: The State in a Changing World* (New York: Oxford University Press, 1997), 27 and 99–102.
3. World Bank, *Can Africa Claim the 21ˢᵗ Century?* (Washington, D.C.: World Bank, 2000), 71.
4. Laure-Hélène Piron and Julius Court, *Independent Evaluation of the Swiss Agency for Development and Cooperation Human Rights and Rule of Law Documents* (London/Bern: Overseas Development Institute and Swiss Agency for Development and Cooperation, November 2003).
5. Stephen Golub, "Battling Apartheid, Building a New South Africa," in *Many Roads to Justice: The Law-Related Work of Ford Foundation Grantees around the World*, ed. Mary McClymont and Stephen Golub (New York: Ford Foundation, 2000).
6. U.S. Office of Democracy and Governance, *Achievements in Building and Maintaining the Rule of Law*, Occasional Papers Series (Washington, D.C.: USAID, November 2002), 136–8.
7. United Nations, *United Nations Millennium Declaration*, resolution adopted by the General Assembly, A/Res/55/2, 2000; and United Nations, *Road Map Towards the Implementation of the United Nations Millennium Declaration*, Report of the Secretary-General, A/56/326, Annex: Millennium Development Goals (New York: United Nations, September 6, 2001).
8. United Nations, *Report of the International Conference on Financing for Development* (Monterrey, Mexico: United Nations, 2002); and Organization for Economic Cooperation and Development (OECD) High Level Forum, *Paris Declaration on Aid Effectiveness: Ownership, Harmonisation, Alignment, Results and Mutual Accountability* (Paris: OECD, 2005).
9. Deepa Narayan et al., *Voices of the Poor: Can Anyone Hear Us?* (New York: Oxford University Press, 2000).
10. Harry Blair and Gary Hansen, *Weighing in on the Scales of Justice: Strategic Approaches for Donor-Supported Rule of Law Programs*, USAID Program and Operations Assessment Report no. 7 (Washington, D.C.: USAID, 1994).
11. K. Biddle, I. Clegg, and J. Whetton, *Evaluation of ODA/DFID Support to the Police in Developing Countries: Synthesis Study* (Swansea, UK: School of Social Sciences and International Development, University of Wales, 1998).
12. International Council on Human Rights Policy, *Local Perspectives: Foreign Aid to the Justice Sector* (Geneva: International Council on Human Rights Policy, 2000).
13. Department for International Development (DFID), *Justice and Poverty Reduction: Safety, Security and Access to Justice for All* (London: DFID, 2000).
14. United Nations Development Program (UNDP), *Access to Justice for All and Justice Sector Reform*, BDP Policy (New York: UNDP, March 2002).
15. United Nations, *The Rule of Law and Transitional Justice in Conflict and Post-Conflict Societies*, Report of the UN Secretary-General, S/2004/616 (New York: United Nations, 2004).
16. World Bank Legal Vice Presidency, *Legal and Judicial Reform: Strategic Directions* (Washington, D.C.: World Bank, 2003), 45–6.

17. UN Millennium Project, *Investing in Development: A Practical Plan to Achieve the Millennium Development Goals* (New York: UN Millennium Project, 2005); UK Commission for Africa, *Our Common Interest: Report of the Commission for Africa* (London: UK Commission for Africa, March 2005).
18. DFID, *Nigeria Access to Justice Program Memorandum* (Institutional Annex) (London: DFID, May 2001).
19. Laure-Hélène Piron with Andy Norton, "Politics and the PRSP Approach: Uganda Case Study," ODI Working Paper no. 240 (London: Overseas Development Institute, March 2004), 31–3.
20. Government of Uganda, *Budget Framework Paper 2005/6 to 2007/8* (Kampala: Government of Uganda, 2005).
21. Penal Reform International (PRI), "The Chain Linked: A Model for Inter-Agency Co-Operation: New Models of Accessible Justice and Penal Reform in Developing Countries" (Paris: PRI, 2000).
22. Human Rights Watch, "Nigeria's 2003 Elections: The Unacknowledged Violence" (New York: Human Rights Watch, June 2004).
23. Thomas Carothers, *Aiding Democracy Abroad: The Learning Curve* (Washington, D.C.: Carnegie Endowment for International Peace, 1999), 162–3.
24. DFID, "Guidance Note on Non-State Justice and Security Systems" (London: DFID, 2004).
25. UNDP, "Somalia 2001 Socio-Economic Survey Data" (New York: UNDP, 2003).
26. Wilfred Schärf, "Non-state Justice Systems in Southern Africa: How Should Government Respond," paper prepared for the UK Department for International Development, London, 2003.
27. For more details on DFID initiatives with traditional justice institutions, see Laure-Hélène Piron and Francis Watkins, "DFID Human Rights Review" (London: Overseas Development Institute, 2004).
28. U.S. Bureau of Democracy, Human Rights, and Labor, *Country Reports on Human Rights Practices: Rwanda* (Washington, D.C.: U.S. State Department, February 28, 2005), available at http://www.state.gov/g/drl/rls/hrrpt/2004/41621.htm.
29. Reports are available on PRI's web site: http://www.penalreform.org/francais/frset_pre_fr.htm.
30. Carothers, *Aiding Democracy Abroad*, 176.
31. Swedish International Development Cooperation Agency (SIDA), *Swedish Development Co-operation in the Legal Sector* (Stockholm: SIDA, 2002), 12.
32. See chapter 5.
33. For example, see DFID, "Fighting Poverty to Build a Safer World: A Strategy for Security and Development" (London: DFID, 2005). This report does not do much more than reiterate DFID's commitment to justice and security, albeit better recognizing the links between military and civilian security as well as human rights and re-emphasizing the need to use aid to promote the security of the poor, not of states.

CHAPTER TWELVE

Measuring the Impact of Criminal Justice Reform in Latin America

LISA BHANSALI
CHRISTINA BIEBESHEIMER

THE NEED TO BE ABLE to measure the changes generated by rule-of-law reform programs in developing countries is becoming increasingly acute. After nearly two decades of work in this area, it is no longer possible to claim that reform experiences are too recent to stand up to critical analysis. There is a growing emphasis in the development field on justifying projects based on measurable outcomes, thus necessitating better evaluation of reform interventions and the creation of specific indicators to measure results. Serious assessments of the impact of rule-of-law reform efforts would also be useful to help rule-of-law assistance practitioners understand how and why positive change does occur in the justice sectors of the countries where they work, and how they can improve their assistance efforts.

Moreover, some analysts have questioned the assumption of a causal relationship among the rule of law, democracy, and economic and social development that has undergirded much rule-of-law aid work.[1] Others have asked hard questions about whether institutional or operational reforms yield behavioral changes that can actually strengthen the rule of law in developing countries and better the lot of ordinary citizens.[2]

The authors thank Natalia Nolan for valuable research assistance and Linn Hammergren for trenchant, useful comments on a draft. The views expressed in this chapter are those of the authors and do not represent the official views of the World Bank.

If the results of rule-of-law reform projects are not being observed and measured to the extent that practitioners would like, this is at least partially because the task is so difficult. Drawing the link between rule-of-law reform interventions and social, economic, and political indicators is empirically challenging. Legal systems, even if they function perfectly, may have an indirect impact on economies and thus on poverty reduction, which has become the central focus of the development community. Better functioning justice systems would seem to be a positive factor for democratization but proving that fact in specific circumstances is a challenge. The impact of rule-of-law programs on crime and violence rates is also surprisingly difficult to ascertain. Causal links between specific interventions and broader societal outcomes is difficult to establish due to the myriad factors that can influence the larger social, economic, and political conditions in a society: For example, the unemployment rate plays an important role in influencing levels of criminal activity, and public attention and political will (which are difficult to control for) are important in reducing the incidence of human rights abuses. Furthermore, there are problems of data availability and reliability. The general dearth of justice sector statistics in developing countries, as well as the lack of comparative studies between pre- and postreform statistics or between jurisdictions, makes it difficult to conduct thorough analyses of results.

In this chapter we take on the challenge of attempting to assess the impact of rule-of-law work in the context of an historic wave of reforms that have been under way for two decades and about which recent studies have begun to provide some empirical data—that is, the broad push for criminal justice reform that has swept through most parts of Latin America. In our view, by focusing somewhat narrowly on the question of how rule-of-law programs affect key indicators of a central element of the rule of law—due process—it is possible to provide at least a preliminary answer to the question of impact. This approach may provide a base for broader analyses of the effects on underlying social, economic, and political conditions, and it raises interesting questions about the relationship between the rule-of-law reform movement and the still problematic state of the rule of law in the region.

Dual Impetus for Reform

Understanding the origins of criminal justice reform in Latin America can shed light on which indicators best measure the reforms' intended results. The wave of rule-of-law reform in Latin America arose and has developed as an integral part of the dual economic and political transitions that the region experienced in the 1980s and 1990s.

Economic Impetus

In the wake of the debt crisis and the collapse of the import substitution development model in the early 1980s in Latin America, most countries in the region adopted market-oriented reforms conforming to the "Washington consensus." These reforms entailed implementing policies aimed at opening markets, deregulating and re-regulating industries, privatizing state-owned companies, and increasing foreign investment. Donors saw improving the performance of legal systems as a key element of attracting greater foreign direct investment, and therefore rule-of-law reforms took on great importance in the minds of politicians and policy makers in the context of development. In addition, the wastefulness and inefficiency of the region's judicial systems, combined with obstacles to accessing justice for the most disadvantaged, started to be seen as contributing factors to the high levels of inequality plaguing the region.[3] Recent research has validated this assumption, showing that costs associated with weak contract enforcement, high levels of crime, and corruption can amount to 25 percent of sales, and that increased security and legal predictability can encourage investment required for economic development.[4] Thus, starting in the 1980s and continuing ever since, justice reform projects are seen as a way to promote social and economic development, growth, and poverty reduction.

Political Impetus

At the same time that most Latin American countries were launching broad-gauged economic reform initiatives designed to move toward market economics, they were also engaged in political transitions from authoritarianism to democracy. Rule-of-law reforms, especially in the criminal law domain, also gained impulse and backing as part of these political developments. Democratic activists and new democratic governments hoped that by bolstering both the independence and efficacy of their countries' justice systems they would help fortify democratic norms, increase public accountability, reduce corruption, and ensure that extra-constitutional actors or tendencies would be curbed. In many countries, jurists and legal scholars have promoted and led criminal process

reforms to strengthen institutional structures in the fight against abuse
and impunity.

Local human rights and academic communities rallied around legal
reforms as a means of linking the transition to democracy with an effort
to improve the human rights records of countries in the region. Furthermore, the reforms took place in a context of an existing and well-
regarded regional human rights system including the Inter-American
Commission and Court of Human Rights. Most countries in the region
are signatories of all the major human rights treaties; as a result, governments in the region are held increasingly accountable both nationally
and regionally and often seek to improve human rights protection for
their citizens. In countries such as El Salvador and Guatemala, which
spent many years waging civil war, the postconflict peace process assisted by the United Nations also produced agreements to make improvements in their justice systems to protect human rights.

Chile presents one example of the close ties between democratic transitions and rule-of-law reforms. There, the legal reform movement arose
as a response to the need to establish controls over the use of power and
to prevent corruption as the country moved away from authoritarian
rule. In 1989, President Patricio Aylwin's administration ushered in the
return to democracy after nearly two decades of military dictatorship.
For this new governing left-of-center coalition in Chile, criminal procedural reform was crucial to dismantling the institutional remnants of
authoritarianism and to balancing power.[5] The strong political right wing
also had vested interests in promoting reform. The reforms gained momentum following a much-publicized scandal where a supreme court
judge was accused of manipulating criminal procedures to allow a well-
known Colombian criminal to flee the country.[6] Another factor was the
highly publicized kidnapping of the son of a wealthy and influential
businessman who became active in pressing for reforms and a stronger,
more professional state capacity to investigate and prosecute crime.

Concerned with the rising levels of crime and violence that have unfortunately accompanied the dual economic and political transitions in
many countries, ordinary citizens throughout Latin America have also
supported criminal justice reforms. Moreover, citizen discontent over
soaring crime rates—Latin America and the Caribbean is one of the most
violent regions in the world—has pushed governments to act.[7] Most of
the citizens involved with the criminal justice system, whether as victims or defendants, are poor (partly because the rich often escape prosecution, partly because crime is more pervasive in poorer sections of

Figure 12.1. Comparison of Homicide Rates in Latin America and Other Regions, 1970–1999 (number of homicides per 1000,000)

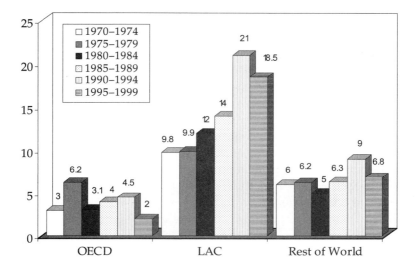

Source: United Nations, *Surveys of Crime Trends and Operations of Criminal Justice (1970–1994)* (New York: United Nations, 1999).

society, and partly because most citizens are poor in Latin America).[8] Nonetheless, during the decade when most reforms began, rich and poor alike were insistent that their government do something about crime and violence. (Figure 12.1 shows Latin America's high homicide rate relative to other regions.) In some cases a partial backlash has occurred against new criminal procedure codes that citizens feel are too liberal regarding the rights of the accused, but in general concern over crime has served as a further element of the impetus for broad justice sector reforms.

Role of External Donors

The modern wave of criminal justice reform in Latin America began in El Salvador in 1981 after the murder of several American Jesuit nuns at the hands of Salvadoran death squads. The crimes resulted in significant international pressure on the Salvadoran government to solve the crimes; the Salvadoran justice system, however, was unable to investigate and prosecute the perpetrators. When the spotlight of international attention was directed at the Salvadoran justice system, it revealed institutions that were unable to carry out professional crime investigations and trials. The U.S. Agency for International Development (USAID) was a primary mover behind the Salvadoran criminal procedure reforms, so it was not surprising that instruments such as oral trials and prosecutor-led investigations—instruments characteristic of the U.S. common law, accusatory system—were proposed as methods to improve criminal prosecution and promote stable democratic regimes. It is surprising that such profound procedural and structural changes were embraced by jurists, legislators, and citizens of El Salvador, and that those changes have spread like wildfire to the rest of the region. Although the original impetus for change may have come from external models and actors, criminal procedure reform has transformed from an exogenous into a locally supported movement. Criminal procedural reform is now under way in various phases in most of Central America, all of the Andean region, and nearly all of South America. Of the twenty civil law countries in the region, more than half are currently overhauling their criminal processes.

The history of donor involvement in criminal justice reform has been more directly linked to democratic institution building than economic enhancement. The largest financier of criminal justice reform initiatives in Latin America over the last decade and a half has been USAID. By the end of 1999, USAID had spent $300 million on justice and police reform projects.[9] According to its own evaluation, USAID considers its investment to be a success story, albeit largely in terms of legislative reforms to promote procedural change within the justice sector. Among the factors cited as contributing to the success of the reforms in law is the fact that the enactment of criminal procedure codes strengthens due process by providing, for the first time, "a right to an oral trial, procedural due process guarantees, a right to confront witnesses, a right to counsel, and other fundamental rights." To date, reformed criminal procedure codes have been adopted in Argentina (in the provinces of Buenos Aires and Cordoba), Bolivia, Chile, Colombia, Costa Rica, Dominican Republic, Ecuador, El Salvador, Guatemala, Honduras, Nicaragua, Paraguay, Peru, and Venezuela.[10]

Since 1991, the Inter-American Development Bank (IDB) has financed judicial reform projects with a strong emphasis on consolidating democratic institutions in Latin America by protecting basic human rights and seeking to promote social development, including a focus on criminal and juvenile justice. Thus far, the IDB has approved approximately $274 million for the implementation of criminal justice reforms in the region.[11]

To date, the World Bank has played only a minor role in financing criminal justice reforms in Latin America. Its justice reform projects have focused on the enhancement of a country's economic performance, and it has directed financing to improvements in court efficiency and productivity through modernization, including automation. Excluding its analytical work, the World Bank has approved approximately $156 million in loans and grants to the region since 1992, including some financing of legal aid and public defender services in countries with ongoing criminal justice reforms (for example, Ecuador, El Salvador, and Guatemala).

The United Nations and a number of other bilateral aid agencies have supported law reform in the context of the transition to peace in post-conflict countries such as Guatemala and El Salvador. Bilateral donors—particularly Spain—have provided aid to modernize police forces. A number of European donors have focused on strengthening human rights protections in the region through working with newly created human rights ombudsman's offices.

Content of the Reforms

Latin America's criminal justice reforms aim for monumental changes. Most countries of the region went through most of the twentieth century with civil and criminal procedure codes modeled after those of early continental European codes—for example, those of Spain, France, and Germany. These early European models were based on entirely written procedures in which the judge oversaw not only the decision-making and sentencing phases but was also responsible for the investigative phase of the criminal process. Over the last fifty years, most of continental Europe has made modifications in this "inquisitorial" process, adding some provisions for an oral trial (in some cases before juries), as well as an expanded role for the prosecutor in the investigative phase of the criminal process. As European countries reformed toward more modern criminal justice systems blending oral and written processes, their former Latin American colonies were slower to follow reform efforts. As European countries began to adopt "hybrid" systems incorporating accusatorial processes from common law England, Latin American codes remained more closely linked to the previous inquisitorial tradition (with the exception of Argentina's Cordoba province in the 1940s).[12] At the heart of the matter was a perceived conflict between defendants' rights and the social hierarchy typical of postimperialism in Latin America:

There was concern that new hybrid codes becoming law in Europe might, if transferred to Latin America, diminish power of the elite in providing "too many guarantees to protect the rights of suspects."[13]

The most recent wave of reforms in Latin America seeks to leap over half a century of incremental progress implemented in European civil law countries. These reforms seek to create a more transparent and fairer criminal justice system through creating an entirely oral trial system in which defendants are guaranteed their due process rights and receive faster justice through more efficient processing of cases. Replacing a wholly written with a wholly oral trial means that police, prosecutors, public defenders, judges, forensic and other expert witnesses, and even victims of crime who testify at trial must have new skills and adopt new roles. This changes the underlying incentives and premises of the criminal system: The prosecutor, in conjunction with the police, must present proof at trial in order to find a defendant guilty, and the nature of oral trials allows for "accusatorial" or adversarial proceedings wherein defendants have the right to contest the evidence against them and cross-examine witnesses. Trials are now public and, as before, defendants can appeal decisions against them.[14] Some countries are making use of juries for the first time, which involves persuading citizens to take on a new type of civic duty.

Changes in the new procedural codes require that countries create entirely new public institutions. Because the key responsibility for managing the investigation of a crime has moved from judges to prosecutors, with whom investigative police forces must now coordinate, many countries have created independent offices of the public prosecutor (*Ministerio Público* or *Fiscalía*). Although less frequently, public defenders, too, are being moved out of departments of the executive or judicial branches into newly created, independent defender's offices directly financed by the legislative branch as public entities.

The flexibility that all of this requires of public and private actors is mind-boggling: Imagine the reaction of the U.S. legal system (based on the Anglo-Saxon tradition of common law) if the government were to propose a change in federal law that would essentially require attorneys and judges to go back to school to learn how to practice in a civil law system!

Measuring Results

Given that criminal justice reform has several long-term objectives, such as contributing to economic development and democratization, an effort to assess these reforms might look for a causal link between the reforms and these broad objectives. Given the complex challenges involved in working out the issue of causality described above, we believe a useful place to start is a more limited first step: To what extent can we measure whether reform initiatives are successful in meeting their stated objective of strengthening the rule of law in the countries in which reforms have been implemented? We focus on this question in large part because it is possible to answer it, given data that are starting to emerge from the region. But we also concentrate on this question because we believe it is a crucial issue, one that may provide knowledge that will help improve the design and implementation of rule-of-law projects and constitute a base for future, broader inquiries into the impact of rule-of-law reforms.

Thus, in choosing to focus on whether these reform projects have had an impact on the rule of law, we do not examine the effect of criminal justice reform on broader socioeconomic or political conditions. We are not looking to measure the impact of criminal justice reforms on indicators such as the amounts of foreign direct investment, incidence of corruption, or rates of economic growth. Nor are we examining the impact on rates of crime and violence. The statistics for crime and violence rates exist before and after criminal procedure reforms, and one of the goals of reformers was to have a positive impact on the region's extremely high crime rates. It might seem natural, therefore, to look to measure the impact of these reforms according to changes in crime and violence rates. But in the countries examined in this chapter, crime and violence rates have not decreased noticeably after reforms were implemented. Crime rates, however, are notoriously volatile according to factors that have little to do with the criminal justice system (the unemployment rate, for example), and so tracing the impact of criminal process reforms on these rates is very difficult. In fact, improvements in the criminal justice system can actually result in higher crime rates: Because crime and violence rates are calculated according to the number of complaints filed in the system, an "efficient" criminal system in which complaints can be more easily filed, and in which the public has enough confidence to bother to register a complaint, can lead to a higher reported crime rate. Recorded increases in crime and violence rates may thus reflect not higher levels of crime, but rather an improved procedural system and the public's response to this improvement. Conversely, when high costs, long delays, and low public confidence in criminal systems discourage citizens from filing complaints, reported crime rates decrease.[15]

Instead, we will examine whether the enormous efforts undertaken toward criminal justice reform in Latin America have brought about significant changes in the administration of justice that the architects of the reform movement believed to be important building blocks to the consolidation of the rule of law. We will focus on the impact of the reforms on due process; in particular, the changes that the reforms have brought about in the speed of trials, the number of accused who are held without trial, the use of sentences alternative to imprisonment, and the provision of public defenders for indigent defendants. Respect for due process is a key component of the rule of law, and the indicators we have chosen span the early and perhaps most critical trial stages—from arrest through investigation to trial where "the criminal process has its widest impact and where the greatest numbers of persons are involved."[16] We have chosen these indicators in part because the impetus for change behind the reforms in Latin America was not economics so much as a concern for human rights, crime and violence, and democratization, such that these indicators are measures loyal to the reforms' original objective. We have also chosen these indicators because, as the discussion below indicates, they are indicators for which there are data available both pre- and postreform, such that change over time can be measured.

Availability and Limitations of Data

Even though we are not attempting to analyze the impact of reform on the broader economic and political objectives or crime and violence rates, we are nonetheless confronted with a series of difficulties in measuring the impact of criminal justice reform on due process, which arguably represents the heart of a country's rule of law.

The major difficulty is the lack of reliable prereform data with which to compare postreform statistics. Statistics by governments, whether pre- or postreform, are scarce and, where they exist, partial. Country data should be improving through the process of reform, given that donor-funded projects nearly all require some baseline data and a means for collecting data on indicators by which to measure project progress and impact. To the extent that data are being collected in the criminal justice sector throughout the region, however, it does not seem to be reflected in public government information sources.

One leap forward in availability of data in the region has been made through the creation in 1999 of the Justice Studies Center of the Americas (usually referred to by its Spanish acronym, CEJA) as a regional organization under the auspices of the Organization of American States. CEJA's membership includes all the countries of the region (all countries with membership in the Organization of American States are also CEJA members), and all of the major donors to the region supported its creation. USAID, the Canadian International Development Agency (CIDA), the IDB, and organizations such as the Ford Foundation, among others, have all provided funding for the center. CEJA was created to be a research and policy advisory institution to assist Latin American and Caribbean countries to analyze, understand, and improve the process of justice reform in the region. Specifically, CEJA's work to improve data-gathering and understanding of justice institutions in Latin America and the Caribbean represents notable progress in measuring the impact of reforms in the region. Because prereform statistics are scarce, however, the data CEJA is making available can only be measured against a limited number of prereform indicators.

The dearth of initial baseline data has several sources. CEJA's studies point out that the most acute source of problems in implementing criminal justice reforms lies in poor administration of the reform process; that is, poor change management. This is not particularly surprising. It is no small task for a group of judges and lawyers to oversee the kind of profound institutional change attempted in the criminal justice reforms being carried out in the region. Many courts, as well as new prosecutorial and defense organizations, are not run by personnel with specialized expertise in public sector management. Better data collection is likely to come about with better management because managers sensitive to the value of data in measuring an institution's responsiveness to users tend to press for the provision of solid, reliable data in an institution. It also appears that donors have not been as helpful as they might in assisting countries to improve data collection in the justice sector. Although donor-funded projects require baseline data and statistics on progress and impact indicators, this kind of information has not become easily and publicly available in most countries of the region.

CEJA's Follow-up Project on Judicial Reform Process in Latin America is currently the most reliable source of data on justice institution performance in the region. This project is carrying out its work in three phases, each involving a different group of countries. The first phase, which is completed, includes Argentina (Cordoba), Chile, Costa Rica, and Paraguay; the second phase, also completed, includes Ecuador, El Salvador, Guatemala, and Venezuela; the third phase, now under way, includes Argentina (Buenos Aires), Bolivia, and Honduras.[17] These reports include statistics on the indicators we track in this chapter: number of prosecutors and public defenders, budget allocations, usage of alternative sentences, and percentages of prisoners awaiting trial. CEJA also collects statistics on the ratio of complaints per prosecutor, the number of courts in a country, number of judges and their ratio per population, number of trials per judge, amount of evidence presented at trial (as a way to examine the diligence with which public defenders and prosecutors are performing the new tasks assigned them), and duration of cases.[18] CEJA's statistics are, in significant part, based on data provided by state entities (courts, prosecutors' offices, and the like) in the countries studied, which may present some concern about quality of the data (despite the fact that all data are reviewed in international workshops attended by governmental and nongovernmental experts). CEJA researchers also generate some of their own statistics based on direct observation of court processes made over certain time periods in the countries under study.[19] CEJA collects these statistics to make cross-national comparison possible, in an effort to evaluate progress in criminal justice reform.

In addition to country statistics and CEJA data, USAID produces reports that include country-by-country reviews and evaluations of USAID's projects, which sometimes provide statistical data on performance of justice institutions. The United Nations Latin American Institute for the Prevention of Crime and the Treatment of Offenders (ILANUD), which was instrumental in code reforms, also provides statistics on the human rights indicators of justice reform, such as percentages of prisoners detained without trial. (ILANUD's main objective is to work with Latin American governments on economic and social development, supporting policy making in the areas of crime prevention and criminal justice.) Although some national research institutions are also beginning to make progress in collecting data, these do not, for the most part, generate their own data but function more as data clearinghouses.

As the discussion that follows indicates, the statistics available do permit measurement of changes in operations of justice systems, in inputs into criminal justice systems in the form of public funds and personnel, and even some impact assessment. Measurement, however, is still partial and basic, and much progress remains to be made in measuring the progress and impact of criminal justice reform.

Preliminary Results and Trends

The due process indicators that we have chosen to measure the impact of reforms in criminal justice include preventive detention, speed of trials, structural changes, and availability and use of alternative sentencing. Measurable changes are observable for each of these indicators.

Preventive Detention

One shocking characteristic of the criminal justice system in many Latin American countries is the overwhelming number of accused persons held in detention without trial. In many countries in the region, a majority of those detained have not yet been tried. The issue is both social and systemic: Those accused of serious crimes and those who the authorities fear may not appear for trial are held in detention for months, even years at a time, due to pretrial delays inherent in the judicial procedures. Because of long delays associated with the written and transitioning systems, many defendants await the equivalent time in "preventive detention" as they would otherwise have had to serve if found guilty. The concept of "innocent until proven guilty" is simply not being implemented according to the reformed codes' objectives, which is unacceptable from the point of view of due process rights.[20] Why are so many of those in prison in Latin America awaiting trial rather than serving their sentences? Due to public outcry over rising levels of crime and perceptions of insecurity, judges have tended to rely overly on the use of pretrial incarceration (or preventive detention), and it has become the norm rather than the exception in a number of Latin American countries. Furthermore, according to some observers, Latin America's legislative history and its application by judges reflects a repressive belief favoring prison (or protecting "the social good") at the expense of individual due process guarantees.[21]

Have criminal justice system reforms had an impact on the number of people imprisoned before trial? They have explicitly sought to do so. For example, new criminal procedures have established roles for oversight judges, or *jueces de garantías* (those who set bail and decide on pretrial detention). The new laws dealing with the role of these judges, however, have often been unclear, and courts do not appear to be clarifying them much. Judges appear to be playing a minimalist intervention in the process rather than the substantial role envisioned in the reforms.[22]

The data available on pretrial detention in Latin America show that the impact of criminal procedure reforms on preventive detention varies considerably by country. According to CEJA figures, improvement has been noted in Guatemala, where pre- and postreform pretrial detention statistics dropped from 54 percent to 47 percent between 1981 and 2002.[23] As shown in figure 12.2, Chile, which has arguably begun the

Figure 12.2. Preventive Detention Statistics over Time

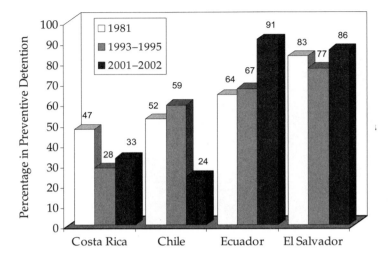

Sources: E. Carranza, *Estado Actual de la Prision Preventiva en America Latina y Comparacion con los Paises de Europa* (San Jose, Costa Rica: ILANUD/Comision Europea, 1996); C. Riego, "Third Comparative Follow-Up Project on Judicial Reform Processes in Latin America" (Santiago, Chile: CEJA, 2004).

Notes: Both sources report share of those in preventive detention per 100,000. Chile and El Salvador 1993-1995 data from 1993; Costa Rica and Ecuador 1993-1995 data from 1995; Chile and Costa Rica 2001-2002 data from 2001; Ecuador and El Salvador 2001-2002 data from 2002.

implementation of criminal reforms quite successfully, boasts some of the lowest preventive detention figures in the region, having decreased the percentage of detainees awaiting trial from more than 50 percent to 24 percent.[24] In the Dominican Republic, where an ambitious USAID-funded reform initiative has taken place, the number of prisoners in preventive detention was reduced from 87 percent of prisoners in 1996 to 73 percent in 1999 (figure 12.3).[25]

Figures 12.2 and 12.3 compare ILANUD data on percentages of prisoners awaiting trial with more recent CEJA data. Of the six countries for which data are available, four countries show an overall downward trend, but in two countries, Ecuador and El Salvador, the percentage of prisoners detained without trial appears to be increasing.

It is possible that the initial rise in percentages of preventative detention shown in figure 12.3 is a result of better data collection since implemention of reform processes. Tracking these percentages over more time will indicate whether the relatively modest decreases will continue and deepen. Preventative detention is an indicator that speaks to the impact

Figure 12.3. Preliminary Postreform Impacts in Two Reforming Countries

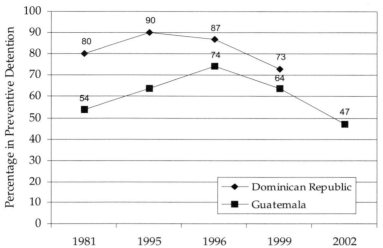

Sources: Dominican Republic data for 1981 and 1995 taken from E. Carranza, *Estado Actual de le Prison Preventiva en America Latina y Comparacion con los Paises de Europa* (San Jose, Costa Rica: ILANUD/Comision Europa, 1996). Dominican Republic data for 1996 and 1999 taken from Management Systems International, *Achievements in Building and Maintaining the Rule of Law* (Washington, D.C.: USAID, November 2002). Guatemala data for all years taken from "Guatemala Follow-Up Report: 2002-2003" (Santiago, Chile: CEJA, 2003) citing information compiled by NGO Justicia Penal y Sociedad in Guatemala City.

of reform, and it comes about as a result of a number of other interim but significant changes such as speed of trial, availability of public defenders, and use of alternative sentencing, all of which are examined below. Impact indicators such as this one thus change more slowly than progress or output indicators.

Although the reform effort does seem to be having the effect of reducing the percentage of prisoners awaiting trial in a number of countries, figure 12.4 shows that the statistics are still alarming, and more progress is required in many countries of the region.

These data taken together also raise the very practical question as to why rates vary as much as they do before and after reforms, and why they have fallen after reform in some cases but not in others.

Speed of Trials

Although it may take more time before reforms significantly impact levels of preventive detention, the conversion to oral trials has substantially decreased delays in justice. Everywhere that prereform data are

Figure 12.4. Share of Accused in Preventive Detention in Latin America (average for 2001–2003)

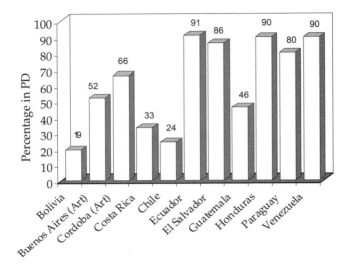

Source: C. Riego, "Third Comparative Follow-Up Project on Judicial Reform Processes in Latin America" (Santiago, Chile: CEJA, 2004).

available to compare with postreform results, the time from arrest through trial has dropped. In Bolivia, for example, the average time to complete a criminal case dropped from four years to five months after reforms.[26] In El Salvador, the average length of time before resolution has been halved; prior to reforms the average duration was two years, but more than 54 percent of cases are now resolved within one year.[27] Reform efforts in Chile have yielded similar results, reducing the average time between an arrest and sentencing to less than 200 days from nearly 600 days under the previous system.[28] Here, too, prereform data are scarce, but CEJA's recent studies establish statistics for 2004 that will provide a baseline against which to measure changes going forward (see figure 12.5).

Structural Changes

As noted earlier, criminal justice reforms entail significant institutional and structural changes, including new legislative frameworks and drastic organizational and behavioral change; new positions are created, new responsibilities are assigned, and the relationships between actors in-

Figure 12.5. Delays in Justice in Select Latin American Countries

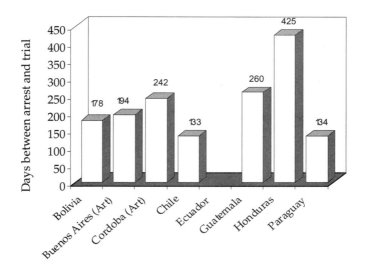

Source: C. Riego, "Third Comparative Follow-Up Project on Judicial Reform Processes in Latin America" (Santiago, Chile: CEJA, 2004).

volved shift dramatically. The change to oral trials is accompanied by the newly acquired right of defendants to more directly challenge their accusers, necessitating a marked increase in the number of public prosecutors and defense attorneys. Countries throughout the region have created new independent agencies of prosecutors and public defenders and have allocated important levels of resources into recruiting and training new staff for them. These are impressive changes considering the short amount of time since the reforms began and the level of training required for this new personnel to carry out their duties.

Bolivia, for example, had only 90 prosecutors in the entire country in 1991. Today, their role is explicitly defined in the legal framework, and their number has risen to 300. The Public Ministry (a new institution of prosecutors created under the reforms) provides training for newly hired prosecutors to oversee criminal investigations and prosecute cases. Likewise, the number of public defenders in the country has increased from only 11 in 1991 to 200 in 2002.[29] In Colombia, the number of public defenders has risen from 150 to 1,125 from the mid-1990s to 2002.[30] Reforms have also had impressive institutional results in Guatemala, which in 1986 had only 30 prosecutors, but by 2002 had 175 prosecutors and 110 public defenders actively working in the new system.

Table 12.1. Incremental Changes in Public Ministry Budgets

Country	Year	Public Ministry Budget ($US million)	Year	Public Ministry Budget ($US million)
Bolivia	1999	6.98	2003	10.64
Chile	2001	18	2003	64
Ecuador	2001	7.65	2002	12.14
El Salvador	1997	8	2000	19
Guatemala	1995	11	2001	45
Paraguay	1998	7.71	2000	20.28

Source: C. Riego, "Third Comparative Follow-Up Project on Judicial Reform Processes in Latin America" (Santiago, Chile: CEJA, 2004), 16.

Some countries have also made substantial increases in budgetary allowances for public prosecutors. Table 12.1 compares incremental increases in budget to the public prosecutor's office in countries undergoing reforms. Chile, El Salvador, Guatemala, and Paraguay more than doubled their budgets following reform implementation.

Hiring and training new personnel does not guarantee better due process protections for citizens, but budgetary increases do indicate country commitment to the reform effort and the likelihood that reforms will be sustainable. In theory, creating independent prosecutor's offices and defense institutions leads to healthy competition and checks and balances among justice institutions. Separate prosecutor and defense institutions are interested in ensuring that judges deal fairly with victims and defendants, and the role of the judge becomes one of keeping prosecutors and defense attorneys within the scope of their appropriate roles.

Availability and Use of Alternative Sentencing

Another legal and institutional change brought about by reforms is making alternative sentencing options available to prosecutors and judges. Prior to the criminal procedural reforms instituted in the last decade, prosecutors and judges either did not have the option of offering alternative sentences or the alternatives were so cumbersome and ill-understood that they went essentially unused. New codes introduce some clarity around alternatives to imprisonment (such as community service sentencing options) and alternatives to trial (such as plea bargaining). Alternatives to imprisonment can be important to restoring the victim and helping defendants reintegrate into society, which may discourage recidivism

Table 12.2. Use of Alternatives to Sentencing in Latin America

Country	Share of Cases that Use Alternatives to Sentencing (percent)
Bolivia	40
Costa Rica	64
Chile	21
Ecuador	2
El Salvador	26
Guatemala	4
Paraguay	10

Source: C. Riego, "Third Comparative Follow-Up Project on Judicial Reform Processes in Latin America" (Santiago, Chile: CEJA, 2004), 22.

and which is certainly less expensive for the state than imprisonment. The availability and use of alternatives to trial and discretionary practices by public prosecutors allow for quicker processing, shorter delays, and more efficient use of time for prosecutors and judges.

Since the reforms, several countries have implemented such options: 40 percent of cases in Bolivia involved the use of alternative case resolution; 64 percent in Costa Rica; and 21 percent in Chile (see table 12.2).[31]

Although figures vary by country and even appear dismal in some (such as in Ecuador or Guatemala), the use of alternative resolutions nevertheless represents an institutional possibility that did not exist prior to reforms. Some countries have yet to fully exploit these instruments, but many have shown significant progress in their implementation.

Conclusions

In spite of the scarcity of data and serious challenges implicit in measuring the impact of justice reform, it is possible to measure positive changes made by criminal justice sector reforms for a variety of due process indicators: number of prisoners being held without trial, speed of trials, number of prosecutors and public defenders funded by countries in the region, and use of sentences alternative to trial and imprisonment. These are not insignificant changes, in that they reflect improvement in the due process afforded to parties in the criminal justice system. Thus criminal process reforms, with significant donor support, are producing some measurable and positive changes. This goes some way toward answering one of the questions posed in the introduction to this chapter: Can institutional or operational reforms yield behavioral changes that strengthen the rule of law in developing countries?

Criminal process reform is generating progress in due process rights. That said, it is hard to draw conclusions about the overall effectiveness of this very ambitious reform effort without measuring more than due process indicators. We have seen that there are two distinctive characteristics of the justice sector in Latin America: Much of the region is engaged in an ambitious reform of the criminal process; and most countries of the region continue to suffer from alarmingly high crime and violence rates. Do these high crime rates mean we are losing the battle in criminal justice reform? Not necessarily. We have noted that crime rates are notoriously volatile according to factors that have little to do with the criminal justice system, such that the effectiveness of these reforms may not be accurately judged according to changes (or the lack thereof) in crime and violence rates. Still, given crime rates that remain stubbornly high—even if those rates are not, in and of themselves, a fair measure of the effectiveness of the criminal justice system—it is critical to find ways to measure whether criminal justice systems are performing effectively.

There remain real limitations on what can be and is being measured in terms of impact of criminal justice sector reforms in Latin America. From a citizen's point of view, it would be important to be able to determine whether or not these reforms mean that a complaint about a crime leads to an investigation that identifies the true culprit, which in turn leads to a prompt trial process that imposes a fair sentence and respects the due process of all those involved—victims, witnesses, and defendants. Are criminals being effectively identified and prosecuted? Has the perceived impunity from prosecution for the elite been reduced such that rich and poor are treated equally under the criminal law? Our discussion of the available data makes it clear that countries are not at present generating statistics that make it possible to measure this sort of impact. This poses questions for both donor agencies and the countries working on reform and may well require greater investment in improving managerial statistics systems.

Countries in Latin America took on criminal process reform without necessarily stopping to consider all of the logistics of preparing to measure the impact of that reform once it took place. This is not really surprising, nor does it constitute evidence that reforms have not been effective. What does seem surprising, and truly impressive, are the magnitude and scale of the reform attempted and the fact that countries are keeping at it in spite of the difficulties. The countries of Latin America have bitten off huge reform goals that require significant public funds and retraining of the whole criminal justice sector, as well as new forms of participation from the public—whether as jurors or as observers of trials that have now become public. Amazingly, there has been very little backsliding. Although public exasperation and weariness with crime has led to some modifications in criminal codes to make sentences for some crimes longer (as in Venezuela and El Salvador), the countries that began this reform process continue to push it forward year after year.

And countries of the region are learning from their experiences as they go. Chile observed the profound reform process carried out in other countries and has decided to proceed with reform on a gradual basis, implementing it region by region and adjusting the process on the basis of experience in each region. Peru and Mexico studied the experience in the rest of region and are adapting reforms to the particularities of their systems. This demonstrates that it is necessary not just to measure change produced as a result of reform but also to understand what it is that produced the change being measured. Why, for example, are the numbers on pretrial detention in Guatemala low before reforms, and why did they go down further after reforms were implemented when percentages in El Salvador went up? This kind of understanding is key to those designing and implementing reforms, and more and better information could be generated to make that sort of understanding possible.

Criminal justice reform has become a hallmark of Latin American justice systems, deriving its strength from local support and some of its funding from external donors, and it is becoming more nuanced and country-specific as it proceeds. Statistics currently available show that the reforms have had positive impact on due process indicators. Now, countries and donors alike need to invest more concretely in collecting the statistics that will allow them to better measure the overall impact of this systemic reform on the effectiveness of criminal justice systems and better explain what factors contribute to a successful change process.

Notes

1. See Thomas Carothers in chapter 2 of this volume.
2. See Stephen Golub in chapter 7.
3. S. Pastor, *New Systems for the Organization and Management of Justice: Myth or Reality?* (Madrid: Centro de Investigaciones en Derecho y Economia, La Universidad Complutense de Madrid, June 2003).
4. See World Bank, *World Development Report 2005: A Better Investment Climate for Everyone* (New York: Oxford University Press, 2004), ch. 4.

5. Nibaldo H. Galleguillos Portales, "The Politics of Judicial Reform in the Democratic Transition: An Analysis of the Chilean Case," *Ciencia Ergo Sum* (November 1998–February 1999): 239–48.
6. Galleguillos Portales, "Politics of Judicial Reform."
7. United Nations, *Surveys of Crime Trends and Operations of Criminal Justice (1970–1994)* (New York: United Nations, 1999).
8. In 2000, 24.5 percent of people in Latin America and the Caribbean were living on less than $2 a day, and 9.5 percent on less than $1 a day. World Bank, *World Development Indicators 2005* (Washington, D.C.: World Bank, March 2005).
9. Margaret Sarles, "USAID's Support of Justice Reform in Latin America," in *Rule of Law in Latin America: The International Promotion of Judicial Reform*, ed. Pilar Domingo and Rachel Sieder (London: Institute of Latin American Studies, 2001). An official at USAID reports that since the early 1990s, USAID spent approximately $420 million on judicial and legal development and about $127 million on human rights–related programs. In fiscal 2004 alone, USAID spent $38 million on rule-of-law activities in Latin America and the Caribbean.
10. USAID, *USAID Promotes the Rule of Law in Latin America and Caribbean Democracies* (Washington, D.C.: USAID, October, 2004), 4–6.
11. C. Biebesheimer and J. Payne, *IDB Experience in Justice Reform: Lessons Learned and Elements for Policy Formulation* (Washington, D.C.: Inter-American Development Bank, November 2001).
12. Duce Perdomo and Perez Perdomo, "Security and the Criminal Justice System," in *Crime and Violence in Latin America: Citizen Security, Democracy, and the State*, ed. Joseph S. Tulchin, H. Hugo Frühling, and Heather Golding (Washington, D.C.: Woodrow Wilson Center Press, 2003), 73.
13. Perdomo and Perdomo, "Security," 75.
14. Ibid., pp. 72–3.
15. See World Bank, *World Bank Development Report 2005*.
16. J. Ferguson, "Enhancing Democratic Governance in Latin America through Prosecutorial Reform," in *Justice and Democratic Governance*, ed. Juan Enrique Vargas and Luis Bates (Santiago, Chile: Justice Studies Center of the Americas and the Ministry of Justice, 2003).
17. Justice Studies Center of the Americas (CEJA), "Follow-Up Project on Judicial Reform Processes in Latin America," (Santiago, Chile: CEJA, 2004), available at www.cejamericas.org.
18. CEJA, *Justice and Democratic Governance*.
19. The methodology for collecting and generating data in this project is described on the CEJA web site: www.cejamericas.org.
20. See International Covenant on Civil and Political Rights (ICCPR) (1966), art. 14; and American Convention on Human Rights (1979), art. 8.
21. N. H. Martinez, "De los Diez Pecados de la Reforma Judicial y Algunos Anatemas," in *Estado y Economia en America Latina: Mexico*, ed. Miguel Angel Prrua (Mexico City: Centro de Investigation para el Desarrollo, 1999), 16.
22. C. Riego, "Third Comparative Follow-up Project on Judicial Reform Processes in Latin America" (Santiago, Chile: Justice Studies Center of the Americas, or CEJA, 2004).
23. CEJA, "Guatemala Follow-up Report: 2002-2003" (Santiago, Chile: CEJA, 2004).
24. It must be noted, however, that Chile has yet to implement reforms in the greater Santiago area where 40 percent of the population resides.
25. Management Systems International (MSI), *Achievements in Building and Maintaining the Rule of Law* (Washington, D.C.: USAID, November 2002), 57.
26. USAID, *USAID Promotes the Rule of Law*, 4.

27. CEJA, "Follow-Up on Criminal Procedures Reform in El Salvador" (Santiago, Chile: CEJA, 2002), 77.
28. "Chile: Reforms Seek to Strengthen Bachelet Candidacy," *Oxford Analytica*, June 7, 2005.
29. MSI, *Achievements*, 39–40.
30. Ibid., p. 50.
31. Riego, "Third Comparative Follow-Up."

PART IV

Conclusions

CHAPTER THIRTEEN

Steps toward Knowledge

THOMAS CAROTHERS

DURING THE PAST TWENTY YEARS, a set of new areas of development aid emerged at the intersection of democracy promotion and support for market-based economic reforms—the twin imperatives that have come to dominate contemporary donor thinking about political and economic development. These new areas, which quickly became the topics for endless discussions within aid organizations and countless projects in developing and postcommunist countries, include good governance, anticorruption, state building, civil society development, legislative strengthening, decentralization, and, the subject of this book, promotion of the rule of law.

These various aid endeavors differ in certain ways, such as in the institutions they primarily target, but they also share some crucial links. Reflecting their place at the nexus of political and economic concerns, each is used simultaneously as a method for advancing both democratization and market-oriented economic reforms. Thus, for example, decentralization programs have multiplied within democracy-related aid portfolios as a means of more directly connecting citizens to their political systems. At the same time, some donors have added decentralization programs to their socioeconomic agenda, as a way of stimulating local economic initiatives and establishing economic policy-making capacity that takes local realities into account. Anticorruption programs are sometimes funded by democracy promoters seeking to foster accountability and transparency in a struggling democratic system and sometimes by economic developmentalists hoping to reduce the economic waste and distortions that corruption produces.

Another common attribute of these new aid areas is that they all enjoy a somewhat nonpartisan appeal. Persons on both the left and right, within donor as well as recipient countries, can find reasons to support them. For example, persons on the left may interpret civil society development as consistent with their philosophy of bottom-up, participatory development while persons on the right may like it as a way to encourage a vigorous independent sector capable of keeping government in check and championing the value of individualism. Rule-of-law strengthening may appeal to those on the left for its ties to the empowerment and protection of rights of disadvantaged populations, but it also strikes a favorable chord with conservatives for its association with securing law and order.

An additional shared element of their appeal is that each area shines as something new and different yet has reassuring roots in the formative "modernization" period of political and economic development work of the 1960s: The current wave of rule-of-law work harks back to the law and development movement, good governance programs link to the earlier enthusiasm for public administration reform, today's decentralization efforts connect to an earlier generation of programs that was labeled "municipal governance," and the civil society focus ties to the earlier rise of concern with citizen participation in development.

As each of these new areas caught on in the 1980s or 1990s, it enjoyed a "boom" of its own—a rush of funding and a multiplication of projects as aid organizations scrambled to get on the map in what appeared as an exciting, fresh domain. Despite little empirical research making the case, donors usually embraced the idea that the new theme in question was a crucial building block, prerequisite, or generator of democracy and market-based economic development. And they often followed relatively standardized or "cookie-cutter" approaches to project development, reflecting the combination of lack of preparatory research and strong pressure to move ahead rapidly.

With the passage of time, however, the booms in these various areas have slowed. Hard questions on various levels about each of these areas have surfaced: about the clarity and coherence of the definition of the actual goal, about the validity of the core rationale for such work, about the amount of impact being produced, and about whether lessons from experience are being learned along the way. In some of the areas, knowledge to answer such questions is starting to be generated by scholars, policy-oriented researchers, and development practitioners. Civil society assistance, for example, is now the subject of a large and rapidly growing body of analytic, critical writings. The same is starting to be true with state building and possibly decentralization.

Accumulation of knowledge about rule-of-law assistance has lagged behind some of these other areas for a variety of reasons: the disinclination toward developmental research among the lawyers who dominate this field; an unusually strong initial sense of certainty, often verging on hubris, about such work; and the fact that law (and by extension rule-of-law promotion) is often perceived by nonlawyers as an unusually "technical" domain that they are not qualified to critique or even study. But as the different chapters of this volume make clear in a range of small and large ways, the gap between knowledge and practice in rule-of-law promotion is starting to be bridged, even if only partially so far. Progress is evident with respect to all four of the key issues mentioned above: definition, rationale, impact, and learning.

Definition

A characteristic feature of the boom in these various new areas of development aid is an apparently widely shared agreement on the definition of the operative concept in question—whether it is civil society development, good governance, decentralization, or the rule of law. In reality, however, ambiguities or uncertainties of definition afflict most of these domains. For example, legions of developmentalists and democracy promoters have embraced the idea of civil society development during the past two decades, and the term *civil society* has come to be treated as something of a magic elixir in the aid world. Yet behind the screen of that apparently broad consensus are quite divergent ideas about what civil society is and of what civil society development should consist. These include contending views of the centrality of nongovernmental organizations (NGOs) within the overall arena of civil society and the wisdom of government funding for civil society. Similarly, legislative strengthening is pursued by many different donors as though they shared a common goal in that domain. Yet ask a British and a U.S. aid representative, for example, about what exactly are the crucial features of a good legislature, and the consensus on the shape of the goal may be less firm than imagined.

Questions and quarrels about basic definitions are also very much present in rule of law work. As Rachel Kleinfeld shows in her chapter, the definition of the rule of law that most donor organizations have adopted does not accord with the main conception that legal scholars and philosophers have traditionally emphasized. Rule-of-law aid practitioners tend to conceive of the rule of law in institutional terms, that is to say, as a certain configuration and manner of functioning of state legal institutions. Legal scholars and practitioners instead think of the rule of law in terms of certain values or ends, such as equality before the law or predictable, efficient justice.

The tendency of aid practitioners to use institutional-based definitions is understandable given that their expertise is often institution-based, for example on subjects such as judicial management or police reform. But Kleinfeld points out that this definitional approach brings problems. Perhaps most important, it encourages practitioners to approach rule-of-law strengthening as a series of what often end up as mechanistic, unproductive efforts to make specific institutions in the target countries resemble their counterpart institutions in developed countries. Her recommendation that practitioners explore and eventually shift to ends-based definitions of the rule of law will not immediately solve the underlying difficulties of this field. But it could open the door to new ways to incorporate social, political, and cultural factors into assistance, to better sort out the tensions and contradictions among different types of rule-of-law aid, and to arrive at measures of success more directly related to the day-to-day well-being of ordinary citizens.

Several chapter authors take Kleinfeld's analysis of definitions a step further, critiquing rule-of-law aid for what they find to be a chronic tendency to translate the very broad idea of the rule of law into a narrow preoccupation with judicial reform. Laure-Hélène Piron and David Mednicoff uncover that tendency in Western rule-of-law programs in sub-Saharan Africa and the Middle East, respectively, and highlight its shortcomings. Wade Channell laments a related sort of formalism in aid for law reform in Central and Eastern Europe—the belief that the rule of law starts from the top, with the right laws, and that is where aid providers should concentrate their efforts. The judicial reform critique is the core of Stephen Golub's broad-gauged attack on the conventional approach to rule-of-law promotion, what he (and Frank Upham) call the rule-of-law orthodoxy. In his view, rule-of-law promoters are mistaken in assuming that a well-functioning judiciary is central to the development of the rule of law, which he sees as something arising from many other things, including positive changes in the structural power relations among different sectors of society. And he contends that practitioners confronted with questions about the centrality of judiciaries to the rule of law should not fall back on the idea that judicial reform is a worthwhile developmental priority in and of itself.

Rationale

The core rationale for various of the new areas of development aid is also a matter of ongoing and sometimes increasing debate. What were initially embraced as vital building blocks of democracy and economic success are starting to appear to some observers as useful but not essential additions to the overall developmental picture. For example, many U.S. aid groups gravitated quickly and enthusiastically in the 1990s to the idea that a vibrant civil society is crucial for democratization. Yet that idea has come under criticism from some analysts, who, pointing to cases such as Japan and France where a relatively weak civil society co-exists with stable democracy, argue that it is a projection of a very U.S.-specific outlook. Similarly, an efficient legislature untainted by money politics can be prescribed as crucial for democratization and economic development, but some established, wealthy democracies seem to manage to survive without one. Aid providers have a hard time not turning idealized endpoints into recommended pathways or even prerequisites. Disentangling correlation from cause in development remains notoriously difficult.

Several of the book's contributors challenge the view put forward by the World Bank and some other development institutions that establishing the rule of law is essential for economic development. Frank Upham notes that China has achieved an extraordinary record of sustained economic growth without the sort of rule-of-law system that Western experts now say is crucial. He then broadens his argument by drawing extensively on the legal and economic histories of the United States and Japan. Neither of what were two of the most successful economies of the twentieth century, he asserts, was built on a foundation of the sort of formalized, apolitical rule-of-law system that some donors are now insisting is essential for development in poor countries.

Matthew Stephenson questions the idea that progress on the rule of law in the commercial domain (which is often thought of as a relatively easy entry point for externally sponsored rule-of-law work) will spill over into progress on the rule of law in more sensitive, political domains, such as constitutionalism and criminal law. He explains in detail why he believes that such a spillover effect is unlikely to occur in China, where Western rule-of-law promoters regularly invoke the idea as a primary justification for their work. Although focused on China, his argument has important broader implications for the overall value of commercial law aid and the underlying conception common in donor circles that law is a kind of unified web in society, in which work on one major strand of it will naturally bolster other strands.

Impact

The question of impact is one of the most vexing issues concerning all these new areas of development aid. Many aid organizations have avoided tackling the hard task of assessing impact of these various lines of work. For the first decade or so of such programs, donors coasted on the fact that their work in these areas was relatively new. As the years passed and that rationale dimmed, many slipped into the appealing but illusory outlook that work in areas as widely appealing as civil society development or anticorruption is both intrinsically valuable and uniquely difficult to submit to conventional evaluative methods. Many of the chapters in this volume deal with the question of impact, and they offer several different views.

Some authors are generally skeptical about the impact of rule-of-law projects focused on state institutions, especially on judiciaries. After reviewing all the evaluative evidence he can uncover, Golub broadly concludes that rule-of-law aid does not seem to have deep impact on the state institutions it tries to affect. And whatever impact it does have on them does not generally translate into tangible improvements in the lives of poor or otherwise disadvantaged citizens, which, he argues, should be the key test of all development work. Channell is also doubtful about impact, hesitating to credit the many law reform projects of the past fifteen years in postcommunist countries with far-reaching effects. Innumerable laws have been updated or rewritten entirely, bringing them in line with contemporary Western models. But often the new laws are only paper creations enforced sporadically or not at all. Or they are hijacked by vested interests to serve unintended ends.

Several authors hold that the rule-of-law work in the regions they study is too new to draw firm conclusions about its impact. Piron describes a kind of take-off phase of Western rule-of-law aid to Africa of the past ten years. She articulates a number of significant concerns about the ability of rule-of-law promoters to rise to the unusually daunting challenges that Africa presents in this domain. In like fashion, Mednicoff notes the rapidly growing Western interest in supporting rule-of-law reform in the Middle East but contends that the hoped-for impact is at best a very distant possibility. Stephenson is equally cautious about the likely consequences of the expanding body of rule-of-law aid to China. He acknowledges that many of these programs may have useful, positive effects on specific institutions or problems. But he is wary of the idea, implicit in many of these efforts, that Western actors can do much to help produce a broader rule-of-law transformation in China.

Several authors writing about criminal justice reforms find grounds for a somewhat more positive view. Matthew Spence determines that U.S. support for criminal justice reform in Russia gave a significant boost to the adoption of a new criminal procedure code, which was one of the most important post-1991 Russian legal reforms. Although the U.S. assistance did not create the top-level impetus for the reform, it did catalyze energy for the reform at the critical juncture, helping key specialists act, providing useful external validation for the reforms, and furnishing some practical comparative knowledge to drafters of the new code.

Lisa Bhansali and Christina Biebesheimer examine the impact of the oldest and broadest set of legal reforms in the developing world: the large wave of criminal justice reform over the past twenty years in Latin America. Bilateral and multilateral aid was critical to the initiation and spread of this reform impulse. Bhansali and Biebesheimer focus on the impact of these reforms on the rule of law itself, rather than on the broader political and economic conditions that reformers hope will benefit from these efforts over time. They chart the impact on a series of indicators relating to the establishment of due process, which they view as central to the rule of law, such as lowered levels of pretrial detention and increased speed of trials. Although the picture is not entirely clear or consistent, they find enough gains to warrant the conclusion that the reforms are having positive effects on the criminal justice systems of the region. At the same time, they acknowledge that better functioning of these systems has not, in many countries, translated into a lowering of Latin America's distressingly high levels of crime. The causal link between the quality of a criminal justice system and crime levels is only a weak one, with many other factors—social, political, and economic—relevant as well.

Learning

All of the analysis and debate in this volume over issues of the definition, rationale, and impact of rule-of-law assistance naturally lead to the further issues of learning and how to do better. The authors have a raft of suggestions for improving rule-of-law aid, which fall into several clusters. Perhaps their most frequent recommendation is that rule-of-law promoters give more attention to the nongovernmental or civil society side of the legal domain. For Piron this means that Western legal specialists need to take seriously the challenge of incorporating traditional, informal African justice systems into their programming, something that only a few aid organizations have yet tried to do. She also advocates finding more and better ways of working closely with African NGOs that are pursuing pieces of the rule-of-law puzzle, such as local legal resource centers, prison reform groups, and media-based legal education programs. Channell presents this same imperative in the law reform context as the need for external actors to fully engage the relevant societal stakeholders in designing, negotiating, and implementing legal reforms. In his view, it is precisely the tendency of aid providers to neglect the societal side of the law reform—to treat it as an insular, top-down process—that leads to the passage of many reformed laws that are never adequately implemented or enforced.

Mednicoff goes a step further in this direction, asserting that rule-of-law aid providers should not just increase their attention to civil society but actually shift their main focus from state institutions to the nongovernmental side. He cautions that the authoritarian context of rule-of-law work in the Arab world imposes sharp limits on what can be expected from aid programs centered on state institutions. Aid providers hoping to use law as an entry point for fundamental political and economic change, he contends, would do better to deemphasize state institutions and concentrate instead on fostering a broad social understanding of law among ordinary citizens. This would involve working with a range of issues and institutions such as revising law school curricula, supporting independent media projects on legal education, and backing indigenous human rights movements.

Golub argues for a similar paradigm shift, away from the state-centric approach to one based on supporting the legal empowerment of the poor and other disadvantaged populations. Such an approach, which he says has been successfully applied on at least a medium scale in various developing countries, not only makes local nongovernmental groups the key partners but also replaces the institution-based definition of the rule of law with an ends-based definition that focuses on improving the lives of everyday people. It employs paralegal activists and law students to spread practical knowledge about how citizens can use law as a tool to improve their own lives. It also seeks to mainstream a rule-of-law focus into the larger, more established areas of development aid, such as health, agriculture, and education, to amplify the impact of what is too often a narrowly self-contained area of work.

Many of the chapter authors also urge aid organizations to be more political in their approach to promoting the rule of law. These authors' broad command to "take politics more fully into account" has many variants. For Mednicoff the importance of a political lens starts at the macro level with a realistic assessment of the prospects for legal change in the overall political systems in which rule-of-law promoters find themselves working. And he highlights not only the Arab world's authoritarian political context but also the political barriers that U.S. rule-of-law promoters face there given Arab anger about U.S. policies in the region. Golub also underscores the role of politics as a frequent source of reform blockage. He stresses that top-down institutional reforms often fail due to entrenched political interests that will be threatened by the proposed changes. In his account, proponents of the conventional approach often try to ignore this factor, to the detriment of their work. Piron presents a similar argument for Africa, underscoring the politically treacherous waters in which rule-of-law promoters must swim. She recognizes that aid providers must often obtain the support of current politicians in a country where they wish to initialize a program, but she urges them to support reforms in ways that will outlast any one government by building coalitions across parties and other power divisions.

Bhansali and Biebesheimer point out that the political side has sometimes been a positive factor in rule-of-law work. The whole criminal justice reform movement in Latin America was given impetus by the pro-democratic winds of change that blew across the region in the 1980s and 1990s. And governments in the region have been able to sustain at least some of this reform drive, despite the frustratingly high crime rates that continue to plague the region, because they continue to find a political mandate for doing so.

In his analysis of the successful adoption of a new criminal procedure code in Russia, Spence emphasizes the unusual political juncture that made reform possible—the arrival to power of a new president who simultaneously decided to pursue legal reform as a way to burnish his reformist credentials and to centralize enough political power around him to make it possible to get such reforms through. And Spence shows that the ability of U.S. rule-of-law aid providers to act nimbly to take advantage of that political juncture was crucial to the success of their efforts.

For Channell also, political issues are frequently paramount in law reform. Too often, he says, aid providers eager to notch up another completed law reform project use their donor leverage to shortcut the local deliberative process and hurry the new or revised law onto the books. Successful law reform requires an immersion in and respect for the substance and forms of local political mechanisms, no matter how slow or frustrating they may be.

Finally, in their recommendations about ways to do better, the authors reinforce the overall theme of this book by urging rule-of-law promoters to engage more actively and deeply in generating practical knowledge and lessons about what they are learning as they go along. As the wide range of insights and information in the different chapters makes clear, the problem of knowledge is being chipped away as experience accumulates. But the process is slower and more haphazard than it should or could be. Bhansali and Biebesheimer note that although some useful statistics about the progress of criminal justice reforms in Latin America are starting to become available, donors who support these reforms have not done enough to build measurement components into their projects. Piron puzzles over why donors are not putting more effort into extracting lessons from their work on justice sector reform in Africa. She finds at least a partial explanation in the lack of interest some rule-of-law promoters show in the broader learning about good practice in development aid and the constant pressure they face to disburse aid quickly and keep moving on to the next project. Channell also examines why some fairly obvious lessons about law reform are persistently not learned by aid providers. He identifies a whole set of wrongful incentives in the aid business regarding the generation and accumulation of knowledge. And he argues that overcoming the tendency of lessons to remain unlearned would require deeper changes in organizational structures and practice than many aid providers realize.

Looking Ahead

Anyone who works in the field of development for more than a few years inevitably becomes aware that it is a domain littered with discarded fads, crisscrossed by swinging pendulums, and afflicted with frequent bouts of group amnesia. Thus, a fundamental question about the various areas of aid that have emerged in the past two decades at the intersection of politics and economics is whether they will burn out within their first generation of existence, be replaced by new donor enthusiasms, or grow into coherent aid subfields with settled operational definitions, well-grounded rationales, proven results, and a capacity for learning lessons from experience. Different hunches or hypotheses could certainly be hazarded about the prospect of each of the different areas. For rule-of-law aid, the proverbial jury remains out. A large, even robust amount of activity is being carried out under the rule-of-law flag. The subject commands strong interest in many quarters and continues to be invested with high expectations. Yet as the essays in this book show, many basic issues about such work, from conceptualization and design through implementation and evolution, are still in flux. The searching nature of many of the critiques herein could give rise to pessimism about the state of progress in this field. At the same time, however, both implicitly and explicitly, the authors make clear that something vital and dynamic lies at the root of rule-of-law promotion, something that will continue to sustain commitment and hope in such work despite the daunting complexities and conundrums that exist all along the way.

Bibliography

Ajani, Gianmaria. "By Chance and Prestige: Legal Transplants in Russia and Eastern Europe." *American Journal of Comparative Law* 43 (Winter 1995): 93–117.

Alkon, Cynthia J. "The Cookie Cutter Syndrome: Legal Reform Assistance under Post-Communist Democratization Programs." *Journal of Dispute Resolution* 2002, no. 2 (2002): 327–65.

Alvarez, José. "Promoting the 'Rule of Law' in Latin America: Problems and Prospects." *George Washington Journal of International Law and Economics* 25, no. 2 (1991): 281–331.

Autheman, Violaine. "Global Best Practices: Judicial Integrity Standards and Consensus Principles." Rule of Law white paper no. 1. Washington, D.C.: International Foundation for Election Systems, 2004.

———. "Global Lessons Learned: Constitutional Courts, Judicial Independence and the Rule of Law." Rule of Law white paper no. 4. Washington, D.C.: International Foundation for Election Systems, 2004.

Autheman, Violaine, and Sandra Elena. "Global Best Practices: Judicial Councils—Lessons Learned from Europe and Latin America." Rule of Law white paper no. 2. Washington, D.C.: International Foundation for Election Systems, 2004.

Ball, Nicole. "Strengthening Democratic Governance of the Security Sector in Conflict-Affected Countries." *Public Administration and Development* 25, no. 1 (February 2005): 25–38.

Biebesheimer, Christina, and Mark Payne. "IDB Experience in Justice Reform: Lessons Learned and Elements for Policy Formulation." Technical Papers Series. Washington, D.C.: Inter-American Development Bank, 2001.

Blair, Harry, and Gary Hansen. "Weighing in the Scales of Justice: Strategic Approaches for Donor-Supported Rule of Law Programs." USAID Program and Operations Assessment Report no. 7. Washington, D.C.: USAID, 1994.

Burg, Elliot M. "Law and Development: A Review of the Literature and a Critique of 'Scholars in Self-Estrangement.'" *American Journal of Comparative Law* 25 (1977): 492–530.

Buscaglia, Edgardo, and Maria Dakolias. "An Analysis of the Causes of Corruption in the Judiciary." Washington, D.C.: World Bank, Legal and Judicial Reform Unit, 1999.

———. "Judicial Reform in Latin American Courts: The Experience of Argentina and Ecuador." Technical Note no. WTP 350. Washington, D.C.: World Bank, 1996.

Cadwell, Charles. "Implementing Legal Reform in Transition Economies." In *Institutions and Economic Development*, edited by Christopher Clague. Baltimore, MD: Johns Hopkins University Press, 1997: 251–69.

Call, Charles T. "Democratization, War and State-Building: Constructing the Rule of Law in El Salvador." *Journal of Latin American Studies* 35, no. 4 (November 2003): 827–62.

Chavez, Rebecca Bill. *The Rule of Law in Nascent Democracies: Judicial Politics in Argentina*. Stanford, CA: Stanford University Press, 2004.

Chodosh, Hiram E. "Reforming Judicial Reform Inspired by U.S. Models." *DePaul Law Review* 52, no. 2 (Winter 2002): 351–81.

Chua, Amy L. "Markets, Democracy and Ethnicity: Toward a New Paradigm for Law and Development." *Yale Law Journal* 108, no. 1 (October 1998): 1–107.

———. *The World on Fire: How Exporting Free Market Democracy Breeds Ethnic Hatred and Global Instability*. New York: Anchor Books, 2003.

Ciurlizza, Javier. "Judicial Reform and International Legal Assistance in Latin America." *Democratization* 7, no. 2 (Summer 2000): 211–30.

Craig, Paul. "Formal and Substantive Conceptions of the Rule of Law: An Analytical Framework." *Public Law* (1997): 467–87.

Dahan, Frédérique. "Law Reform in Central and Eastern Europe: The 'Transplantation' of Secured Transactions Laws." *European Journal of Law Reform* 2, no. 3 (2000): 369–84.

Dakolias, Maria. "Legal and Judicial Development: The Role of Civil Society in the Reform Process." *Fordham International Law Journal* 24, symposium (2000): S26–S55.

———. "Strategy for Judicial Reform: The Experience of Latin America." *Virginia Journal of International Law* 36, no. 1 (Fall 1995): 167–231.

Dakolias, Maria, and Kim Thachuk. "The Problem of Eradicating Corruption from the Judiciary," *Wisconsin International Law Journal*, no. 2 (Spring 2000): 353-96.

Davis, Kevin E. "What Can the Rule of Law Variable Tell Us about Rule of Law Reforms?" New York University Law and Economics Research Paper no. 04-026. New York: New York University Press, 2004.

Davis, Kevin E., and Michael J. Trebilcock. "Legal Reforms and Development." *Third World Quarterly* 22, no. 1 (February 2001): 21–36.

deLisle, Jacques. "Lex Americana? United States Legal Assistance, American Legal Models, and Legal Change in the Post-Communist World and Beyond." *University of Pennsylvania Journal of International Economic Law* 20, no. 2 (Summer 1999): 179–308.

Dezalay, Yves, and Bryant Garth. "Law, Lawyers, and Social Capital: 'Rule of Law' Versus Relational Capitalism." *Social and Legal Studies* 6, no. 1 (1997): 109–41.

Dezalay, Yves, and Bryant G. Garth. *Global Prescriptions: The Production, Exportation, and Importation of a New Legal Orthodoxy*. Ann Arbor: University of Michigan Press, 2002.

Dietrich, Mark K. "Legal and Judicial Reform in Central Europe and the Former Soviet Union: Voices from Five Countries." Washington, D.C.: World Bank, Legal Vice Presidency, 2000.

Domingo, Pilar, and Rachel Sieder, eds. *Rule of Law in Latin America: The International Promotion of Judicial Reform*. London: University of London, Institute of Latin American Studies, 2001.

Elena, Sandra, Buruiana Procop, and Violaine Autheman. "Global Best Practices: Income and Asset Disclosure Requirements for Judges–Lessons Learned from Eastern Europe and Latin America." Rule of Law white paper no. 3. Washington, D.C.: International Foundation for Election Systems, 2004.

Elster, Jon. "Constitution-Making in Eastern Europe: Rebuilding the Boat in the Open Sea." *Public Administration* 71 (Spring/Summer 1993): 169–217.

Faundez, Julio, ed. *Good Government and Law: Legal and Institutional Reform in Developing Countries*. New York: St. Martin's Press, 1997.

Franck, Thomas M. "The New Development: Can American Law and Legal Institutions Help Developing Countries?" *Wisconsin Law Review* (1972): 767–801.

Friedman, Lawrence M. "On Legal Development." *Rutgers Law Review* 24 (1969): 11–64.

Garcia-Sayan, Diego. "The Role of International Financial Institutions in Judicial Reform." In *CIJL Yearbook: The Judiciary in a Globalized World* 7. Edited by Mona A. Rishmawi, 31–50. Geneva: Center for the Independence of Judges and Lawyers, 1999.

Gardner, James. *Legal Imperialism: American Lawyers and Foreign Aid in Latin America*. Madison: University of Wisconsin Press, 1980.

Garth, Bryant G. "Building Strong and Independent Judiciaries through the New Law and Development: Behind the Paradox of Consensus Programs and Perpetually Disappointing Results." *DePaul Law Review* 52, no. 2 (Winter 2002): 383–400.

Gillespie, John. "Transplanted Company Law: An Ideological and Cultural Analysis of Market-Entry in Vietnam." *International and Comparative Law Quarterly* 51, no. 3 (July 2002): 641–72.

Gloppen, Siri, Roberto Gargarella, and Elin Skaar, eds. *Accountability Function of Courts in New Democracies*. London: Frank Cass, 2003.

Golub, Stephen. "The Growth of a Public Interest Law Movement: Origins, Operations, Impact and Lessons for Legal System Development." In *Organizing for Democracy: NGOs, Civil Society and the Philippine State*. Edited by G. Sidney Silliman and Lela Garner Noble, 254–79. Honolulu: University of Hawaii Press, 1998.

Gray, Cheryl W. "Reforming Legal Systems in Developing and Transition Countries." *Finance and Development* 34, no. 3 (September 1997): 14–7.

Gupta, Poonam, Rachel Kleinfeld, and Gonzalo Salinas. "Legal and Judicial Reform in Europe and Central Asia." Washington, D.C.: World Bank, Operations and Evaluation Department, 2002.

Hager, Barry. *The Rule of Law: A Lexicon for Policy Makers*. Washington, D.C.: Mansfield Center for Pacific Affairs, 2000.

Hammergren, Linn A. "Code Reform and Law Revision." USAID Document no. PN-ACD-022. Washington, D.C.: USAID, Center for Democracy and Governance, 1998.

———. "Do Judicial Councils Further Judicial Reform? Lessons from Latin America." Carnegie working paper no. 28. Washington, D.C.: Carnegie Endowment for International Peace, 2002.

———. "Institutional Strengthening and Justice Reform." USAID Document no. PN-ACD-020. Washington, D.C.: USAID, Center for Democracy and Governance, 1998.

———. "Judicial Training and Justice Reform." USAID Document no. PN-ACD-021. Washington, D.C.: USAID, Center for Democracy and Governance, 1998.

———. "Political Will, Constituency Building, and Public Support in Rule of Law Programs." USAID Document no. PN-ACE-023. Washington, D.C.: USAID, Center for Democracy and Governance, 1998.

———. *The Politics of Justice and Justice Reform in Latin America: The Peruvian Case in Comparative Perspective.* Boulder, CO: Westview Press, 1998.

Hay, Jonathan, Andrei Shleifer, and Robert W. Vishny. "Toward a Theory of Legal Reform." *European Economic Review* 40, no. 3 (April 1996): 559–67.

Henderson, Keith, and Violaine Autheman. "Global Best Practices: A Model State of the Judiciary Report—A Strategic Tool for Promoting, Monitoring and Reporting on Judicial Integrity Reforms." Rule of Law white paper no. 6. Washington, D.C.: International Foundation for Election Systems, 2004.

Henderson, Keith, Angana Shah, Sandra Elena, and Violaine Autheman. "Regional Best Practices: Enforcement of Court Judgments—Lessons Learned from Latin America." Rule of Law white paper no. 5. Washington, D.C.: International Foundation for Election Systems, 2004.

Hendley, Kathryn. "Legal Development in Post-Soviet Russia." *Post-Soviet Affairs* 13, no. 3 (July/September 1997): 228–51.

Hewko, John. "Foreign Direct Investment: Does the Rule of Law Matter?" Carnegie working paper no. 26. Washington, D.C.: Carnegie Endowment for International Peace, April 2002.

Hoeland, Armin. "The Evolution of Law in Eastern and Central Europe: Are We Witnessing a Renaissance of 'Law and Development'?" In *European Legal Cultures.* Edited by Gessner Volkmar, Armin Hoeland, and Csaba Varga. Brookfield, VT: Dartmouth Publishing Company, 1996.

Hu, Martin G. "WTO's Impact on the Rule of Law in China." In *The Rule of Law Perspectives from the Pacific Rim*, 101–6. Washington, D.C.: Mansfield Center for Pacific Affairs, 2000.

Huggins, Martha. *Political Policing: The United States and Latin America.* Durham, NC: Duke University Press, 1998.

International Crisis Group (ICG). "Building Judicial Independence in Pakistan." ICG Asia Report no. 86. Brussels: ICG, 2004.

Islam, Roumeen. "Institutional Reform and the Judiciary: Which Way Forward?" Policy Research working paper no. 3134. Washington, D.C.: World Bank, 2003.

Jarquin, Edmundo, and Fernando Carrillo, eds. *Justice Delayed: Judicial Reform in Latin America.* Washington, D.C.: Inter-American Development Bank, 1998.

Jayasuriya, Kaniskha, ed. *Law, Capitalism and Power in Asia: The Rule of Law and Legal Institutions.* London: Routledge, 1999.

Jensen, Erik G., and Thomas C. Heller, eds. *Beyond Common Knowledge: Empirical Approaches to the Rule of Law.* Stanford, CA: Stanford University Press, 2003.

Krasnov, Mikhail. "Is the 'Concept of Judicial Reform' Timely?" *East European Constitutional Review* 11, nos. 1/2 (Winter/Spring 2002): 92–4.

Kritz, Neil J., ed. *Transitional Justice: How Emerging Democracies Reckon with Former Regimes,* vols. I, II, III. Washington, D.C.: United States Institute of Peace, 1995.

Lawyers Committee for Human Rights. "Building on Quicksand: The Collapse of the World Bank's Judicial Reform Project in Peru." New York: Lawyers Committee for Human Rights, 2000.

———. "Halfway to Reform: The World Bank and the Venezuelan Justice System." New York: Lawyers Committee for Human Rights, 1996.

Lippman, Hal, and Jan Emmert. "Assisting Legislatures in Developing Countries: A Framework for Program Planning and Implementation." USAID Program and Operations Assessment Report no. 20. Washington, D.C.: USAID, 1997.

Mani, Rama. "Contextualizing Police Reform: Security, the Rule of Law and Post-Conflict Peacebuilding." In *Police Reform and Peacebuilding.* Edited by Espen Eide and Tor Tanke Holm. London: Frank Cass, 2000.

———. "The Rule of Law or the Rule of Might? Restoring Legal Justice in Post-Conflict Societies." in *Regeneration of War-Torn Societies.* Edited by Michael Pugh. London: Macmillan Press, 2000.

Maraval, José María, and Adam Przeworski, eds. *Democracy and the Rule of Law.* Cambridge: Cambridge University Press, 2003.

Mathernová, Katerína. "The World Bank and Legal Technical Assistance: Initial Lessons." Policy Research working paper no.1414. Washington, D.C.: World Bank, 1995.

Mattei, Ugo. "Efficiency in Legal Transplants: An Essay in Comparative Law and Economics." *International Review of Law and Economics* 14, no. 3 (September 1994): 3–19.

McAdams, James. *Transitional Justice and the Rule of Law in New Democracies*. Notre Dame, IN: University of Notre Dame Press, 1997.

McClymont, Mary, and Stephen Golub. *Many Roads to Justice: The Law-Related Work of Ford Foundation Grantees around the World*. New York: Ford Foundation, 2000.

Mendez, Juan E., Guillermo O'Donnell, and Paulo Sergio Pinheiro. *The (Un) Rule of Law and the Underprivileged in Latin America*. Notre Dame, IN: University of Notre Dame Press, 1999.

Merryman, John H. "Comparative Law and Social Change: On the Origins, Style, Decline and Revival of the Law and Development Movement." *American Journal of Comparative Law* 25 (1977): 457–83.

Messick, Richard E. "Judicial Reform and Economic Development: A Survey of the Issues." *World Bank Research Observer* 14, no. 1 (1999): 117–36.

Messick, Richard E., and Linn Hammergren. "The Challenge of Judicial Reform." In *Beyond the Washington Consensus: Institutions Matter*, 109–19. Washington, D.C.: World Bank, 1999. Edited by Shahid Javed Burki, and Guillermo Perry.

Miller, Jonathan M. "A Typology of Legal Transplants: Using Sociology, Legal History and Argentine Examples to Explain the Transplant Process." *American Journal of Comparative Law* 51 (Fall 2003): 839–85.

Neild, Rachel. "Themes and Debates in Public Security Reform: A Manual for Civil Society." Washington, D.C.: Washington Office on Latin America, 1998.

Oakley, Robert B., Michael J. Dziedzic, and Eliot M. Goldberg, eds. *Policing the New World Disorder: Peace Operations and Public Security*. Washington, D.C.: National Defense University Press, 1998.

O'Donnell, Guillermo. "Why the Rule of Law Matters." *Journal of Democracy* 15, no. 4 (October 2004): 32–46.

Ohnesorge, John K.M. "The Rule of Law, Economic Development, and the Developmental States of Northeast Asia." In *Law and Development in East and Southeast Asia*. Edited by Christoph Antons. London: Routledge Curzon, 2003.

Open Society Institute (OSI). "Monitoring the EU Accession Process: Judicial Independence." EU Accession Monitoring Program. Budapest: OSI, 2001.

Örücü, Esin. "Law as Transposition." *International and Comparative Law Quarterly* 51, no. 2 (April 2002): 205–23.

Peerenboom, Randall. "Globalization, Path Dependency and the Limits of Law: Administrative Law Reform and Rule of Law in the People's Republic of China." *Berkeley Journal of International Law* 19, no. 2 (2001): 161–264.

———. "Let One Hundred Flowers Bloom, One Hundred Schools Contend: Debating Rule of Law in China." *Michigan Journal of International Law* 23 (Spring 2002): 471–544.

Pistor, Katharina, Philip A. Wellons, and Jeffrey Sachs. *The Role of Law and Legal Institutions in Asian Economic Development: 1960–1995.* Oxford: Oxford University Press, 1999.

Popkin, Margaret. *Peace without Justice: Obstacles to Building the Rule of Law in El Salvador.* University Park: Pennsylvania University Press, 2000.

Pouligny, Beatrice. "UN Peace Operations, INGOs, NGOs, and Promoting the Rule of Law: Exploring the Intersection of International and Local Norms in Different Postwar Contexts." *Journal of Human Rights* 2, no. 3 (September 2003): 359–77.

Prillaman, William C. *The Judiciary and Democratic Decay in Latin America: Declining Confidence in the Rule of Law.* Westport, CT: Praeger, 2000.

Rose, Carol V. "The 'New' Law and Development Movement in the Post-Cold War Era: A Vietnam Case Study." *Law and Society Review* 32, no. 1 (1998): 93–140.

Russell, Peter H., and David M. O'Brien. *Judicial Independence in the Age of Democracy: Critical Perspectives from around the World.* Charlottesville: University of Virginia Press, 2001.

Sachs, Jeffrey, and Katharina Pistor, eds. *The Rule of Law and Economic Reform in Russia.* Boulder, CO: Westview Press, 1997.

Sajó, András. "Universal Rights, Missionaries, Converts, and 'Local Savages.'" *East European Constitutional Review* 6, no. 1 (Winter 1997): 44–9.

Schauer, Frederick. "The Politics and Incentives of Legal Transplantation." CID working paper no. 44, Law and Development Paper no. 2. Cambridge, MA: Harvard University, Center for International Development, 2000.

Schedler, Andreas, Larry Diamond, and Mark F. Plattner, eds. *The Self-Restraining State: Power and Accountability in New Democracies.* Boulder, CO: Lynne Rienner Publishers, 1999.

Schwartz, Herman. *The Struggle for Constitutional Justice in Post-Communist Europe.* Chicago: University of Chicago Press, 2000.

Seidman, Ann Wilcox, and Robert B. Seidman. "Using Reason and Experience to Draft Country-Specific Laws." In *Making Development Work: Legislative Reform for Institutional Transformation and Good Governance.* Edited by Ann Wilcox Seidman, Robert B. Seidman, and Thomas W. Wälde. The Hague: Kluwer Law International, 1999.

Seidman, Robert B. "The Lessons of Self-Estrangement: On The Methodology of Law and Development." In *Yearbook of Research in Sociology of Law.* Edited by Rita Simon. Greenwich, CT: JAI Press, 1978.

Sevastik, Per, ed. *Legal Assistance to Developing Countries: Swedish Perspectives on the Rule of Law.* The Hague: Kluwer Law International, 1997.

Sharlet, Robert. "Legal Transplants and Political Mutations: The Reception of Constitutional Law in Russia and the New Independent States." *East European Constitutional Review* 7, no. 4 (Fall 1998): 59–68.

Shihata, Ibrahim F.I. *Complementary Reform: Essays on Legal, Judicial and Other Institutional Reforms Supported by the World Bank.* The Hague: Kluwer Law International, 1997.

Sidel, Mark. "Law Reform in Vietnam: the Complex Transition from Socialism and Soviet Models in Legal Scholarship and Training." *UCLA Pacific Basin Law* Journal 11 (Spring 1993): 221–59.

Sieder, Rachel. "Renegotiating 'Law and Order': Judicial Reform and Citizen Responses in Post-War Guatemala." *Democratization* 10, no. 4 (Winter 2003): 137–60.

Strohmeyer, Hansjörg. "Collapse and Reconstruction of a Judicial System: The United Nations Missions in Kosovo and East Timor." *American Journal of International Law* 95, no. 1 (January 2001): 46–63.

Sunshine, Russell B. "Technical Assistance for Law Reform: Cooperative Strategies for Enhancing Quality and Impact." *European Journal of Law Reform* 2, no. 1 (2000): 61–93.

Tamanaha, Brian Z. "The Lessons of Law-and-Development Studies," *American Journal of International Law* 89, no. 2 (April 1995): 470–86.

———. *On the Rule of Law: History, Politics, Theory.* Cambridge: Cambridge University Press, 2004.

Trubek, David M. "Toward a Social Theory of Law: An Essay on the Study of Law and Development." *Yale Law Journal* 82, no. 1 (1972): 1–50.

Trubek, David M., and Marc Galanter. "Scholars in Self-Estrangement: Some Reflections on the Crisis in Law and Development Studies in the United States." *Wisconsin Law Review* 4 (1974): 1062–102.

Tshuma, Lawrence. "The Political Economy of the World Bank's Legal Framework for Economic Development." *Social and Legal Studies* 8, no. 1 (1999): 75–96.

Ungar, Mark. *Elusive Reform: Democracy and the Rule of Law in Latin America*. Boulder, CO: Lynne Rienner Publishers, 2002.

U.S. Agency for International Development (USAID). "Guidance for Promoting Judicial Independence and Impartiality," Washington, D.C.: USAID, Office of Democracy and Governance, 2002.

U.S. General Accounting Office (GAO). "Foreign Assistance: Promoting Judicial Reform to Strengthen Democracies." Report no. GAO/NSIAD-93-149. Washington, D.C.: GAO, National Security and International Affairs Division, 1993.

———. "Foreign Assistance: U.S. Rule of Law Assistance to Five Latin American Countries." Report no. GAO/NSIAD-99-195. Washington, D.C.: GAO, National Security and International Affairs Division, 1999.

Van Puymbroeck, Rudolf V. *Comprehensive Legal and Judicial Development: Toward an Agenda for a Just and Equitable Society in the 21st Century*. Washington, D.C.: World Bank, 2001.

Wälde, Thomas W., and James L. Gunderson. "Legislative Reform in Transition Economies: Western Transplants—A Short-Cut to Social Market Economy Status?" *International and Comparative Law Quarterly* 43, no. 2 (April 1994): 347–78.

Welch Jr., Claude. "Human Rights NGOs and the Rule of Law in Africa." *Journal of Human Rights* 2, no. 3 (September 2003): 315–27.

Widner, Jennifer A. *Building the Rule of Law: Francis Nyalali and the Road to Judicial Independence in Africa*. New York: W.W. Norton, 2001.

———. "How Some Reflections on the United States' Experience May Inform African Efforts to Build Court Systems and the Rule of Law." *Democratization* 10, no. 4 (November 2003): 27–45.

World Bank. "Guatemala: The Role of Judicial Modernization in Post Conflict Reconstruction and Social Reconciliation." Social Development Notes no. 21. Washington, D.C.: World Bank, Conflict Prevention and Reconstruction Unit, February 2005.

———. "Initiatives in Legal and Judicial Reform." Washington, D.C.: World Bank, Legal Vice Presidency, 2004.

———. "Legal and Judicial Reform: Strategic Directions." Washington, D.C.: World Bank, Legal Vice Presidency, 2003.

Index

Contributors

Rachel Kleinfeld is codirector of the Truman National Security Project. She has served as a consultant on police, judicial, and legal reform in Latin America, Eastern Europe, and Asia for various private and nonprofit organizations. She is currently writing on U.S. and EU strategies to build the rule of law abroad.

Lisa Bhansali is a senior public sector management specialist at the World Bank, where she works in the Poverty Reduction and Economic Management department for Latin America and the Caribbean. Her areas of focus include managing projects on legal and judicial reform, governance, anticorruption, and public administration. She has also worked on rule-of-law programs for the Open Society Institute, the Inter-American Development Bank, and the United Nations Development Programme. She is an adjunct professor at the Washington College of Law at American University, where she teaches on rule of law and the administration of justice.

Christina Biebesheimer is chief counsel of the Justice Reform Practice Group in the Legal Vice Presidency at the World Bank, which contributes to Bank research and to project development to help ensure that Bank justice projects constitute effective reform processes responsive to local needs. Having worked on justice reform issues at the Inter-American Development Bank for more than a decade, she has particular expertise in justice reform in Latin America and the Caribbean in the context of good governance, transition to democracy, and human rights.

Wade Channell is an independent consultant specializing in legal reform and economic development issues in developing and transition countries. Since graduating from Southern Methodist University Law School in 1985, he has lived in Eastern Europe, Western Europe, Latin America, Africa, and the United States, and has worked in more than thirty-five countries. He is currently based in Brussels.

Thomas Carothers directs the Democracy and Rule of Law Project at the Carnegie Endowment for International Peace. He has worked on democracy promotion programs with many U.S. and European organizations and has written extensively on the subject, including *Uncharted Journey: Promoting Democracy in the Middle East* (Carnegie Endowment, 2005), *Critical Mission: Essays on Democracy Promotion* (Carnegie Endowment, 2004), and *Aiding Democracy Abroad: The Learning Curve* (Carnegie Endowment, 1999).

Stephen Golub teaches international development and law at Boalt Hall Law School of the University of California at Berkeley. He also consults and conducts research for organizations that fund international development activities concerning civil society, legal systems, and governance, and for NGOs that carry out such activities. These organizations include the Ford Foundation, the Open Society Justice Initiative, the Asia Foundation, the International Council on Human Rights Policy, the United Kingdom Department for International Development, the World Bank, and the Asian Development Bank.

David Mednicoff is assistant professor in the Department of Legal Studies at the University of Massachusetts—Amherst. A lawyer and political scientist, his areas of expertise include public international law and Middle Eastern politics. He has published on the endurance of Arab monarchies and on indigenous human rights activism in the Middle East. His chapter in this volume is part of a larger study in progress on the political contestation of the rule of law in contemporary Arab politics.

Laure-Hélène Piron is a research fellow at the Overseas Development Institute, London, where she manages the Rights in Action Program. She specializes in providing policy and programming advice to aid agencies in the areas of human rights, justice sector reform, and political development. She has a particular focus on Africa, and has undertaken field work in Ghana, Kenya, Malawi, Nigeria, Rwanda, Somalia, and Uganda, as well as Latin America and the Balkans. She has published papers on human rights-based approaches to development, social exclusion, politics and aid, available at www.odi.org.uk/rights.

Frank Upham is a professor of law at New York University School of Law and a specialist in comparative law. He has published extensively on the interaction of law with politics, society, and culture in Japan, including his book *Law and Social Change in Postwar Japan* (Harvard University Press, 1986). In recent years, his research has moved from Japan into the general area of law and development with a particular reference to the development of the Chinese legal system.

Matthew Spence is codirector of the Truman National Security Project and associate world fellow at Yale University. He has served as a lecturer in international relations at Oxford University, a fellow at the Stanford Center on Democracy, Development, and the Rule of Law, and an elections monitor in Kosovo. His commentary has appeared in the *Los Angeles Times, International Herald Tribune, New Republic*, the *Baltimore Sun*, and on BBC radio. He is currently writing a book about U.S. democracy promotion.

Matthew Stephenson is an assistant professor of law at Harvard Law School. His research interests include administrative law, environmental law, positive political theory, and the reform of legal institutions in developing countries. His most recent publications are "Public Regulation of Private Enforcement: The Case for Expanding the Role of Administrative Agencies," *Virginia Law Review*, 2005, and "Court of Public Opinion Government Accountability and Judicial Power," *Journal of Law and Economics and Organization*, 2004.

THE CARNEGIE ENDOWMENT FOR INTERNATIONAL PEACE is a private, nonprofit organization dedicated to advancing cooperation between nations and promoting active international engagement by the United States. Founded in 1910, Carnegie is nonpartisan and dedicated to achieving practical results. Through research, publishing, convening and, on occasion, creating new institutions and international networks, Endowment associates shape fresh policy approaches. Their interests span geographic regions and the relations between governments, business, international organizations, and civil society, focusing on the economic, political, and technological forces driving global change. Through its Carnegie Moscow Center, the Endowment helps to develop a tradition of public policy analysis in the states of the former Soviet Union and to improve relations between Russia and the United States. The Endowment publishes *Foreign Policy*, one of the world's leading journals of international politics and economics, which reaches readers in more than 120 countries and in several languages.